INDUSTRIAL RELATIONS RESEARCH
ASSOCIATION SERIES

Industrial Relations
in a Decade of
Economic Change

AUTHORS

Roy J. Adams   Kenneth McLennan
Richard N. Block   John Niland
William Brown   José Pastore
Braham Dabscheck   Richard B. Peterson
Otto Jacobi   Francois Sellier
Hervey Juris   Thomas E. Skidmore
Solomon B. Levine   Koji Taira
Mark Thompson

EDITORIAL BOARD

Hervey Juris
Mark Thompson
Wilbur Daniels

First Edition

Library of Congress Catalog Card Number 85-80520
ISBN 0-913447-30-7

Price $15.00

INDUSTRIAL RELATIONS RESEARCH ASSOCIATION SERIES

PROCEEDINGS OF THE ANNUAL MEETING (Spring publication)
PROCEEDINGS OF THE SPRING MEETING (Fall publication)
ANNUAL RESEARCH VOLUME (Fall publication)
   (MEMBERSHIP DIRECTORY every sixth year in lieu of research volume)
IRRA NEWSLETTER (quarterly)

INDUSTRIAL RELATIONS RESEARCH ASSOCIATION
7226 Social Science Building, University of Wisconsin
Madison, WI 53706 U.S.A. Telephone 608/262-2762

Pantagraph Printing, 217 West Jefferson, Bloomington, IL 61701

CONTENTS

PREFACE

The IRRA last published a research volume with a comparative industrial relations theme in 1967.[1] Since then many of the issues that attracted the attention of industrial relations practitioners and scholars have changed. So has the environment in which industrial relations takes place. The prolonged period of economic prosperity which had lasted from the end of World War II until the end of the 1960s was supplanted by a decade of economic turmoil. In choosing the theme for the 1985 research volume, the editors and the Executive Board felt that the membership and other readers would welcome a volume which looked at how major industrialized nations coped with the changes that occurred during the 1973–1983 decade.

The book begins with an outline of the economic conditions faced by the major industrialized nations during the decade. Individual chapters were then commissioned for eight developed nations—Australia, Canada, France, Germany, Japan, Sweden, the United Kingdom, and the United States. Apart from the U.S., these nations were selected for their economic importance, their intellectual interest to North American readers, and the variety of responses by their industrial relations systems. Brazil, a major industrial power among developing nations, was also included to give one example of the problems faced by one of the new competitors.

The reader will find that the editors' desire for illustrating a variety of alternative approaches to a common set of problems has been met. The variety here could scarcely have been greater.

For the first time, an IRRA research volume is composed equally of materials written by North American and non-North American scholars. The IRRA is indebted to all of our authors for their contributions. The book has benefitted from the editorial assistance of Barbara Dennis and Sanna Longden and the help of Tracy Ayres

---

[1] Solomon Barkin, William Dymond, Everett M. Kassalow, Frederic Myers, and Charles Meyers, eds., *International Labor* (New York: Harper & Row, 1967).

v

and Julia Taylor. Invaluable financial assistance was provided by Labour Canada's University Research Committee, the Faculty of Commerce and Business Administration at the University of British Columbia, the Center for Urban Affairs and Policy Research at Northwestern University, and from funds generated by the Pepsico Research Professorship at the Kellogg School, Northwestern University.

Hervey Juris
Mark Thompson

The Market Economies Tack Against the Wind: Coping with Economic Shocks 1973-1983*

PIERRE TABATONI
University of Paris Dauphine

The purpose of this chapter is to highlight the economic changes of the 1973-1983 decade, illuminate similarities and differences in how market economies coped with these changes, and speculate on the forces which not only led the market economies into these troubles, but also led them out of the decade. Finally, I will discuss some implications of these underlying forces for our economic future.

In attempting to understand the 1973-1983 decade, it is useful to recall features of the late 1960s and early 1970s, as they explain much of the change of the later period. For OECD countries, the average annual growth rate of real gross domestic product (GDP) dropped by 2.0 percentage points in the period 1973-1979 compared to 1961-1973. This was quite a shock in itself for nations used to an unprecedented high growth rate since the war. The growth of productivity dropped from a record 4.3 percent in 1961-1973 to an annual rate of around 2.3 percent from 1973 to 1979. Inflation, which had accelerated after 1965, exploded during 1968-1969 and was kept at a high level from 1973 to 1979: Europe's average annual rate was 10.9 percent; in the U.S. it was 8.5 percent. This is to be compared with 3.7 and 2.6 percent, respectively, in the period 1961-1969.

---

* I wish to express my gratitude to Professor F. Roure for extended collaboration on the preparation of several parts and for careful reading of the drafts, and to the Russell Sage Foundation which provided facilities for work and opportunities for useful discussions.

The decade in question started with the first oil shock in 1973, which reinforced a rise in prices of the world's basic commodities, particularly from mid-1975 to mid-1977; it was followed by a second oil shock in 1979. Both resulted in serious recessions. In the industrial countries, the annual rate of growth of real gross national product (GNP) dropped from 6 percent in 1973 to −1 percent in 1975, and from 3 percent in 1979 to −1.25 percent in 1982.

Due to the deterioration in the terms of trade, our economies had to transfer huge amounts of real resources to the oil and basic material producers. It is estimated that from 1970 to the end of 1980 this transfer amounted to 8.5 percent of GDP in Japan, 7 percent in Italy, about 4 percent in Germany and France, and 3 percent in the U.S.; for Great Britain it was 4 percent in the first oil shock.

After 1980, the sudden increase in the value of the dollar also had a strong impact on the terms of trade and on the foreign debt service. But the decade ended with decreasing prices on basic commodities and a drop in the 1983 oil price from $35 to $29 per barrel, with further drops expected.

A second major characteristic of the decade was significant technological developments in electronics, biology, computer science and software development, space and underseas exploration, telecommunications, and energy savings. It was a time of extending the frontiers of knowledge and economic space.

It was also a period of change in world trade and finance. There was an internationalization of production and consumption involving nearly all countries, although the volume of world trade increased by only 3.6 percent a year on average, compared with 8.7 percent in the previous decade. The major change was a redistribution of international activities, reducing the share of industrial countries in world exports from 70.8 percent in 1973 to 63.5 percent in 1981, and, to a lesser degree, reducing their imports (from 71 to 67.3 percent). For the OECD, Western Europe's share of the world's commodity exports decreased from 50 to 47 percent between 1971 and 1983, Japan's share (3.2–3.4 percent) and the U.S. (13.4–13.1 percent) being less affected (OECD, Foreign Trade by Commodities, 1985).

Even more significantly, the "comparative advantage" in world trade of high technology products increased in Japan (from 0.87

percent in 1970 to 1.41 percent in 1980), while decreasing in the U.S. (from 1.27 to 1.20 percent) and in the European community (from 0.94 to 0.88 percent). As calculated by the European community, "comparative advantage" is the share of exports of a particular product related to total exports, by any country. The less developed countries (LDCs) increased their share of manufacture exports as did the Eastern European socialist countries, all having increased their foreign debt.

A major change occurred in the international monetary system in 1972-1973 when the Bretton Woods fixed exchange rates collapsed under pressure from the inflationary distortions of the late 1960s and 1970s. The new flexible exchange rate, combined with a strong expansion of the flow of capital markets (Euromarkets) which had to recycle the OPEC oil surplus, submitted the domestic economies to increasing international pressure.

The average monthly change in real exchange rate (nominal rate corrected by inflation differential between two countries) was quite a new experience for business and government, when it suddenly passed from 0.82 percent in 1970-1972 to 2.9 percent in 1973-1975, and 2.24 percent in 1976-1978. On balance, while the new flexibility in exchange rates, according to theory, permitted each country to have more autonomous national policies than with fixed rates, large and frequent fluctuations in exchange rates put stress on government policies. These policies increasingly became foreign-exchange value-minded, especially in the most inflationary countries. In fact, flexible rates allowed more divergence in inflation experience, which ultimately led to anti-inflationary converging policies.

The consequences for business were harsh. In general, profits were squeezed between high labor and material costs and the effects of exchange rates and increased international competition. The average annual rise of unit wage cost in 1973-1980 was larger than in 1960-1970: for the U.S., 7.5 vs. 1.5 percent; for Europe (EC), 11.2 vs. 3 percent; for Japan, 3.6 vs. 2.7 percent. The investment efficacity, which relates the investment effort to GNP growth, dropped between 1960-1973 and 1974-1984—in the U.S. from 0.21 to 0.14, and in Europe from 0.21 to 0.08 (*European Economy*, November 1984, p. 21). Those inflated costs aggravated the loss of world competitiveness for a number of our basic and traditional industries.

The new uncertainties about growth and inflation made business more cautious. And anti-inflation policies gradually reduced domestic demand.

Finally, unemployment increased throughout the period, even though between 1960 and 1982 the U.S. created 33.5 million jobs and Japan 12 million; the European community, however, created only 3.4 million (*European Economy*, November 1984). At the same time the labor force increased due to demography and to increased participation of youth and women, while the previous strategy of importing unskilled foreign personnel as guest workers contributed to further industrial relations problems, particularly in Europe.

After the second oil shock, these attitudes which had begun to develop in the seventies towards fighting inflation and restoring international competition were reinforced; the psychological and political costs of high unemployment and interest rates faded before them.

Debt was necessary and easier to get, at least for companies and governments having access to international financial markets. The fact that real rates of interest were kept low until 1979 generated—in combination with tax investment incentives—an acceleration of capital-labor substitution which contributed to rising unemployment and higher debt. National investment, especially in manufacturing, still declined as a percent of GDP. Business was investing in labor cost saving and productivity, rather than expansionary investment, and government sacrificed public investment to social subsidies.

The United States added its own "policy shock" in 1979 with its new monetary and budget policies that generated high real rates of interest and a high exchange value for the dollar. While this meant a higher foreign debt burden, it also meant a strong economic recovery after 1982, which brought exceptional support to European and LDC exports as well as to Japanese ones.

The end of 1984 is filled with contradictory messages. On the positive side, recovery seemed on its way and, in the U.S., growth and reduced unemployment appeared to be sustainable, even if at slower rates. Everywhere else inflation had receded to unexpected levels and interest rates declined. In addition, the developing countries, through their own rigorous efforts, negotiated international arrangements to alleviate their debt burden; with an economic world recovery, they have resumed their export drive.

On the negative side, however, many uncertainties remain. What is the future of interest rates, of the dollar rate, of the growth rate itself? How durable is low inflation and, above all, the future level of unemployment, given the new technology and the rise of the service sector relative to the manufacturing sector? With persistent low growth rates, Europe's prospect is for even greater unemployment. What will happen to the increasing—although often disguised—practice of "protectionism" and barter trade?

The lessons of the seventies and eighties may have lasting effects, having focused on the longer term strategies of technological competitive restructuring, and on the strategic role of microlevel decisions. In the sections that follow, we will look more closely at measures of economic performance, major trends affecting performance and the policy implications of past performance, and the major trends.

Comparative Performance Measures: 1973-1979-1984

Economic Performance: Growth, Productivity, Prices

In the 1973–1979 period, the rate of real growth of the industrial market economies was 2.8 percent (see Table 1), and we see (in Table 2) the diversity of growth in different industrial countries. It is also interesting to compare the higher growth rates of the developing countries (Table 1), particularly in the newly industrializing countries of East Asia and the Pacific and in Latin America. The negative impact of the recession on the oil exporters and in Latin America is visible. The outstanding performance of the East Asian and Pacific countries, when considered jointly with Japan and the western and southern parts of North America (defined as the Pacific Area), explains why this area is often seen as the new high growth center for the world.

Labor productivity also slowed. There was a drop in the average annual rate of increase of output per hour in the periods 1960–1973 and 1973–1982: U.S. from 3 to 1.7 percent; Canada, 4.5 to 1.6; Germany, 5.7 to 3.6; Great Britain, 4.4 to 1.8; France 6.7 to 4.5; Sweden, 6.6 to 2.7; and Japan, 10.7 to 7.2 (*Monthly Labor Review*, January 1984).

From 1981 to 1984, especially after 1982, this growth rate (measured more simply by GNP/employment) recovered: U.S.

from 1.4 to 2.5 percent; Japan, 3.2 to 5.25; and Western Europe, 0.4 to 2.5 (OECD *Economic Outlook*, December 1984, p. 50).

TABLE 1
Comparative Growth

	1980 GDP per Capita in $	Annual Rate of Growth of Real GDP in %				
		1973–79	1980	1981	1982	1983
Industrial market economies	10.440	2.8	1.3	1.3	−0.5	2.3
Middle East oil exporters	1.330	4.9	−2.4	2.4	1.3	−0.7
Latin America	1.840	5.0	5.8	−2.3	−1.4	−2.5
Middle East & North Africa	.800	3.0	4.2	−2.4	2.4	1.7
East Asia & Pacific	1.100	8.6	3.6	6.7	4.0	6.1
Low income countries	.250	4.8	5.9	4.8	5.2	7.2

Source: World Bank, *World Development Report*, 1983.

TABLE 2
Annual Real Growth of Industrial Countries GNP
(in percent)

	1973	1975	1977	1979	1981	1983	1984[a]
United States	5.5	−0.7	5.2	2.4	3.0	3.6	6.75
Japan	8.8	2.3	5.3	5.1	4.2	3.0	5.75
Germany	4.6	−1.7	3.1	4.2	0.0	1.0	2.5
France	5.4	0.2	3.1	3.3	0.2	1.0	1.75
Great Britain	2.9	−0.7	1.0	2.1	−1.1	3.3	2.0
Italy	7.0	−3.6	1.9	4.9	0.2	−1.2	3.0
Canada	7.5	1.1	2.2	3.4	4.0	3.3	4.25
Netherlands	5.7	−1.0	2.4	2.4	−0.7	0.6	1.25
Switzerland	3.0	−7.3	2.4	2.5	1.5	0.7	2.5
Sweden	4.0	2.6	−1.6	3.8	−0.5	2.1	3.25
Australia	6.2	2.2	0.9	3.3	3.9	0.6	6.25

Source: OECD *Economic Outlook*, December 1982, pp. 43, 166.
[a] 1984 evaluations by OECD.

Inflation (see Table 3), which for total OECD countries jumped from 4.8 percent in 1969 to 13.4 percent in 1974, was still at 12.9 percent in 1980, but dropped to 5.3 percent in 1983.

Changes in Unemployment and Employment

Unemployment rates differed markedly across the industrial economies through both time periods (OECD Employment Prospects 1984). Lower rates were maintained in Japan and Sweden; the Netherlands and Great Britain showed the highest increase in the decade (see Table 4).

TABLE 3
Inflation: Increase in Consumer Prices
(percent per year)

	1967	1971	1975	1979	1983	1984
United States	2.8	4.3	9.1	11.3	3.2	3.25
Japan	4.0	6.1	11.8	3.6	1.9	2.25
Germany	1.4	5.3	6.0	4.1	3.3	2.5
France	2.7	5.5	11.8	10.8	9.6	7.25
Great Britain	2.5	9.4	24.2	13.4	4.6	5.0
Italy	3.7	4.8	17.0	14.8	14.6	11.0
Canada	3.6	2.8	10.8	9.2	5.9	4.25
Netherlands	3.5	7.5	10.2	4.2	2.8	3.25
Switzerland	4.0	6.6	6.7	3.6	3.0	2.75
Sweden	4.3	7.4	9.8	7.2	8.9	7.75
Australia	3.2	6.1	15.1	9.1	10.1	6.75

Source: OECD *Economic Outlook*, December 1984, Table R-10, and estimates for 1984 in each country section.

TABLE 4
Unemployment Rates
(as percent of labor force)

	1973	1975	1977	1981	1983	1984
United States	4.8	8.3	6.9	7.5	9.5	7.5
Japan	1.3	1.9	2.0	2.2	2.6	2.75
Germany	0.8	3.6	3.6	4.4	8.0	8.25
France	2.6	4.1	4.7	7.3	8.0	9.25
Great Britain	3.3	4.6	6.4	10.6	13.1	11.75
Italy	6.2	5.8	7.0	8.3	9.7	10.0
Canada	5.5	6.9	8.0	7.5	11.8	11.5
Netherlands	2.2	5.2	5.3	8.6	13.7	15.75
Sweden	2.5	1.6	1.8	2.5	3.5	3.25
Australia	3.4	4.8	5.4	6.5	8.3	9.25

Source: OECD *Economic Outlook*, December 1984, p. 51.

Unemployment concentration among women and young people was higher where population growth combined with cultural factors to increase labor force participation (see Table 5). In most countries from 1975 to 1981, the labor force participation of women increased; in addition, almost everywhere the younger generation increased in numbers, although youth participation in the workforce tended to decrease with the lengthening of studies or with new job-training program developments.

The severity of the recession also increased the duration of unemployment. For instance, the percent of people unemployed over one year, comparing 1979 to 1983, are: U.S., 4.2–13.3 percent; Canada, 3.5–9.5; Sweden, 6.8–10.1; Japan, 17.2–14.3; Germany, 19.9–28.5; Great Britain, 24.5–36.2; France, 30.3–42.6; and the Netherlands, 27.1–43.7 (OECD Employment Prospects, September 1984, Annex Table H).

TABLE 5
Labor Force Participation
(in percent)

Country	1975			1981		
	Men	Women	Youth (16–24)	Men	Women	Youth (16–24)
United States	78.0	46.3	64.6	77.0	52.1	67.7
Japan	81.0	44.8	47.4	79.6	46.7	43.2
Germany	72.0	37.4	61.9	69.3	38.5	57.1
Great Britain	81.3	46.8	69.6	77.7	46.6	73.2
France	73.2	42.5	54.6	69.9	43.0	50.3
Canada	78.4	44.0	62.9	78.3	51.6	67.9
Sweden	77.0	55.0	70.8	74.0	60.5	68.9

Source: Constance Sorrentino, "International Comparisons of Labor Force Participation," Monthly Labor Review (February 1983). Figures are percentages of numbers in each group.

Shifting economies led to an interindustry shift in the distribution of employment. The share of industrial employment from 1970 to 1982 decreased everywhere: U.S., 34.3–28.4 percent; Canada, 30.9–25.6; Japan, 35.7–24.9; Germany, 48.5–42.7; Great Britain, 44.7–34.7; and European Community, 42.5–36.3. Conversely, service employment grew: U.S., 61.1–68 percent; Canada, 61.4–68.2; Great Britain, 52–62.6; Japan, 46–56.1; Germany, 42.9–51.7; and European Community, 46–56.1 (OECD Labor Force Statistics 1984).

Political and Social Environment

Within each country certain factors contributed to increased politicization of the economic and social debate, and to changes in the ruling majorities: controversies about employment policies, the extension of taxes and regulation, and the frustrations resulting from increasing differentiation in purchasing power, job security, and protection against competition.

Intranational dimensions. Out of 23 elections in the OECD area, 12 shifted to more conservative majorities and 11 to more social-hyphenated or socialist ones. After 1979, the conservative drift prevailed in the U.S., Great Britain, Canada, the Netherlands, Denmark, and Germany. The social-democracies lost some positions but regained others (Sweden, Spain, Portugal, Australia). Socialist majorities prevailed in France and Greece.

The events of the past 15 years have progressively created frustrations among political interest groups. As policies shifted to deflation, to limiting budget support for the public sector and social transfers, and to reductions in protection from international competition, persons in large organized manufacturing and public service, farmers, small business, unskilled workers, foreign (guest) workers, and even professional groups reacted politically. In addition, new social movements not related to economics (environment protectionists, those concerned with nuclear energy use, those concerned with foreign policy, and all sorts of particular interests) have created a new activism and new political con-stituencies at the same time that the homogeneity of the labor force has decreased.

These sources of internal division were enhanced by more "fundamentalist" injections on the right and on the left. The traditional foundations of social consensus which economic growth and the welfare state had made possible were disrupted. Mediating forces were at work, however. The pursuit of less ambitious social policies ameliorated some dissent. Uncertainty about unemploy-ment reduced the number and duration of labor conflicts, and also generated some major labor agreements.

In short, the policies of stabilizing national purchasing power in the 1980s, which were accepted by practically all governments, contrasted with the pre-1980 social policies. While the former looked more closely for the support of labor and consumer groups, the new policies forged coalitions which look more complex in their composition, more ambiguous in their objectives, and possibly more unstable.

International dimensions. The worsening of the international situation since the mid-1970s has reinforced the politicization of domestic social life. Variations in East-West relations and grave regional conflicts in the Far East, Middle East, Central America, and Africa have had mixed effects on international cooperation.

On one hand, these crises have reinforced solidarities within the broad alliances and generated a stronger interdependence between economic negotiations, political, and military strategies. On the other hand, these crises enhanced particularities of interest as well (Europe vs. the U.S., Western vs. Eastern Europe, the U.S. vs. Japan, Western countries vs. LDCs, etc.).

The relations with less developed countries in trade, finance, and technology transfers were also sensitive to international politics. In the 1980s, new points of view tend to deemphasize the role of international multilateral agreements, or of multilateral institutions of finance, and to favor more direct deals, more private investment, and more reliance on market mechanisms. Although some postwar institutions, such as the International Monetary Fund (IMF) have played a strategic role since 1982 in avoiding major world financial crises linked with LDC debt, there is now uncertainty about the future of the relations between the industrial world, the new industrializing countries, and the poorer LDCs, and about the possibilities of multilateral cooperation. Every country will have to rely more on its own capacity to export and compete, and to fight against "neo-protectionism." The longer term impacts of such trends on the LDC growth, and on the level and structure of employment in all countries, must be understood as strategic ones.

Major Trends Impacting Employment

Demographic, cultural, and ideological change, technological innovation, and increasing internationalization of the market economies converged during the 1973-1983 decade, severely constraining the behavior of the economic actors and putting pressure on governments to respond.

Demographic, Cultural, and Ideological Changes

Demography plays an important role in the supply of labor through the growth of the age-eligible population. Of most current concern is the "young" group (16-24) looking for employment. The average annual rate of growth of the age-eligible population was generally higher in 1975-1979 than in 1979-1982 and 1983. But

diversity is observed: U.S., 1.7–1.2–0.8 percent; Canada, 2.0–1.6–
0.9; Germany, 0.4–1.4–1.0; Great Britain, 0.4–0.8–0.7; France, 0.7–
1.1–0.8; and Sweden, 0.2–0.4–0.3 (OECD Employment Prospects
1984, Annex Table E). For 1980–2000 such growth will be smaller
than in 1970–1980, but the population will become older in our
industrial nations. By the year 2030, in the U.S. the 65+ age group
will represent 18.1 percent of the population, compared with 11.1
percent in 1982 and 12 percent in 1990 (*Monthly Labor Review*,
May 1983, p. 15). In Japan the figure will jump from 9.5 percent
now to 16 percent in the year 2000. The economic consequences
of an aging population on social security health expenditures are
well known. By contrast, in LDCs the rate of population growth
will increase, particularly for the younger workers, with dramatic
pressures on their own employment and export drive, and with
obvious consequences on the international division of labor on trade
and on our production structure, immigration, and employment.

Besides population structure, we also have to look at
participation rates in the labor force. The most probable scenario,
at least in the U.S., is a stable participation of the younger group,
and particularly of the women's share due to education, family
organization, new attitudes towards life, and economic reasons.
Consequences on the organization of worklife are expected.

Cultural changes are also important, especially with regard to
their implications for worklife, lifestyle, and individual vs.
collective interests. As we know, the baby-boom generation
entering the workforce in the 1970s introduced its need for
expression, differentiation, and self-development, and its concern
with social and political issues. The new young generation at work
in the 1980s, chastened by the employment history of the 1970s,
is seen as more self-reliant, more pragmatic and risk-taking, but
also concerned with concrete political and social problems.

The changing attitudes of women, which brought them en masse
into the workforce in the 1970s, is probably the most important
cultural revolution of that decade. Older people are also asserting
their needs, and are looking for more specific use of their
experience, more flexibility in retirement, and more concern for
their health.

Contrary to public opinion, it seems that people indeed want
to work and that work occupies a central position in their lives,
although a somewhat less exclusive one than before (Aspen Institute

1983, Yankelovitch 1979, Yoshihiro 1983). There is a desire for more flexibility in the workplace, for better harmonization between the worklife and the non-worklife, and for better training. There is also more concern with job design and perhaps employee involvement.

The reduction in the duration of work is also a fact of the 1980s. Weekly hours have been reduced everywhere (U.N., Yearbook of Labor Statistics 1983). Internationally, the workyear is still quite diverse: 1850 hours in the U.S.: 1770 in Germany; 2100 in Japan (1982 data). Furthermore, the traditional concept of a life of full-time employment may not be as relevant now as it was 20 years ago and job mobility is better accepted. Modern telecommunications may permit more work away from the office in the service functions and "professionalize" more employees.

A final, but no less important, cultural change in the last decade is the shift in attitude towards less direct public interference in private life, and a shift in the public's attitude towards the welfare state, public goods, and taxes (Gooby 1982). Behind these shifts in attitudes are some new developments in economics, sociology, political science, and decision theory. One is a renewed emphasis on "micro" decision-making, on its importance for productivity, innovation, risk, and labor relations.

Microlevel analysis focuses on the behavior of the individual consumer, investor, worker, voter, bureaucrat, or political agent, and on his or her interest group behavior.

In economics, microanalysis has benefited from spectacular advances in mathematical economics, in information theory—especially its developments concerning asymmetric information, signaling, information disclosures, and efficient markets, and in the analysis of market segmentation and of new marketing methods that aim directly at particular groups of purchasers. Within neoclassical economics, the vigorous rational expectation theorists (Barro 1984, Sheffrin 1983) are challenging the neo-Keynesians (Malinvaud 1978, Meade 1983, Tobin 1983). They argue that government intervention distorts the clearing power of markets and reduces individual and societal welfare.

Sociology and political science have also increasingly turned their interests to microlevel behaviors. The field of public choice and of new currents in political economy (Frey 1978, Mueller 1983, Van Winden 1983) have their foundations in the self-interest of specific groups of voters, specific groups of civil servants and bureaucrats, specific political parties, specific pressure groups, etc. Sociologists of organizations also have contributed actively to the understanding of how organizational structures and communication systems can permit innovative decentralized actions.

This leads to a second major level of theoretical development: the level of collective action. At the center of the study of collective action has been the analysis of strategy, especially in the work of management theorists who incorporated perspectives from the different social sciences. Their models of strategic planning and management and their models of negotiation look at the relationships within and between collectives.

This multidiscipline reliance on the microlevel paradigm constitutes a powerful ideological vector. Needless to say, it has drawn critical reactions from other traditions of thought rooted in the historical approach to macro structures and choices. Examples include Marxian theories of social class conflict and power structures as well as other approaches to social issues that have links with moral philosophy and that do not accept the neglect of altruistic points of view or of social utility functions. Since it is well established that collective criteria cannot, theoretically, reconcile the diversity of individual utilities, solutions have usually been proposed in the form of incrementalist policies (Fellner 1981). Such approaches do not try to build up as rigorous a formulation as maximizing models, and instead lean more on the concept of bounded rationality and on satisficing behaviors, along the lines by Herbert Simon (1983).

Where microeconomic foundations of macroeconomic behavior are acknowledged, it has been as it relates to the study of productivity, innovations, and the understanding of rigidities brought about by monopolistic structures in the goods and labor markets. For neo-Keynesians, the acceptance of micro strategies does not extend to the minimization of a role of government: they believe that macroeconomic policies are necessary to compensate for the effects of market dysfunctions and to support long-term growth and employment.

It is not surprising then that in the absence of a consensus on models of growth, policy-makers did not have a "right" way to meet the emergencies of the inflation and competition. We return to this important point in our last section on policies.

Technological Change and the Costs of Innovation

In addition to having to cope with changes in demography, culture, and ideology, practitioners and policy-makers have also had to cope with new technological processes and the strains they have placed on existing relationships, even as they improve prospects for the future.

New technologies. In the past ten years new technologies have significantly lowered costs and improved productivity and quality in the so-called declining industries (steel, coal, textiles) as well as generating new growth sectors. Electronic microprocessors, genetic engineering, optics (lasers), new composite materials, and new energy-saving processes are revolutionizing business, industry, education, health care, and other services (Ayres 1984).

The combination of computers and telecommunications will permit more interactive communications and improved treatment of information. The Japanese, Americans, and, to a lesser degree, Europeans are already placing these computer and communication technologies at the core of their industrial, military, and societal strategies.

Diffusion of innovation. The utility of these new technologies and their impact will depend on the delays of diffusion or innovation (Rosenberg 1981). Networks are created through which technologies are transferred and also made to work together. The role of networking becomes more important as production and markets become segmented and specialized.

Networking can be improved through research, education, professional organizations, government support of innovations, and joint actions between companies (Kamien and Schwartz 1982, Ken'Ichi 1983, Rosenberg 1981). In the past 20 years networks have improved significantly. Mergers and joint ventures in research, production, and marketing have been undertaken explicitly for networking, especially where new technologies were at stake. Networking has also occurred between major firms in computer manufacture, software, and telecommunication: in automotive and machine tools; in agro-industries, pharmaceuticals, and biotechnology; in measurement instruments and optics; and in computers and publishing. Government support to science and technology has fostered new information processes and some longer term evaluations of new market opportunities at the precompetitive level. This is illustrated by the new industrial policies in Japan, Europe, and the U.S. (see the Policy section).

Diffusion of innovation can take time and is subject to bottlenecks. Cultural traditions and nationalistic barriers can reduce innovation and information flow. National fragmentation of markets—as in the European Community—also limits scale economies in research, production, financing, and marketing of innovation. Services in telecommunications, insurance, thrift management, and education are more than often reserved to domestic suppliers, as are military and economic innovations financed by national governments. Judicial systems may also reduce the flow of information and innovation through the regulation of technology transfers, mergers, joint actions, patents, "intellectual property," etc. Finally, the implementation of innovation and technology is heavily dependent on the preparedness of human resources and organization systems to accept change. People may prove yet to be the greatest bottleneck of all, with institutional barriers not far behind.

There is another dimension to the question of innovation that leaves policy-makers confused. It is the micro-macro debate: where are we on the "long-wave" or Kondratieff cycle? Theoreticians of long waves in the economy, or of cluster innovations in the Schumpeterian sense, contend that there are phases of long cycles when networking is more intense, wider, and more quickly influenced. At these times the crucial linkages between technical invention and markets happen more easily. In other phases, new techniques appear too infrequently, the content of the basic inventions is too limited, or entrepreneurial and management processes are not capable of connecting the invention with new product markets (Rosenberg and Frischtak 1984, Serge 1982, Van Duijn 1983). Many would agree that the period 1948–1973 may have seen one of these long waves of innovation and sustained growth (Van Duijn) in which both capital and employment have been extended (Serge). Between 1973 and 1983 we may have experienced a phase of capital-labor substitution, investment in some basic innovations, and lower growth. But now, after the strong recession of the early 1980s, are we entering a new long-term upward trend with cumulative innovation and a new investment drive? Or are we in a period of cautious, slow innovation with continued capital-labor substitution?

What will be the effects on people's mobility, on education and training, on human resource management methods? What effect on employment and its level, structure, and form? The present forecast for the U.S., for instance, estimates that by 1995 employment in manufacturing might be 23.5 million, compared with 20.4 million in 1969. Services, however, would reach 68.6 million, compared with 36.5 million (*Monthly Labor Review*, November 1983, p. 26). Figures do not tell, of course, which qualifications would be required by new techniques and new relations.

Internationalization of the Market Economies

Since the 1960s, successful efforts to reduce trade barriers and organize international free capital markets have created a new world division of labor, intensified specialization, and increased market segmentation. As a consequence, intraindustry trade has expanded relative to interindustry trade (Bergstrand 1982). In the sections that follow we examine this process more closely.

Internationalization of production and distribution. Import penetration (imports as a percent of domestic markets) increased for manufactured goods in all industrial countries during 1970–1983. Penetration was much greater in Canada, Germany, Great Britain, France, and Italy than in the U.S.; Japan remained relatively closed. Exports as a percent of GDP increased as well (*European Economy*, July 1983). The oil shocks forced these countries to export to the LDCs to pay the energy and raw material bills, even if they saved on energy consumption. Economic policies to lower inflation and limit internal demand has forced businesses to turn to foreign markets since the middle 1970s. And the increasing foreign debt, in countries where the domestic rate of saving is very often low, has reinforced the need to export to pay the debt burden. Recently the disinflated economy of the 1980s has increased the pressure for competitive exports.

Domestic and international competitive pressures and the rising costs of domestic production have led many businesses to invest in cheap labor countries and to "outsource" their production (i.e., buy more of their components or even the product itself from outside the country). In addition, in the 1960s and 1970s businesses have begun to rely more on foreign workers, and now illegal immigrants are supplying manpower in unskilled jobs.

Practically all large companies and an increasing number of firms of all sizes have developed their international operations. The largest ones have become multinational corporations, not only in the industrialized OECD area, but in the developing countries and state-controlled and socialist economies as well (IRM 1983 and 1984, United Nations Organization 1983). Their expansion strategies have not been alike. European multinationals invested largely within Europe itself, as a way to go around the national trade barriers that still existed within the Common Market. In the last five years their investments in other parts of the world, and especially in North America, have accelerated. Japanese multinationals have oriented their main foreign production and investments in the developing countries of Asia and Latin America as a base for cheaper production and exports (IRM 1983). Since 1982, however, the Japanese have increased investments in the U.S. and Europe, partly to get around protectionist measures and partly to increase profits. Contrary to Europe and Japan, the major part of U.S. direct investment abroad in 1983 was located in industrialized countries— $169 billion out of $226 billion: $100 billion in Europe, $47 billion in Canada, $51 billion in LDCs (Survey of Current Business 1984).

It is clear that consideration of the international dimensions of marketing and technology problems have become an important part of management's long-term strategy (Davidson 1983). There has been a notable expansion of joint production, research, and distribution companies from different parts of the industrialized world—Japan, Europe, North America. Firms lagging in new technology are exchanging their marketing positions for access to new technical processes. Governments (as in the so-called "North-South" dialogue) as well as companies are pursuing these relationships (OECD World Economic Interdependence, 1982). The outcomes seem to be less direct investment than joint agreements or jointly owned affiliates. The multinationals provide engineering, managerial expertise, marketing, and financing in exchange for markets and production.

All this is a challenge of growing importance for the industrialized world, for it requires balancing the requirements of worldwide marketing (for economies of scale), growing needs for specialization and segmentation, and the broader strategy of developing satisfactory relations with foreign environments in all their cultural, political, trade, and technology particularities.

Informing this balancing act is the framework of the United Nations, ILO, OECD, and EEC directives and codes of conduct (Rowan and Campbell 1983, Hamilton 1984). While contested and controversial, they are considered as steps towards preserving proper social and development policies as well as a condition of industrial transformation, although their monitoring actions could disturb the international investment climate.

Internationalization of capital. Although during the 1970s many domestic capital markets maintained obstacles to the free movement of capital, the extension of the Eurodollars market (Johnston 1983) in the broader form of "xenomarkets" benefited from some exceptional factors (OECD Capital Markets Quarterly 1982–84, IMF Annual Reports 1982–84, Bank of International Settlements Annual Reports 1983–84).

First, supply was abundant. Oil exporting countries were pouring funds into Western banks. Furthermore, increased competition among those banks generated exceptional innovation in the collection and use of funds. In addition, the deficit in the U.S. basic balance of payments (current account deficit plus net export of long-term capital) increased from $-3.7 billion in 1966–1970 to $-15.6 billion in 1976–1980.

Second, demand was strong. Money was needed to finance the increased volume of international trade, to cover the price increase of foreign traded goods, and to meet the demands of foreign debt, particularly by governments and businesses who pursued debt in anticipation of continued inflation and a low real debt cost. From 1972 to 1983, about 67 percent of the gross borrowing in the international markets was by the industrial OECD countries, and 28 percent by the developing countries.

Since 1981 the picture in the international capital markets has changed. The recession, the reduction in inflation in the industrialized countries, and the reduction in the growth of international trade have decreased the demand for funds everywhere, except among the LDCs, whose needs in managing their debt burden were enhanced, and also in the U.S. where a strong expansionist policy after 1982 required an influx of foreign capital. There was a strong reduction in the supply from oil exporters, and restrictive monetary policies generally limited credit expansion.

A major change was the reassertion of the dominance of U.S.

financial institutions in the world markets. Dynamism and innovations such as options markets and futures markets as well as the sheer size of the U.S. market and its worldwide networks have helped reduce the $-15.6 billion negative basic balance in 1976-1980 to $-4.7 billion in 1980-1983.

Another major change in the world capital markets corresponds to the new international position of Japan. With its current account surplus ($35 billion in 1984), its impressive savings (19 percent of disposable income, compared with 6 percent in the U.S.), and its policies of "controlling" internal consumption and imports, Japan is becoming a major partner in international finance. Japan is now the second most important borrower, after the U.S., as well as the major exporter of capital, borrowing short-term largely in Europe and lending at longer term to the U.S. From 1981 to August 1984, Japan exported $70 billion of long-term capital.

In order to obtain a larger internationalization of the yen, with the hope that a greater demand for the yen would reverse its continued undervaluation, the U.S. and European countries have pressed for reforms to encourage capital flows into Japan. At the same time, however, the reforms realized inside the financial markets in Japan, and the attractions of investing in U.S. assets, have contributed to massive capital exports to the U.S. which have supported the dollar. Such trends in foreign investment could quickly make Japan the first creditor of the world and lead to a real internationalization of the yen for trade as well as for financial transactions.

International monetary system and the role of the dollar. Any international monetary system must not only provide enough international liquidity—that is, enough "reserve" acceptable for payment in international operations, but also provide a regulatory function. This regulation works by pressuring domestic economies to reduce their foreign account deficits, meanwhile giving them temporary loans in order to avoid cumulative reduction of trade (Levi 1983).

Since the end of the war, the U.S. dollar has played a determining role in the international monetary system. The dollar has been used largely as a means of payment in world trade (50 percent of payments in 1977), but also as a basis of international financial flows. This is why it is impossible to appreciate the functioning of the system without considering its connection with the internationalization of capital markets and the leadership of the American credit institutions.

In international liquidity, the ratio of private international resources to the volume of international trade was rather stable in the 1960s and 1970s (11–15 percent), but jumped to above 50 percent after 1983. The reason for the very high preference by the private sector for investing its international reserves in dollars is based much more on its need for international capital management than on seeking working capital for trade. The share of U.S. dollars in those private reserves reached 88 percent in 1983. The dollar's share of the central banks' foreign reserves was 71 percent (Krediet Bank *Bulletin*—N43, 1984).

In other words, during the mid-1960s and 1970s the U.S. policy of benign neglect of the value of the dollar (because of its foreign deficit) discouraged private holders. Therefore, the flow of dollars had to be bought by central banks (mainly European). After 1982, however, many factors (economic, financial, and political) dramatically restored the confidence in the dollar, driving foreign capital into the U.S. This contributed to the strong reevaluation of the dollar, as the supply of dollars was not large enough to meet demand.

Since more than three-quarters of private dollar holdings have been short-term investments, a change in the opinion of investors might quickly bring about a massive shift of funds into other moneys (yen, Deutsche mark, Swiss francs, or the European Currency Unit [ECU]), if those assets were thought more secure and profitable. This leads to a brief discussion of the problems of exchange rates.

The result of the 1971 U.S. decision to suppress the dollar's convertibility into gold and the general adoption in 1973 of flexible exchange rates meant that everyone had to learn to operate again with variable rates of exchange. This meant inventing new forms of hedging and using more intensely and rationally the new technical facilities of the international capital markets in order to better manage foreign exchange positions (*IMF Report* 1982, Levi 1983, McCulloch 1983).

Because of the uncertainties of this change, the members of the European community decided in 1979 to create their European Monetary System (EMS). It is a joint float designed to maintain a better stability between the values of the European moneys, although each one fluctuates with the dollar and other nonmember exchanges according to the market situation. The results have been positive, even if seven negotiated internal readjustments within the EMS have been necessary. As a result, the European Currency Unit is becoming more popular among international investors (Svoboda 1983).

The regulatory function of the flexible exchange rate system is simple in principle. It is based on the autonomy of each nation to design its own economic policy in order to avoid a domestic inflation rate higher than its foreign competitors. For example, if the U.S. price level increases in a year by 10 percent and Great Britain by 15 percent, the value of the pound, expressed in dollars, should fall by $0.05/(1 + 0.15)$—that is, by 4.4 percent. This is the famed purchasing power parity principle which should work at least on a long-term equilibrium basis (Levi 1983).

Variations in exchange rates by themselves exercise some regulation on trade balances through their effects on the costs, in foreign money, of exports and imports (McCulloch 1983). The experience with inflation differentials and exchange rates in the 1970s and 1980s once more illustrates that many factors create divergencies between the inflation differentials and the variation of exchange rates. This has led to overshooting—overvaluation by reference to the purchasing power parity—or undershooting (undervaluation) (Buiter and Miller 1982, *IMF Report* 1982). And in those cases the mechanisms of regulation by which a depreciation of exchange in a country should generate restrictive policy are rendered more difficult to implement.

The intervention of expectations about the evolution of exchange rates, interest rates, and prices has generated cumulative exchange depreciation as well as an increasing rate of inflation. This is why all countries are watching their real rate of exchange, that is, rates corrected by the inflation differential. The real rate is an expression of the divergence from the purchasing power parity, and is a measure of foreign competitiveness; an increased real rate makes exports less attractive. Conversely, if the U.S. shows a 5 percent inflation compared with a British 15 percent, as long as the depreciation of the pound is greater than the inflation differential, British exporters to the U.S. can still remain competitive (Levi 1983).

From 1972 to 1978, the Swiss franc, the yen, and the Deutsche mark appreciated in real terms, while the dollar, the lira, and the French franc depreciated. The pound fluctuated over the period 1976–1981 with a strong reevaluation and a serious drop since. Of course, the dollar jumped vigorously. Since 1980 its real exchange rate vis-à-vis the rest of the world had increased 55 percent by mid-1983 and more than 40 percent in late 1984 (by 63 percent with Germany, 46 percent with Japan, but about stable with the pound).

The prospect for high growth, low inflation, and higher profit opportunities, combined with the higher rates of interest brought about by American economic policies, have attracted foreign funds into the U.S which are invested in U.S. securities and into direct investment for production and marketing. Political uncertainties in the East-West and North-South confrontations have also played some role in those transfers to North America. Such a shift of funds has largely permitted the U.S. to support its expansion with foreign resources, covering the increasing budget and trade deficit at a high before-tax long-term real rate of interest, which increased from 2 percent in early 1980 to 7 percent in early 1984, and at a high dollar value.

From this experience it is clear that a monetary system largely based on the dollar, with an international capital market in which U.S. institutions are the most active and a flexible exchange rate which can quickly respond to all the anticipations of foreign exchange markets, does not put too much pressure for quick readjustment on U.S. policies and rates. Still, the corrective effects are building up, through the increasing reaction of U.S. exporters who are badly hit (and who are afraid of losing world markets over the long term, even after a correction), through the changing anticipations of dollar holders about the dollar's future value, and through internal and external reactions against the high real rate of interest which penalizes certain sectors more than others (heavy industries, construction, agriculture).

On the other hand, of course, the U.S. economy could expand its new technology, create new markets, and maintain its high growth rate, thus permitting more flexibility in resource allocation, more innovation, and greater productivity. Many Pacific countries have been able to keep up along the growth track.

But other countries with competitive weaknesses have had to adjust and reinforce their industrial restructuring under strong pressures from the world trade and finance systems. Their domestic policies became dependent on their international monetary position, and their prolonged low growth by itself made industrial restructuring more painful and more doubtful.

International trade redistribution and the balance of payments. As a result of the internationalization of production and finance in a world with flexible exchange rates, major changes have occurred in the distribution of trade and in the balance of payments for industrialized and nonindustrialized countries. In Table 6 we see some of these changes in the developed world.

TABLE 6
Current Payments Balances
(in billion $)

	1978	1979	1980	1981	1982	1983	1984
European Community (EC)							
At current prices:							
Balance of trade in goods and services	+32	+6	−17	+10	+13	+25	+18
Investment income and transfers (net)	−13	−17	−20	−24	−29	−30	−21
Current balance	+19	−9	−37	−14	−16	−5	−3
Japan							
At current prices:							
Balance of trade in goods and services	+17	−10	−10	+7	+7	+18	+45
Investment income and transfers (net)	0	+1	−1	−2	0	0	−10
Current balance	+17	−9	−11	+5	+7	+18	+35
United States							
At current prices:							
Balance of trade in goods and services	−31	−26	−22	−22	−30	−47	−107
Investment income and transfers (net)	+16	+25	+22	+27	+19	+17	+6
Current balance	−15	−1	0	+5	−11	−30	−101

Source: European Community *Annual Economic Review*, p. 134. Estimates for 1984 from OECD, EC, and U.S. sources.

The U.S. trade deficit is now mostly in the industrialized countries. In 1984, deficit with the LDCs was only three-fourths of the deficit with the industrial world, compared with four times in 1979. Japan and the East and South Pacific nations accounted for 35 percent of the total deficit (15 percent in 1979); OPEC's share fell from 71 to 11 percent; Latin America's share jumped from 4 to 11 percent. Europe, West and East, previously the source of a very large surplus, contributed 13 percent in the 1984 deficit. The traditional surplus in revenues brought by investment income has decreased due to the interest paid on debt, but there are positive balances in a number of goods and services integrating new technologies, managerial and financial networks (Sveikauskas 1983).

Japan has been in current surplus since 1982. While her exports are growing, exporters of manufactured goods to Japan face many obstacles, not only with respect to competitiveness, but also due to administrative and cultural impediments. Not facing such obstacles in the past decade, Japanese firms have built up their market share in the 11 most industrial countries at a rate of 6.5 percent a year for manufactures. These Japanese exports, concentrated in five or six new technology products in automotive, electronics, and bioproducts, finally generated strong defensive reactions from, and voluntary limitations of exports negotiated with, Europe and the U.S.

To pay for its oil and other basic goods, the European community had to increase its exports of manufactures, and also part of its agricultural surplus (41 percent of its 1982 exports compared with only 30 percent in 1972). Its exports to other industrial nations have been stable, with Japan and Southeast Asia at a low 5 percent, and decreasing to the U.S. from about 18 to 15 percent. This included a strong revival of its exports to the U.S. in 1984, largely due to real rates of exchange very favorable to Europe as well as new penetration efforts. A major characteristic of the EC trade is still its regional concentration within itself (53 percent in 1982) and with other European countries, the Middle East, the Mediterranean countries, and the African continent. Another characteristic is that, even within the Common Market, many obstacles to the free circulation of goods and services are fragmenting the so-called internal market, a major issue for European firms' strategies. All in all, besides a persistent deficit in investment income and transfers, the current balance deficit has been decreasing.

OECD trade relations with the European socialist countries have followed economic and political cycles of the 1970s and 1980s. They have been marked by many conflicts about technology transfers, barter, trade credit conditions, and the broader political environment of East-West relations. This trade has also been regulated by the Eastern countries' policy to reduce their hard currency net debt ($76.5 billion at its peak in 1981, reduced to $65.5 billion in 1983). The Eastern exports of manufactures to OECD, which represented 40 percent of socialist exports in 1970, have decreased to 28 percent in 1982, while the energy share in exports climbed from 21 to 55 percent because of the famous Siberian gas deal with Western Europe (Economic Commission for Europe, Annual Report 1984).

In summary, we can say of the developed countries that their future growth and trade potential will rely more on sets of manufactured goods and services that will integrate new technology as well as scientific and managerial talents, therefore providing greater added value, than on the standardized capital-intensive equipment industries or labor-intensive manufactures. The Japanese speak of the softening of their economy in the 1990s.

Looking back at this discussion, one must conclude that the development of world trade through the reduction of trade barriers is a priority item. The interdependence of growth between developed and developing countries demands it. It will not be easy.

In the 1970s a large number of agreements were negotiated which were supposed to combine greater access to products of developing countries with protection of the receiving country's own most sensitive sectors (e.g., the "multifibre agreement," the "General System of Preference," the "Lome agreement" countries, and other regional agreements). But other agreements organized voluntary constraints on some exports (autos, steel, some electronic products), especially among Japan, Europe, and the U.S. In addition, disguised protectionism arose in many forms through the national regulation of standards, through customs, through legal and fiscal procedures, etc. (OECD World Economic Interdependence 1982).

Of course, the extension of the General Agreement on Tariff and Trade (GATT) in the 1960s and 1970s (essentially concerning manufactured goods) has provided monitoring mechanisms, but the 1980 recession made its implementation less efficient. A rather major sticking point concerns agricultural trade and services exchanges, which remain largely under national or regional jurisdiction. Today, 2 percent of the world farmers provide 75 percent of world agricultural exports.

The service sector industries (banking, finance, insurance, telecommunications, engineering, software, management consultancy, etc.), which are becoming the most important areas of growth in advanced countries and crucial items of development everywhere, are heavily protected. During the November 1984 meeting of GATT, participants had bitter discussions while trying to prepare a next phase of international trade extension after the "Kennedy Round" and the "Tokyo Round." The extension of free trade in services is meeting especially strong resistance from the developing countries. Other practices, such as the amazing expansion of barter trade, will be even more difficult to dismantle. There is a risk of other nonofficial, and even negotiated, restrictive practices. The less favorable the prospect for reducing unemployment, the more active might become the tenets of proposals to "reduce the external constraint" on domestic growth. Another scenario could be the breakdown of worldwide multilateral efforts and the explosion of bilateral, regional, or sectoral market arrangements.

Government Policy Responses

Since 1945 macroeconomic policy, particularly fiscal policy, has been governments' preferred way of stabilizing economic fluctuations, controlling aggregate demand, and avoiding severe recessions. It was also a way of contributing to the continuation of the welfare state, symbolic of longer term social consensus.

The stagflation of the 1970s, however, caused serious questions about the efficacy of fiscal policy in coping with the kinds of problems we have discussed in this chapter. Industrialized countries faced with economic turmoil, and with no dominant economic theory to guide them, tried multiple responses.

Theoretical Controversies

The two contenders for theoretical dominance were the "neoclassical" mainstream and the "neo-Keynesian" mainstream.

The two diverge essentially on the degree to which they accept the idea that price and wage flexibility permit adjustments in the supply of and demand for goods and factors of production, how they see the dynamics of expectations contributing to that adjustment, and how they view the impact of public policies on real growth and employment.

Both schools of thought believe that stimulation of the economy (through monetarist or fiscal intervention) will lead to real spurts of growth in output and employment. A difference between them is the extent to which each believes that there is a lasting effect. Each understands that in an inflationary period nominal wages will rise while real wages will fall. Thus, workers will supply labor at a lower price, increasing employment. They differ on how long this "nominalist illusion" can persist. Both agree that as the pace of inflation increases, adjustment will happen more quickly, eventually eliminating any gain and stabilizing at a Nonaccelerating Inflation Rate of Unemployment (NAIRU).[1]

Within the neoclassical school, the rational expectations group says this will happen quite quickly. In this framework economic agents act rationally on the basis of their anticipation of all major events in the markets, including economic policy (see, for example, Barro 1984). They use all available information immediately and correctly, and they quickly imitate the moves made by the better informed agents. This is a characteristic of a highly developed communication society, one with enough experts that analyses and forecasts are quickly made available. When people can anticipate new policies, they will quickly adjust their supply and demand behaviors through the markets. In this framework, macroeconomic policy becomes useless: it can generate more inflation when it is expansionary, but has no "real" effects even in the short run. No government can be supposed to be more rational and better informed than any other best informed actors in the economy. It is only when events cannot be anticipated that policy can generate real effects in growth and employment: "shock" policies—that is, major and sudden shifts—when they can demonstrate their commitment to last, can have real effects, until anticipations adjust to them.

---

[1] Efforts to measure NAIRU in the U.S. and Great Britain conclude that such a level of unemployment has been raised since the 1960s to levels now ranging between 7 and 10 percent of the workforce (Englander and Loss 1983 and 1984, Metcalf 1984; see also Gordon 1982).

A related neoclassical "micro"-based argument against using macropolicy to reduce unemployment is the neoclassical view of the employment decision by workers (see, for example, Brown 1983). In this framework workers weigh the cost of acquiring information in searching for a new job, the uncertainties associated with a new job, and the cushion provided by unemployment insurance and transfers against the possibility of only finding a job with lower wages or worse conditions, in which case they continue to search for better opportunities.

Neo-Keynesians admit that anticipation can limit the real effects of inflation on employment. However, in their framework appropriate government incomes policies can regulate the relative growth of wages and profits and limit inflation, thus extending the benefit (for example, see Okun 1980).

Another neo-Keynesian, Edmond Malinvaud (1978), concludes in his theoretical analysis of product market and labor market rigidities that the end of the 1970s may have seen a Keynesian unemployment situation with classical contamination. It is Keynesian in the sense that excess supply of goods and labor was created by insufficient buying (insufficient government spending and autonomous investment). But it is partly classical as a sharp drop in productivity and the accumulation of social tensions contributed to maintain real wages too high for the given level of budget and investment.

Political economists have also contributed to this debate by emphasizing the role of competing interest groups on policy-making and on support or deterrence in implementation (Mancur Olson 1982, Minsky and Ferri 1984).

As we can see from this brief summary, since the 1970s economic policy-makers could no longer rely on a widely accepted theoretical model as Keynesian doctrine had provided before. All Western governments operating within internationally agreed-upon norms of trade and finance had to meet this unquestionable mix of inflation and loss of competition at a time when market specilizations, trade, and innovations required an upsurge of initiative and entrepreneurship.

We shall see how, in a convergent way, they tried to meet those constraints, focusing "macro" policies on inflation while seeking cyclical supports to their recessions and unemployment.

The Practice of Budget and Monetary Policies

Table 7, which refers to the aggregate OECD countries from 1971 to 1984, illustrates the successive moves of macroeconomic policies for the whole region, but does not differentiate by countries.

TABLE 7
Macroeconomic Policies 1971-1984—OECD Countries

Expansionist Changes		Restrictive Changes		Opposite Changes	
M+ B+	M+	M— B—	M—	M+ B—	M— B+
74–75	82–83	78–79	72–73	71–72	76–77
81–82		83–84	73–74	75–76	77–78
			79–80	80–81	

Source: OECD Economic Studies (Spring 1984), Graph VII.

Note: M+ is real monetary expansion from one year to the other. B+ is budgetary expansion through increased deficit.

Budget policies have largely been used everywhere to support demand and compensate for the consequences of the recessions, but in different ways, in different degrees, and at different times in different countries. A general tendency since the mid-1970s, and in a stronger way in the 1980s, has been to reduce the budget deficit or at least reduce the rate of growth of the so-called "structural" deficit (as we shall see below). Monetary policies became more firmly anti-inflationist. Several countries, especially social democracies or socialist countries, combined their use of monetary and budget policies with incomes policies, price and exchange controls, and foreign trade regulations in order to reduce the inflationary impact of their social and economic policies.

It is clear that the real effect of those budget and money policies were different, depending upon the general climate, clarity of purpose and perceived commitment of each government. These issues affect anticipations and the initiatives taken at microlevels, and therefore the efficiency of structural adjustment.

Budget policies. The budget deficits shown in Table 8, column 1 (defined as central and local government deficits plus social security measured as a percent of the national product) increased

TABLE 8

Budget Balances as a Percentage of National Product

		General Administrative Budget Balance (%)	
		(1) Total Balance	(2) Cyclically Adjusted Balance
United States	1973	0.6	−0.2
	1979	0.6	1.2
	1984	−3.1	−1.5
Japan	1973	0.5	0.6
	1979	−4.8	−4.3
	1984	−2.3	−1.3
OECD Europe	1973	−0.6	0.9
	1979	−3.2	−2.9
	1984	−4.4	−1.1
European Community	1973	−1.3	−1.6
	1979	−3.6	−3.3
	1984	−4.7	−1.0
Germany	1973	1.2	1.3
	1979	−2.7	−2.3
	1984	−1.4	1.7
Great Britain	1973	−2.6	−3.6
	1979	−3.2	−3.2
	1984	−2.8	2.0
France	1973	0.9	0.4
	1979	−0.7	−0.8
	1984	−3.5	−0.1
Sweden	1973	4.1	4.0
	1979	−3.0	−1.7
	1984	−3.5	−1.1

Source: Study by R.W.R. Price and P. Muller in OECD *Economic Review* (Autumn 1984).

Note: "General administrative total budget" includes central and local government plus social security as percent of GNP or GDP. "Cyclically adjusted balance" is the total deficit minus the impact of cyclical variations on spending and receipts.

considerably in most of the countries or regions reported from 1973 to 1979. From 1979 to 1984, Germany, Japan, and Great Britain seemed to have gained some control, while the rest showed additional increases. Column 2 reports the same data but eliminates from the total deficit (or surplus) the impact of the business cycle on the spending and taxes. As we can see, this adjusted balance is quite different from the unadjusted balance, shifting everywhere in the direction of a reduced deficit (or even a surplus as in Germany and Great Britain). This means that most governments have worked to reduce their so-called structural deficits (Lipp 1984).

The prospect for reducing structural deficits, however, is not terribly bright. On the expenditure side we can anticipate that interest payments on the national debt will continue to remain high, that social security payments will remain high as the populations of these countries age, and that new technologies will continue to put pressure on health and national defense budgets where that is an important consideration. On the plus side, there is increasing attention to putting pressure on public businesses to operate more profitably, or to privatize parts of them.

In a period where many factors in these societies are leading to pressure for stabilization or reduction of taxes, the political problems concerning expenditure reductions are enormous, especially as they have to deal with transfer expenditures which mobilize special interest groups and affect the long-term perception in each society of the degree to which there is solidarity or disaffection. Therefore, while there are pressures to reduce taxes or provide special incentives to increase investment, fiscal reality and an aversion to increased deficits raises serious obstacles to tax reform.

Monetary policies. Monetary policy refers to control of the money supply (defined differently in different countries) within some pre-established ranges of money growth rates. In the 1970s, governments engaged in a practice called "monetization" of the debt. The monetary goal was to keep real interest rates low, so money was printed to finance the public debt (monetization of the debt). Especially after 1979 several monetary authorities have tried to limit the increase of budget deficits and of the public debt by refusing to finance treasury needs with money creation. Thus, from 1970 to 1978 average nominal interest was around 5.5 percent and real interest rates close to zero (and negative in 1974–75). The change in orientation was strongly influenced by the new U.S. monetary policy since 1979 (Friedman 1984).

In the summer of 1979 the U.S. Federal Reserve System turned to a more restrictive monetary policy to fight inflationary anticipation and the deterioration of the dollar's value (it had dropped in real exchange value by about one-third from 1973 to

1980). When the Reagan economic program included a strong increase in the federal budget deficit, the Federal Reserve refused to monetize the debt, fearing the prospect of a new inflationary surge. Thus, nominal interest rates were allowed to rise to a record level of 20 percent. By the end of 1982 money had become "easier"; the recession had helped dampen inflation and inflationary anticipation. By the beginning of 1985 nominal long-term rates were down to 11.6 percent (compared to 12 percent in Great Britain, 7.5 percent in Japan, 7.4 percent in Germany, and 5.2 percent in Switzerland).

The effect of U.S. policy on the industrialized countries. High interest in the U.S., along with its strong economic recovery and world political uncertainties, attracted considerable foreign capital investment into the U.S. and at the same time made U.S. banks (in 1984) strongly reduce their foreign investments. The availability of these foreign and domestic funds permitted the pursuit of a bolder expansionist policy in the U.S.

Foreign financing compensated the reduction of U.S. household savings, which by itself reinforced private consumer demand. The high value of the dollar boosted imports of foreign goods into U.S. markets, at lower dollar prices than domestic production, and reinforced foreign competition, all of which helped lower inflation in the U.S. The reduction of oil prices and basic commodities also added to disinflation.

Another characteristic of this new monetary policy was the rejection of any targeting of foreign exchange rates. The flexible exchange rates of the 1970s and 1980s provided mechanisms of adjustment which forced countries with weaker foreign exchange positions to more vigorous anti-inflationary policies. They had to avoid excessive deterioration of their exchange rate, which would increase their import prices and reinforce inflationary expectations.

In theory, markets and flexible exchange rates are expected to adjust quickly to changes in trends, with each country taking responsibility for its own domestic policies. In practice, however, the control of the money supply is no easy matter. Since 1983 U.S. authorities have had to pay a great deal more attention to internal and foreign credit markets.

Because of the strength of the U.S. market, many other countries had to adapt their monetary policies to the constraints of the international monetary system. The members of the European

Monetary System (EMS) have negotiated seven readjustments of their rates among themselves since 1979. Great Britain frequently had to support the pound in foreign exchange since it is not a full member of EMS and its sterling value depends much on the price of its oil and on the dollar. France, after its Socialist reform of 1981, adopted a much more austere budget and monetary posture in 1982–83, as it decided to stay within the European Monetary System. Sweden, after its unilateral decision to devaluate in 1982, had to go back to direct freeze of prices and wages for a while, and its 1984 monetary policy was very strict. Japan, Switzerland, and Germany were able to maintain relatively lower rates of interest, thanks to their vigorous disinflation and their strong export positions.

The result of countries' caring about their international monetary positions is that the inflation differential among countries has gradually been reduced. The 1984 estimates of annual consumer price increases are 3.2 percent in the U.S., 2.2 percent in Japan, 2.2 percent in Germany, 5.0 percent in Great Britain, and 7.0 percent in France.

In summary, while there is no unambiguous theoretical framework for the appropriate way out of stagflation, the realities of world trade considerations have forced all governments to utilize monetary policy and, to the extent possible, fiscal policy, to move towards disinflation. In doing so, however, each country has borne costs with respect to structural changes in unemployment in their domestic economies. In the next section we look at how various countries have attempted to deal with these internal consequences.

Structural Unemployment Policies

Although there is no consensus on the definition of structural unemployment and on the significance of the concept itself, all countries have developed policies to reduce obstacles to their long-term international competition as well as to improve their mutual adaptation of supply and demand in their labor markets (for example, see Abraham 1983, Standing 1983, Yankelovich 1979). These policies have had to deal with unemployment in many so-called declining industries, often linked with regional concentrations of unemployment or with concentrations of unemployment in particular groups, such as young people without a proper education, women with no labor market training, aging people unable to find new jobs, and immigrants.

Such policies, whether legislated or designed through collective negotiations, are properly seen as a significant part of industrial relations. Each country has its own traditions and institutions. But everywhere the need for restructuring and innovations has challenged industrial relations systems to be able to communicate an understanding of a longer term perspective and the need for adjustments in employment relationships, which make longer term competitiveness possible.

This is not an easy task. It involves innovative strategies for unions as well as for managements. New forms of work organization require decentralized discussions at lower levels, changes in the division of labor among workers, supervisors, and managers, and perhaps increased flexibility in the compensation package—shifting some of the variable portion or risk down farther in the employment relationship.

Leaving to subsequent chapters the task of defining how each country's industrial relations system dealt with these challenges, let us here just consider briefly two major issues with which all countries seem to be dealing: increased flexibility in the operation of the labor market and industrial policies to generate new job opportunities.

Reducing institutional rigidities in labor markets. As we know, declining employment opportunities associated with shifts in demand as well as increases in supply of younger workers and women have put pressure on labor market institutions. Rule changes have been sought to increase the fluidity of the market: changes in layoff procedures, increased freedom to hire part-timers, efforts to facilitate early retirement, efforts to make wage systems more flexible, changes in unemployment compensation, etc. From the management side have come proposals to reassess seniority and to make workrules more flexible. From the union side have come pressures for reduced hours of work in order to create jobs. Governments have proposed various training and retraining schemes, and better, perhaps more job-relevant, public education.

The intent of all these proposals is to ease hiring, facilitate job search, and improve mobility. Incumbent workers (both union and nonunion) assess each of these proposals from a self-interest perspective. Changes will not come easily, but it appears that these will be the kinds of issues that institutions will have to deal with in all countries whose international competitive position must be improved.

Industrial and social policies. Industrial policies deal with the basic factors of innovation, productivity, and competition. They often imply the intervention of public authorities who provide a long-term orientation and who make institutional changes to create more innovative frameworks. In their most modern form, these policies represent the product of close cooperation among government, business, scientific organizations, and the finance sector. It would be better perhaps to talk of "industrial and science policies," whose main objectives are, first, to develop information networks among the main actors, and second, to provide long-term support and finance which, in fact, help distribute the high risk of such new adventures over the whole collectivity.

Supporting employment in the so-called declining industries by subsidizing their cost or investment or by maintaining protected high prices is a mixture of social and industrial policies. Its social component has in the past ten years often been dominant with public support, granted on the condition that it would facilitate the technological changes needed to make those sectors more competitive, while permitting a progressive reduction of manpower. Experience has shown how difficult it is to monitor the use of public funds for these purposes. Moreover, there is the risk of perpetuating subsidies in new sectors, of cartelization at high prices in basic industries, and of political inequities such as those felt by people laid off elsewhere. Finally, public resources used to support the existing sectors may also reduce funds available for new technological processes. On the other hand, basic industries are also large markets for new techniques.

A dominant theme of industrial policy is direct aid for new technology. Direct aid of this type (electronics, biotechnologies, space industries, new materials, optics) is usually a research-development support system focusing on precompetitive applied research and on cooperation between advanced technology firms, universities, defense, and finance. The institutional arrangements are different in each country. In the U.S. defense project funding and science support to firms and universities are the principal forms. In Japan, the role of the MITI is to organize the targeting of a limited number of major technological breakthroughs, where government clearly indicates to the business, banking, and academic communities the direction of its support for the long term, and where business cooperates on precompetitive research but still remains very competitive. Europeans, on a national scale or within the new ESPRIT program of the European community (1984), have been working about the same way as the Japanese within their own traditions.

Other steps to supplement an industrial policy include regional development policies to foster industries favoring small and middle-sized firms, a size class associated with innovation, exports, and jobs. There are also steps to increase competitiveness through antimonopolistic control, or deregulation, and through measures to promote joint research among firms who are otherwise competitors. In Europe one of the most important issues is still how to create a really common market by suppressing barriers at each national border, and how to control subsidies and reduce the scope of protected markets.

How countries go in the future will depend on the basic quality of their science systems, their ability to develop applied fields, the quality of management talent, and the way in which they combine social objectives and industrial structure objectives.

Conclusion

For our market economies, 1973–1983 has been a period of collective learning, of new constraints and opportunities brought about in the world economy by a major redistribution of potentials in technology, trade, finance, and politics.

The recipe for high growth rates developed in the 1950s and 1960s based on cheap energy, growing urban consumer markets, large-scale investment industries, and oligopolistic structures in many goods and labor markets, with the safety belt of public welfare and transfer payments, met their limits in a period of more competitive production and exchange. For a time, growing inflation and growing debt—domestic as well as foreign—provided a stagflation answer to the shocks of the 1970s. But this led to successful anti-inflationary policies towards the end of the period. In 1984 the general prospects seemed to be for noninflationary cautious growth, with stable or decreasing oil and commodity prices, closely controlled public spending, wages restraint, market regulation to weaken monopolistic practices, and a high level of noninflationary unemployment.

The problem now is for all agents to adjust to these disinflated economies. This requires a longer term outlook, a rejection of the illusions and hidden protections of purely nominal expansions, an adjustment to the real burden of debts, and a focus on productivity and more risky investments. These adjustments will change the way business is conducted and, therefore, the framework within which industrial relations systems will function.

One major change will be the need for innovation, quality, and competitive cost structures. To achieve this change there will be increased emphasis on "micro" units (individuals, small firms, decentralized parts of large firms), and the necessity for flexibility in market relationships. The increasing specialization of production and exchange, and the subsequent development of exchange on a worldwide basis, will reduce the attractiveness of protectionist defense as a means of supporting particular domestic sectors. These changes will affect bargaining.

The changes in society will also affect how people manage the risks inherent in living. Increased efficiency in financial markets and institutions should provide the large middle and upper classes more diversified ways to manage cash flows and longer term risks in employment, health, retraining, retirement, relocation, etc. The question then is, "What institutions, and what collective supports, will represent the solidarity of the society towards new types of proletariats which may be brought about by unexpected poverty or lasting involuntary unemployment?" If, as it seems probable, personnel adaptation to new jobs through training and other means might take a longer time, as employees may have to overcome real cultural shocks, shifting from jobs based on physical handling of material and tools to jobs whose information-processing dimensions require more abstract capacities or better understanding of the system in which one operates, or having to shift to jobs in services requiring nonspecialized aptitudes in communications and relations, how will the industrial relations system provide for these people's needs?

Finally, business and workers will be affected by other trends that cannot be ignored as a background for industrial relations. The priority given to the regulation of working life may be increasingly challenged in the future by other major concerns of people about their health, their overall security, their cultural life (with more leisure available), and even by more fundamentalist concerns about ethics and politics.

However, all of the above notwithstanding, the dominant factor may well be that sectoral negotiators will need to evaluate more systematically the impact of international life on domestic or sectoral decisions. Events at the international level will more often set the boundaries of domestic product and labor markets. Such an improved understanding of world interactions for growth, employment, and welfare might enlarge the practice of international cooperation beyond the present status of crisis management, especially as the role of the developing countries in world economic growth and political balance becomes clearer to all.

References

Abraham, Katharine G. "Structural/Frictional vs. Deficient Demand Unemployment: Some New Evidence." *American Economic Review* 73 (September 1983): pp. 708–24.

Aspen Institute of Humanistic Studies. *Work and Human Values: An International Report on Jobs in the 1980s and 1990s.* September 1983. Pp. 41–78.

Ayres, Robert. *The Next Industrial Revolution: Reviving Industry Through Innovation.* Cambridge, MA: Ballinger, 1984. Chs. 3, 6, 8.

Bank of International Settlements. *Annual Report.* 1983, 1984.

Barro, Robert J. *Macroeconomics, Theories, Policies.* New York : Wiley, 1984. Parts II and III.

_____. "Rational Expectations and Macroeconomics in 1984: Discussion." *American Economic Review* 74 (May 1984): pp. 416–17.

Bergstrand, Jeffrey. "The Scope, Growth and Causes of Intra-industry International Trade." *Federal Reserve Bank of Boston Bulletin* 1 (October 1982): pp. 45–51.

Brown, Clair. "Unemployment Theory and Policy, 1946–1980." *Industrial Relations* 22 (Spring 1983): pp. 164–85.

Buiter, W. H., and M. Miller. "Real Exchange Rate Overshooting and the Output Cost of Bringing Down Inflation." *European Economic Review* 19 (May/June 1982): pp. 85–123.

Davidson, W. "Structure and Performance in International Technology Transfer." *Journal of Management Studies* 4 (1983).

Englander, A. S., and A. C. Loss. "The Stability of the Phillips Curve and Its Implications for the 1980s." Research paper. New York: Federal Reserve Bank of New York, January 1983. P. 58.

_____. "Potential Output Growth and the Long Term Inflation Outlook." Research paper. New York: Federal Reserve Bank of New York, Summer 1984. Pp. 15–24.

European Economy. "The External Constraint: Price and Income Elasticities of External Trade in EC, USA and Japan." 16 (July 1983): pp. 134–59.

Fellner, William, et al. "Shock Therapy and Gradualism: A Comparative Approach to Anti-Inflation Policies." Paper of the Group Thirty. New York: 1981. Pp. 9–18.

Franco, L. G. *The Threat of Japanese Multinationals: Now the West Can Respond.* Wiley/IRM Series on Multinationals. Geneva: Wiley, 1984.

Frey, Bruno S. *Modern Political Economy.* Oxford and New York: Oxford University Press, 1978. Chs. 1, 4, 5, 7.

Friedman, Milton. "Lessons from the 1979–82 Monetary Policy Experiment." *American Economic Review* 74 (May 1984): pp. 397–400.

Gooby, P. Tayler. "Two Cheers for the Welfare State: Public Opinion and Private Welfare." *Journal of Public Policy* (October 1982).

Gordon, Richard. "Inflation, Flexible Exchange Rate and the Natural Rate of Unemployment." In *Workers, Jobs, Inflation*, ed. M. Bailey. Washington: Brookings Institution, 1982. Pp. 89ff, 127–45.

Hamilton, G. *The Controls of Multinationals: What Future for the International Codes of Conduct in the 1980s*. Wiley/IRM Series on Multinationals. Geneva: Wiley, 1984.

International Monetary Fund (IMF). *Annual Report*. 1982, 1983, 1984.

IRM (Institute for Research and Information on Multinationals, Geneva). See entries under L. Franco (1984), G. Hamilton (1984), and S. Lall (1984).

Johnston, R. B. *The Economics of the Euro Markets: History, Theory and Policy*. London: MacMillan, 1983. Chs. 2, 3, 6, 7, 11.

Kamien, Morton J., and Nancy J. Schwartz. *Market Structure and Innovation*. Cambridge Surveys of Economic Literature. Cambridge and New York: Cambridge University Press, 1982. Chs. 1, 2, 4.

Ken'Ichi, Imai. "Japan's Industrial Policy: Technical Innovation and Formation of a Network Society." *Journal of Japanese Trade and Industry* 4 (1983): pp. 43–48.

Krediet Bank. *Weekly Bulletin*, No. 43, 1984.

Lall, Sanjaya. *The New Multinational*. Wiley/IRM Series on Multinationals. Geneva: Wiley, 1984.

Levi, Maurice. *International Finance, Financial Management and International Economy*. New York: McGraw-Hill, 1983. Chs. 4, 6, 8, 11, 12.

Lipp, Ernst Moritz. "Measurement and Policy Implications of Structural Budget Deficits." International Institute of Public Finance, 40th Congress, 1984.

Malinvaud, Edmond. *The Theory of Unemployment Reconsidered*. Barry Blackwell Yrgo Johnson Lectures, 1978. Ch. 2, pp. 55–75; Ch. 3, pp. 83–87, 91–97, 107–14.

McCulloch, R. "Unexpected Consequences of Floating Exchange Rates." In *Essays in International Finance*, No. 153. Princeton, NJ: Princeton University, 1983.

Meade, J. "A New Keynesian Approach to Full Employment." *Lloyds Bank Review* (October 1983): pp. 1–20.

Metcalf, D. "On the Measurement of Employment and Unemployment." *National Institute Economic Review* (London) (August 1984): pp. 62ff.

Minski, H. P., and P. Ferri. "Prices, Employment and Profits." *Journal of Post Keynesian Economics* 6 (Summer 1984): pp. 489–99.

Monthly Labor Review. "The Job Outlook Through 1995." (November 1983a).

_____. "The Aging of the U.S. Population: Human Resources Implications." (May 1983b).

_____. "Post Recession Productivity Gain Helps Curb Labor Cost Growth." (December 1984a).

_____. "Productivity Trend in Manufacturing in U.S. and Eleven Countries, 1960–1982." (January 1984b).

Mueller, Dennis C. *The Political Economy of Growth*. New Haven, CT: Yale University Press, 1983.

OECD Publications—Series. "Capital Markets." Paris: 1982, 1983, 1984.

_____. "Employment Prospects," annual reports. Paris: 1983, 1984.

_____. "Labor Force Statistics." Paris, 1984. Annex Table VII.

_____. "Foreign Trade by Commodities." Paris: 1985.

OECD Publications—Studies. "World Economic Interdependence and the Evolving North-South Relationships." Paris: 1982.

_____. "Exchanges Between Industrial Countries and Developing Countries in the Next Decade." *Economic Review* (Autumn 1984).

_____. "Medium Term Financial Strategy: The Coordination of Fiscal and Monetary Policies." *Economic Studies* 2 (Spring 1984): pp. 7–50.

Okun, Arthur S. *Prices and Quantities: A Macroeconomic Analysis.* Washington: Brookings Institution, 1980. Chapter on "The Labor Market."

Olson, Mancur. *Rise and Decline of Nations: Economic Growth, Stagflation, and Social Rigidities.* New Haven, CT: Yale University Press, 1982. Chs. 2, 7.

Rosenberg, Nathan. *Inside the Black Box: Technology and Economics.* Cambridge and New York: Cambridge University Press, 1981. Pp. 154–59.

Rosenberg, Nathan, and Claudio L. Frischtak. "Technical Innovation and Long Waves." *Cambridge Journal of Economics* 8 (March 1984): pp. 7–24.

Rowan, R., and D. Campbell. "The Attempts to Regulate Industrial Relations Through International Codes of Conduct." *Columbia Journal of World Business* (Summer 1983).

Serge, Peter M. "The Economic Long Wave: A Survey of Evidence." Paper D 3262-1. Cambridge, MA: Sloan School, Massachusetts Institute of Technology, April 1982. P. 30.

Sheffrin, Steven M. *Rational Expectations.* Cambridge Surveys of Economic Literature. Cambridge and New York: Cambridge University Press, 1983. Pp. 6–11 and Ch. 2.

Simon, Herbert. *Reason in Human Affairs.* Stanford, CA: Stanford University Press, 1983.

Standing, Guy. "The Notion of Structural Unemployment." *International Labor Review* 122 (March/April 1983): pp. 137–52.

Survey of Current Business. "Direct Investment Abroad" (August 1984).

Sveikandkas, Leo A. "Science and Technology in United States Foreign Trade." *Economic Journal* 93 (September 1983): pp. 542–54.

Svoboda, Alexander K. "Exchange Rates Regimes and US/European Policy Interdependence." IMF Staff Papers, March 1983.

Tobin, James, ed. *Macroeconomics, Prices and Quantities.* Washington: Brookings Institution, 1983. Chapter on "Labor Markets" and pp. 21–137, 147–51.

United Nations Organization. *Transnational Corporations and World Development,* 3d Survey. New York: 1983.

_____. *Yearbook of Labor Statistics.* New York: 1983.

United Nations Organization, Economic Commission for Europe. *Annual Report,* 1984.

Van Duijn, J. J. *The Long Wave in Economic Life.* London: George Allen, 1983.

Van Winden, F. A. *On the Interaction Between State and Private Sector.* Amsterdam: North Holland, 1983.

Yankelovich, D. "Work, Values and the New Breed." In *Work in America, the Decade Ahead,* eds. Clark Kerr and Jerome M. Rosow. New York: Van Nostrand Reinhold, 1979.

Yoshihiro, Kogane. "Changing Value Patterns and Their Impact." In *Interface.* Paris: OECD, 1983. Pp. 15–80, 188–211, 215–25.

Chapter 2

Australian Industrial Relations and the Shift to Centralism*

Braham Dabscheck and John Niland
University of New South Wales

Like most Western economies in the past decade, Australia faced the twin problems of high inflation and rising rates of unemployment. In periods of full employment, such as the 1960s and the early 1970s, or when the economy showed signs of recovery, as with Australia's short-lived resources boom of the early 1980s, industrial relations proceeded on a decentralized, industry-by-industry basis. However, stagflation dominated most of the period between 1974 and 1985, and the basic Australian response to such economic adversity has been to centralize regulation of industrial relations, especially national-level wage determination.

There have, of course, been other developments and areas of interest in Australian industrial relations over the past decade:[1] antidiscrimination legislation (Ronalds 1979, Bedwell 1981, Thornton 1982); attempts to develop a legislative and arbitral base for redundancy protection (Yerbury and Clark 1983); concern about issues relevant to occupational health and safety (Cunningham 1984); legislation designed to bring greater controls on certain forms of trade union behavior, such as secondary boycotts (Mitchell 1979 and 1983, Hughes 1984); the preparation and hearing of submissions to an inquiry on the reform of Australian industrial relations law and systems (Conference on Alternatives 1984); and the formation in 1977 of the Confederation of Australian Industry (CAI) to act as a single spokesperson on behalf of employer interests (Plowman 1978, Ford, Plowman, and Lansbury 1978) and the emergence of the Business Council of Australia (BCA) as a second peak-level employer body. Despite these developments, the dominant issue in Australian industrial relations over the last decade

---

* This is a revised and lengthened version of Dabscheck and Niland (1984).

[1] For a regular survey of developments in Australian industrial relations, see the Annual Review section in the March issue of *The Journal of Industrial Relations*.

has been centralism and the development of a national wages policy. This trend has involved unions, tribunals, and more recently the Hawke Labor government (but not the employers) seeking to achieve industrial relations stability and recovery via the preservation of real wages. There has been relatively less emphasis on redundancy. Also surprising in an era of high unemployment has been the waning influence of employers. In these respects, recent trends in Australian industrial relations vary from the experience of most other Western market economies.

This chapter is divided into four parts. The first section outlines Australia's unique form of industrial relations regulation and recent changes.[2] The second section deals with performance and operation in the Australian economy over the last decade, particularly unemployment, inflation, and industrial conflict. The third section examines the industrial relations responses to these problems, focusing on the development of a centralized wages policy. And in the final section we assess the main trends and briefly look at possible future developments.

The Institutional Setting

While any national system of industrial relations has some unique features, the very foundation of the Australian system, which emphasizes conciliation and arbitration, is unusual. The key role played by industrial tribunals is a major difference from other industrialized countries. While most nations have established public agencies to deal with problems arising between labor and management, the number of such bodies in Australia, and their pervasive influence over day-to-day industrial relations, sets them apart. The large number of such bodies demonstrates the willingness of governments to regulate economic and industrial problems through tribunals. The federal system of government is also important, since the national parliament shares power to create tribunals with six state parliaments and the two main territories. By counting only bodies whose primary responsibility is to regulate some aspects of employment relationships, one finds 18 Commonwealth tribunals and 89 in the states and territories, for a total of 107 tribunals with a labor force of 6 million workers.

---

[2] For a more detailed examination of the intricacies and nuances of Australian industrial relations, see Dabscheck and Niland (1981) and Plowman, Deery, and Fisher (1980).

There are several significant aspects of the federal system for industrial relations. First, the federal government cannot become directly involved in industrial relations except for its own employees and all workers in the territories. Federal power in industrial relations derives from the Australian Constitution which empowers it "to make laws for the peace, order and good government of the Commonwealth with respect to . . . Conciliation and Arbitration for the prevention and settlement of industrial disputes extending beyond the limits of any one State"[3]

In effect, this provision bars the federal government from passing laws that directly regulate industrial relations. Instead it delegates this function to industrial tribunals, which exercise powers of "conciliation and arbitration." While most tribunals are independent of one another, the Australian Conciliation and Arbitration Commission (Arbitration Commission) has gradually assumed a leading role.

Tribunals, particularly the Arbitration Commission, are also quite independent from governments, so much that a leading arbitration judge once referred to himself and his colleagues as the "economic dictators of Australia."[4] Arbitration Commission members hold tenured appointments, and they have never responded meekly to the federal government. The Commission hears submissions from the various parties, including the federal government, and hands down a decision based on its own view of the best response to particular industrial relations problems. Consequently, the Arbitration Commission has an important role in the development of national wage policy. If the federal government wishes to implement a wages (and incomes) policy, it cannot use legislation; rather, the Arbitration Commission and the major tribunals operating within the respective states must cooperate. On the other hand, the Arbitration Commission is able to operate a wages policy without the cooperation of the federal government, notwithstanding the latter's control over fiscal and monetary policy. For example, from December 1975 to July 1981 the Arbitration Commission implemented a wages policy based on indexation (see below) despite the lack of cooperation and support of Prime

[3] For an examination of other constitutional powers available to the federal government, see Dabscheck and Niland (1981), pp. 187–90.

[4] Quoted in Perlman (1954), p. 32.

Minister Fraser's Liberal National government.[5] In the end, however, the failure of the government to support the Commission with policies on taxation and other issues contributed to the collapse of indexation. Thus, while the Arbitration Commission has considerable discretion in the short run, checks and balances between it and the federal government build up, and over the long run there is a quasi-bargaining relationship between these two parties.

Second, the Constitution does not limit state governments in the same way that it restrains the power of the federal government. Since state governments can legislate directly on wages and working conditions, political methods to achieve industrial relations objectives are more prevalent there than at the federal level. While these governments have created numerous industrial tribunals, they also have the power to override these bodies. For example, state governments have used legislation to introduce a 40-hour work-week, health and safety standards, and, more recently, requirements that tribunals under their jurisdiction follow the Arbitration Commission's national wage standards. Approximately 40 percent of workers are covered by federal awards, 50 percent by state awards, with 10 percent having no award coverage.

The pivotal role of the High Court in interpreting the Australian Constitution is the third significant aspect of the federal system. This body's decisions in effect determine the division of powers between the state and federal governments and, as a result, define and limit the powers of the Arbitration Commission vis-à-vis other tribunals and the state and federal governments. Two recent decisions illustrate the importance of the High Court.

Traditionally, the High Court took a narrow view of the term "industrial dispute" in the Constitution, which effectively denied access to the Arbitration Commission to certain groups, primarily white-collar workers in areas which are not technically "industrial" in nature. Equally significant has been the High Court's view that disputes over managerial prerogatives lie beyond the federal tribunal's constitutional jurisdiction. Such disputes were nonetheless regulated through a combination of conciliation and voluntary or private arbitration, in which the parties waived any legal objections to the tribunal's involvement.

---

[5] See Plowman (1981), pp. 126–38 and 157–60 for details.

In the 1983 *Social Welfare Union* case the High Court revised its interpretation of the meaning of the term "industrial disputes," with the effect that groups of workers who have hitherto been denied access to the Arbitration Commission can now, if they wish, have it determine their wages and conditions (assuming the dispute crosses state boundaries).[6] Also, the Arbitration Commission now has the constitutional authority to hear disputes involving managerial rights, and has widened its coverage in respect of such issues as dismissal and redundancy. Following these decisions, the Arbitration Commission handed down landmark decisions in 1984 dealing with both principles and standards to apply in situations of termination, change, and redundancy.[7]

On a more general level, the High Court heard an environment dispute in 1983 between the federal and Tasmanian government over the latter's right to build a dam in the Tasmanian wilderness. The High Court ruled in favor of the federal government on the basis of its authority over external affairs.[8] As a signatory to an international treaty, the federal government acquires legislative powers to achieve the objectives of that treaty. The significance for industrial relations is that Australia has ratified many of the Conventions established by the International Labor Organization,[9] and it is conceivable (though currently not probable) that the federal government could legislate to further the aims of those Conventions. One obvious example is in the area of occupational health and safety, an issue of growing importance in Australia.

These two High Court Cases paved the way for a significant realignment of power and coverage between the various legislatures and industrial jurisdictions. The decisions favored the federal government and the Arbitration Commission over state-based bodies, including legislatures as well as tribunals. This authority conferred on federal bodies will make centralism easier to sustain.

Another factor in the shift to centralism is Australia's system of wage determination. In the federal jurisdiction a three-tier

---

[6] *Social Welfare Union* case (mimeo), pp. 13–14, reported 47 *Australian Law Reports* 225.

[7] Australian Conciliation and Arbitration Commission, *Termination, Change and Redundancy* case, 2 August 1984, Mis 250/84 MD Print F6230; and 14 December 1984, Mis 505/84 MD Print F7262.

[8] 46 *Australian Law Reports* 625.

[9] For a list of these, see Dabscheck and Niland (1981), pp. 206–209.

structure exists. There are national wage cases, industry cases, and over-award negotiations, the importance of each tier varying over time and between sectors. In national wage cases a panel of senior members of the Arbitration Commission determines or adjusts wages for all workers covered by federal awards, setting minimum levels consistent with broad industrial, social, and economic changes. Since the 1950s major considerations in national wage cases have been the state of the economy and the equitable distribution of the benefits of economic growth, given the levels of inflation, productivity, investment, employment, and the balance of payments. Usually, though not invariably, the various state tribunals ratify national wage case decisions, passing the increases on to workers in their jurisdictions.

In industry cases the Arbitration Commission (or the appropriate state commission) deals with wages of workers covered by a particular award. These are usually handled by individual tribunal members who take into account circumstances that affect the industry or the workers covered by their award. Wage increases gained at this level are added to those determined in national wage cases.

Beyond the tribunals and depending on economic and political circumstances, unions and employers may negotiate over-award wages and benefits. Although the tribunals are not involved initially in this process, unions and employers often register their agreements with a commission to achieve greater legal and economic standing for the document. If the tribunal considers the settlement is too generous and breaches its operating principles of wage determination, such registration may be denied. While cases of such over-award negotiation have been common, particularly prior to the mid-1970s and during a brief period in the early 1980s, bargaining over a total economic package occurs only in isolated instances (e.g., metals in 1981–82, coal in 1982–83, oil in 1983, and, to a lesser extent, building in 1983–84). A key strategy in enhancing centralism is the promotion of the first tier—national wage cases— and the downgrading of the other two, particularly over-award negotiations.

The long-standing system of tribunals has fostered a high degree of organization among workers and employers. The effective operation of the tribunals basically depends on the collective representations of workers, so there is an incentive for them to organize. Australian trade union membership is approximately 55 percent of the labor force. The highest density is in blue-collar industries or occupations, plus the public sector. While there are over 300 unions in Australia, the 10 largest organizations include almost half of all members and operate in all six states. Most unions are occupational; that is, they include persons in jobs in a genetic category, such as work closely related to electricity, of various skill levels. A few large unions are industrial. Because of this structure, managers naturally must deal with multiple unions in a firm.

There is one major peak association for Australian labor, the Australian Council of Trade Unions (ACTU). It acts as a national coordinating body, but does not engage in bargaining or represent its members before the tribunals. The locus of power is at the state and union levels within the Council. Unions affiliate with the Australian Labor Party (ALP) at the level of the state branch. Affiliation is common, though not universal, so the labor movement is a major source of support to the ALP.

The influence of the tribunals on employer organization has also been strong. Individual employers, faced by strongly organized workers and complex rules imposed by tribunals in separate awards for each union, found organization convenient, if not imperative. A vast array of bodies emerged, divided by the variety of industrial relations functions performed, industrial sector represented, and geographic scope. While it is possible for an individual employer to appear before a tribunal, small firms find it especially useful to delegate this responsibility to an association.

The Confederation of Australian Industry (CAI) is the major peak association for employers. It includes a large number of individual associations and performs industrial relations functions as well as representing its members on issues of commerce, industry, and trade. It has become a major voice for Australian employers in national wage cases. In 1983, a number of large employers formed the Business Council of Australia as a competing peak association with functions similar to the CAI (Dabscheck and Niland 1981).

The effect of this system is to guarantee about 90 percent of Australian workers an arbitrated floor below which wages and conditions may not fall or be agreed to by the industrial parties. Trade unions usually pursue further wage increases and other concessions through two main avenues: From decisions of the industrial tribunals or, beyond this, through over-award bargaining.[10] Speaking generally, when the economy is healthy and prosperous, unions are able to gain (or employers are willing to grant) wage and other concessions via direct negotiations with employers. Under conventional collective bargaining, a recession would probably shift the balance of power in favor of employers because of their ability to reduce the level of concessions gained by unions and/or obtain "givebacks." When the Australian economy is depressed, however, unions turn to industrial tribunals to gain desired concessions, thereby seeking protection from the rigors of the market.

The declining influence and power of employers in industrial relations during the last decade is directly related to the decisions of the Arbitration Commission to implement a centralized system of wage determination based on wage indexation. While employers have voiced strong and continuing opposition to centralized wage determination, at least when full adjustment for price movements is involved, they are not without their defenses. Employers are more likely to accept arbitrated wage increases "not because employers generally are more law-abiding than unions, but because they have an easier escape route from unfavorable awards by raising prices or transferring capital."[11] In addition, employers have used their influence, often with union support, to obtain aid from both state and federal governments in the form of tariffs, subsidies, and tax concessions.

Unemployment, Inflation, and Industrial Action

The performance of the Australian economy deteriorated substantially during the 1970–1984 period, although there were signs of recovery in 1984. The economy suffered high levels of inflation and unemployment.[12] Table 1 shows employment by industry 1971–1983, during which period the size of the Australian workforce grew

---

[10] Other avenues are also available. Unions can make use of political lobbying and play off the various state and federal tribunals against each other. For a more complete analysis, see Dabscheck (1981).

[11] See Isaac (1975), p. 409.

[12] For regular surveys of the Australian economy and labor market, see *The Australian Economic Review and Australian Bulletin of Labour*, respectively. And for a recent survey of the Australian economy by a group of American academics, see Caves and Krause (1984). Also see Blandy and Richardson (1982), Blandy and Covick (1982), and Chapman, Isaac, and Niland (1984).

TABLE 1

Employment by Industry: Persons 1971–1983 (in thousands)

	Year (at August)												
	1971	1972	1973	1974	1975	1976	1977	1978ᵃ	1979	1980	1981	1982	1983
Agriculture	413	442	426	405	398	385	400	377	399	407	414	410	411
Mining	89	81	70	74	79	80	80	80	82	84	98	91	94
Manufacturing	1365	1330	1382	1374	1263	1282	1277	1185	1221	1234	1131	1193	1134
Construction	471	466	503	506	511	494	482	485	466	483	472	464	388
Wholesale/retail trade	1113	1163	1187	1166	1157	1157	1185	1239	1224	1265	1266	1240	1215
Transportation, storage	294	286	312	313	330	321	316	327	344	342	349	374	365
Finance	395	399	410	429	431	456	467	466	483	511	555	583	573
Community services	616	664	692	747	793	852	895	919	940	1008	1022	1050	1074
Recreation	322	350	356	356	372	370	373	365	367	386	396	400	389
Other industries	429	429	453	485	508	502	520	528	515	526	553	544	591
Total employment	5516	5610	5783	5855	5841	5898	5995	5970	6042	6247	6356	6348	6233
Unemployment	93	144	106	141	278	293	359	396	374	391	377	459	684
Workforce	5608	5754	5889	5996	6120	6191	6355	6365	6315	6639	6733	6806	6917
Participation rate (%)	61.0	61.3	61.6	61.4	61.6	61.3	61.8	60.7	60.1	61.1	60.7	60.1	59.8

Source: Reserve Bank of Australia, *Australian Economic Statistics 1949/50 to 1982/83: I Tables,* Occasional Paper No. 8A, January 1984.

ᵃ Break in continuity of series.

from over 5.6 million to 6.9 million, a 23 percent increase. In the same period total employment grew from 5.5 million to 6.2 million, an increase of only 13 percent. The obvious result has been a spectacular growth in unemployment from 93,000 to 680,000, a 635 percent increase. Accompanying the high level of unemployment has been a gradual decrease in the labor force participation rate,[13] especially among older males (Merrilees 1982).

The table shows that the major areas of employment growth in this period are in the tertiary/service industries, finance and community services, where employment approximately doubled. On the other hand, both manufacturing (especially metals, cars and white goods) and construction have experienced both absolute and relative declines in employment. In 1971, 25.6 percent of employed persons were in manufacturing; by 1983 that figure had fallen to 18.2 percent. And in the construction industry the figures were 8.4 and 6.2 percent, respectively.

TABLE 2
Australian Unemployment Rate, 1971–1983

Year (at August)	Unemployment Rate (%)
1971	1.7
1972	2.5
1973	1.8
1974	2.4
1975	4.6
1976	4.7
1977	5.7
1978[a]	6.2
1979	5.8
1980	5.9
1981	5.6
1982	6.7
1983	9.9

Source: Reserve Bank of Australia, *Australian Economic Statistics 1949/50 to 1982/83: I Tables*, Occasional Paper No. 8A, January 1984.
[a] Break in continuity of series between 1977 and 1978.

Table 2 provides information on the Australian unemployment rate in the period 1971 to 1983. In the early 1970s a relatively low unemployment rate prevailed, hovering around the 2-percent level. This all changed dramatically in the second half of 1974. Australia found itself caught up in a world-wide inflation and experienced

---

[13] It has also been argued that there is a significant number of hidden unemployed not included in official statistics. See Stricker and Sheehan (1981).

substantial increases in both prices and average weekly earnings. The federal government's attempt to use the Keynesian tools of fiscal and monetary policy to control inflation merely boosted unemployment throughout the rest of the 1970s. Unemployment levels stayed fairly constant, at approximately 6 percent. Accompanied by a short-lived resources boom, the rate of unemployment declined slightly between January and June 1981.[14] In 1982 and 1983 the economy moved back onto a downtrend and unemployment rapidly increased. However, with growth in 1984 the unemployment rate that year again began to fall, to approximately 8.5 percent of the labor force.

TABLE 3
Unemployment Rates (Percent) by Age and Sex, 1971–1983

	Males		Females		Persons	
Year (at August)	Aged 15-19	Aged 20+	Aged 15-19	Aged 20+	Aged 15-19	Aged 20+
1971	3.2	1.0	4.3	2.3	3.7	1.4
1972	5.6	1.6	5.9	3.2	5.8	2.1
1973	4.6	1.0	4.9	2.3	4.7	1.4
1974	5.0	1.4	6.7	2.9	5.8	1.9
1975	10.8	2.8	15.1	4.8	12.9	3.5
1976	12.7	3.0	15.8	4.5	14.2	3.5
1977	15.8	3.5	20.3	5.0	18.0	4.0
1978[a]	16.5	4.3	17.2	5.7	16.8	4.8
1979	14.7	3.7	20.4	5.4	17.4	4.3
1980	14.8	3.9	18.9	5.4	16.7	4.5
1981	11.2	4.0	17.1	5.5	13.9	4.5
1982	16.4	5.4	17.1	5.9	16.7	5.5
1983	23.0	8.7	22.2	7.9	22.6	8.4

Source: Reserve Bank of Australia, *Australian Economic Statistics 1949/50 to 1982/83: I Tables*, Occasional Paper No. 8A, January 1984.

[a] Break in continuity of series between 1977 and 1978.

Table 3 shows how unemployment has been distributed between men and women and between teenagers and adults in the years 1971 to 1983. Except for 1983, the unemployment rate of women had exceeded that of men. Teenagers have a substantially higher unemployment level than adults. Almost one in four teenagers were unemployed in 1983, compared to one in 12 adults. Also, individuals' time in unemployment has increased sharply. In 1973 the average duration unemployed was 9.3 weeks;

---

[14] Australian Bureau of Statistics, *The Labour Force, Australia*, January 1982, No. 6203.0.

in 1983 this figure had increased to 41.5 weeks, an increase of almost 350 percent.[15] Further, the unemployed themselves are segmented, with approximately 2 percent of the labor force accounting for 50 percent of measured unemployment, largely because some spend periods exceeding 70 continuous weeks out of work, while many others have only quite brief encounters with joblessness (Gregory and Foster 1984).

TABLE 4

Annual Movements in Consumer Price Index and
Average Weekly Earnings, Australia, 1971–72 to 1982–83

Year	% Change in CPI	% Change in AWE
1971–72	6.8	10.1
1972–73	5.9	9.0
1973–74	13.1	16.2
1974–75	16.7	25.4
1975–76	12.8	14.5
1976–77	14.0	12.4
1977–78	9.4	9.9
1978–79	8.2	7.7
1979–80	10.1	9.9
1980–81	9.4	13.5
1981–82	10.4	n.a.
1982–83	11.5[a]	11.4

Source: Reserve Bank of Australia, *Australian Economic Statistics 1949/50 to 1982/83: I Tables*, Occasional Paper No. 8A, January 1984.

[a] Break in continuity of series.

n.a. Not available.

Causes of Australian unemployment have been variously assessed. One line of argument, closely associated with the Australian Treasury, is that labor cost increases which exceed productivity growth are a source of rising unemployment (Johnson et al. 1978). Relevant to this concern are movements in the consumer price index (CPI) and average weekly earnings (AWE), details for which are given in Table 4. Since 1973–74, changes in the CPI each year have been around 10 percent. Only in the years 1977–78, 1978–79, and 1980–81 did it fall below this figure. Real wages, for the most part, have been maintained, or increased; AWE for most years increased at a faster rate than the CPI. The major

[15] Australian Bureau of Statistics, *Employment, Underemployment and Unemployment 1966–1983*, Catalogue No. 6246.0.

exception was the period of the nine-month wage pause, beginning in December 1982.

While economists generally acknowledge the potential dis-employment effect of the so-called "real wage overhang," many question whether it has been a dominant cause of unemployment. But even if an overhang had existed, unemployment may not necessarily respond to a reduction in wages.

The natural level of unemployment—the point at which unemployment is relatively insensitive to increasing demand and price stability no longer depends on easing demand pressures—has been the subject of considerable debate. Australian estimates vary between 2 and 7 percent (Dornbush and Fisher 1984, Mitchell 1984, Trivedi and Baker 1982).

Thus, while unit labor costs do matter, they do not link to unemployment in the straightforward fashion implied in Treasury analysis. The conclusion of Trivedi and Baker (1982), and one endorsed by the Department of Employment and Industrial Relations (DEIR), is that "variations in frictional unemployment are really just a small part of the story. Most, if not all, of the increase in unemployment in the 1970s is explained by real wages and capacity utilization with the latter variable causing most of the movements in the past five years" (DEIR 1984, p. 18). The DEIR, often at odds with Treasury economic policy, has emphasized the need to contain wage increases, but through an effective prices and incomes policy rather than through deflationary monetary and fiscal policy.

Beyond the debate over the appropriate macroeconomic policy, two further lines of attack have been mounted against unemploy-ment. Concern for the problems of special groups such as youth, Aborigines, and women, caused the federal government to sponsor special training programs in the 1970s. However, these represented essentially ad hoc responses to the manifest political liability of burgeoning unemployment. Overall, there is no integrating philosophy, and it is possible that such measures do little to create new jobs (Niland 1984).

The second development is the provision of procedures and standards of compensation to apply in situations of redundancy. Such arrangements have lagged behind European standards. Because of constitutional difficulties, job protection was initially based in state legislation, but with the recent expansionist mood of the High Court (Yerbury 1984), the Australian Arbitration Commission is more assured (though still not guaranteed) jurisdiction in this area. A pair of landmark decisions in 1984 established comprehensive principles and standards for termination, change, and redundancy. Initially, the decisions apply only to the Metal Industry Award, but probably will follow a typical Australian pattern and transfer to other federal awards. Employers covered by federal awards now cannot dismiss employees unfairly, but must notify workers and unions of significant production, organizational, and technological changes which will have serious employment effects. They must also consult with unions to minimize the hardship for the workers concerned. The decisions establish minimum amounts of severance pay, to a maximum of eight weeks pay, subject to the employer's ability to pay.

Downturns in the economy, together with the Arbitration Commission's second period of wage indexation (see below), has led to a decline in strike activity, although the trend was not uninterrupted. Australia averaged 2318 strikes per year, or 0.634 working days lost per employee, in the years 1971–83. As Table 5 shows, strike activity was generally higher in the earlier part than in the latter part of the period, with the upsurge in 1980–81 reflecting the mini-resources boom and, more importantly, the release of pressures built up over the six or seven years of relatively

TABLE 5
Strikes in Australia, 1971 to 1983

Year	Number of Disputes	Workers Involved Directly and Indirectly (000)	Working Days Lost (000)	Working Days Lost per Employee
1971	2,404	1,326.5	3,068.6	0.693
1972	2,298	1,113.8	2,010.3	0.449
1973	2,538	803.0	2,634.5	0.570
1974	2,809	2,004.8	6,191.5	1.320
1975	2,432	1,398.0	3,509.9	0.742
1976	2,055	2,189.9	3,799.2	0.803
1977	2,090	596.2	1,654.8	0.350
1978	2,277	1,075.6	2,130.8	0.432
1979	2,042	1,862.9	3,964.4	0.785
1980	2,429	1,172.8	3,320.2	0.650
1981	2,915	1,251.8	4,192.2	0.800
1982	1,060	722.9	2,158.0	0.396
1983	1,787	470.5	1,641.4	0.249

Sources: Australian Bureau of Statistics, Monthly and Quarterly Summaries of Industrial Disputes, Catalogue Nos. 6321.0 and 6322.0.

tight wage controls in the first wage indexation experiment. The number of workers involved in strikes (directly and indirectly) ranged from a high of 2.2 million in 1976 to less than half a million in 1983. Total working days lost ranged from a high of 6.3 million in 1974, also the year of highest inflation in this period, to a low of 1.6 million in 1983. The highest figure for working days lost per employee in this period was 1.320 in 1974, with the lowest being 0.249 in 1983.

Thus, despite an arbitration system dedicated to replacing strike activity with "a new province for law and order," working days lost through strikes are no less, and in some cases much greater, than in other OECD countries (Clarke 1980). Where there is a difference, however, is in the duration profile. Australia has a large number of relatively short strikes. Between 40 and 50 percent are terminated/resolved within one day, with between 70 and 80 percent terminated/resolved within three days. Other forms of industrial conflict, by definition difficult to measure, are bans and limitations on the normal performance of work. One indication of a long-run rising trend here is in the apparent increase in employer applications to industrial tribunals for permission to suspend employees not working to direction.

Assuming that the typical length of the working year in this period was 226 days (Steinke 1983), each Australian worker on average in the years 1971 to 1983 spent 0.281 percent of the time available for work on strike. While doubtless there are situations where strikes threaten the economic viability of particular firms or industries, it is useful to put aggregate time lost through overt industrial activity into a broader context. Finding permanent jobs for 30,000 individuals would add more than 6 million working days per year of production. It has been estimated that strikes constitute 5.5 percent of temporary nonapproved absences from work. This compares with other causes of lost time such as industrial accidents (excluding industrial deaths), 6.3 percent; off-the-job accidents, 12 percent; drug and alcohol abuse, 18 percent; the odd day or two off work sick (usually up to a maximum of 10 per year), 19 percent; and general illness, 39 percent (Crawford and Volard 1981).

Wages Policy

Pre-indexation

Throughout the 1950s and 1960s industrial disputes in Australia were regulated by a combination of bargaining, conciliation, and arbitration, with arbitration having a less significant role. This was the period of consent determinations, where tribunals readily registered agreements between the parties, and of conciliation, where industrial tribunals sought to accommodate their decisions to the needs of the parties (Yerbury and Isaac 1971). When tribunals became involved in disputes, they devised solutions to satisfy the *particular* needs of the parties before them rather than seeking a *uniform* solution to be applied in all situations.[16] The parties desired and industrial tribunals permitted, if they did not encourage, the resolution of disputes at the industry or firm level, rather than at the national level. Industry-wide awards and over-award negotiations were common. This period features a decentralized approach to industrial relations regulation—a period unique in modern Australian history, which may never be repeated.

The corollary of this pattern, of course, was a decline in the importance of national wage cases. Between 1969–70 and 1974–75, their contribution to total increases in the weighted average minimum wage for males fell from 51.6 to only 21.2 percent (Howard 1977, p. 271).

The Centralized Indexation Approach

Late in 1974 Australia began to experience world-wide economic problems. As the economy weakened, the ACTU mounted a national claim before the Arbitration Commission, seeking increases in wages and the (re)introduction of automatic cost-of-living adjustments. A similar approach, but applying only to the basic (or minimum) component of wages, had been abandoned in 1953 after 30 years because it was thought to be inflationary.[17] The 1975 case turned on an assessment of whether automatic (or almost automatic) indexation would improve or worsen the

---

[16] For an account of how Sir Richard Kirby, the Arbitration Commission's President from 1956 to 1973, approached industrial relations regulation, see Kirby (1970) and d'Alpuget (1977).

[17] *Commonwealth Arbitration Reports* 477. Also see Dabscheck (1983).

Australian economy. In 1974 wages had risen an average of 24 percent, largely through direct negotiation. Consequently, the Arbitration Commission would not order wage indexation unless the ACTU agreed that increases outside national wage case adjustments (i.e., wage indexation) would be kept to a minimum. Eventually, the ACTU gave the desired undertaking.[18]

The Commission's decision in April 1975 effectively linked wage adjustments with CPI movements. It became the key element in the national strategy for settling wages and industrial relations issues during the subsequent decade of inflation, recession, and unemployment. The Commission concluded that a central and orderly system of wage determination would help solve Australia's economic, industrial, and social problems. It permitted wage reviews after each publication of the CPI, but only if wage increases from other sources were negligible. The Arbitration Commission also warned that "violation even by a small section of industry whether in the award or non-award would put at risk the future of indexation for all."[19] The Commission's guidelines allowed exceptional wage increases for change in work value ("a significant net addition to work requirements"); for the catch-up of community movements (for those who had missed out on the wage round before indexation's introduction); anomalies (added in May 1976) and inequities (added in September 1978).[20]

Wage indexation lasted for six years in the first instance—from April 1975 to July 1981. Table 6 provides details of the various decisions of the Arbitration Commission. Only seven of the 19 decisions handed down provided full indexation. Others were either partial indexation, where adjustment was less than CPI movement (e.g., June 1977), or plateau indexation where the Arbitration Commission awarded a percentage increase up to a certain wage level and a flat amount beyond this level. Work-value increases provided a cover for safety valves to meet pressures that inevitably build up in a centralized wage policy. In mid-1978, for

---

[18] For the background to this original undertaking by the ACTU, see Dabscheck (1975), pp. 298–303, and for a discussion of the relationship between the ACTU and its affiliates, see Dabscheck (1977).

[19] 167 *Commonwealth Arbitration Reports* 18, p. 39.

[20] The original indexation decision implied that productivity cases would be heard annually; however, the ACTU never mounted a productivity case in the first six years of wage indexation's operation.

instance, waterside workers gained a work-value increase of about $8.00 per week. However, with a centralized system, particularly where any one union has members across many industries, the irresistible force of comparisons saw this flow to other workers. By April 1981 the Arbitration Commission estimated that the waterside workers' $8.00 had been extended to 80 percent of the workforce, which negated the inherent logic of work value as "a significant net addition to work requirements."

The Arbitration Commission wished to ensure that national wage cases were the major, if not the only, source of wage movements in the economy. With some success it urged the parties,

TABLE 6
Alterations to Total Wage Under Wage Indexation, 1975–1981

Date	CPI Variation (%)	Wage Variation
1975 March	3.6	3.6%
June	3.5	3.5%
September	0.8	nil
December	5.6	(5.8% + 0.8%) = 6.4%
1975 March	3.0	3.0% to $125 per week; $3.80 thereafter
June	2.5	2.5% to $98 per week, then $2.50 to $98–$166 per week; 1.5% thereafter
September	2.2	2.2%
December	6.0	$5.70
1977 March	2.3	1.9% to $200 per week; $3.80 thereafter
June	2.4	2.0%
September	2.0	1.5%
December	2.3	1.5% to $170 per week; $2.60 thereafter
1978 March	1.3	1.3%
June/September	4.0	4.0%
December/March 1979	4.0	3.2%
1979 June/September	5.0	4.5%
December/March 1980	5.3	4.2%
1980 June/September	4.7	3.7%
December/March 1981	4.5	3.6%

Source: National Wage Case decisions. After June/September 1978 the hearings were changed from four a year to two a year.

other tribunals, and governments to follow its lead in responding to economic problems. Strong bargaining activity in the early 1970s had meant that national wage decisions then had accounted for only 20–30 percent of increases in the total wage. This picture changed dramatically with the onset of wage indexation. As Table 7 shows, over 95 percent of wage increases between August 1976 and June 1978 came from indexation decisions. After June 1978 the figure declined to less than 90 percent for males, and in July 1980 to less than 90 percent for females, a reflection of the work-value round described in the previous paragraph. The apparent success of wage indexation—the Arbitration Commission's ability to maintain its grip on wages—was due largely to the depressed state of the economy, which reduced the ability of trade unions to gain other concessions.

TABLE 7

Wage Indexation Increases as a Percentage of
Change in Total Wages, Australia 1975 to 1981

Year	Male (%)	Female (%)
August 1976	92	94
August 1977	94	96
June 1978	98	99
December 1978	89	97
June 1979	86	95
January 1980	86	96
July 1980	81	86
January 1981	83	70
May 1981	91	79

Source: Australian Bureau of Statistics, *Wage Rate Indexes (Preliminary)*, Catalogue No. 6311.0.

Strains of Centralism

A centralized system of wage determination inevitably produces stresses and strains.[21] Not all participants within the industrial relations system saw the need for such an approach or else doubted the wisdom of following the Arbitration Commission's economic policies. The government of Prime Minister Malcolm Fraser did not share the Arbitration Commission's enthusiasm for wage indexation, for example. As unemployment rose, it maintained that the Com-

---

[21] For a more detailed critique of the problems associated with Australia's system of compulsory arbitration, see Niland (1976 and 1978), Brown and Rowe (1983), Tilling and Wheeler (1984).

mission should develop a wages policy to support the federal government's budgetary policy, that is, to keep wages below the rate of increase in the CPI, even to grant no raises at all.[22]

The Arbitration Commission, for its part, urged the federal government to devise economic policies consistent with the maintenance of a system of wage indexation (Isaac 1977). For example, it urged the government not to make decisions which would raise prices (such as increasing indirect taxes) because of their impact on wages (and hence further price increases). However, the Commission and the Fraser government never did agree on economic policy. Plowman has estimated that from December 1975 to September 1979 policy-induced price increases of the Fraser government added 2.25 to the annual rate of inflation (Plowman 1981, p. 159).

Some state tribunals found the wage indexation guidelines overly restrictive. Occasionally the major tribunals of Western Australia and South Australia handed down decisions different from the Arbitration Commission (Nieuwenhuysen 1981). Also, tensions developed among members of the Arbitration Commission itself. Two justices clashed openly (Staples 1979 and 1980), and a number of conciliation commissioners also expressed misgivings about the strictures of wage indexation. In fact, a case was mounted in the High Court to test whether individual members of the Arbitration Commission had to follow the wage indexation guidelines. The Court ruled that Commissioners were obliged to follow the principles determined by a full bench of the Arbitration Commission.[23]

The CAI and other employer bodies, while supporting a centralized system of wage determination, objected to wage indexation. They preferred to tie wages to increases in national productivity rather than to prices. Employers in sectors experiencing growth and/or wishing to innovate following technological change objected to indexation because it restricted their ability to alter wages to attract labor, while those employers in declining sectors maintained that wage indexation imposed increases which

---

[22] For an examination of the Fraser government's approach to wage indexation, see note 5. Regarding the support offered by the Whitlam Labor government, see Yerbury (1981).

[23] *Australian Telephone and Phonogram Officers Association*, 56 *Australian Law Journal Reports* 228.

forced them to lay off workers. Unions, for their part, objected to Arbitration Commission decisions granting less than full indexation. Generally speaking, however, most unions supported wage indexation because it guaranteed wage increases during a period of economic decline. With wages centrally determined, some unions applied the resources and energy that they would have used in wage campaigns to pursue other objectives with employers. The most important of these initiatives was a campaign for the 35-hour week pursued by metal trades unions during 1980 and 1981. In many ways the eventual adoption of the 38-hour workweek as national standard can be attributed to this aspect of wage indexation.[24]

Late in 1980 and through 1981 the Australian economy began to recover. The Fraser government pointed to an emerging mining and resources boom. The demand for skilled workers increased and employers bid wages up to attract or hold onto their labor force. A number of employers and unions in both the private and public sectors negotiated agreements involving wage increases in the vicinity of $20.00 per week. Besides the mining/resources sector, the most conspicuous of these were in road transport, New South Wales rail, the Melbourne waterfront, and sections of the Australian public service. When a new wage round was unleashed, it was difficult to contain; at the end of July 1981 the Arbitration Commission faced the inevitable and ended wage indexation.

Towards a Social Contract Approach

By Australian standards, a decentralized system of industrial relations and wage determination emerged again. Wages, rather than being determined nationally by the Arbitration Commission, were adjusted on a case-by-case, or award-by-award, basis with different sets of unions and employers negotiating changes in wages and working conditions (in some situations with the aid of tribunals). Undoubtedly the metal trades industry agreement in 1981 was the most significant.

After the end of wage indexation, the metal trades employers (the Metal Trades Industry Association) found that they had to negotiate with the metal unions over a demand for the 35-hour week. A December 1981 agreement contained four key elements: a

---

[24] It should be noted that the 40-hour working week was introduced during a period when wartime and postwar regulations placed restrictions on wages. See Sheridan (1973).

basic increase, a mid-term adjustment to be paid from June 1982 unless "there is an unforeseen change of an extraordinary nature in the economic circumstance," a 38-hour workweek to be introduced in mid-March 1982, and an agreement by the unions not to make any extra claims for increased wages during the 12-month life of the agreement. The no-extra-claims clause constituted a major innovation by the standards of Australian industrial relations and partly explains the decline in strikes which occurred after 1981 (see Table 5). These features quickly spread, facilitated by the trade union structure. The Arbitration Commission estimated that, by May 1982, 75 percent of employees had received wage increases since the end of wage indexation in July 1981.

In the second half of 1982 the condition of the Australian economy deteriorated substantially. Both unemployment and the rate of inflation increased (see Tables 2 and 4). Since awards set minima on the parties, temporary working arrangements can be approved only through a tribunal hearing, a rare event. There were, however, many rumors of workers who had agreed to work at less than award rates and had forgone over-award pay, often over the strenuous objections of their union officials. By the end of 1982, federal, state, and territory governments initiated moves to freeze wages in both the private and public sectors.[25] Following one of the regular conferences between federal and state leaders in December, the federal Minister for Employment and Industrial Relations applied to the Arbitration Commission to freeze wages of workers covered by federal awards.

In December 1982 the Arbitration Commission expressed concern about the deteriorating condition of the economy and noted approvingly the united position of the various governments on the need for a wages pause. It decided to introduce a six-month pause (which, in fact, lasted a total of nine months), during which the Commission itself would refuse to grant increases and would expect other industrial tribunals to follow the same course. The major exception was to allow wage adjustments for workers who had not received an increase in the metal-trades-type round. This decision once again reflected strong pressures towards wage uniformity in the Australian system. In handing down its decision,

---

[25] For details of the legislative initiatives of the various governments, see Australian Conciliation and Arbitration Commission, *National Wage Case Decision, December 1982*, Mis 550/82 MD Print F1600, pp. 22–29.

the Arbitration Commission noted that "the pause is the beginning of a process of re-establishing a centralized wage fixing system";[26] it was indeed the Arbitration Commission's first step towards regaining some authority in national wage determination.

In March 1983 the ALP, under the leadership of former ACTU president, Bob Hawke, was elected on a platform of national reconciliation and consensus. An important feature of the ALP campaign was an Accord, the result of four years of negotiation between the ALP and the ACTU. The Accord committed a federal Labor government and the ACTU to a centralized system of wage determination which had "the maintenance of real wages . . . [as] a key objective."[27] The Accord also included a wide range of social and industrial reforms that would be pursued by a federal Labor government. After the election, the new government's first act was to call a National Economic Summit Conference in April 1983 of representatives of unions, employers, government, and community groups to devise a program of national reconstruction. The Conference was the focus of great public interest (including live national television coverage) and occurred against the background of Australia's worst economic crisis since the 1930s: inflation was running at 11 percent, and unemployment exceeded 10 percent.

The final communique of the Summit Conference stressed the need for the attainment of sustained economic growth through a centralized system of wage determination, the mechanics of which were to be determined by the Arbitration Commission at a subsequent national wage case. An important function of the Summit was to give broad community endorsement of the Accord between the ALP and its union allies and helped establish the framework for a social contract approach to wages policy.[28] However, a prominent businessman lamented to Prime Minister Hawke near the end of the Summit that

> . . . it would be only an extension of the spirit of this Summit if business were incorporated as the third party of this accord, as an equal partner . . . . [M]ost of us felt during the early days of this Conference, as though we had been

---

[26] *Ibid.*, p. 10.

[27] Statement of Accord by the Australian Labor Party and the Australian Council of Trade Unions Regarding Economic Policy (mimeo), p. 5.

[28] For a stimulating analysis of the Summit, see Kemp (1983).

invited to play singles tennis against a championship doubles combination.[29]

The spirit of compromise and consensus associated with the National Economic Summit established the climate for a national wage case to determine the future course of Australian wage determination. In September 1983 the Arbitration Commission announced that it had decided to reintroduce a centralized system of wage determination based on a six-monthly indexation for a period of two years, declaring that

> . . . it would be in the public interest for the Commission to try once again to operate a centralized system based on *prima facie* full indexation. We do so in the expectation that it would lead to a more stable environment and that it would provide the basis for a more rapid economic recovery than would occur in any alternative system.[30]

With inflation and unemployment in double figures, the Arbitration Commission acknowledged that Australia was experiencing its most serious economic problems since the Depression. It feared, however, that if it did not grant workers an immediate increase of 4.3 percent—equivalent to the previous six-monthly move in the CPI—it would endanger the emerging consensus and national reconciliation which had been generated following the election of the Hawke government and the Summit.

The six-monthly indexation principles announced by the Arbitration Commission in September 1983 was a substantial tightening of the previous wage indexation guidelines. The new principles reflected lessons learned from the Arbitration Commission's 1975–81 wage-indexation experiment: fewer loopholes were allowed, and a strong emphasis was placed on self-enforcement to ensure that the principles were observed. In an unprecedented move, the Arbitration Commission required each union to give a formal undertaking of compliance with the Commission's wage-fixing principles before granting each group the 4.3 percent wage increase. National wage case adjustments were to be the major

---

[29] *National Economic Summit Conference,* 11–14 April 1983, Documents and Proceedings, Vol. 2, *Record of Proceedings* (Canberra: Australian Government Publishing Service, 1983), p. 194. The final communique appears on pp. 196–200.

[30] Australian Conciliation and Arbitration Commission, *National Wage Case Decision, September 1983,* 1 Mis 300/83 MD Print F2900, p. 16.

source of wage movements, and sectional wage claims, by definition, were to be minimized, if not abolished. As the Arbitration Commission observed, ". . . the requirements of the new centralized system . . . impose obligations and responsibilities on unions, employers, governments, and tribunals. They must all accept commitment to these requirements for the system to work."[31]

In April 1984, consistent with its September 1983 decision, the Arbitration Commission increased wages by 4.1 percent— corresponding to the previous six-monthly movement in the CPI. There was no case in the second half of 1984 due to a slight fall in the CPI, mainly resulting from an adjustment to inflation calculations after the introduction of Medicare, a national health insurance system which relieved individual workers of the cost of private health insurance.

Conclusion

Although Australia has experienced the serious economic problems common to other countries in the past decade, public policy responses to their problems and their impact on the major industrial parties have been unusual. Other Western market economies have experienced decreases in the rate of unionization, cuts in real wages, "give-backs" or concession bargaining, and a general decline in the power and influence of unions. Australian unions, however, have been able to maintain, if not improve, their position, despite the general economic decline. The rate of unionization of Australian workers has remained fairly constant at 55 percent through that period,[32] real wages have been maintained (see Table 4), the length of the standard working week has been reduced to 38 hours, redundancy rights have been established, and Medicare introduced. With Labor Parties in office federally and in four of the six states, the political influence of unions, both individually and collectively, probably has not been greater since before World War I.

The key difference between Australia and other Western market economies is the existence of a well-developed system of industrial tribunals. Unions and workers whose wages and working conditions

---

[31] *Ibid.*, p. 48.

[32] Union-based surveys report a higher rate of unionization than those based on household surveys. See Hill (1984).

are determined in the market will ultimately be forced to make concessions to employers in periods of economic decline. The same thing does not necessarily apply where industrial tribunals act as a buffer between unions and employers. In the last decade the Arbitration Commission, except for some partial indexation decisions and the wages pause, has given income protection in exchange for a centralized system of wage determination and industrial regulation administered by itself. For their part, unions accept the Arbitration Commission's wage indexation packages so long as unemployment is high, primarily because they would not do as well if left to their own devices with employers in the market. This view is illustrated, for example, by the following extract from the ACTU's Wages and Salaries Policy developed at its September 1983 Congress:

> Congress declares that the maintenance of the real value of wage standards won over many years of struggle is essential, particularly in this period of serious economic decline. . . . The . . . Accord . . . is the labor movement's direct response to those which have attempted to force wage negotiations into the marketplace where wages would be determined on the basis of the so-called free labor market criteria.[33]

When economic conditions are brighter, unions traditionally move beyond industrial tribunals and augment award conditions through direct negotiations with employers.

Employers generally have been unhappy with wage indexation. Opposition falls into two main categories: those who oppose regulation per se and would like to see much freer bargaining between labor and management without the guaranteed floor provided by the award network; and those who support the concept of industrial tribunals to achieve high uniformity in wage structures, but with adjustments at something less than full indexation for inflation. Both groups are critical of having cost-of-living adjustments forced on them during periods of economic decline. Other opposition to the Accord-based wages policy has been on the grounds that the formal system is an alliance of self-interests which protects the wage of those who already have a job;

---

[33] Minutes of the ACTU 1983 Congress, 12–16 September 1983, p. 152.

in 1983 the unemployment rate of teenagers was 22.6 percent (Table 3), up nearly 380 percent in the previous decade.

Australia has developed a unique system of national level bilateral bargaining in the last decade. The key bargain is that between the ACTU and the Arbitration Commission. During the recession the ACTU has sought to protect real wages while the Arbitration Commission has sought a commitment from the ACTU and other parties to the dictates of a centralized system. By taking the initiative in wage-setting activity, the Arbitration Commission has usurped the role of employers in this process. This is the fundamental source of the waning influence and power of employers in the period since the mid-1970s. The importance of the Accord negotiated between the ACTU and the ALP was that the ACTU, by locking in a federal government to support its basic position, gained a powerful ally in submissions to the Arbitration Commission that it should once again maintain the real value of wages via a centralized system of wage determination. Equally, it enabled the ALP to derive political capital from an agreement negotiated between the ACTU and the Arbitration Commission.

The Australian system of industrial relations places great trust and store in the personnel of the Arbitration Commission (approximately 40 presidential and commissioner members). The tribunal's unique constitutional position gives its members considerable scope for independent action in responding to the numerous and varied problems associated with industrial relations regulation. One plausible conclusion, therefore, is that the development of a centralized system of wage determination reflects the value system and professional ideas of the Commission's current personnel, coupled with the pragmatism of unions to make use of industrial tribunals during periods of economic adversity. Both effects are reinforced by the High Court's recent expansionist mood in favor of federal power. Also important is the fact that the federal government, which is responsible for filling Commission vacancies when they occur, is dominated by a leader and other senior ministers strongly committed to the centralist style. President of the Commission since 1973, Sir John Moore, is due to retire by the end of 1985. Even if his successor, and the successors of other members who will reach statutory retiring age in the next few years, show an unexpected interest in decentralism, regulatory theory[34] suggests

_____
[34] For a survey of regulatory theory and its application to Australian industrial relations, see Dabscheck (1983), pp. 1-19.

they will still strive to maintain independence from government policy, while facing the strong centralist pressures generated by the Commission's own paramount need to ensure survival.

Australian industrial relations are highly regulated, and Wilson (1978) proposes that regulatory bodies are motivated by the need to increase their autonomy and gain control over their environment. He argues that "autonomy is acquired by eliminating rival organizations that might wish to perform some or all of the same tasks as one's own bureau and acquiring sufficient good-will and prestige so as to make attacks on oneself and one's agency costly for one's critics" (p. 165). Elimination of rival organizations in this context appears unlikely; it may be more appropriate in Australian industrial relations to see the prime strategy as one of domination and control.

How can a regulatory body dominate and control its rivals? The answer is that it must be prepared to take the initiative in devising and implementing new programs by which it responds to the demands of regulation. Such programs should not be designed simply to solve the problems of the moment; they should lay down a plan or blueprint for the future, predetermining and preempting future decision-making. It will also be necessary to accompany the announcement of the program with an aggressive marketing campaign. Claims must be made that the plan of action is the best means available to resolve relevant issues. Rival regulatory bodies thus will be forced to follow the lead of the innovative body to avoid the charge that they are a brake on progress and out of step with a program heralded as vital to society's well-being. In addition, the plan of action will create expectations among the clients of rivals for similar treatment. In the hands of a suitable aggressive regulatory body, the forces of comparison can be used as a weapon to dominate and control rival regulatory bodies.

Both wage indexation periods introduced by the Arbitration Commission are examples of this approach. Both have had the object of ensuring that CPI-focused national wage cases are the major, if not the only, source of wage increases. Indexation was also promoted as necessary for resolving Australia's industrial, social, and economic problems. The Arbitration Commission's guidelines and principles seek to eliminate competition with the market, the source of so-called sectional wage increases. Wage indexation simultaneously enables the full bench to control other members of the Commission and places pressure on other tribunals to adopt a similar approach if they wish to maintain their relevance to the traditional clients.

Two other examples of the Arbitration Commission's propensity to attempt to dominate and control rival regulatory bodies can be given. Sir John Moore, in his submission to the Hancock Committee of Review into Australian Industrial Relations Law and Systems, argued for the welding of state and federal systems under a national industrial relations tribunal. And in the recent *Termination, Change and Redundancy* case the Arbitration Commission ruled that it would hear dismissals involving discrimination, a matter previously the preserve of (mainly state) antidiscrimination bodies.[35]

It appears that centralism will be a continuing feature of Australian industrial relations. The Arbitration Commission itself is certainly comfortable with this approach, recent High Court decisions have favored the federal government over the states, and the current federal Labor government is committed to centralism. Although the report of the Hancock Inquiry is awaited with some considerable interest, probably the only real threat to centralism is sustained economic growth and recovery reflected in relatively low unemployment levels. If the past is any guide, trade unions able to gain enhanced concessions from employers in the marketplace would turn their back on industrial tribunals. One longer-run factor to bear in mind is that the federal Opposition is becoming more aggressively deregulatory in its policy and, if elected to office in 1988, could try to carry out its policy of reducing the Arbitration Commission's power and influence. However, this is speculation. What is established is that in Australia the main response to the economic difficulties of the past decade has been a shift to centralism.

References

Australian Bulletin of Labour.
Bedwell, Pamela, "Women and Work: The NSW Anti-Discrimination Act." Bachelor of Arts Honors Thesis, University of New South Wales, November 1981.
Blandy, Richard, and Owen Covick, eds. *Understanding Labour Markets in Australia.* Sydney: George Allen and Unwin, 1984.
Blandy, Richard, and Sue Richardson, eds. *New Labour Markets Work: Case Studies in Adjustment.* Melbourne: Longman Cheshire, 1982.

---

[35] Under Section 109 of the Australian Constitution, if there is a clash between a federal and state law the former shall prevail.

Brown, W. G., and L. G. Rowe. "Industrial Relations in Australia: The Need for Change." *Australian Bulletin of Labour* 9 (September 1983): pp. 247–87.

Caves, Richard E., and Lawrence B. Krause, eds. *The Australian Economy: A View from the North.* Sydney: George Allen and Unwin, 1984.

Chapman, B. J., J. E. Isaac, and J. R. Niland, eds. *Australian Labour Economics: Readings.* 3rd ed. Melbourne: Macmillan, 1984.

Clarke, R. O. "Labour-Management Disputes: A Perspective." *British Journal of Industrial Relations* 18 (March 1980): pp. 14–25.

Conference on "Alternatives to the Present Arbitration System: Needs, Options and Strategies." Little Bay, Sydney: Industrial Relations Research Centre, University of New South Wales, and National Institute of Labour Studies, Flinders University, October 29–30, 1984.

Covick, Owen. "Productivity-Geared Wages Policy, Labor's Share of Gross Product, and the Real Wage Overhang." In *Australian Labour Economics: Readings*, eds. B. J. Chapman, J. E. Isaac, and J. R. Niland. Sydney: Macmillan, 1984. Pp. 315-34.

Crawford, Bob, and Sam Volard. "Work Absence in Industrialized Societies: The Australian Case." *Industrial Relations Journal* 12 (May/June 1981): pp. 50–57.

d'Alpuget, Blanche. *Mediator: A Biography of Sir Richard Kirby.* Carlton: Melbourne University Press, 1977.

Dabscheck, Braham. "The 1975 National Wage Case: Now We Have an Incomes Policy." *The Journal of Industrial Relations* 17 (September 1975): pp. 298–309.

————. "The Internal Authority of the ACTU." *The Journal of Industrial Relations* 19 (December 1977): pp. 388–403.

————. "The Australian System of Industrial Relations: An Analytical Model." *The Australian Journal of Industrial Relations* 22 (June 1980): pp. 196–218.

————. *Arbitrator at Work: Sir William Raymond Kelly and the Regulation of Australian Industrial Relations.* Sydney: George Allen and Unwin, 1983.

Dabscheck, Braham, and John Niland. *Industrial Relations in Australia.* Sydney: George Allen and Unwin, 1981.

————. "Recent Trends in Collective Bargaining in Australia." *International Labour Review* 123 (September-October 1984): pp. 631–46.

Department of Employment and Industrial Relations (DEIR). "The Feasibility of Restoring Full Employment." Supplementary Submission to the Committee of Inquiry into Australian Industrial Relations Law and Systems, Canberra, December 1984.

Dornbusch, R., and S. Fischer. "The Australian Macro Economy." Paper presented to the Brookings Survey of the Australian Economy Conference, Australian National University, Canberra, 1984.

Ford, G. W., June M. Hearn, and Russell D. Lansbury, eds. *Australian Labour Relations: Readings.* 3rd ed. South Melbourne: Macmillan, 1980.

Ford, G. W., David Plowman, and Russell D. Lansbury. "Employer Associations: An Introduction." In *Australian Labour Relations: Readings*, eds. G. W. Ford, June M. Hearn, and Russell D. Lansbury. Melbourne: Macmillan, 1984. Pp. 413–24.

Gunningham, Neil. *Safeguarding the Worker: Job Hazards and the Role of the Law.* North Hyde: Law Book Co., 1984.

Hill, John D. "Australian Union Density Rates 1976-1982." *The Journal of Industrial Relations* 26 (December 1984): pp. 435–50.

Howard,, W. A. "Australian Trade Unions in the Context of Union Theory." *The Journal of Industrial Relations* 19 (September 1977): pp. 255–73.

Hughes, Kerwyn. "Employment Security in the Commonwealth Public Sector: The CE(EP) and CE(RR) Acts." Kensington: Industrial Relations Research Centre Monograph, University of New South Wales, April 1984.

Isaac, J. E. "Wage Determination and Economic Policy." *The Australian Economic Review* 39 (3rd Quarter 1977): pp. 16–24.

Johnson, H. N., R. G. Campbell, and R. N. Simes. "The Impact of Wages and Prices on Unemployment." *Proceedings*, Winter School of the New South Wales Branch of the Economics Society of Australia and New Zealand, Sydney.

Kemp, D. A. "The National Economic Summit: Authority, Persuasion and Exchange." *The Economic Record* 59 (September 1983): pp. 209–19.

Kirby, R. "Conciliation and Arbitration in Australia—Where the Emphasis?" *Federal Law Review* 4 (September 1970): pp. 1–29.

Merrilees, William J. "The Mass Exodus of Older Males from the Labour Force: An Exploratory Analysis." *Australian Bulletin of Labour* 8 (March 1982): pp. 81–94.

Miller, Paul W. "The Economic Position of Migrants: Facts and Fallacies. A Preliminary View." *Australian Bulletin of Labour* (September 1982): pp. 229–48.

Mitchell, D. J. B. "The Australian Labour Market." Paper presented to the Brookings Survey of the Australian Economy Conference, Australian National University, Canberra, 1984.

Mitchell, Richard. "Industrial Relations under a Conservative Government: The Coalition's Labour Law Programme 1975 to 1978." *The Journal of Industrial Relations* 21 (December 1979): pp. 435–65.

————. "The Development of Federal Labor Law Policy under the Coalition Government: Some Comments on the 1982 Bill." The Australian National University, Research School of Social Sciences, Industrial Relations Papers, 1983.

Nieuwenhuysen, John. "The South Australian Industrial Commission and the Demise of Wage Indexation." *The Journal of Industrial Relations* 23 (December 1981): pp. 508–15.

Niland, John. "The Case for More Collective Bargaining in Australia." *The Journal of Industrial Relations* 18 (December 1976): pp. 365–90.

————. *Collective Bargaining and Compulsory Arbitration in Australia.* Kensington: New South Wales University Press, 1978.

————. "Special Labour Market Adjustment Measures." In *Australian Labour Economics: Readings*, eds. R. J. Chapman, J. E. Isaac, and J. R. Niland. Melbourne: Macmillan, 1984. Pp. 531–47.

Perlman, Mark. *Judges in Industry: A Study of Labour Arbitration in Australia.* Melbourne: Melbourne University Press, 1954.

Plowman, David. "Employer Associations: Challenges and Responses." *The Journal of Industrial Relations* 20 (September 1978): pp. 237–63.

————. *Wage Indexation: A Study of Australian Wage Issues 1975–1980.* Sydney: George Allen and Unwin, 1981.

Plowman, D., S. Deery, and C. Fisher. *Australian Industrial Relations.* Sydney: McGraw-Hill, 1981.

Ronalds, Chris. *Anti-Discrimination Legislation in Australia: A Guide.* Sydney: Butterworths, 1979.

Sheridan, Tom. "Labor v. Labor: The Victorian Metal Trades Dispute of 1946–47." In *Strikes: Studies of Twentieth Century Australian Social History*, eds. John Iremonger, John Merritt, and Graeme Osborne. Sydney: Angus and Robertson, 1973.

Staples, J. F. "Conciliation and Arbitration Amendment Bill 1979." *The Australian Quarterly* 51 (December 1979): pp. 51–58.

————. "Uniformity and Diversity in Industrial Relations." *The Journal of Industrial Relations* 22 (September 1980): pp. 353–62.

Steinke, John. "The Long-Term Decline in the Standard Working Year." *The Journal of Industrial Relations* 25 (December 1983): pp. 415–30.

Stricker, Peter, and Peter Sheehan. *Hidden Unemployment: The Australian Experience.* Parkville: Institute of Applied Economic and Social Research, University of Melbourne, 1981.

The Australian Economic Review.

The Economic Record.

Thornton, Margaret. "Perspectives on Sex Discrmination Legislation in Australia." *The Australian Quarterly* 54 (Summer 1982): pp. 393–403.

Tilling, John, and Kenneth Wheeler. *Toward Collective Bargaining: The Fixed Contract Approach.* Kensington: Industrial Relations Research Centre Monograph, University of New South Wales, January 1984.

Treadgold, N. L. "Aboriginal Incomes: An Aggregate Analysis of the 1976 Census Results." In *Australian Labour Economics: Readings,* eds. B. J. Chapman, J. E. Isaac, and J. R. Niland. Melbourne: Macmillan, 1984. Pp. 602–19.

Trivedi, P. K., and G. M. Baker. "Equilibrium Unemployment in Australia: Concepts and Measurement." Canberra: Centre for Economic Policy Research Discussion Paper No. 59, Australian National University, 1982.

Wilson, James Q. *The Investigators: Managing FBI and Narcotics Agents.* New York: Basic Books, 1978.

Yerbury, D. "The Government, the Arbitration Commission and Wages Policy: The Role of the 'Supporting Mechanism' under the Whitlam Government." In *Incomes Policy in Australia,* ed. Keith Hancock. Sydney: Harcourt Brace Jovanovich, 1981. Pp. 195–234.

_____. "The High Court's Current Expansionist Approach to Australia's Industrial Powers." Kensington: Australian Graduate School of Management Working Paper 84-001, January 1984.

Yerbury, D., and Robert Clark. "Redundancy and the Law: The Position in Mid-1983." *The Journal of Industrial Relations* 25 (September 1983): pp. 353–75.

Yerbury, D., and J. E. Isaac. "Recent Trends in Collective Bargaining in Australia." *International Labour Review* 103 (May 1971): pp. 421–52.

Chapter 3

Brazilian Labor Relations: A New Era?*

José Pastore
University of São Paulo

Thomas E. Skidmore
University of Wisconsin-Madison

Brazil has long been known for the rigidity of its labor relations. Foreign observers have often remarked on how easily the Brazilian government seems to be able to control unions through an interventionist Labor Ministry, a network of government-appointed labor court judges, and direct repression when necessary.

At no time did this picture seem more true than during the authoritarian regime installed after the military-led overthrow of President João Goulart in 1964. Militant labor union leaders were among the prime targets for dismissal and harassment of the first "revolutionary" government. From 1964 until 1977 those governments kept union leaderships under control by using the existing laws and regulations as well as by repression. The single important exception was the 1968 outbreak of wildcat strikes in Minas Gerais and São Paulo, and they were quickly repressed. Otherwise labor protest was limited to brief work-to-rule actions.

Beginning in 1977, however, two new trends appeared. One was a gradual liberalization by the military government, a process that Brazilians call *abertura* (opening). Although the country has hardly become an ideal democracy, it has moved toward a more

* We wish to thank Helio Zylberstajn for research assistance and for preparation of the tables. The Ministry of Labor kindly supplied unpublished data. Finally, we thank Mark Thompson, James Stern, and Margaret Keck for their helpful comments on an earlier draft. Final responsibility is, of course, ours. This article was completed in early 1985, before the change of government.

73

constitutional system by restoring habeas corpus, ending censorship, and allowing an opposition candidate to win the presidential
election in January 1985.

The second trend after 1977 was the appearance of a new labor
union militancy. It began in São Paulo, the principal center of
Brazilian industry (see Table 1). The leaders came from the Metalworkers (*Metalúrgicos*) in the giant car and truck factories of
Volkswagen, Ford, and Scania-Vabis. These leaders had an
authentic grassroots following—something their earlier counterparts had usually lacked. They led a series of strikes in 1978 and
1979 (described below) that resulted in direct bargaining with the
employers. Many in the union movement thought Brazilian labor
relations were entering a new era. In this chapter we will attempt to
evaluate how far that prediction has been fulfilled.

TABLE 1
São Paulo's Role in Brazil's Industrial Economy

São Paulo's Share of Brazil's	
Total population (1980)	21.0%
Economically active population (1980)	24.1
Total value added in manufacturing (1975)	54.8
Labor force employed in manufacturing (1975)	47.0

Sources: 1980 figures, *Censo Demografico* 1980, FIBGE; 1975 figures, *Censo Industrial* 1975, FIBGE.

One factor that has not changed is the legal structure: the labor
code and the legal powers of the protagonists—the workers, the
unions, the employers, the Ministry of Labor, and the labor courts.
On the other hand, there are new factors: (1) the government's
occasionally relaxed attitude in applying the labor laws; (2) a new
generation of union leaders who seek power in order to improve the
workers' lot in the workplace (the "bread and butter" approach so
often scorned by older leaders and by leftist intellectuals); (3) an
increased union ability to carry out tightly organized and well
disciplined work actions, including strikes; (4) an increased resort to
direct bargaining between unions and employers, especially at the
plant level; (5) increasingly sophisticated agreements resulting from
such bargaining; (6) workplace-level labor-management committees (*comisões de fábrica*) and shop stewards, both virtually
unknown before 1977; and (7) frequent government manipulation

of the official wage structure to meet economic, social, or political goals.

None of these changes could have gone far without *abertura*, which itself was a product of the combined forces of liberalizing policies from within the government and strong pressures from key groups in Brazilian society. Unfortunately another, far less favorable trend was also at work: Brazil's most serious economic recession in half a century. From 1980 to 1983 Brazil lost 9 percent of its per capita GNP. Only in mid-1984 did signs of recovery begin to appear. This painful slump brought sharply increased unemployment and spiraling inflation. Both worsened the unions' bargaining position. Thus, the impact of world economic change acted to undermine the domestic trend toward greater activism by workers and unions.

Here we will examine how these contradictory forces interacted, how workers and employers struggled to defend their interests in the midst of an economic maelstrom, and how the present-day realities of Brazil's labor relations differ from those under a repressive military regime. The first section describes the impact of recent world economic change on Brazil. New developments in the labor relations system between 1978 and 1984 are outlined in the second section. The third section focuses on the responses of government, unions, and management to the new socioeconomic environment. Finally, in the fourth section we explore future scenarios, looking especially at the possibility of movement towards a labor relations system less legalistic and more geared to negotiation.

The Effects of World Economic Change on Brazil: 1978-1984

An inquiry into Brazil's labor relations since 1978 offers an interesting case study in Third World experience. The post-1964 Brazilian governments, brought to power by a military-civilian coup that year, made their country into an aggressive participant in the world economy. They promoted exports and attracted foreign capital, both private and public. In the first half of the 1970s Brazil achieved an annual economic growth rate of 10.9 percent (see Table 2). Although from 1975 to 1979 it dropped to

TABLE 2
Annual Rates of Growth by Sector

	Agri-culture	In-dustry	Com-merce	Trans-portation and Commerce	Financial Inter-mediaries	Govern-ment	Gross Domestic Product
1971	11.3	12.0	13.1	10.1	—	—	12.0
1972	4.1	13.0	11.4	13.5	—	—	11.0
1973	3.6	16.3	12.9	21.0	—	—	13.6
1974	8.2	9.2	9.7	17.5	—	—	9.7
1975	4.8	5.9	2.7	13.7	—	—	5.4
1976	2.9	12.4	7.3	14.5	—	—	9.7
1977	11.8	3.9	4.7	9.4	—	—	5.7
1978	−2.6	7.2	4.2	9.6	—	—	5.0
1979	5.0	6.4	5.4	13.9	—	—	6.4
1980	6.3	7.9	6.8	10.1	10.2	2.5	7.2
1981	6.4	−5.5	−2.8	0.2	8.0	0.0	−1.6
1982	−2.5	0.6	0.9	5.6	4.5	2.5	0.9
1983	2.2	−6.8	−3.5	0.1	3.7	0.0	−3.2

Source: Conjuntura Econômica 38 (June 1984).

an average of 5.6 percent, 1979 recorded a 6.4 percent rate and 1980 was even better at 7.2[1]

Brazil badly needed to maintain high growth in order to provide jobs to meet the explosive increase in its labor force (see Table 3). For the 1960s Brazil's labor force grew at 3.3 percent a year. In the 1970s the rate was even higher, reaching 3.9 percent. The greatest need for jobs was in the cities, as Table 3 indicates. That point is underlined in Table 4, which shows that from 1950 to 1980 employment in the primary sectors dropped by 50 percent, while

TABLE 3
Brazilian Labor Force

	Urban	Rural	Total
Size (in millions)			
1960	10.3	12.4	22.8
1970	16.5	13.1	29.6
1980	30.2	13.0	43.2
Annual geometric rate of growth (percent per year)			
1960/1970	5.51	0.23	3.26
1970/1980	6.27	−0.08	3.88

Source: FIBGE, Censos Demograficos, 1960, 1970, 1980.

[1] For background on the contemporary Brazilian economy, see Baer (1983, forthcoming).

TABLE 4
Employment Distribution in Brazil (in percentages)

	Primary	Secondary	Tertiary	Total
1950	59.9	14.2	25.9	100.0
1960	54.0	13.2	32.8	100.0
1970	44.3	18.4	37.4	100.0
1980	30.0	25.5	44.6	100.0

Source: FIBGE. *Censos Demograficos*, 1950, 1960, 1970, 1980.

TABLE 5
Income Distribution

	Percent of the Population		
	Lower 60 Percent	Higher 5 Percent	Higher 1 Percent
Percentage of Income			
1960	23.4	30.7	13.0
1970	21.0	34.1	14.7
1980	18.4	36.4	15.4
Real increase in average income of the group			
1960/1970	7.1%	33.0%	35.4%
1970/1980	86.0	125.3	122.4

Source: FIBGE, *Censos Demograficos*, 1960, 1970, 1980.

in the secondary and tertiary sectors it grew by 80 and 72 percent, respectively. The distribution of income resulting from growth favored the highest deciles, although all groups increased their absolute incomes (see Table 5).

By the end of the 1970s, however, the world economic scene was darkening. Brazil, a dependent economy on the periphery of the capitalist world, has always been closely influenced by decisions at that world's North Atlantic center. Such a decision came in September 1979 when U.S. monetary policy changed abruptly. The prime objective of the new policy was to reduce U.S. inflation, which in 1979 had reached 11.3 percent.[2] That goal was achieved. By mid-1984, U.S. inflation had dropped to about 4 percent. But the cost was high, as the U.S. plunged into its most severe recession

[2] For analyses highly critical of U.S. policy-makers' insensitivity to the effects of U.S. policy abroad, see Dornbusch (1983, 1984) and Tobin (1984).

since the Great Depression. It also brought the world economy down with it.

In the U.S. and other industrialized countries, workers' economic pain was reduced by unemployment compensation and welfare programs. The story was very different in the Third World. First, the recession hit harder in per capita terms because Third World populations were growing faster. Brazil's population, for example, was increasing at 2.4 percent a year, as compared to 0.8 percent in the U.S. The combined effect of the world recession and high population growth hit Brazil with a per capita GNP decline of 9 percent from 1980 to 1983. The world recession also brought a drastic worsening in Brazil's terms of trade (Economic Commission for Latin America 1984). By the end of 1983 that ratio had deteriorated by 42 percent, as compared to 1979. It all added up to a severe decline in Brazil's markets both at home and abroad.

The world debt crisis added yet another unwelcome dimension in 1982. In the 1970s Brazil, like most Latin American countries, had borrowed heavily from multinational agencies and commercial banks. Fortified with these loans, Brazil was able to maintain rapid growth. This strategy had been based on the assumption that the low interest rates would continue. That assumption was rudely upset, however, by the steady rise in Eurodollar interest rates, which went from 8.7 percent in 1978 to 17 percent in 1981.[3] As inflation declined in the U.S. and Western Europe, real interest rates hit record levels.

Those rates were especially damaging to major debtors such as Brazil. Just as export prices and markets shrank, the cost of the debt service jumped. The borrowers' plight was dramatized in August 1982 when Mexico announced it could no longer make amortization payments on its foreign debt. In plain terms, Mexico was verging on default.

Alarm spread through the world financial community. As the U.S. government and multilateral agencies rushed in to prevent a Mexican default, Brazil's creditor banks, many of which had lent heavily to Mexico, now shied away from giving new loans to Brazil. Although the Brazilian government had tried hard to demonstrate its credit worthiness, its short-term financial plight was soon

---

[3] Lance Taylor (1982) compares the bankers to sheep as they followed leaders in granting more and more loans. Data may be found in Economic Commission for Latin America (1983, 1984).

identified with Mexico's. Shortly after Brazil's national elections of November 1982, the government of President João Figueiredo (1979-85), meeting a stone wall from the banks, turned to the International Monetary Fund (IMF) for help. The IMF's price was adoption of a stringent stabilization program (as in virtually all cases of IMF assistance), subordinating all else (such as employment or economic growth) to an improved balance of payments.

These measures reinforced the recession already under way. In 1981 the growth rate had fallen sharply to −1.6 percent. The following year, 1982, brought a barely positive figure of 0.9 percent, and 1983 was far worse, at −3.2 percent. Furthermore, inflation had doubled during 1983, to 211 percent. In short, Brazil was faced with its most serious economic crisis since World War II. Not surprisingly, the effects on labor relations and its participants were great.

The data available can be summarized briefly.[4] By December 1983, employment in the greater metropolitan regions of São Paulo and Rio de Janeiro had both fallen 15 percent, as compared to their August 1978 averages (see Table 6). Industry was hit especially hard. By February 1984 industrial production had dropped 14 percent from its average level during 1980 (*Conjuntura Economica* 1984). Industrial employment was hit even harder (see Table 6).

---

[4] Unfortunately the Brazilian government has only recently begun collecting data for some of the key indicators the editors of this volume have asked us to discuss. For example, data on employment are available only for the major urban areas and the series only goes back to 1978. For agricultural and service sectors there are no data. Data on unemployment are available only from 1980, monthly for six major metropolitan regions of the country. But the methodology was changed in 1982, making even the brief time series noncomparable. These official unemployment data, gathered by IBGE, are considered by many informed observers to understate seriously the actual level. For income distribution there are data from the censuses of 1960, 1970, and 1980. A wealth of information and interpretation on income distribution may be found in Morley (1982). Researchers should note that Morley's work appeared before data from the 1980 census were available. Historic trends, as revealed in the censuses, can be seen in Table 5. It is impossible with these limited data to establish a time series for 1978-1983. The same must be said of labor participation rates, which also can be extracted only from the census and PNAD data. The employment data which will be cited shortly are gathered by the Sistema Nacional de Emprego (SINE) of the Ministry of Labor. It should be noted that in a labor surplus and relatively poor economy such as Brazil, unemployment is inherently difficult to measure. First, there is no unemployment compensation and only a rudimentary national employment service. Second, many urban workers in Brazil are recent migrants from the countryside or have close ties there. When work in the city is scarce, they often return to the rural sector, where no employment or unemployment data are gathered. In short, the Brazilian case presents severe data problems for the analysis of labor relations, but it is no less interesting and important for that.

As compared to its August 1978 average, December 1983 industrial employment was down 26 percent in greater São Paulo and 30 percent in greater Rio. Real wages in São Paulo manufacturing held up through 1982, but fell sharply in 1983 and early 1984 (see Table 7). These data on average wages in fact understate the decline, since in a recession the lower paid workers were laid off first. Those earning only the minimum wage in Rio or São Paulo suffered even greater losses (see Table 8).

TABLE 6
Employment Level: Metropolitan Areas
of São Paulo and Rio de Janeiro
August 1978 = 100

	Manufac-turing	Con-struction	Com-merce	Services	Total
	São Paulo				
Dec. 1978	99.6	96.0	102.6	101.7	100.2
Dec. 1979	101.8	79.9	106.8	105.6	101.9
Dec. 1980	100.5	76.1	111.0	106.8	101.3
Dec. 1981	83.8	72.6	107.0	108.7	91.3
Dec. 1982	82.3	65.1	106.4	114.0	91.3
Dec. 1983	74.4	50.7	103.9	113.2	85.1
Sept. 1984	n.a.	n.a	n.a.	n.a.	93.3
	Rio de Janeiro				
Dec. 1978	99.6	90.6	105.4	101.1	99.4
Dec. 1979	97.9	77.6	111.0	102.4	98.0
Dec. 1980	91.6	80.8	115.0	102.8	96.9
Dec. 1981	79.6	71.7	112.6	102.1	92.2
Dec. 1982	77.9	62.1	117.1	102.8	90.1
Dec. 1983	69.7	50.9	122.2	99.9	84.9
Sept. 1984	n.a.	n.a.	n.a.	n.a.	85.0

Source: Ministry of Labor.
Note: These figures include employment in the formal sector only.

TABLE 7
Real Wage Index in São Paulo Manufacturing Industries

1979	1980	1981	1982	1983	1984
107.7	116.7	122.2	125.1	109.7	96.4

Source: FIESP (Manufacturing Employers Federation of São Paulo).
Note: 1984 figures are for February. All other figures are year averages. Base 100 = 1978.

TABLE 8
Minimum Wage Adjustments for São Paulo and Rio de Janeiro
and Inflation Rates

	Minimum Wage		Inflation	
Year	Annual Adjustments (%)	Index	Annual Rates (%)	Index
1970	20.0	100.0	20.7	100.0
1971	20.5	120.5	21.9	121.9
1972	19.1	143.5	17.7	143.5
1973	16.1	166.6	15.3	165.4
1974	21.4	202.3	29.8	214.7
1975	40.7	284.6	23.6	265.4
1976	44.1	410.1	39.9	371.3
1977	44.1	510.0	47.1	546.2
1978	41.0	833.3	35.1	737.9
1979	45.4	1,211.6	45.5	1,073.6
1980	83.0	2,217.2	94.7	2,090.3
1981	104.0	4,523.1	120.3	4,605.0
1982	96.2	8,874.3	91.2	8,804.8
1983	109.4	18,582.8	118.5	18,238.5
1984	179.4	51,920.5	235.5	64,545.2

Note: All figures are annual and refer to changes since May of the preceding
year. Inflation rates as calculated by Fundação Getúlio Vargas (IGP-DI).

Within the context of a deep recession, some pockets did better
than others. Enterprises linked to export trade did well, some even
showing growth, as the government continued to pay high export
subsidies (Veja 1984). The agricultural crops that benefited were
soybeans, sugar, coffee, and oranges; in industrial products it was
shoes, vehicles, and a range of intermediate goods.

The effect of these prosperous export pockets on labor relations
was not as obvious as might first appear. Union activity did become
more frequent in these pockets than in the recession-hit sectors.
Also, collective agreements became more complex and sophisticated. In addition, new mechanisms for conflict resolution at the
plant level began to be created in the export sector. This meant a
decentralization, away from the *município*-wide union activity
(explained below). Although these changes did not transform the
labor relations system, especially the excessive role of the state, they
represent the frontier of labor relations innovations in Brazil today.

One sector that deserves special analysis is the alcohol (from
bio-mass) sector. Forced to substitute for oil which in the late 1970s
was 75 percent imported, Brazil has increased annual alcohol

production from 900 million liters in 1979 to 9 billion liters in 1984, with the product going largely to supply alcohol-fueled automobiles. This huge increase, based on an equally huge increase in sugar cane cultivation, had greatly affected labor relations in those areas. Workers involved in alcohol production—both sugar-cane cutters (*bóias-frias*) as well as mill workers—have become aggressive. In rural regions where both workers and managers lack experience with unions, such as in São Paulo, this has increased open labor conflicts, in turn pushing the system towards more organization and innovation. In regions where rural unions have a long history, such as the northeastern state of Pernambuco, the recurrent strikes have proved more manageable.

The net impact of the world economic crisis and the national recession on Brazilian labor relations after 1980 was mixed. In the depressed sectors, the effect was to strengthen both the bargaining hand of employers and the government's control over unions and over the entire labor relations system. In the export and energy sectors, workers won more space and bargaining power.

Old System in a New Era

Labor relations in Brazil take place within a framework created by a labor code (CLT, or *Consolidação das Leis do Trabalho*), issued in 1943 during the dictatorial regime of President Getúlio Vargas (1937–45). It covered almost every aspect of a worker's life: the mechanism for wage adjustments, terms of employment, health, safety, union organization and operation, strike procedures, etc. Despite subsequent swings of Brazil's political pendulum, that legal structure has remained largely intact.[5] The following is an account of how the system operated from 1965 to 1978–79. As will be explained later, 1978–79 brought changes, both in the law and in its application.

---

[5] For a brief description of the legal framework of the Brazilian labor relations system, see Magano (1982). The classic historical analysis of the system is Moraes (1952). For developments in the system's operation in the early 1960s, see Erickson (1977). The heavy hand of the government as of 1972 is carefully described in Mericle (1974). Another valuable analysis is given in Souza (1975). For information and analysis of the labor scene since 1978, see especially Almeida (1975, 1981, 1983a, 1983b) and Souza and Lamounier (1981). The motor vehicle industry has been a crucible of labor relations conflict since 1978. For the overall economic context, see Mericle (1984) and for an excellent analysis of the shop-floor labor relations, see Humphrey (1982).

Role of the State

The most important feature of this system was the state's central role in every phase of labor relations. Most terms of employment and pay were established by law rather than by direct bargaining between employees and employers. Under this framework industrial conflict was ultimately reduced to legal issues for the labor courts (discussed below) to decide. In practice, the government and Labor Ministry were able to dictate results, rather than facilitating bargaining between the parties.[6]

What the Vargas dictatorship had sought to create was a hierarchical structure of parallel *sindicatos* (associations), representing trades or economic sectors. On the workers' side it was to be the labor unions (*sindicatos trabalhistas*), and on the employers' side the businessmen's associations (*sindicatos patronais*). Holding power over both was the federal government, through the Ministry of Labor and the labor courts (*tribunas trabalhistas*). Representation on issues of collective agreement had to go through the respective workers' *sindicatos*, providing the latter had been officially recognized by the government. This structure followed the corporatist model established earlier in Portugal, Spain, and Italy. The entire system was based on the assumption that neither management nor labor should hold sway, so the government would always have the last word. In fact, the employers never took to the idea of forming their *sindicatos*. Where the latter existed they often represented all industry in a state, not just one industry, as the CLT provided (Alexander 1962, pp. 60–62).

This intricate system had developed as a response to the industrial conflict in the early decades of this century in São Paulo and Rio de Janeiro. Protest then was often led by immigrant workers of anarchist persuasion (Skidmore 1979). By the 1930s the communists had displaced the anarchists. In that decade the government passed more and more laws to prevent or control conflict in the workplace. In practice it protected employers from effective union pressure, both by subordinating unions to

---

[6] After comparing several Latin American countries over the last 20 years, Erfren Cordova (1981) concluded that Brazil is the most backward country in the effective use of collective bargaining for conflict resolution.

government supervision and by channeling most disputes to labor courts staffed by government-appointed judges.

In practice the *sindicato* of employers has seldom functioned as such. Nor did they need to, since they could normally just go along with government-announced wage increases, which between 1965 and 1978 greatly favored the employers. Our analysis of 1965-1978/79 will therefore emphasize the workers' unions (*sindicatos trabalhistas*).

Geographic Definition of Unions

By law, Brazilian labor unions were defined by a geographical unit—the *município*, a level of local government roughly similar to a U.S. county or township. The Metalworkers of the *município* of São Paulo, for example, included by the late 1970s over 200,000 workers. Nearby were three other *municípios* (Santos André, São Bernardo, and São Caetano), all within the greater metropolitan area of São Paulo and each with its own metalworking industry. Each had its own Metalworkers union, which normally dealt with metalworking firms only in its *município*. This compartmentalization effectively divided the workers, even within a major metropolitan area, and aided employers' divide-and-rule tactics towards the unions.

Under this system only the *município* level counted. Paid union officers existed only there. There was virtually no union presence at the plant level. Shop stewards (*delegado sindical*) were practically unknown and none were formally recognized by the employers. This structure applied to all of Brazil, whatever the size of the workplace or the population of the *município*.

Unions in the same state could form a federation (a few trades, such as maritime workers, had national federations), but collaboration on that level was sporadic and largely ineffectual. The state federations could in turn form a national confederation, but these were usually little more than paper organizations.

As for any horizontal alliance of unions, such as the CGT in France or in Argentina, Brazil's labor code was silent. Attempts to create them occurred in the early 1960s, but they were quickly suppressed by the post-1964 military governments. Recent attempts to form such alliances, such as CUT (Central Unica de Trabalhadores) and CONCLAT (Coordenação Nacional da Classe Trabalhadora), remain of dubious legality.

Worker Coverage

All employees in the formal sector—that is, those with a *carteira* (worker's card) registered with the Labor Ministry—were covered by the labor code, which guarantees minimum standards in pay, working conditions, and terms of employment. These guarantees were a government responsibility, whether or not the employee had a union. In return for this coverage each worker had to pay, via a salary "check off" (*impôsto sindical*), the equivalent of one day's pay per year.

Union Status

As noted above, the CLT provided for unions on the *município* level, and by trade or craft (*categoria*), such as metalworkers, bank clerks, or petroleum workers. Once a union was recognized by the Ministry (representation was exclusive), it fell under Ministry regulations. First, its officers had to be Ministry approved. Second, its funds came from the compulsory contribution paid to the Ministry by each worker in the union's jurisdiction. The Ministry could channel up to 80 percent of these funds to the unions, while the remaining 20 percent stayed in the Ministry. At any time the Ministry could, on finding that the CLT had been violated, stop funding the union, remove any or all officers, appoint outsiders in their stead, and run the union from the Ministry. Government intervention gave birth to a special kind of union officer—the *pelego*, or government hack. They were usually elected only because of a Ministry veto of rival candidates and by a generous use of Ministry-controlled patronage and funds to buy votes.

Bargainable Issues

From 1965 to 1979 the military governments applied the labor code and wage laws so that virtually nothing was bargained. In theory, however, anything not prohibited by law could have been bargained. Among the issues that workers were soon to find most urgent were wages, overtime, job security, seniority, sick leave, and job-related health hazards.

Conflict Resolution

Where unions and employers reached a settlement, it was recorded with the regional labor office (*Delegacia Regional de*

Trabalho), and then took the form of a legal contract enforceable by the labor court. If the union and employers failed to agree, either party could take the case to the labor court, whose decision was binding, unless an appeal was made to the higher labor courts.

Conflict could also arise between an individual worker and his employer. Such cases were sometimes handled by the union, but often workers contracted their own lawyer (who got paid only if the worker won a cash award).

Labor Courts

As seen above, these bodies were a key to conflict resolution in the Brazilian system. Judges on these courts were government appointed and vulnerable to government pressure. Obviously the judges had discretion in deciding individual grievances, although even here the authoritarian atmosphere must have worked against plaintiffs, especially at the margin.

The court had in each case first to decide its jurisdiction. Its guideline was the CLT, which was silent on such potentially important questions as the rights of shop stewards. If the court decided it lacked jurisdiction, then the parties had no further legal recourse. One party, usually the employer, thereby won by default.

Right to Strike

The CLT made it very difficult to carry out a legal strike. The union had to appeal to the labor court. If the issue was wages, as in most cases, the court followed government cues, which went against the unions. Or if the union had already risked a strike (very rare between 1965 and 1978), management had the right to request a court ruling on the strike's legality. If declared illegal, the strike had to stop immediately. If the strikers disobeyed, then (a) management had the right to deny pay for the strike days (in Brazil, unlike the U.S., striking workers have expected their pay to continue); (b) the Ministry of Labor could intervene the union and remove the elected leaders; (c) the police could use force to protect property and to protect workers wanting to work.

Job Security

The CLT gave job security (*estabilidade*) to all workers employed for ten years or more. Such workers could be dismissed only for "due cause," which the labor courts had interpreted so narrowly as to make inapplicable. Dismissal without "due cause" involved a large fine, so employers protected themselves by routinely dismissing workers in their ninth year and then often rehiring them on a new seniority track.

The Castelo Branco government (1964–67) began a phaseout of this law in favor of a severance pay scheme by which both worker and employer would contribute via a payroll deduction to a fund (*Fundo de Garatia de Tempo do Serviço* or FGTS) that the worker could draw on when, having been dismissed without "due cause," marrying, buying a house, suffering unemployment, or retiring. The more militant workers rejected this change as a thinly disguised assault on job security.

Wage Policy

In 1965 the government pushed through a law giving itself the power to set wage levels for both the public and private sectors. Most important was the calculation of the minimum wage, which was a benchmark for all wages. To call it a "minimum" was certainly a misnomer. In 1968, 59 percent of the labor force was not even earning the minimum wage (Morley 1982, p. 55). Even those earning more had their salaries calculated in multiples of the minimum wage.

As part of its economic stabilization program, the Castelo Branco government (1964–67) imposed a complicated formula for the annual adjustment of the minimum wage. It was composed of three separate calculations: (1) inflation since the last adjustment; (2) inflation expected for the coming year; and (3) the productivity gain since the last adjustment. Between 1965 and 1979 the formula— as calculated by the government—was simply imposed, to the detriment of the workers in the late 1960s, when the variable for expected inflation was consistently underestimated. In the 1970s the adjustments more closely followed inflation (see Table 8), although the workers received a small share, at best, of the considerable gains in productivity.

In fact, the latter was a loophole in the law because it left unspecified how the productivity gains would be calculated and distributed. Should the government ease its total control of the wage adjustment process, the workers and employers might negotiate directly over the wage increase allowable because of past productivity gains.

In practice, this system removed conflict from the workplace and transferred it to a tripartite court which represented the state. In effect this system either aborted the dispute or resolved it far from the point of conflict. Thus the system successfully preempted confrontation between labor and capital and left little room for direct bargaining.[7] This explains why successive governments have found the CLT structure so easy to live with. In the late 1940s President Dutra used the law to purge the union leadership of all leftists. In his 1951–54 presidency Getúlio Vargas used the law, via his young Labor Minister João Goulart, to encourage labor mobilization in São Paulo. When Goulart was later president (1961–64), the unions assumed a major role in the game of populist politics.[8] Some observers believed that the frequent strikes of those years represented an upsurge of labor militancy. Although the latter certainly existed, the worker mobilization came almost invariably from the top down. The union leaders tried to turn out worker support for the Goulart government (1961–64). They were interested primarily in moving the government to the left, not in more successful bargaining with employers. In fact, these leaders owed their positions to President Goulart, not to support among their members. When the military coup struck in 1964 they were rapidly deposed by the new military government. The repression also hit hard the Brazilian Labor Party (PTB or *Partido Trabalhista Brasileiro*), created by Getúlio Vargas in 1945 and later used to mobilize political support for populist candidates and programs.[9]

The long dominance of corporatist institutions led to much passivity and paternalism in Brazilian society. A good example was the widespread tendency to look to the state to solve every

---

[7] The building of this system of co-optation took place even before the approval of the CLT. "Between 1930 and 1943, Vargas achieved his major goals in the labor sector. First, he prevented any significant unrest during the economic crisis. Second, he built a whole system of state controls and almost eliminated progressive elements within the movement. The Labor Ministry and its agents could manipulate labor organizations through intervention, nonrecognition, and control over finances. A constantly expanding bureaucracy within the Ministry and Social Security (Previdência Social) apparatus provided jobs used to co-opt labor leaders." (Spalding 1977, p. 182.)

[8] Alexander points out that Brazilian unions were not conceived as organizations for collective bargaining. "The function of the *sindicato* in relation to the employer was thus reduced to providing the worker with legal representation before the labor courts." (Alexander 1962, p. 61)

[9] For general view of the role of the state in Brazil's labor relations system, see Rodrigues (1981).

problem.[10] Such attitudes seem to overtake even those who favor change in labor relations. Union leaders and management, for example, have talked much about collective bargaining in recent years. In the end, however, both seem to prefer having their conflicts handled by the law. That sentiment (reinforced for union leaders by an awareness of their weak bargaining position in many sectors) explains the preference for automatic wage indexation rather than negotiation over wages.[11]

Under this corporatist system, the impulse to bargain was stunted. Many wage adjustment mechanisms were incorporated into the labor laws and the labor courts developed a "normative" role in settling wage disputes. The frequent recourse to legislation in order to set wages reinforced the expectation that solutions were to be found in laws.

Changes Since 1978

The past six years have seen change in the political and economic framework. In the political sphere the break came in 1978 in São Paulo. President Ernesto Geisel, who had promised to restore a democratic regime, was nearing the end of his term (1974–79). His promise had coincided with the growing demands of key groups in the civil society, such as lawyers (through their bar associations), clergy and concerned laymen (through their action-oriented "pastorals"), and business (through their industrial and commercial federations). The Geisel government in effect encouraged this awakening of civil society, while warning that the process of liberalization must not be too rapid or it would frighten the "hard line" military, still powerful behind the scenes. Geisel's regime had not hesitated to use censorship or suspension of political rights to maintain control. Now, however, liberalization had picked up its own momentum.

It was inevitable that union leaders, long frustrated by repression, would join in the chorus demanding change. The most immediate issue angering workers was the government's failure to

---

[10] A fuller description of these expectations may be found in Pastore (1984).

[11] This preference has been expressed by several union organizations, such as CUT (Central Unica dos Trabalhadores), a fledgling alliance of unions from different industrial sectors; CONCLAT (Coordenação Nacional de Classe Trabahaldora), a national assembly of unions; and DIEESE, an interunion research organization. The latter has argued for the right to a wage adjustment equal to 100 percent of the inflation rate, plus an additional range within which to bargain.

adjust wage rates to compensate fully for inflation. The most blatant case had been in 1973, when Finance Minister Delfim Netto established the official inflation rate at 15 percent when in fact it was 20 to 25 percent. This distortion had a continuing effect on wages because the base for all subsequent adjustments was understated.

Discontent over this issue was skillfully channeled by a new generation of union leaders who began to denounce the corporatist CLT structure and wanted to build a new independent union movement (*novo sindicalismo*) by throwing out the old pro-government bosses (*pelegos*). The most prominent of those leaders was Luis Inácio da Silva, known by his nickname "Lula," who was president of the Metalworkers union of São Bernardo, a São Paulo industrial suburb. São Bernardo included key industries, especially the motor vehicle companies. The following analysis will concentrate on the São Paulo industrial sector, which produced the most significant worker militancy. Some series of events will be described more than once in order to bring out all their implications for the labor relations system. Because Lula was the president of a key metallurgical workers union, and because of the strength of his personality and his following, he became the leading labor spokesman in these years.

The 1978 worker actions began with a carefully planned sit-down strike in a São Bernardo truck factory. It quickly spread to 90 firms involving 500,000 workers in greater São Paulo (Veja 1978). The metalworkers involved decided to bargain directly with their employers and for an extra 11-percent one-time pay increase (they had demanded 34 percent) to adjust base pay for the past understatement of inflation. Future calculations of inflation would start with this base. This strike, and especially the subsequent direct bargaining, was heavily reported by the press, much of which depicted the movement as the workers' response to President Geisel's *abertura*.

The following year, 1979, brought a much longer São Paulo metalworkers' strike (the one-year working agreements normally expired in March, although a few expired in September), once again led by Lula. The metalworkers' example emboldened other union leaders, many of the new generation, and more than 400 strikes occurred between January and October 1979. About 30 involved key economic sectors: metalworking, urban transportation, ports, steel, trucking. In other sectors such as banking, electricity, and telecommunications, the mere threat of a strike (without a strike being carried out) was sufficient to alarm employers and the government. This time the government "intervened" the union and removed Lula from office. Not surprisingly, the eventual wage settlement fell far short of workers' demands.

The next major industrial strike action, and the last one until 1983, was in 1980. The São Paulo metalworkers again set the pace, striking for a 15 percent real wage increase, along with 12-month job security (which would have been indefinite tenure since the contracts were for one year) and recognition of shop stewards. The bargaining team for management represented the automakers and a spectrum of metal mechanical industries. This team initially offered the workers 3.6 percent (later raised to 5.9 percent) and no job security. This time the labor court stepped in, granting 7 percent and refraining from declaring the strike illegal—itself a minor victory for the workers.[12] Lula decided to continue the strike (the government had allowed him to return to his union presidency), which attracted great support from the Catholic church laymen and the press. Once again the employers asked the labor court to rule on the strike, and this time they declared it illegal (April 14, 1980). The strikers now suffered severe repression, as pickets were attacked by police and Lula and 13 union leaders were jailed for a month. This did nothing to shake Lula's following among the metalworkers. After 41 days, however, the workers returned to work with most of their demands unmet and their strike days unpaid. The "new unionism" had been defeated, at least for the short run, by a powerful government, determined employers, and the lack of an adequate structure within which direct bargaining might occur. When the time for the wage adjustment again rolled around in March 1981, there was no metalworkers' strike. Nor did they strike in 1982 or 1983 when the deep recession in Brazil had weakened their bargaining strength. As a result, they had to accept the wage adjustment laid down by the government.[13]

[12] For a detailed description of this strike from the standpoint of the Labor Ministry, see Macedo (1981, pp. 217–68).

[13] The 1982–83 period was marked by only a few strikes at the plant level, usually against firms in the export sector. In 1984 this trend reached the rural areas, most notably the sugar cane areas producing for the alcohol program.

Responses to Economic and Political Problems

Government Responses

The 1979–1984 period in Brazil was marked by frequent changes in economic policy, especially wage policy. These changes were formulated in the turbulent atmosphere generated by political liberalization, rising inflation, and the deepening economic slump.

After 1979 the key word in Brazilian politics became "negotiation." The trend towards negotiation went beyond the political arena. Political parties, congressmen, the press, and many interest groups demanded the right to participate in the government's response to inflation and recession. Labor also shared this desire. We shall now look again at the strikes by São Paulo metalworkers to see how the government reacted to the union resurgence.

The 1978 metalworkers' sit-down strike against the auto industry and its suppliers lasted only 12 days. But the union and Lula gained surprising visibility, with the press picturing him as a legitimate spokesman for a small but strategic part of the working class. Lula had quickly become Brazil's best known labor leader since 1945. The argument in much of the press was that since the government itself was moving towards redemocratization, a move towards direct negotiation between labor and capital was highly appropriate. The political opening was therefore used to justify union activism and the government response became a test of its real intentions.[14]

None of these events produced any changes in the legal structure of labor relations. The government had simply become less rigorous in enforcing the labor code (CLT). In 1979 that attitude changed when the metalworkers again led a strike in São Paulo. After 28 days of paralysis in the giant car factories, the Minister of Labor invoked the CLT, intervened in the metalworkers' union, and replaced its officers with civil servants. A strong reason for government intervention was the dwindling supply of vehicles needed to fill export orders. Thus the government soon made clear the limits of its tolerance for the "new unionism." It was well short of allowing the kind of long, drawn-out, union-management struggles that have marked the development of unionism in the

---

[14] For a description of the basic arguments used by the metalworkers' leadership in the strikes of 1979–80, see Moisés (1982).

industrialized countries. To show that the *abertura* was still alive, the Minister pardoned Lula, who could thus return to his union and organize an even longer strike (42 days) in April 1980. Once again the legal mechanisms were activated and Lula was removed. This time there was no pardon. By the CLT, Lula could no longer run for union office.

This exclusion only reinforced Lula's determination to turn to party politics (Souza 1985). He had already helped found the PT—Partido dos Trabalhadores (Workers Party) in October 1979. He became the party's first president and in 1982 ran on the PT ticket for governor of the state of São Paulo (as discussed below). Although finishing in fourth place, he won more than a million votes. The fact that he could be eligible to run for governor but not for union president is another example of the archaic nature of Brazilian labor law, which has successfully resisted change even in time of political liberalization.

The government's stop-and-go pattern of intervention and pardon in the case of the metalworkers and Lula did not stem from a desire for change. It was more a political strategy—something had to be done to cope with the growing public sympathy for Lula and the strikers. The government did not hesitate to prosecute the leaders. Lula fought the multiple charges against him and won in every case except his second removal from the São Paulo union presidency. He and other union leaders charged with political crimes (inciting to riot, etc.) have been much helped by the political climate of *abertura*. Indeed, even removal from his union officership has not stopped Lula from remaining a leader in his union's deliberations. Here, too, the enforcement of the Labor Ministry decision showed traces of *abertura*.

It is possible that the worker militancy of 1978–1981 (at a level unknown since the early 1960s) convinced the military that any attempt to close the political system would be costly. Those strike mobilizations created a network of sympathizers, led by São Paulo Cardinal Arns and well-organized Catholic laymen. The new union activity also attracted interest and support from Western European (especially West German) foundations controlled by labor unions and political parties. The U.S. had long had a program to introduce Brazilian union leaders to the U.S. system of labor relations. The U.S. labor attachés around Brazil were in close touch with Brazilian leaders. All this foreign involvement would also mean that a government crackdown was likely to alienate U.S. and Western European opinion—an outcome the Brazilian governments preferred to avoid.

On the economic scene, inflation was on the rise again. In 1979 it hit 46 percent, compared to 35 percent in 1978. Nonetheless, the economy was still booming in 1979. Together inflation and the political opening created an atmosphere favoring labor mobilization. For the government, however, too much mobilization might endanger the political opening.[15]

The government responded to growing union demands by a series of wage bills approved and then amended between October 1979 and October 1984.

Government Wage Policies in 1979-1984: The new union militancy impressed the new Figueiredo government (1979–85). Its principal response, duly approved by Congress, was Law 6,708 which provided: (1) automatic semiannual wage adjustments based on the cost-of-living index; (2) a differential inflation adjustment according to wage level. Workers earning the equivalent of one to three times the minimum wage would receive an adjustment of 110 percent of the cost of living. For those earning three to ten, the adjustment would be 100 percent; for those earning above ten, 80 percent. The law was an important concession to labor. Making the adjustment semiannual had been a frequent union demand. The differential cost-of-living adjustment was designed to make income distribution more equal.[16]

The "solution," once again, came from a law rather than from bargaining. This new wage law limited bargaining to discussion of a wage increase based on productivity gains.

With the automatic indexation taking care of inflation, the more aggressive unions complained that they had little left to bargain for. They would thus find it more and more difficult to attract new members and to organize demonstrations and strikes. In fact, strikes declined from 429 in 1979 to 42 in 1980, 34 in 1981, and 36 in 1982. Collective disputes taken to São Paulo labor court—the

---

[15] In 1984 Lula ran for office in the metalworkers' union again and won. In the ensuing legal battle the Federal Court of Appeals (Tribunal Federal de Recursos) ruled that he could assume the union office. It was a historic decision, since it directly challenged the powers of the CLT.

[16] Detailed justification of the new wage policy can be found in Macedo (1981, 1983).

center of most labor disputes—also fell, from 289 cases in 1979, to 89 in 1980, 60 in 1981, and 42 in 1982. In general, the 1979 law produced relative peace on the level of collective labor struggle.

But Law 6,708 lasted only two years. Conservative economists, starting in mid-1980, began a campaign against wage indexation, arguing it was a major stimulus to inflation because of the 100 percent adjustment at the lower levels. A new law was passed (Law 6,886) in December 1980 which left untouched the 110 percent rate but slashed the adjustment for those in the top brackets.[17]

The critics continued their attack on the 110 percent adjustment at the 1–3 times the minimum wage levels, which included about 70 percent of the labor force (although only 30 percent of the total wage bill).[18] In January 1983—when Congress was in recess—President Figueiredo issued Decree-Law 2012 which reduced the 110 percent adjustment to 100 percent and reduced the adjustment for 3–7 times the minimum wage to 95 percent and for 7–15 to 80 percent. The rest were unchanged. This was the most severe cut to the upper wage categories yet seen, as well as an abandonment of the bonus for the lowest paid. In May 1983 the government had to backtrack, under Congressional pressure, and issued Decree-Law 2024 which established the 100 percent adjustment for 1–7 times the minimum wage, thereby restoring full cost-of-living adjustment for those in the 3–7 times the minimum wage category. In July 1983 the government reversed its field again, as it gave in to the IMF pressure to reduce the wage bill. Decree-Law 2045 now established an 80 percent adjustment for all brackets and declared illegal any negotiated settlement above that level. It was the first time since 1979 that the adjustment formula did not favor the lowest paid. This move was highly unpopular. The

---

[17] Law 6,708 provided for an automatic, semiannual wage adjustment according to the following formula: 110 percent of the cost-of-living index for those making 1-3 times the minimum wage, 100 percent for those making 3-10 times the minimum wage, and 80 percent for those making more than 10 times the minimum wage. Law 6,886 then stipulated 80 percent for 10-15 times the minimum wage, 50 percent for 15-20, and 0 percent for those earning more than 20 times the minimum wage. The latter group received the adjustments equivalent to those at up to 20 times the minimum wage but nothing beyond.

[18] Although Law 6,708 was attacked as being a central cause of inflation, virtually all the empirical studies found other causes (the public sector deficit, indexation in the financial sector, etc.) to be more important than the wage increase. See Camargo (1984), Bacha and Lopes (1983), Cunha (1983), World Bank (1984), and Knight (1981).

government had to declare a state of emergency in Brasília during Congressional debate over the bill in order to prevent massive demonstrations by the opposition.

Decree-Law 2045, like all the other recent wage laws, had a short life. In October 1983, only three months later—in a calmer political atmosphere—the Congress passed Decree-Law 2065, reestablishing a 100 percent adjustment for 1-3 times the minimum wage, and fixing the adjustment at 80 percent for 3-7 times and 50 percent for 7-10 times the minimum wage. In October 1984 yet another wage law was passed, improving the inflation adjustment for the 3-7 minimum wage equivalent from 80 to 100 percent and the over-7 minimum wage equivalent from 50 to 80 percent.

The dizzying changes in the indexation formulas had only served to arouse new bargaining demands. None of the formulas had succeeded in pleasing everyone. The net effect of all these wage bills (except Law 2,045) was to shift significantly the distribution of wage and salary income, to the benefit of the bottom (in income) two-thirds of workers and to the detriment of the top 1.6 percent, with varying shifts in between (see Table 9). The Figueiredo government received little credit from the unions for this income redistribution, while middle and upper income earners were indignant over the relative losses. In part this was because the workers understandably paid most attention to the declining purchasing power of their nominal wages.[19] Meanwhile, the IMF continued to demand wage austerity, stipulating that total wages should increase at a rate no greater than 80 percent of the official cost of living.

Other Government Policies Towards Labor: What of the oft-discussed role of bargaining? Congress had kept it well in mind. Decree-Law 2,065 (of October 1983) provided that automatic indexation would apply only until mid-1985. For the rest of 1985 the indexation adjustment would fall to 70 percent, then 60 percent for 1986 and 50 percent for 1987. The parties would be free to bargain for anything beyond the indexation adjustment until mid-

---

[19] The independent interunion research institute (DIEESE) published its own data (gathered in its own surveys) on the number of hours of work (at the minimum wage) needed to buy the basic foodstuffs, as defined by the federal government. These data were published monthly, as in DIEESE (1983).

TABLE 9
Distribution of Wage and Salary Income
(Formal Sector Only)

	Percent of Earnings		Percent of Employment	
	1979	1983	1979	1983
Income as a multiple of the value of the minimum wage:				
Up to 3 × minimum wage	25.4	31.2	67.6	67.1
3 to 10 × minimum wage	43.3	39.4	26.6	27.0
10 to 15 × minimum wage	9.2	11.0	2.9	3.2
15 to 20 × minimum wage	5.7	6.7	1.3	1.4
More than 20 × minimum wage	16.4	11.6	1.6	1.4
Total	100.0	100.0	100.0	100.0

Source: RAIS (Relação Anual de Informações Sociais), Ministry of Labor.

1988, after which wage increases would be left completely to bargaining.

This law marked the first time in 50 years that the government explicitly promoted collective bargaining as a way to settle wage disputes. The new posture did not last long. After six months Decree-Law 2,065 was under attack, not surprisingly, for having reduced the wages of the middle class. In October 1984 the Congress passed a new law restoring the 100 percent indexation adjustment for the 1–7 times the minimum wage. The adjustment was to be 80 percent for all higher brackets, with bargaining permitted only up to 100 percent of the indexation formula. This new law eliminated the plan to move gradually towards bargaining. In short, Brazil went back to a simple indexation adjustment for 90 percent of the labor force.

Wage adjustments have continued to be settled by government action. Faced with a deep recession after 1981, even the best organized unions were hesitant to give up the minimum gain guaranteed by automatic indexation in exchange for an unknown collective bargaining scheme. It should be added that this attitude also reflects a corporatist mentality of looking to the state for solutions.

To complicate matters further, inflation skyrocketed. It went from 95 percent in 1980 to 119 percent in 1983, and to 236 percent in 1984. As a result, losses in real wages under the various indexation systems have been substantial over the last four years. Not surprisingly, these losses explain most of the resort to strikes by the

Metalworkers and other key unions in late 1983 and 1984.[20] Most have been limited to individual firms, particularly the exporters. These firms have frequently disregarded the official wage limits. Their success in paying higher wage rates has furnished a demonstration effect for other sectors and thereby stimulated a return to militancy among the new generation of union leaders.

Many of these resurgent unions have a new characteristic: they are closely linked to party politics. This should not be surprising. Indeed, experience elsewhere seems to show that labor relations systems that lack the flexibility to allow bargaining over economic issues tend to encourage a recourse to politics (Scoville 1973). Since achieving political objectives requires different mechanisms than attaining economic goals, it is common for unions to support political parties or join interunion organizations (Millen 1963).

Brazil's rigid legal structure and lack of bargaining room have recently pushed the unions towards either total support of the government (carried out by *pelegos*), or the creation of an opposition political party, such as the PT. Both "peleguismo" and "petismo" can be seen as the products of a rigid labor relations system.

> Where collective bargaining dominates the scene, trade unionism is the main or only form of labor organization. When a political party is created by the unions . . . the party is primarily intended to supplement and support union action. In contrast, primary emphasis on political activity tends to call for the formation of political parties of the working class—often ahead of unions, which are then created for specific action in the industrial relations field. Such unions are then usually subordinated, at least in their earlier stages, to the political branch of the movement. . . . (Spalding 1977, p. 3) Where legislation or courts prevent the workers from organizing effectively for the defense of their interests, the main thrust of any workers' movement will almost inevitably be directed at a basic change of the institutions, and the means available to the workers will be political: mass demonstrations, violence, sabotage, political strikes, etc. (Spalding 1977, p. 24)

---

[20] More than 200 strikes were registered in the first six months of 1984.

Nonetheless, this corporatist labor relations system has been functional for a half-century and is still functional for some regions and social sectors where only legal protection can guarantee at least minimally acceptable wages and working conditions.

Yet large segments of the labor force appear ready for collective bargaining, particularly in industrial sectors such as vehicles, chemicals, transportation, and printing. The highly heterogeneous Brazilian labor market requires both the protection of the corporatist system and the flexibility of collective bargaining. How to meet these two conflicting needs? Two laws?

In the Brazilian juridical tradition, labor law is federal law and the constitution does not permit adaptations to state or regional needs. For instance, when Decree-Law 2,065 (a federal law) established a timetable for a gradual transition to collective bargaining, this was supposed to be obeyed equally by unions and employers in, for example, São Paulo, Pernambuco, and Amazonas. Yet this is quite unrealistic, given the low level of union organization in the latter two states.

An alternative solution was suggested in 1983 by technical staff of the Ministry of Labor. They proposed that any move towards collective bargaining be voluntary. For example, the creation and use of grievance procedures and arbitration would have to be approved by both employees and employers. This proposal would circumvent the need for a single federal labor law covering the entire labor market.

This plan was immediately criticized by both union spokesmen and management leaders, as well as by labor lawyers and labor court judges who rightly feared that an alternative system for resolving labor disputes would undermine their exclusive authority. The proposal did not even have enough support within the Executive to be sent to Congress.

Finally, there are some other recent economic policies that have notably affected labor. One of the most important is the general effort towards de-indexation and removal of subsidies. Credit subsidies to agriculture were removed in 1982–1983, and export subsidies were to be removed in 1984–1985. This effort greatly pleased the IMF, which has been pushing since 1982 for de-indexing the entire economy. But the social consequences of such a policy are unlikely to be even. The sector where de-indexation was first tried is labor. The results are instructive. The wage adjustment formula has kept wage rate increases well below Brazil's rate of inflation for the 1981–1984 period. The workers have thus paid a heavy price for the supposed policy of de-indexation.

Union Responses

Trends in union organization of the past five years are related to the world economic crises in only a secondary manner. The principal link is Brazil's economic slump, with its international origins, as described earlier. Otherwise, most changes are best seen as the product of a combination of primarily internal forces, namely, the reactions to *abertura*, recession, and government application of the corporatist code. Union penetration is a good example.

Union Penetration: By the labor code (CLT), any formally recognized employment, that is, where the employee carries a *carteira* (worker's registration card), is automatically covered by all the CLT's legal and financial provisions. If the *município* of the workplace has no recognized union, the workers can form one and petition the Ministry of Labor for recognition. What is important to note is that workers gain the basic protection of the labor code not through unionization, but through government regulation of the workplace. One cannot therefore cite union penetration as a measure of either the state of the economy or of the degree of union militancy.

One can, however, look at who has won the union officerships.

Internal Union Politics: When the government's political liberalization allowed for greater union activism after 1978, more elections of union officers were contested. There were roughly three groups of contenders: the *pelegos*, the communists, and the *petistas*.[21] The latter, with their aggressive leadership and partial success in São Paulo in 1978, seriously threatened the long-time leadership dominance of the communists and *pelegos*. Indeed, the latter two had worked out a comfortable coexistence over the years, dividing up the union officerships and readily collaborating with the government during the darkest days of the repression. That record had helped by 1977–1978 to discredit the incumbent leaders in the eyes of the workers and to give the *petistas* a special appeal.

---

[21] The label *petista* is used here to describe the independent union militants who formed the PT in October 1979. *Petista* is a useful label for these militants as long as one remembers the party (and therefore the word) came later.

The *petistas* were backed by an increasingly important social force: radical Catholics, who gave strikers valuable logistical support, drawing on the support of the outspokenly pro-labor Cardinal Arns and on the cadres of lay volunteers in greater São Paulo. The status quo forces were far from ready to surrender, however. A new movement, *Unidade Sindical* (Labor Union Unity), emerged, made up of *pelegos*, the orthodox communists (Partido Comunista Brasileiro, or PCB) and two smaller groups, the Chinese-line communists (Partido Comunista do Brasil, or PC do B) and MR-8 (Movimento Revolucionário 8 de Outubro—the day of Guevara's death), the remnants of an urban guerrilla movement. Such a heterogeneous coalition was unlikely to last long. The very fact of its creation showed how threatening the *petistas* appeared.

By mid-1984 the *petistas* showed steady gains in the electoral fight to control union *diretorias*. The *pelegos*, although losing ground, still controlled about two-thirds of the union *diretorias*. The communists were holding steady, controlling about 15 percent. For those who preferred industrial peace—if only for the short run—the *pelegos* were the ideal labor leaders. The communists were a close second, since they had a long established reputation for prudent action in day-to-day dealings. The *petistas* were the most troublesome because they were fighting to transform the system into one where worker representatives could gain real power and force direct negotiation with employers.

Worker Militancy: We have seen how worker militancy surged forth in 1978–1980 in the São Paulo industrial heartland. The initial demands were for wage increases, a demand that continued for all three years. Very soon, however, they added a demand for increased job security, an area where the law gave the employer an advantage. They added also a demand for worker representation at the plant level, either through shop stewards or through labor-management committees—another issue on which the labor code was silent. Finally, as the recession deepened, there was a demand that the government undertake job creation—such as public works—to absorb the growing mass of unemployed. An alternative demand by some unions was to shorten the workweek from 48 to 40 hours, thus necessitating new hires.

As noted earlier, after 1980 the incidence of strikes declined until late 1983. There were several reasons. The new wage law (6,708) of 1979 was one. Since it provided for an annual wage increase of 10 percent above the inflation adjustment for those earning between 1 and 3 times the minimum wage—the majority of workers—it undoubtedly undercut rank-and-file support for wage-oriented strikes. Second, a recession after 1981 created a large pool of surplus labor. They were a direct threat to take jobs of would-be strikers. The third reason was the cautious attitude of many workers, even in the more militant unions. They lacked a long experience of union activism, and they were understandably skeptical about the union's ability to protect them from employer retribution. The latter was a real threat, as could be seen when the employers fired many workers who led the 1978–1980 strikes.

Other Issues: A relatively new area of worker activism that has survived the recession is the creation of workplace-level labor-management committees. The law makes no provision for such institutions, so they can only be established by union-employer consensus. Workers in a few plants have, through direct negotiations, succeeded in getting such committees recognized by their employer. A leading case is the Ford plant in São Paulo (Brito 1983). The greatest potential for worker representation by such committees is in negotiations over workplace-specific working conditions, which the *município*-level union normally neglected. In the short run such committees will probably remain restricted to the more highly organized industrial workers.

Management Responses

Although the legal framework of Brazil's labor relations system is basically unchanged, employers have sometimes reacted in new ways to the challenges presented by the *abertura*, the new union activism, and the economic crisis (Cardoso 1983). First, they have demanded a role in governmental decision-making. This has been expressed through lobbying by the two national business confederations—CNI (National Confederation of Industry) and CNC (National Confederation of Commerce)—as well as the key state federations of industry such as in São Paulo, Rio de Janeiro, Rio Grande do Sul, and Minas Gerais. The second employer reaction has been the creation of professional associations in the area of human resources and personnel management, with the aim of improving employment recruitment and promotion. Third, the growing unionization has stimulated the creation of new mechanisms, such as quality circles and labor-management committees, especially in export-oriented firms. Fourth, new attempts have been made at training industrial relations personnel at Brazilian and foreign universities and training centers, aimed especially at producing competent negotiators. These four types of management response merit more detailed examination.

Lobbying: The deepening recession and the steady increase in domestic interest rates made life much more difficult for businessmen. Management and government had traditionally enjoyed a symbiotic relationship. Recession and interest rates were supposed to be taken care of by the government, as they had in the past. But this time they were not. This prompted vigorous lobbying from management's federations and confederations. They demanded that the federal government ease its pressure on the domestic economy. Business wanted both lower wages and lower interest rates. The federal government, trying to please all sides, responded with a series of measures aimed at gradually de-indexing both interest rates and wages. But the former lasted no more than three months (beginning in 1983), while under-indexation of wages is still in effect. Thus management's lobbying partially achieved one of its goals.

Management also became zealous about labor law enforcement. At several critical junctures the employers' associations quickly requested that the labor courts declare a strike illegal, further requesting that the Labor Ministry intervene the striking unions and revoke the political rights of the union leaders. The employer associations were thus ready to interpret the *abertura* in a highly self-interested manner.[22]

Personnel Administration: As we saw earlier, the 1979 wage law required semiannual salary adjustments based on a formula that favored the lowest wage-earners. At the beginning, the pressure for a larger adjustment was extended also to the higher wage levels. As the unions became more aggressive, the employers could not, as they had in the past, rely on dismissals as a means to reduce the effect of the indexation formula and to undermine the pressure

---

[22] During the strikes the employers' associations have often agreed to establish training programs for negotiators as well as to consider the idea of labor-management committees and grievance procedures. Once the strike is over, however, usually little has been done. A study by FIESP (the São Paulo Industrial Federation) has shown the employers to be evenly divided over the creation of mechanisms for grievance accommodation and conflict resolution. As a result, FIESP decided against any attempt to move in the direction of bargaining.

from strategic unions. Another management response to union pressure was the organization of personnel associations to improve recruitment and promotion of employees. Standards for personnel selection and promotion became tougher and based on more scientific criteria. Today these associations are highly active, and many managers credit them for much of the increase in labor productivity in recent years.

Quality Circles and Labor-Management Committees: In the past five years unions have pressed hard, especially in the export sector, to participate in decisions about firing, hiring, working hours, etc. About 70 percent of the 1982 bargaining demands in São Paulo had to do with recognizing shop stewards (*delgado sindical*) or labor-management committees as extensions of the unions. Both management and the labor courts systematically rejected this demand. Management did agree, however, to implement quality circles, productivity committees, and social clubs to cover everything except the economic issues (wages, hours of work, and firing). A study still under way shows that more than 50 quality circles were created after 1979 in Brazil's industrial sector.[23] This trend is hardly surprising. The acceptance (or promotion) of such innovations has been typical of employer behavior in the advanced industrial economies. Brazilian employers undoubtedly hoped, as had their earlier counterparts in the U.S. and Europe, that these "noneconomic" concessions would undercut worker support for the unions. That seems confirmed by the fact that in the same period not a single shop steward was recognized at the plant level.

Training in Industrial Relations: Brazilian management has traditionally dealt with labor problems by dispatching their lawyers to the labor courts. The increasing union pressure after 1979, along with the climate of *abertura*, induced the large corporations—the multinationals at first—to recruit and train industrial relations experts. In the metalworking sector, FIESP promoted the training of negotiators for its sector as well as for many enterprises. Based on a tripartite agreement, managers and workers have created a new institute to sponsor training and research in the area of labor relations: IBART (Instituto Brasileiro de Relações do Trabalho), which has the support of the Ministry of Labor and the International Labor Organization.

---

[23] The study is sponsored by the Ministry of Labor, Brasilia, 1984.

Basic Changes

Moving Towards Negotiation

Despite the rigidities of the legal system, the interaction between unions and management has increased in the last five years. A few firms and their employees have come up with sophisticated agreements and new strategies to circumvent laws both sides find troublesome.[24]

Inflation and recession have played an important role in bringing these changes, particularly for unions in strategic sectors such as ports, transportation, and the metal and chemical industries. Data from a 1982 survey show that in São Paulo about 75 percent of the bargaining efforts reached agreement, meaning that only 25 percent went to the labor courts. In 1979 the results had been precisely the reverse: about 75 percent of the disputes went to the labor courts.

Does this mean a strengthening of the union movement and a decisive shift towards bargaining, or does it indicate only a lack of room to disagree? Probably some of each. On the one hand, the new unionism has pushed managers towards negotiation. On the other hand, the wage laws and the labor code have limited the room for taking a case to the labor courts. Any settlement beyond the law will be disregarded by these courts, as has happened, for instance, with job security claims.

In 1982, 42 percent of the disputes in São Paulo centered on seniority issues. The labor court judges systematically rejected union demands, arguing that such demands violated the CLT. Such a decision was, of course, a de facto ruling in favor of employers.

Another example is the reduction of the workday. About 40 percent of the disputes centered on the reduction in working hours as a strategy to avoid layoffs in a recession. Managers agreed to that measure, providing the wages were prorated, but the workers insisted on no wage cuts. On this issue the labor courts once again refused to arbitrate, arguing that it violated the CLT.[25]

---

[24] The wide range of agreements reached in the 1979–1982 period is analyzed in Souza (1983).

[25] Any attempt to strike over these issues would be declared illegal (as has happened several times), since they are not covered by the CLT. This type of claim can be resolved only through agreement between labor and management. In case of an impasse, the question cannot be resolved by the court or by a strike. In short, if management does not agree, the issue ends up being resolved in management's favor.

The final 18 percent of the disputes centered on the criteria for hiring and firing workers; direct agreement was reached on hiring but not firing. Following the logic of their ruling on seniority, the labor judges refused to consider the union appeals.

On the issue of real wage increases (based on productivity gains), the union demands ran from 10.8 to 15 percent. Where bargained, the range of settlements was between 0.8 and 6 percent.[25] But when taken to the labor courts, the range of awards was between 4 and 7 percent—which meant an advantage for those who had appealed to the courts. The subsequent wage laws reduced the margin for bargaining, however.

Overall, we can conclude that most of the labor force continued to be guided by the labor code on the collective disputes. Indeed, in most cases disputes did not even arise. The key item—wage adjustment—was taken care of by the 1979 law. For most workers, the option to bargain was at best remote.

Bargaining and unionism have gained some ground, however, in a few strategic sectors, such as the automobile industry. There direct negotiation has increased substantially, and the labor law has occasionally been bypassed. Management and labor have learned that direct agreement can offer more alternatives for settling their disputes. They have learned also that the creation of specific mechanisms and the training of negotiators are crucial elements in successful bargaining.

There is other learning about bargaining going on in these strategic sectors. Management knows that labor court decisions on collective disputes tend to favor them, but they avoid turning too quickly to the courts. In these restricted sectors strikes and boycotts do occur today, independently of the CLT and the court decision. They are the products of a new political environment and new union leadership. If a sector is doing well economically, unions will push hard and even strike—challenging management, the CLT, and the government. Knowing that, management in these sectors has been more receptive to bargaining, and innovations are occurring in bargaining procedures, grievance mechanisms, and labor-management committees. Here labor relations now require a professional attitude rather than recourse to the police or the labor courts.

---

[25] For an overview of the most common disputes and resolutions, see *Boletim* (1982–84)

Political Changes

By May 1978, after just a year of the new worker militancy, Lula and his leaders had begun to think that activism in the workplace might not be enough. Although they had just carried out a successful strike, they were highly suspicious of the employers, who had responded in a more unified way than the union leaders had expected. Over the next year, Lula and company debated whether the workers ought to enter politics. Under the repressive military regime of the 1970s, that could only be done by voting for the broad-front MDB (Movimento Democrático Brasileiro), the "official" opposition party. In the 1974 Congressional elections, for example, the MDB won a massive working class vote in the industrial sectors of São Paulo. The MDB leaders had made the military government's labor policies a target for blistering attack. Notwithstanding these MDB efforts, the union militants thought the time had come to create a new party, a workers' party.

Why? Why not continue working through the MDB, which was growing stronger by the day, especially in São Paulo? Partly because these union militants deeply distrusted the MDB, not least because it was supported by the Brazilian Communist Party (PCB), the break-away Maoist communists (PC do B), and the *pelegos*, all enemies of the *petistas* in the battle for union control. The PCB communists strongly opposed the creation of the PT (*Partido dos Trabalhadores*), arguing that Lula and his lieutenants should stick to union organizing. But Lula argued that the workers could never gain political influence until they had a party that spoke *exclusively* for them. Whatever its virtues, the MDB represented widely contradictory interests, of which only one was workers. As in any coalition, the workers might find *their* interests sacrificed at the key points. As for the PCB, the *petistas* regarded it as a discredited and tiresome bureaucracy whose rigid dogma rendered it unable to speak for workers.

The debate over creating the PT followed predictable lines. Lula and his allies argued that the workers must find a political voice. Since the structure of labor relations was government-created and government-enforced, only those in control of the government could change it. That logic aroused angry opposition from some of Lula's lieutenants and fellow leaders in other unions. These dissenters argued that priority *must* go to strengthening the still highly fragile structure of new independent union leadership. The *pelegos* and the communists remained strong and could be ousted only by systematic and patient organizing. What point was there in a Workers' Party if the petistas did not even control the industrial unions?

Some of the nay-sayers suspected that Lula's national fame had gone to his head. He was a fascinating figure to the public—the man who challenged the giant auto companies, the old labor bosses, the communists, and the government. The new PT would have to rise on Lula's name, at least at the outset, and that reinforced his personal role. Thus the PT's creation opened a rift between the PT organizers and those who opted to concentrate on union organizing.

Disregarding the many warnings, Lula and his allies founded the *Partido dos Trabalhadores*, or Workers' Party, in 1979. It created a new pole of leadership in labor relations, especially in São Paulo. In the short run it diverted from the union scene some valuable *petista* manpower. That would necessarily weaken *petistas* in their battles to win control of key unions. On the other hand, it offered an alternative outlet for action by leaders such as Lula whom the government had purged from their union positions.

In the short run the new party could not hope to have a major electoral impact, except in São Paulo state. This simply reflected the fact that the strongest PT support would come from the strongholds of the industrial unions in that state. The chance to influence national politics anytime soon was remote. But the PT enthusiasts optimistically plunged into the formidable task of registering the party *município* by *município*.

The Figueiredo government was at first pleased with the PT's creation, believing it would divide the opposition, thereby improving the electoral chances of the government's own ailing party, the PDS. Political tensions rose as the November 1982 election neared. At stake were all the governorships, all federal deputies, two-thirds of the federal Senate, and all state legislators, mayors, and town councils.

The PT's natural base was the industrial heartland—above all São Paulo, but also urban areas in Rio de Janeiro, Minas Gerais, Paraná, and Rio Grande do Sul. A new electoral regulation required every party to run a gubernatorial candidate in every state. The PT complied, but the fledgling party was forced to spread its resources throughout Brazil, most of which was far from ready for a Workers' Party.

Since the PT's base was in São Paulo, this nationwide party organizing necessarily cut into the *petista* forces available for the labor struggles there. But this may not have been a net loss. The recession that began in 1981 drastically worsened bargaining conditions for the workers. Thus, the drain on manpower and resources probably did not significantly influence the bargaining outcomes in 1981–1984.

Did the PT influence national party politics in these years? Minimally. In the 1982 elections PT succeeded in electing only two candidates for national office (a federal deputy from Minas Gerais and a federal deputy from Rio de Janeiro) outside of the state of São Paulo, where it elected six federal deputies. Lula ran for governor of São Paulo and lost to Franco Montoro, a highly popular PMDB (the MDB repackaged to meet new electoral requirements) senator. The party did manage to elect scattered state deputies, mayors, and city councilmen, largely in the state of São Paulo.

Impact on Labor Relations

What difference could these electoral victories make in decision-making about labor relations? In the short run, virtually none. In the 1982 elections the government party, the PDS, emerged with 235 federal deputies, five votes short of the absolute majority of 240. At first glance the eight PT deputies might seem a possible swing vote. In practice, however, the PT was hardly likely to strike a deal to vote with the PDS. That kind of leverage was more likely from the PTB, another splinter party (13 seats) and far more pragmatic. In fact, in 1983 the PTB did negotiate a short-lived coalition with the PDS.

On the state and local level it was the PMDB which had swept the elections in most of the Center-South, with the exception of Rio, where the new party (PDT) of Leonel Brizola carried the day. The PT was generally competitive only in areas won by other opposition parties. The most striking example was São Paulo, where even in its areas of strongest support the PT often ran second to the PMDB.

In the end none of this made much difference to the structure and content of labor relations. That structure could be altered only by massive change in the federal labor laws (or by their nonenforcement—a less likely outcome). The military government had placed that possibility far beyond the realm of the politically possible in the 1982 elections. The same was true of the repressive apparatus, which at the state and local level was still controlled by the SNI (*Serviço Nacional de Informações,* or national intelligence) and the military. Thus, by mid-1984 the PT had produced little political impact. Its leaders and enthusiasts were not discouraged, however. They saw these difficult years as sowing the seeds of a major new political force.

The PT was not the only political vehicle for union activists. Since the *pelegos* prospered from the existing union structure, they were pragmatic in party politics, obviously avoiding the PT but ready to make deals with the PDS or the PMDB for short-term advantage. The communists (the orthodox PCB) strongly supported the PMDB. By so doing, they hoped to achieve their primary short-term goal: the legalization of the Communist Party. That, in turn, would enable them to organize the working class politically, take control of the national government, and transform Brazil into a socialist society. Obviously, that would also transform the labor relations system. Since the PMDB had no influence over the national labor relations system, the PCB's support for the PMDB had no short-term political payoff.

The PCB has been active on another front. Like Lula, they believe in parallel lines of action: one in party politics and the other on the shop floor. Active in union organizing for 40 years, the communists had entrenched themselves in key unions such as the petroleum workers and the dock workers.

The year 1984 has seen an upsurge of PT influence among the union movements in São Paulo and Rio Grande do Sul, where several elections have been won by PT union leaders. The PT movement has also targeted rural workers, particularly the São Paulo "boias-frias" (day laborers) who generally have a weak union tradition but are capable of violent forms of strike and protest. These movements have given visibility to the PT and dramatized its influence as a militant opposition party. As a result, the PT is now seen as Brazil's most authentically left-wing party. Equally important, the PT has become a new and potentially critical factor in the evolution of Brazil's labor relations system.

Conclusion

Brazil has seen more change in its labor relations system in the past five years than in the preceding 40. Yet change occurred not in the legal structure, but in its application. The federal government gave unions more leeway after 1978, allowing more confrontation and direct bargaining than at any time since 1964. This coincided with the remarkable upsurge of worker and unionist activism starting in 1978. The result was a sharp increase in direct bargaining—an important departure for Brazil's traditionally state-dominated labor relations.

How much momentum does this trend have? The new activism is not likely to die out soon, at least at the level of the better organized unions. Its resilience through the jarring 1981-1984 recession is testimony to its strength. There is also reason to believe that employers in the more specialized plants might prefer a direct bargaining relationship, in order to satisfy the special needs of their skilled workers.

Is Brazil ready for a pluralist labor relations system? The short answer is that key laws still favor a corporatist, not a pluralist, system. Given the character of Brazil's labor force and the surplus labor pool, and given the tradition of statist manipulation, it hardly seems likely that the elite will spontaneously promote union autonomy. Changes will have to be fought for, as they have been in the industrialized countries. Prospects for union success on that front will, in turn, depend on the continued openness of Brazil's political system.

What of the PT? The PT is a gamble on the future. It has minimal leverage in Brazilian politics today and its prospects will depend on its ability to attract voters from the PMDB, which has developed voter loyalty due to its antigovernment stand since 1965.

There is an undeniable dynamic spirit among Brazilian workers, at least in the industrial sectors. How that spirit will make itself felt—through union or party activity—cannot be foreseen. Yet even the skeptics must agree that elements of Brazilian labor have escaped the limits that Brazil's political elite had so carefully laid out for them.

References

Alexander, Robert J. *Labor Relations in Argentina, Brazil and Chile*. New York: McGraw-Hill, 1962.

Almeida, Maria Hermínia Tavares de. "O Sindicato no Brasil: Novos Problemas, Velhas Estruturas." *Debate e Crítica* No. 6 (Julho de 1975), pp. 49-74.

————. "Tendencias Recentes da Negociação Coletiva no Brasil." *Dados* 24, No. 2 (1981), pp. 161-89.

_____. "Novas Demandas, Novos Direitos: Experiências do Sindicalismo Paulista na Ultima Dêcada." *Dados* 26, No. 3 (1983a), pp. 265-90.

_____. "O Sindicalismo Brasileire entre a Conservação e a Mudança." In *Sociedade e Politica no Brasil pos-64*, eds. Bernardo Sorj and Maria Hermínia Tavares de Almeida. São Paulo: Brasiliense, 1983b. Pp. 191-214.

Bacha, E., and F. Lopes. "Inflation, Growth and Wage Policy: A Brazilian Perspective." *Journal of Development Economics* 13 (1983), pp. 1-20.

Baer, Werner. *The Brazilian Economy: Growth and Development*, 2nd ed. New York: Praeger Publishers, 1983.

_____. "Political Determinants of Brazil's Economic Development." In *Politics, Policies and Economic Development in Latin America*, ed. Robert Wesson. Forthcoming.

Boletim de Negociação. São Paulo: FIPE, 1982-84.

Brito, Jose Carlos Aguiar. *A Tomada da Ford: O Nascimento de um Sindicato Livre*. Petrópolis: Editora Vozes, 1983.

Camargo, José Marcio. "Salário Real e Indexação no Brasil." *Pesquisa e Planejamento* 14 (April 1984), pp. 137-60.

Cardoso, Fernando Henrique. "O Papel dos Empresários no Processo de Transição: O Caso Brasileiro." *Dados* 26, No. 1 (1983), pp. 9-28.

Conjuntura Econômica 38 (April 1984).

Cordova, Erfren, ed. *Las Relaciones Collectivas de Trabajo en America Latina*. Geneva: International Labor Organization, 1981.

Cunha, Paulo Vieira da. "Reajustos Salariais na Indústria e a Lei Salarial de 1979: Uma Nota Empírica." *Dados* 26, No. 3 (1983), pp. 291-314.

Departamento Intersindical de Estatística e Estudos Sócio-Econômicos (DIEESE). *Boletim do DIEESE*, Ano 11 (January 1983).

Dornbusch, Rudiger. "U.S. Monetary and Fiscal Policy, the Dollar and the International Financial System." São Paulo: Instituto de Pesquisas Económicas, 1983. Mimeo.

_____. "The International Debt Problem: The Latin American Dimension." *Challenge* 27 (July/August 1984), pp. 4-11.

Economic Commission for Latin America. *Economic Survey of Latin America 1981*. Santiago: United Nations, 1983.

_____. "Notas sobre la economía y el desarrollo de américa latina." No. 387/388. January 1984.

Erickson, Kenneth Paul. *The Brazilian Corporative State and Working-Class Politics*. Berkeley: University of California Press, 1977.

Fishlow, Albert. "The United States and Brazil: The Case of the Missing Relationship." *Foreign Affairs* 60 (Spring 1982), pp. 904-23.

Humphrey, John. *Capitalist Control and Workers' Struggle in the Brazilian Auto Industry*. Princeton, NJ: Princeton University Press, 1982.

Knight, Peter T. "Brazilian Socio-economic Development: Issues for the Eighties." *World Development* 9 (Nos. 11/12, 1981), pp. 1063-82.

Macêdo, Murillo. *Trabalho na Democracia: a Nova Fisionomia do Processo Político Brasileiro*. Brasília: Ministério do Trabalho, 1981.

_____. *Negociação no Mundo do Trabalho*. Brasília: Ministério de Trabalho, 1983.

Magano, Octávio Bueno. *Organização Sindical Brasileira*. São Paulo: Editora Revista dos Tribunais, 1982.

Mericle, Kenneth S. "Conflict Regulation in the Brazilian Industrial Relations System." Ph.D. dissertation, University of Wisconsin, 1974.

_____. "The Political Economy of the Brazilian Motor Vehicle Industry." In *The Political Economy of the Latin American Motor Vehicle Industry*, eds. Rich Kronish and Kenneth S. Mericle. Cambridge, MA: The MIT Press, 1984. Pp. 1-40.

Millen, Bruce H. *The Political Role of Labor in Developing Countries*. Washington: The Brookings Institution, 1963.

Moisés, José Alvaro. *Lições de Liberdade e de Oppressão: Os Trabalhadores e a Luta pela Democracia*. Rio de Janeiro: Paz a Terra, 1982.

Moraes Filho, Evaristo de. *O Problema do Sindicato Unico no Brasil*. Rio de Janeiro: Editora A Noite, 1952.

Morley, Samuel A. *Labor Markets and Inequitable Growth: The Case of Authoritarian Capitalism in Brazil*. Cambridge, England: Cambridge University Press, 1982.

Pastore, José. "Em Direção a um Novo Sistema de Relações do Trabalho para o Brasil." São Paulo: FIPE, 1984. Mimeo.

Rodrigues, Aloisio. *O Estado e o Sistema Sindical Brasileiro*. São Paulo: Editora LTR, 1981.

Scoville, James G. "Some Determinants of the Structure of Labor Movements." In *The International Labor Movement in Transition*, eds. Adolf Sturmthal and James G. Scoville. Urbana: University of Illinois Press, 1973.

Skidmore, Thomas E. "Workers and Soldiers: Urban Labor Movements and Elite Responses in Twentieth-Century Latin America." In *Elites, Masses, and Modernization in Latin America, 1850-1930*, ed. Virginia Bernhard. Austin: University of Texas Press. 1979.

Souza, Amaury de. "The Nature of Corporative Representation: Leaders and Members of Organized Labor in Brazil." Ph.D. dissertation, Massachusetts Institute of Technology, 1975.

_____. "A Nova Politica Salarial e as Negociações Coletivas de Trabalho no Brasil, 1979-1982: Um Estado Exploratório." Rio de Janeiro: IUPERJ, 1983. Mimeo.

Souza, Amaury de, and Bolivar Lamounier. "Governo e sindicatos no Brasil: A perspectiva dos anos 80." *Dados* No. 2 (1981), pp. 139-59.

Souza, Isabel Gomez de. "Labor and Politics: An Analysis of the 'New Unionism' in Brazil." Ph.D. dissertation, University of Wisconsin, 1985.

Spalding, Hobart S., Jr. *Organized Labor in Latin America: Historical Case Studies of Urban Workers in Dependent Societies*. New York: Harper & Row, 1977.

Sturmthal, Adolf. "Industrial Relations Strategies." In *The International Labor Movement in Transition*, eds. Adolf Sturmthal and James G. Scoville. Urbana: University of Illinois Press, 1973.

Taylor, Lance. "Back to Basics: Theory for the Rhetoric in the North-South Round." *World Development* 10 (No. 4, 1982), pp. 327-35.

Tobin, James. "Unemployment in the 1980s: Macroeconomic Diagnosis and Prescription." In *Unemployment and Growth in the Western Economies*, ed. Andrew J. Pierre. New York: Council on Foreign Relations, 1984. Pp. 79-112.

"Em Paz, mas em Greve." *Veja*, May 31, 1978.

"Com o Pé na Tábua." *Veja*, July 11, 1984.

World Bank. "Labor Market Developments and Wage Policies." Ch. 3 in *Brazil: Economic Memorandum*. Washington: World Bank, 1984.

CHAPTER 4

Industrial Relations and the Economic Crisis: Canada Moves Towards Europe*

ROY J. ADAMS
McMaster University

The industrial relations systems of Canada and the United States have much in common. "International" unions represent both Canadians and Americans. Since World War II Canada and the United States have implemented similar labor policy frameworks, and the practice of collective bargaining in the two countries is alike. Indeed, because of such outstanding similarities, foreign observers sometimes have concluded that Canada and the United States may be considered parts of a coherent North American industrial relations system (Ross and Hartman 1960). Twenty years ago that observation was more accurate than it is today. As a result of the economic shocks that commenced in the latter half of the 1960s, the two systems have been evolving in quite dissimilar directions. In Canada, movement has been towards more cooperation by labor, management, and government in search of consensus and the expansion of workers' participation by right. Contrarily, large numbers of employers and intellectuals in the United States have abandoned their commitment to unions and collective bargaining as the preferred instruments of industrial democracy in favor of management controlled and initiated participation schemes (see Barbash 1983, Kochan and Piore 1984). Instead of being embraced as a social partner, organized labor finds itself to be the object of the most forceful assault on its integrity in more than a half-century. Although many labor leaders would be prepared to

* I would like to express my deep appreciation to Joe Rose, Mark Thompson, Peter Doyle, and Noah Meltz for their comments on an earlier version of this paper.

participate in cooperative, consensus-seeking exercises, government and business by and large are uninterested.[1]

This chapter is divided into four parts. The main attributes of the Canadian industrial relations system as it stood in the early 1960s are outlined in the first section, and the second section documents the primary economic shocks as they manifested themselves in Canada. The third section is a review of the emergence and course of tripartism—labor, management, and government cooperation in regard to public policy. The fourth section is devoted largely to a discussion of the emergence in Canada of two enterprise-level institutions designed to provide universal equity and participation at the enterprise level—works councils and labor courts. In the final section a model is presented that appears to be the likely destination towards which the Canadian system is evolving and the direction of movement in Canada is compared with that in the United States.

The Traditional System

In the early 1960s the Canadian industrial relations system had settled into a distinctive pattern.[2] Although the major labor federation—the Canadian Labour Congress (CLC)—officially supported the moderately socialist New Democratic Party (NDP), on a day-to-day basis unions behaved very much as Selig Perlman,

---

[1] After surveying the attitudes of business and labor elites in the United States and Canada, Maital and Meltz (1985) came to the conclusion that prospects for a "social contract" were much better in Canada. In the United States, while labor was in favor of seeking consensus, management was opposed. Both management and labor in Canada were skeptical about achieving a social contract, but "while both labor and management opposed it, they are close to being balanced in their views. Only a small shift is required among those who disapprove to achieve a favourable view."

[2] Canada is a large country, geographically, and it has a federal form of government. As a result, there is a considerable amount of internal variation. British Columbia, for example, has a history (not unlike that of California) of broad swings politically from left to right and a tendency towards tumultuous labor-management relations. In Quebec the French heritage has produced a sense of separate identity which has had significant effects on industrial relations practices. For example, a separate union federation grounded in French Quebecois culture (Confederation des syndicats nationaux) has posed a serious challenge to the mainstream labor movement throughout most of the 20th century. A comprehensive review of Canadian industrial relations would have to pay considerable attention to such internal variation. My objective in this chapter, however, is to produce an exhaustive treatment neither of the Canadian system nor of the myriad of changes that have occurred in the system during the past two decades. Instead of focusing on internal variation, I have tried to abstract critical industrial relations dimensions common to most Canadian jurisdictions. Rather than attempting a comprehensive review of industrial relations developments, I have selected a few for analysis which seem to me to be likely to have the most dramatic and enduring results.

the theorist for North American unionism, would suggest (Perlman 1928). They sought to protect and enhance the terms and conditions of employment of their members via negotiations with employers. Radical rhetoric, although by no means absent, was a minor phenomenon. Bread and butter today rather than pie in the sky tomorrow was the primary strategy of unions in practice. The labor movement had little direct influence on government policy. Under certain circumstances it could muster sufficient support to block the passage of onerous legislation, but it had little capacity to achieve policy objectives opposed by influential interest groups (Kwavnick 1973, pp. 433–41).[3]

Canadian employers, unlike those in most European countries, were fragmented in their approach to organized labor. Many associations, some organized on an industrial, some on a provincial, and some on a national basis, did exist. Not infrequently these associations would take on a leadership role in representing the point of view of their members in regard to employment issues. There was, however, no common strategy for dealing with unions, nor was there any generally recognized national organization which could authoritatively express the business viewpoint on employment issues.

Because of the general unwillingness of employers to bargain collectively unless forced to do so, relations between labor and management were, in general, strained and distant. The actors were adversaries, not social partners as their counterparts were sometimes referred to in Europe. The job of the union was to negotiate the best conditions possible for its members to the practical exclusion of other concerns. The role that management had assumed in industrial relations was to bargain hard with certified unions while attempting to defend, as best it could, its ability to make unfettered decisions. To employers beyond the pale of collective bargaining, remaining "nonunion" was an accepted management policy.

The government considered its primary role to be that of protecting the public from the disruptions that could result from

---

[3] Pressure generated by the NDP is generally considered to have been instrumental in the adoption of the Wagner-Act-model policy framework in Canada (a goal sought by unions) and in the development of a widespread social welfare net. For example, universal health care was first introduced by a government in Saskatchewan controlled by the Cooperative Commonwealth Federation, the predecessor to the NDP.

industrial conflict (Woods 1973). The fundamental philosophy of Canadian governments was voluntarism. Labor and management should be allowed to work out their own arrangements, but only so long as the public was left in peace. In practice, the concern with conflict led to a good deal of intervention.

Unlike in the United States, labor law in Canada is primarily a provincial responsibility. Nevertheless, after World War II a labor policy model very similar to the U.S. Wagner Act model was adopted in all Canadian jurisdictions. Under that model if a union sought to bargain with an employer who refused to cooperate, it could, if it had majority support of the employees involved, compel the employer to negotiate by acquiring certification from a labor relations board. It could not, however, strike for "recognition." This policy model, which initially had strong union support, had the unplanned effect of exacerbating adversarialism because it condoned employer opposition to unions so long as the employer did not blatantly attempt intimidation or coercion (Arthurs, Carter, and Glasbeek 1981).

Government intervention also extended to the collective bargaining relationship. Unlike under the U.S. model, in Canada the parties could negotiate on essentially any issue. However, the ultimate union recourse to an impasse was, as in the United States, the strike. That aspect of the model insured that only key wage and benefit issues would be included in collective agreements. Many issues—not considered to be strike issues—"fell off the table" and thus remained within the ambit of management's reserved rights. It was the rare agreement that contained stipulations on issues such as training, occupational health and safety, the introduction of technological change, and the criteria for plant shutdowns (Adams 1984a). To the outside observer such issues might appear to be very important to employees but, in general, they were not strike issues and therefore could be kept by management within its domain of unilateral discretion.

Should union-management negotiations reach an impasse, Canadian jurisdictions required the parties to postpone conflict while government-appointed conciliators attempted to find an acceptable solution to the dispute. When an agreement was reached, it had to last for a specified period of time, usually for at least a year. Strikes were made illegal during the life of a contract. Contrary to U.S. practice, disputes over the interpretation of a collective agreement were required by legislation (rather than by contract) to be submitted to binding arbitration for resolution. The arbitration process was, however, under the control of labor and management rather than government, for two reasons. First, labor and management jointly chose the single arbitrator or arbitration board. Second, the mandate of the arbitrator was to resolve disputes over the interpretation of a written collective agreement freely concluded by labor and management.

By 1960 approximately 32 percent of Canadian employees were in trade unions, a rate almost identical to that in the United States (see Table 5, p. 125). As in the U.S., blue-collar workers in the private sector—manufacturing, construction, and transportation in particular—were much more highly organized than the average. In most of the public sector, governments as employers had avoided Wagner-Act-style bargaining. Instead, consultation took place between government representatives and employee associations, with impasses resolved unilaterally by the employer. That system, however, was nearing the end of its time. Government employees, dissatisfied with consultation, were demanding the same rights as private-sector workers, and legislation towards that end was about to be introduced in several jurisdictions (Ponak 1982).

The government did not limit itself entirely to facilitating labor-management relations. Ideally, if collective bargaining had become universal in scope, the parties would have worked out their own tailor-made substantive agreements in each case. However, in practice, collective bargaining was restricted. Despite its rapid spread during the 1930s and 1940s, most Canadian paid workers remained (and continue to remain) outside the coverage of collective agreements (Adams 1984b). In order to reduce the disparity in the conditions of work of the organized and the unorganized, Canadian governments, like governments in all Western countries, established general minimum requirements on issues such as income protection in the event of unemployment, injury, and superannuation. Maximum hours, minimum wages, job safety standards, and (like most of the industrial world but unlike the U.S.) universal paid holidays and vacations were also legislated (Christie 1980). Those initiatives were, however, considered to be subsidiary to the primary policy of encouraging full collective bargaining.

In the early 1960s this system appeared to be reasonably stable.

After much turmoil in the 1930s and 1940s, relations between labor and management had settled into a pattern of ritualistic normality. Industrial conflict was at a low level compared to what it had been in the preceding decades. But the system was about to be placed under a great deal of strain because of events originating outside of the borders of Canada.

Shock Waves

The "traditional" industrial relations system, outlined above, was shaken by the waves of change which shocked the world political economy between the 1960s and the 1980s. The key events are well known. The war in Vietnam precipitated a trend towards rising prices which was accelerated by massive oil price increases in the 1970s. The transfer of wealth from the oil-consuming to the oil-producing countries led to a reduction in the pace of economic growth and, combined with demographic developments, an increase in the rate of unemployment. After the second oil shock in 1979, very stringent fiscal and monetary policies designed to bring inflation under control produced the worst economic downturn since the 1930s. The increasing competitiveness of goods from Japan and other countries of the Pacific Rim placed additional pressures on the Western economic system (Zoeteweij 1983).

Canada's situation, in contrast to that of the United States and the other major OECD countries, is illustrated by data in Table 1. In most respects Canadian developments followed those in the other countries. However, a few aspects of the Canadian experience are notable. First, employment growth from 1966 to 1982 was more than double that of the seven major OECD countries as a group. This growth was due in part to the coming of age of a "baby boom" generation born in the two decades following World War II, and in part to a large increase in the proportion of adult women participating in the labor force. The increase in the size of the Canadian labor force put tremendous pressure on government to create jobs—a challenge that it met with only partial success. As indicated by the data in the table, although employment increased at notable rates, unemployment in Canada was, and continued to be, considerably higher than in the major OECD nations.

A second outstanding Canadian development has to do with the reaction of the economy to the recent recession. In the U.S. and the OECD big-seven countries as a whole, the economic

TABLE 1
OECD Economic Indicators 1966-1983

	1966	1966-73	1974-82	1981	1982	1983
Growth in real GNE or GDP						
Canada	7.0	5.5	2.1	3.4	−4.4	3.0
United States	6.0	3.9	1.9	2.6	−1.9	3.4
OECD, 7 major countries[a]	5.7	5.4	2.2	1.9	−0.3	2.4
Consumer price inflation						
Canada	3.7	4.3	9.0	12.5	10.8	5.9
United States	2.9	4.4	9.8	10.3	6.1	3.2
OECD-7 major countries	3.2	4.7	9.6	10.0	6.9	4.4
Unemployment rate						
Canada	3.3	4.8	7.7	7.6	11.0	11.9
United States	3.6	4.5	7.3	7.6	9.7	9.6
OECD-7 major countries	2.6	3.2	5.7	6.5	8.1	8.2
Employment growth						
Canada	4.1	2.9	2.1	2.6	−3.3	0.7
United States	3.0	2.3	1.8	1.1	−0.9	1.3
OECD-7 major countries	1.5	1.4	1.0	0.5	−0.7	0.6

Sources: 1966: Historical Statistics (1960-1980), OECD Economic Outlook; 1983; OECD Economic Outlook (July 1984); other years: Canada Department of Finance, The Canadian Economy in Recovery (February 1984).

[a] The seven major OECD countries are Great Britain, France, United States, West Germany, Italy, Japan, and Canada.

downturn of 1981-1982 was relatively shallow compared to Canada where the economy contracted by 4.4 percent in 1982. Not until 1984 did Canadian economic activity return to the level it had reached in 1981. However, by 1984 the Canadian economy was growing at a substantially faster rate than were those of the countries of Western Europe and the unemployment rate was falling (OECD Economic Outlook, July 1984).

Inflation unsettled the relationship between wages and prices in all of the countries of the West. Attempting to keep up with price increases, labor demanded higher wages and backed its demand with a willingness to resort to open conflict. In Canada, time lost due to industrial conflict as a percent of working time doubled in 1966 over 1965 and remained at very high levels until the great recession of 1981-1982. Table 2 presents two indicators of the level of labor militancy. The data on percent of working time lost to strikes are sensitive to the number of collective agreements negotiated each year. The second series—percent of large unit settlements involving a work stoppage—overcomes that problem. The two series are, however, consistent in the story they tell. Except for 1977 and 1978—years in which mandatory controls on wages and prices were in effect—industrial conflict in Canada was at high levels continually between 1966 and 1982. During the 1970s Canada had the second highest level of time lost due to strikes in the Western world (see Table 3). The Canadian rate was more than double that of the U.S., a reversal of experience in the earlier decades.[4]

TABLE 2

Indicators of Labor Militancy,
Selected Years 1963–1983

	Strikes and Lockouts as Percent of Estimated Working Time[a]	Percent of Large Unit Settlements Involving a Work Stoppage[b]
1963–65	0.12	10.4
1966–70	0.35	12.2
1971	0.16	14.4
1972	0.43	13.0
1973	0.30	18.3
1974	0.46	15.6
1975	0.53	12.7
1976	0.55	13.5
1977	0.15	5.5
1978	0.34	6.3
1979	0.34	11.2
1980	0.38	12.3
1981	0.37	13.9
1982	0.25	6.1
1983	0.19	7.1

[a] 1963–1980: Labour Canada. *Strikes and Lockouts in Canada* (Ottawa: annual); 1981–1983: Labour Canada, *Work Stoppages December 1983* (Ottawa: 1984).

[b] 1963–1980: Labour Canada, *Collective Bargaining Review* (Ottawa: annual); 1981–1983: Labour Canada, *Work Stoppages December 1983* (Ottawa: 1984). Large unit settlements refer to bargaining units with 500 or more employees.

TABLE 3

Days Lost Per 1000 Employees,
1971–1981 Annual Average

Canada	906	Japan	116
France	215	Sweden	142
Germany	50	U.K.	551
Italy	1199	U.S.	442

Source: Wood and Kumar, *The Current Industrial Relations Scene in Canada, 1983*, p. 398.

---

[4] Analysis of the composition of industrial conflict in Canada indicates that strikes occur much more frequently than in some countries (e.g., Sweden, The Netherlands, West Germany), but much less frequently than in others (e.g., Italy, France). However, strike volume in Canada tops the charts because Canadian strikes last, on average, longer than in any other major country. See Adams (1982b).

The high level of militancy contributed to wage settlements from the late 1960s to the mid-1970s which substantially exceeded the rate of inflation (see Table 4). This development led some professional economists, many quasi-economists, and a gaggle of pundits to conclude that prices of goods and services were being pushed up by excessive wage increases. Organized labor generally claimed that it was merely trying to (1) make up for past losses, (2) insulate its members against price increases expected to occur during the life of the collective agreement, and (3) make sure its members got a fair share of the increasing economic product.

Whatever the truth of the matter, the high level of industrial conflict and the wage-price spiral associated with it in the private and institutional mind became a prime focus of debate and policy during the 1970s and early 1980s. Several approaches were tried by governments to control or influence the outcomes of collective bargaining. In 1969–1970 a wage-price guideline policy was tried, in 1975–1978 mandatory general wage-price controls were in effect, and in 1982–1983 public-sector compensation was controlled by law in the federal and several provincial jurisdictions (Wood and Kumar

TABLE 4

Settlements in Major Collective Agreements and Inflation,
Selected Years 1967–1983

Year	Wage Settlements[a] Average % Change	CPI[b] Average % Change	Net Change in Real Wages
1960–64 (average)	8.0	1.4	6.6
1965–69	8.0	3.7	4.3
1970	8.6	3.3	5.3
1971	7.8	2.9	4.9
1972	8.8	4.8	4.0
1973	11.0	7.5	3.5
1974	14.7	10.9	3.8
1975	19.2	10.8	8.4
1976	10.9	7.5	3.4
1977	7.9	8.0	−0.1
1978	7.2	9.0	1.8
1979	8.7	9.1	−0.4
1980	11.1	10.1	1.0
1981	13.3	12.5	0.8
1982	10.0	10.8	−0.8
1983	5.9	5.8	0.1

[a] Data refer to wage settlements in collective agreements covering 500 or more employees which do not contain a cost-of-living adjustment clause. Data were collected by Labour Canada and are reported in *Economic Review* (Ottawa: Canada Department of Finance, annual).

[b] CPI = consumer price index. Data from *Consumer Price Index* (Ottawa: Statistics Canada, annual).

1976, Swimmer 1984). The unilateral imposition of controls on wages and prices in 1975 gave rise to a good deal of opposition from both labor and management. As a result, the federal government entered into a series of discussions with representatives of labor and business in hopes of achieving a voluntary, tripartite agreement on restraint. Although no agreement could be reached in the 1975–1978 period, the process of consultation in search of consensus would be used with increasing frequency.

In addition to mandatory controls and consultation in search of consensus, another approach to the nexus was to seek ways to make the bargaining process work better. A good deal of debate focused on broader-based bargaining. Experiments with fact-finding, choice of procedures, first contract arbitration, grievance mediation, and bargaining by objectives were also tried (Craig 1983).

Another approach was to address the conditions that were believed to give rise to worker discontent. A great deal of new legislation was passed in order to improve substantive conditions of work (Christie 1980). Occupational health and safety was a major focus. Human rights codes forbidding discrimination for a growing list of reasons were introduced in all Canadian jurisdictions (Jain 1982). New standards were developed in regard to plant shutdowns and group terminations (Adams 1983). To enable employees to participate in the making of decisions concerning these and other employment issues, a new institutional form emerged in Canada— the works council. These institutions, while common in Europe, had generally been considered inappropriate and unnecessary in North America. Their appearance came, therefore, as a surprise to many.

As collective bargaining matured and expanded, the process designed to resolve disputed interpretations of collective agreements became more complex and the basis of strife. Grievance arbitration as a system was predicated on values of speed, low cost, and informality. By the advent of the 1970s the process (especially in Ontario) had become slower, more expensive, and increasingly legalistic (Weiler 1980). Labor demanded reform. Coupled with the problem of integrating disputes procedures regarding occupational health and safety, employment standards, and human rights with grievance arbitration, the result was a trend towards the European institution of labor courts.

Militant unions, apparently able to win substantial improvements at the bargaining table and through the political process, became attractive to many previously unorganized workers during this period. Unlike in the United States, trade union density in Canada increased substantially during the turbulent 1960s and 1970s (see Table 5).

TABLE 5

Union Membership as a Percent of Nonagricultural Employment, 1956–1980

Year	United States	Canada
1956	33.4	33.3
1960	31.4	32.3
1964	28.9	29.4
1968	27.8	33.1
1972	26.4	34.6
1976	29.1	37.3
1978	26.2	39.0
1980	24.6	37.6

Source: Rose and Chaison (1985); U.S. data from U.S. Department of Labor, Handbook of Labor Statistics, and Canadian data from Labour Canada, Directory of Labour Organizations in Canada.

As in all industrialized countries, the deep recession of 1981–1982 had significant effects on the dynamics of Canadian industrial relations. Union membership growth slowed and the volume of industrial conflict fell. Employers adopted a tougher stance at the bargaining table. Lacking a nonunion hinterland to which they could easily relocate, Canadian employers did not, however, embrace the "nonunion alternative" to collective bargaining as vigorously as their U.S. counterparts. Moreover, Canadian unions resisted more effectively demands for "givebacks" and "concessions" even in industries such as automobile manufacture where the U.S. branch of the United Auto Workers Union had agreed to reductions in wages and working conditions. Whereas in the United States as many as three or four agreements in ten contained concessions, in Canada the rate during 1982 and 1983 was probably no more than one in ten[5] The Canadian system was not, however,

[5] On the United States, see Kochan and Piore (1984, p. 185). In order to make an estimate for Canada I reviewed all of the collective agreements reported in Canada's publication, Collective Bargaining Review, during the months of March, June, September, and December of 1982 and 1983. Agreements covering 500 or more employees are reported in the Review. In 1982, only 4 of 183 agreements contained a negotiated deferred increase, a wage freeze, or a wage deduction. In 7 of the agreements there was a temporary wage reduction required by statute. The concession rate increased somewhat in 1983. Of 206 collective agreements reviewed, 22 (11 percent) contained wage concessions. Construction industry agreements were not included in the 1982 survey but were added in 1983.

inflexible in the face of economic pressures. Wage and price increases slowed significantly during 1983 and by early 1984 wages and prices were advancing at the slowest rate in two decades (Wood and Kumar 1984).

It is impossible to do justice to all of these issues in an essay of modest proportions. Instead of trying to do so I will concentrate on a few topics that illustrate the proposition that Canadian industrial relations are evolving towards forms and patterns common in Europe and away from United States practice with which it has been associated historically.

Tripartism

The term *tripartism* is generally used to refer to formal or quasi-formal decision-making structures in which representatives of labor, business, and government attempt to reach consensus on policy issues of mutual concern (Giles 1982). Although examples of tripartite efforts may be found scattered throughout Canadian 20th century history, the latest episode began in the early 1970s (Waldie 1984). Two factors gave rise to government initiatives to involve labor and management in socioeconomic decisions: labor militancy and the wage-price spiral believed to stem from it.

In the Fall of 1974 the federal Liberal government began to develop a control program despite an election pledge to avoid controls. Opinion polls indicated that the public wanted forceful action and that controls would be accepted. However, instead of immediately imposing the program, the federal Minister of Finance, John Turner, approached representatives of labor and business and sought to achieve a voluntary tripartite agreement on restraint. Turner's initiative was very unusual and caught both labor and management unprepared (Lang 1977). No agreement was reached, and in October 1975 the federal government imposed controls over the objection of both business and labor. That action led to responses that changed the nature of Canadian industrial relations.

The most prominent and numerically dominant labor organization in Canada is the Canadian Labour Congress (CLC). The CLC came into being in 1956, the result of a merger between a federation composed largely of traditional craft unions affiliated with the American Federation of Labor (AFL), and a federation composed primarily of industrial unions which were also part of the Congress of Industrial Organizations (CIO) in the United States. Like the AFL-CIO, the Canadian Labour Congress was a loose and very weak federation. The power in the Canadian labor movement rested with the sovereign national and international unions and in varying degrees at the local union level. The primary function of the CLC was to look after labor's interest at the national level. Research suggested that it could, under certain circumstances, block negative legislation, but that it rarely had the power to compel legislation over the opposition of other consequential groups (Kwavnick 1973).

The federal government's decision to impose controls gave the CLC, as an institution in its own right, an opportunity to expand its role in the industrial relations system. Controls had the effect of shifting the focus of decision-making away from local bargaining to the national level.

The initial reaction of the CLC was to demand immediate removal of controls. Towards that end, a national anticontrols campaign was put into effect. The top leadership of the CLC was not opposed to tripartism in principle. Some of the top officers, including president Joe Morris, were familiar with European experience. Morris believed that a strategy of pure protest against controls would be ineffective as well as contrary to the long-range interests of the labor movement. Instead, influenced by developments in Europe, he and a few others believed that it was crucial for the labor movement to formulate a positive set of proposals and to demand a say in government decisions. As they saw it, decentralized collective bargaining had become less effective because of the increasing intervention of government. Minor changes in fiscal and monetary policies, without labor's consent or participation, could completely undermine the results of collective bargaining. In order to represent its members effectively, organized labor had to develop a capacity to influence government policy effectively (Lang 1977).

The principal response was the production of a document entitled *Labour's Manifesto for Canada* which was approved by the CLC convention in the Summer of 1976. In that document, and in subsidiary papers fleshing it out, the CLC called for a tripartite National Council for Social and Economic Planning (NCSEP) which would have on its agenda all of the following policy issues: investment, housing, manpower planning, income distribution, industrial development, transportation, social security, and health services. Under the council there would be boards and agencies which would carry out "administration and planning functions for which the council had responsibility as set out in the terms of reference" (*Position Paper* 1976).

For example, a Labour Market Board was envisioned which "must have authority for forecasting, training and retraining, mobility grants, immigration and unemployment insurance." The job of the board would be to ensure full employment. Towards that end it "must have the power and authority to channel investment funds . . ." (*Position Paper* 1976). In essence, the Labour Market Board would have made redundant the federal Department of Employment and Immigration and the Unemployment Insurance Commission.

The Social and Economic Planning Council apparently was modeled on a scheme that existed in the Netherlands. The Labour Market Board proposal was similar to institutions in West Germany and Sweden (Adams 1982a). The proposal was quite different from anything existing or contemplated seriously in the United States. National labor-management advisory committees were not unknown in the U.S., but they had far less power and influence than the institutions envisioned in the CLC proposal (Moye 1980).

The federal government did not reject the proposal out of hand. It did, however, express serious reservations. Key government leaders wanted to establish a system of consultation that might lead to consensus. They also were impressed by the intensity of labor opposition to controls. But they were very reticent about ceding to labor the degree of power that it demanded in the Manifesto and related documents.

In order to back its demands for immediate withdrawal of controls, the CLC developed an action plan which had at its core a proposal for a "national day of protest"—a one-day national work stoppage. This technique, which is commonly employed in Italy to influence government policy, had never before been used in North America as a calculated national strategy. On October 14, 1976, approximately 1 million working people failed to show up for work as a gesture of protest against the controls program. At the time approximately 2 million employees belonged to unions affiliated to the CLC. The Day of Protest was judged to be neither a great success nor a total failure. It indicated to the government that the CLC could mobilize a demonstration of considerable proportions.

On the other hand, it illustrated the inability of the CLC to move as a single undivided entity.

As a result of these developments the government continued to talk to representatives of the CLC. Alternate proposals for a policy forum were discussed, but no agreement was reached.

The unilateral imposition by government of controls also had a major impact on business. For some time prior to the controls era, business leaders had discussed, on and off, the possibility of forming a national organization capable of representing their perspective to government (MacLaren 1976). The imposition of controls, despite the opposition of most corporate leaders, illustrated the weakness of industry's fragmented structure. Statements by the Prime Minister that the free market could no longer be relied upon and that the government would have to intervene more vigorously in the economy speeded up the process of institution formation (Giles 1982).

During 1976 the chief executive officers of major corporations formed a loose organization which officially became the Business Council on National Issues (BCNI) in the Spring of 1977. The BCNI quickly attracted the CEOs of most major corporations as well as the top executives of the Chamber of Commerce and the Canadian Manufacturers Association. This organization, despite modest protestations that it was only one of many business associations, quickly became the most influential business actor at the national level (Archbold 1977, Waldie 1984).

In the Spring and Summer of 1976 a number of talks were held between the BCNI and the CLC, between government and the CLC, between government and the BCNI, and among all three. All of the parties agreed that it would be useful to establish a forum in which policy issues could be discussed on a regular basis, but beyond that there was no consensus. Both the BCNI and the CLC wanted controls removed immediately, but neither party was willing to commit its constituents to the voluntary restraint demanded by government as the quid pro quo. The BCNI and the government preferred a consultative multipartite forum with groups such as consumers, farmers, and professionals represented instead of the tripartite, decision-making council proposed by the CLC (Giles 1982). Negotiations broke down in the Summer of 1977, and in 1978 the government unilaterally dismantled its controls program.

During 1977 internal opposition within the CLC to the tripartite initiative began to grow. There were several reasons for it. First, Marxists within the labor movement considered tripartism to be consorting with the enemy and unacceptable for that reason. Other unionists opposed tripartism because they saw in it a shift in power from the rank-and-file worker at the shop floor to a distant centralized bureaucracy. To many unionists, rank-and-file control of collective bargaining was a sacred tenet of the North American labor movement. The tripartists countered with the argument that rank-and-file control was an illusion. Because of the impact of government policies, labor needed influence at both levels.

Another basis of labor opposition was the claim that, because it lacked resources, the CLC would be a weak sister in any tripartite setup. The tripartist's response was that labor could participate effectively if it had sufficient input into the structure and process of decision-making.

A fourth basis of opposition had to do with the relationship between the CLC and the moderately socialist New Democratic Party (NDP). At the national level the NDP was a small third party which occasionally held the balance of power between the Liberal and Conservative parties. Many unionists considered the NDP to be the political voice of labor, and it was CLC policy to support the NDP. Strong NDP supporters within the ranks of labor generally felt that the unions should focus primarily on collective bargaining with employers. Many considered the CLC initiative to be inappropriately competitive with the NDP.

Finally, some unions equated tripartism with the corporatist political structures that existed under the totalitarian fascist regimes of pre-World War II Europe. From that perspective, corporatism undermined the sovereignty of parliament and was therefore antidemocratic. That argument acquired many followers not only within the ranks of labor, but also among business leaders, government officials, and the general public. It overlooked, however, the widespread existence of tripartite decision-making in the democracies of Western Europe after World War II.

At the CLC convention in 1978 the antitripartists carried the day. The Manifesto was discarded as CLC policy and, with that development, many commentators concluded that tripartism was dead (e.g., Craig 1983). They were wrong, however. Although the term is no longer in favor, the practice has continued to develop.

In 1977 the federal Department of Industry, Trade and Commerce decided to set up 23 task forces to look at the problems and prospects of 23 industries. At first there were no labor representatives on these committees, but when the CLC protested, trade unionists were added to each of them. The task forces, known as Tier I committees, published 23 reports which were reviewed by a Tier II committee composed of equal numbers of labor and business representatives. The Tier II committee published its own report recommending several government initiatives. On many issues labor representatives and business delegates were able to agree. Traditionally contentious issues (e.g., union recognition and certification) were, however, put off for consideration at a later date (Waldie 1984).

Another example of tripartism subsequent to the controls era was the Major Projects Task Force. This agency developed out of the Tier I construction task force. Its job was to develop a comprehensive strategy for implementing major construction projects. Like the Tier II committee, it was composed of equal numbers of labor and business representatives. At its peak it had a staff numbering more than 20, mostly loaned from corporations and unions (Waldie 1984). In June 1981 it issued a consensus report containing some 50 recommendations. Unfortunately the report coincided with the onset of the severe recession of 1981–1982 which resulted in major project development being placed on the far back burner. Nevertheless, the exercise demonstrated a capacity by business and labor to address successfully an important policy issue of mutual concern in a nonadversarial, cooperative manner.

In 1984 a National Labour Market and Productivity center came into existence. This agency may be traced back to the Labour Market Board proposal originally put forth by the CLC (Adams 1982a). The inception of this agency is an indication of the continuing vitality in Canada of the concept of tripartism. When the tripartite talks of 1977 collapsed, and especially after the Manifesto was abandoned by the CLC convention in 1978, it appeared that the Labour Market Board was a dead issue. In the course of Tier I and II talks of 1978 and 1979 and the megaprojects task force, the CLC leadership convinced the BCNI to support a joint proposal for a labor market board structured, like the Tier II and megaprojects committees, with equal labor and management participation. The CLC withdrew its initial Manifesto-era demand that the board have

administrative decision-making functions and accepted a consultative model. The BCNI, in turn, dropped its initial stance regarding
a multipartite structure. The government, however, continued to
hold out for a multipartite forum, agreeing to the joint labor-
management request only in 1983.

In the early 1980s productivity entered the political arena as a
key political issue in Canada, just as it did in many countries. During
the 1970s Canada's productivity performance was dreadful (see
Table 6). The recession of 1981–1982 moved the issue up the list of
policy priorities.

TABLE 6
Growth of Productivity, Annual Percent Change

	1966–1973	1974–1982
Canada	2.5	0.0
United States	1.5	0.1
Japan	9.3	3.2
Germany	4.3	2.3
France	4.8	2.3
United Kingdom	3.1	1.2
Italy	5.6	1.3
Seven major OECD countries	3.9	1.2

Source: Department of Finance, *The Canadian Economy in Recovery*,
February 1984.

Noting the success of national productivity centers in Europe
and Japan, the federal government put forth a similar proposal in
1983 (Walkom, February 3, 1983). Instead of two centers,
representatives from the CLC, the BCNI, and the federal
government worked out a structure for melding together the
productivity and labor market agencies (Waldie 1984). The new
center will have 50-50 representation from labor and business. It
will be only advisory in nature, but it will have a substantial budget
and staff with financing coming from government. How much
influence this new agency will have is impossible to say at this point
in time. Its birth and continuation (despite a change in government)
indicates that tripartism continues to develop in Canada.

The road to tripartism has not been a smooth one. Nor is its
future guaranteed. It has suffered two recent setbacks. First, in 1982
the federal government unilaterally, and against the opposition of
the CLC, imposed a new wage-control program (Swimmer 1984).

Instead of general controls on the economy as a whole, a cap of 6 percent in 1982 and 5 percent in 1983 was placed on the remuneration of federal government employees. The objective of this initiative was to demonstrate the commitment which the government had to controlling its own costs so that the private sector would be prompted to do the same. The federal government strongly urged provincial governments to follow suit, and most of them did. It also set up a private-sector committee, with a prominent BCNI member as its head, to cajole corporations to use moderation (Canada Department of Finance, August 28, 1982).

Although no in-depth research into BCNI-CLC-government relations in regard to "6 and 5" has been reported, it is clear that despite labor's opposition, the BCNI (and some other business groups) favored the initiative. Indeed, "6 and 5" was a positive government response to a proposal made public by the BCNI in 1982 (Adams 1982a). While the CLC vigorously condemned the government action, it said little about the support of business for the program. Presumably, it did not want to upset the progress of labor-business cooperation. The relatively quiet response of the CLC also may have been a reflection of disagreements within the Congress between public- and private-sector unions. Although firmly opposed to legislative controls overriding free collective bargaining, many private-sector unionists were not deeply chagrined by the substance of the controls program. Initially, the "6 and 5" decision removed, to some extent, coercive pressure from private-sector negotiations. By 1983, however, it began to appear that the controls decision had produced a perverse effect as wage increases in the public sector led those in private industry.

The future of tripartism would seem to be dependent, in part, on business practicing discretion in regard to stances considered to be inimical to the fundamental interests of organized labor. Indeed, one of the landmark developments of the past decade has been the much greater acceptance by business that organized labor has a legitimate and positive role to play in society. The calculative strategy of law-breaking in order to defeat employee efforts to establish collective bargaining is much less prevalent in Canada than it is in the United States. Moreover, heavy-handed attempts by U.S.-based firms to export such tactics to Canada have been dealt with firmly by Canadian labor relations boards (Meltz 1985, Weiler 1980). The long-term vitality of tripartism would seem to be dependent upon Canadian business refraining from following U.S. practice.

The second present threat to tripartism in Canada is the action of certain provincial governments, particularly very conservative governments in Western Canada. In addition to acceptance of labor by business, the success of tripartism would seem to be contingent even more critically upon the willingness of government to accept and, indeed, foster a strong and confident labor movement. Trade union organizations which consider themselves to be victims of right-wing assaults on their integrity are not too likely to be receptive to pleas that they be cooperative in the public interest. During the past few years some governments, in Western Canada particularly, have pursued policies that had both the intent and effect of weakening the labor movement.

In British Columbia, for example, a right-wing Social Credit government was reelected in 1983 and shortly thereafter introduced a legislative program with the formal objective of reducing spending and increasing government efficiency. But the package included proposals that would have overridden provisions in collective agreements concerning dismissals for cause and stripped public-service unions of their rights to bargain over a wide range of topics. Human rights and tenants' rights legislation also would be weakened, and there would be cuts in the education budgets and welfare programs (Errington and Finn 1983, Thompson 1983).

The B.C. Federation of Labour led the political protests against the draft legislation and planned escalating strikes by public-sector unionists. First, some 35,000 civil servants struck, and were followed by teachers and support staff and employees of public enterprises. As the threat of a general strike loomed, the government agreed to withdraw parts of its program and consult with interest groups on other legislation. The government remained determined to cut government spending.

Developments such as these have truncated what appeared to be a trend away from the tradition of suspicious adversarialism in B.C. towards more cooperative labor relations. They may also have seriously weakened the resolve of those B.C. union leaders who previously had been willing to experiment with consensus at the federal level. Similar, though less harsh, attacks on public employees in Alberta and Saskatchewan may have the same impact.

Because of such counter-trends, it is too soon to say that

tripartism has become a permanent feature of Canadian industrial relations. It is unlikely, however, that there will be a complete reversion to the bellicose anarcho-syndicalism of the past. Most prominent federal politicians from all parties continue to argue the need to firmly establish regular systems for achieving consensus. During the past decade the federal government has increased enormously its consultation with labor and business, and there is reason to believe that these efforts will continue.

Despite reservations by many unionists about neocorporatism, the CLC has increased its efforts and refined its techniques for influencing the government. Intervention by government in the economy has increased, requiring a labor response. The principal choices would seem to be quiet acquiescence, pure protest, or tripartite participation. In practice, the CLC has chosen to pursue participation.

The development of tripartism has altered the character of business in the system substantially. The BCNI has maintained a fairly low profile with the result that many Canadians have never heard of the organization or are only vaguely aware of it. Nevertheless, from the perspective of labor and government, the BCNI has emerged as the dominant, if not the only, voice of the business community[6] Its policy has been and continues to be cooperation with labor and government. While it is opposed to the grandiose scheme outlined in the CLC Manifesto, it is in favor of efforts to reach consensus on "carefully defined issues . . ." (Frazee and d'Aquino 1983, p. iii).

The development of Canadian tripartism has been somewhat ironic. The initial impetus was a desire by government to get control of a wage-price-conflict helix. No agreement could be reached by labor and business on wage or price moderation or on government action to be taken in return for restraint. Nevertheless, in the process

---

[6] The BCNI has not tried to play precisely the same role in the system as that taken by the powerful employer federations in continental Europe. General organizations such as the Chamber of Commerce, the Canadian Manufacturers Association, and the Canadian Federation of Independent Business (the most outspoken voice of small business) as well as important associations representing employer interests in banking, mining, construction, and retail, to name only a few, all vie more or less successfully for the attention of governments. Thus, while the BCNI cannot be regarded as the uncontested voice of business, nevertheless, as an organization composed of Chief Executive Officers whose organizations control over 50 percent of all private-sector activity in Canada, it is certainly the most influential of the lot.

of trying the parties discovered issues on which they could fruitfully cooperate in search of a solution. Most likely they also have come to understand the perspective of each other to a greater degree.

Institutional Change at the Enterprise Level: Works Councils and Labor Courts

The wave of industrial conflict that engulfed Canada from the late 1960s caused Canadian governments to rethink many of their labor policies. At the federal level the department of labor developed a wide-ranging program of reform which became widely known as Munro's 14 Points, after the Minister of Labour, John Munro (Waldie 1984). The program provides a useful starting point to illustrate the range of government initiatives during the period. Although the program was specifically a federal one, many of the issues embodied in it were also addressed simultaneously in several of the provinces.

First, the program contained measures designed to improve collective bargaining. To reduce disputes over data, a collective bargaining information center was proposed and eventually created. It would be a central agency available to both sides. Presumably if both parties could agree to use the same data base, it would be easier for them to reach accord on collective agreement terms. The education and training of union officials was to be supported both as a matter of equity (trade unionists argued that government historically supported management education but not labor education) and on the theory that well-trained unionists would carry out their duties in a more professional and responsible manner. New initiatives were to be undertaken to provide more and better trained mediators, conciliators, and arbitrators.

In order to reduce the opportunity for conflict, broader based bargaining was to be encouraged. Throughout the 1970s broader bargaining and how to achieve it was to be a major focus of debate (Craig 1983). In some jurisdictions (e.g., Ontario and Quebec), broad-based bargaining was to be compelled by law in the very conflict-prone construction industry (Rose 1984). In British Columbia the Labour Relations Board was given the power to impose new bargaining units where it considered that action to be advisable. In most provinces labor laws permitted councils of unions and associations of employers to become certified bargaining agents of their constituents (Weiler 1980). However, after more than a decade of debate and action, broader based bargaining outside of construction was still more of a dream than a reality. The structure of bargaining units showed very little change (Craig 1983). Indeed, after the recession of 1981–1982, notable broad-based units in the railway industry and in meatpacking began to break up and employers sought to end province-wide bargaining in the British Columbia pulp and paper industry. In meatpacking, employers insisted on negotiating decentralized agreements that would reflect regional economic differences.

The federal ministry of labor, Labour Canada, was also the department where the logic of tripartism first began to be worked out. In the Summer of 1976 the department sponsored a tripartite Canadian Labour Relations Council (CLRC) whose mission it was to investigate ways of improving labor-management relations. However, when the government refused to remove controls, the CLC withdrew from the council. Because of the development of BCNI-CLC relations, the CLRC was not revived.

Although not mentioned in the Labour Canada program, a few other initiatives designed to remove irritants giving rise to conflict deserve mention. In a few jurisdictions (e.g., Ontario, Quebec, British Columbia) professional strikebreakers were outlawed because of the animosity and conflict frequently resulting from their use (List, June 13, 1983). Several jurisdictions also introduced provisions which required employers, at the union's request, to deduct union dues from the paychecks of all employees in the bargaining unit and to remit them to their union. This provision, known in Canada as the Rand formula and in the U.S. as the agency shop, was often included in collective agreements. However, in cases where employers refused to agree to such clauses, very emotional and destructive strikes often ensued (Craig 1983).

Because of the propensity of some employers to oppose collective bargaining vigorously, conflict and unrest often accompanied negotiations following the employees' decision to unionize. In hopes of achieving a solution to this problem, several Canadian jurisdictions introduced provisions for binding arbitration of first contracts where employers failed to bargain fairly and in good faith (Craig 1983, Weiler 1980).

In addition to having the intention of improving the structure and process of union-management relations, the Munro program also set out to improve the substantive conditions of work for employees whether or not they engaged in formal collective bargaining. Unorganized workers in the federal jurisdiction were to be provided with the legal right to be dismissed only for just cause, a right that most unionized employees enjoyed because of the widespread existence of contract clauses to that effect. By the early 1980s three Canadian jurisdictions (federal, Quebec, Nova Scotia) had introduced such a right (Adams 1983).

Labour Canada also set out to improve the satisfaction of employees with their work by encouraging enterprises to experiment with a variety of new forms of work organization, referred to generally as quality of worklife (QWL) programs (Srinivas 1980). Similar efforts were made within some of the provincial jurisdictions. In Ontario, for example, a Quality of Worklife Centre, reporting to a tripartite board, was established.[7]

Other substantive issues included on the Canada agenda were occupational health and safety, paid educational leave, and pensions. Each of these issues would be debated extensively. Paid educational leave and the broader issue of labor market training and retraining were to be the subject of several public inquiries as well as major policy revisions. Pensions also were the subject of several in-depth studies (Stone and Meltz 1983).

Two substantive issues not mentioned in the Canada program which were to be of major significance during the 1970s and 1980s were human rights and redundancy. Human rights at work became an increasingly salient issue due in large part to the increased participation of women in the labor force. By the end of the 1970s all jurisdictions had well-developed human rights statutes and programs which forbade discrimination on the basis of many attributes considered to be repugnant and largely irrelevant with regard to job performance (Jain 1982). By the latter 1970s layoffs and redundancies became key issues resulting in new statutes making it more difficult for employers to discharge employees at will (Stone and Meltz 1983).

Many of these issues—concern for occupational health and safety, human rights, job and income security, training, and the quality of worklife in particular—were not unique to Canada. Instead they elicited debate and action in several countries.

---

[7] It should be noted that many unionists did not approve of the participation of organized labor in this center. At the convention of the Ontario Federation of Labour in November 1984, the delegates passed a resolution to withdraw.

Although Canada developed somewhat unique approaches to each of these issues, Canadian solutions were not so remarkable as to warrant extended discussion here. Two additional developments do require close consideration because they were more clearly indicative of the transition of Canadian industrial relations away from the general North American pattern towards European practice.

In several European countries there is legislation which requires that works councils, with representatives chosen by employees, be established in each enterprise that meets specified criteria (Cordova 1982). In most countries the councils initially had only a consultative role. Employers were required to provide councillors with information about the nature of key decisions which would affect employees and to solicit employee views before making major decisions. During the 1970s the councils in many countries were provided with enhanced power. On some issues they acquired the power of co-decision. Employers were precluded from making decisions unless they had the councillors' approval. Deadlocks in such cases usually had to be settled by arbitration.

North American industrial relations experts have generally considered works councils to be irrelevant (Adams 1984a). Decentralized plant-by-plant bargaining was held to be analogous to, and usually superior to, decision-making via works councils. Historical research on the councils suggested that they generally had little real power. Too often they were or seemed to be co-opted by employers, making it particularly difficult for independent unions to achieve influence at the plant level. North-American-style collective bargaining appeared to be far superior in its ability to provide rank-and-file employees with the capacity to participate in decisions that critically affected their working lives.

However, as the 1970s and 1980s progressed, it became increasingly clear that there were serious flaws in Wagner-Act-style collective bargaining. First, despite several decades of experience with it, the majority of relevant employees did not engage in collective bargaining, largely because the model required them to take the initiative to establish bargaining in the face of the almost certain disapproval of their employers (Weiler 1983). Second, although the parties theoretically could negotiate over any issue of mutual concern, in reality collective agreements addressed only those issues over which employees were prepared to stop work and, thereby, forgo income. Collective agreements were usually silent in regard to several of the key issues of the 1970s and 1980s, such as occupational health and safety, human rights, training, and technological change.

As a result, Canadian governments began to search for new ways to ensure participation on such issues. The result was the emergence of an approach similar to European practice. The basic parameters of the emerging Canadian system are these (Adams 1984a):

1. Joint employer-employee committees are to be set up in all enterprises above a certain size.

2. Each committee will have a mandate to look at a specific issue, such as health, redundancy, technological change, profit-sharing, pension management, training, and human rights.

3. If a union already holds bargaining rights for the relevant employees, it designates worker members of the committee. If employees are not represented by a union, they elect representatives to the joint committee.

4. Committee impasses are to be settled by reference to some form (e.g., med-arb, final-offer-selection) of binding arbitration.

This model (with some variation of the key elements) has already been mandated in several provinces for occupational health and safety and in the federal jurisdiction with respect to mass layoffs and plant shutdowns. It has been proposed for use in regard to technological change, profit-sharing, pension management, training, and employment equity (Adams 1984a, Abella 1984). There is little reason to believe that its use will not continue to spread. Only a modest amount of research has been carried out on its functioning, but in general the results have been positive. In the occupational health and safety committees, the parties have been able to fashion solutions in a cooperative and productive manner. Few of the feared negative consequences have occurred.

A second remarkable Canadian development has to do with the evolution of dispute-settlement procedures during the 1970s and early 1980s. In the traditional North American collective bargaining system, if the parties disagreed about the interpretation of the written collective agreement, they would submit their dispute to an arbitrator. The arbitrator (or three-person arbitration board) was chosen jointly by the parties. His job was to interpret the collective agreement. Although most arbitrators had legal training, the arbitration hearing was supposed to be conducted in an informal manner. This process, it was believed, would be faster, cheaper, and more responsive to the realities of the labor-management relationship than a court procedure would be, with its centuries-old paraphernalia of legal custom and tradition. Arbitration was also a procedure controlled by the parties rather than by the state, and most observers considered that attribute to be a positive one. It was one aspect of industrial self-government as opposed to a state regulation of industry (Weiler 1980).

According to many assessments of the grievance arbitration process made in the 1950s and 1960s, North American arbitration was a great success. Nevertheless, it was not problem-free. Labor and management were very careful to select arbitrators who had proven records, and it became difficult for newcomers to break in. The "demand" for proven arbitrators was very high. Often the parties would be willing to wait three to six months for a seasoned hand rather than trust a potentially precedent-setting issue to an untried rookie. As the demand for a small number of arbitrators went up, so did their bills. Instead of cheap and quick, arbitration became longer and more expensive (Weiler 1980).

There also developed, over time, a body of arbitral jurisprudence. Arbitration awards were collected, published and referred to in subsequent cases. Employers hired lawyers to present their cases, and unions were often required to do the same. Although arbitrators were not compelled by law to follow precedent, they did so nevertheless, and a body of custom, tradition, and procedure nearly as complex as common law began to accumulate. As a result, the process no longer met the standards of informality and responsiveness to shop floor realities in many cases. These problems drew the most attention in Ontario where about 30 percent of the unionized workforce was to be found (Weiler 1980).

By the late 1970s a new problem began to surface. Legislation with regard to issues such as occupational health and safety, human rights at work, and new employment standards such as the right to return to work after maternity leave all provided for dispute-resolution procedures (Christie 1980, Tarnopolsky 1982). As the pace of redundancies picked up in the late 1970s, more and more executives, professionals, and others decided to take their employers to court to sue for wrongful dismissal (Adams 1983). Unlike U.S., but like British practice, Canadian common law requires employers to provide redundant employees with notice or pay in lieu of notice.

The relationship between each of these dispute-settlement procedures and grievance arbitration became increasingly complex. For example, if a woman, subsequent to maternity leave, were to be refused her old job back, what should she do? Should she complain to the employment standards administration that one of her statutory rights was being infringed? Should she ask her union to file a grievance? Should she complain to the human rights agency that she was being discriminated against because of her sex? Could she use more than one procedure simultaneously, or in some specified order? To date, questions such as these have produced an expanding body of ad hoc administrative rules, but no unifying legal theory has yet emerged. Nevertheless, from out of the chaos one may dimly perceive the development of a coherent model that is more similar to European than to American practice.

It is common in Europe for disputes over all employment standards, whether based in law or contract, to be submitted to a labor court (Aaron 1982). Statutory works councils commonly have a mandate to oversee the application of both relevant statutes and terms of collective agreements. Canadian practice appears to be evolving towards a similar model.

As long ago as 1963 British Columbia introduced a statutory provision that permitted either labor or management to submit a contract grievance to the Labour Relations Board. In most cases the Board attempted to mediate the problem. If unsuccessful, the Board usually referred it back to the parties, although it could arbitrate a solution if it deemed that course to be advisable. The procedure did not, necessarily, override the voluntary, self-government aspects of grievance arbitration because the parties to any collective agreement could legally agree not to be bound by the statutory provisions (Weiler 1980).

Ontario went further down the road towards a labor court in the mid-1970s when it revised its labor relations statutes to permit expedited arbitration of grievances in the construction industry. Despite provisions in the collective agreement, either party could submit a grievance to the Labour Relations Board for binding resolution. The Board had to set up a hearing within 14 days of receiving a request. It charged a very modest fee for its services.

In 1979 Ontario extended this option to all of the private sector, with a few modifications. As with the construction industry process, either party may initiate expedited arbitration. Any clause to the contrary in the collective agreement is null and void. Instead of a decision by the Board, the Minister appoints a single arbitrator from a list maintained by an agency of the Labour Ministry. The agency develops and applies standards regarding qualifications. The arbitrator must hold a hearing within 21 days of his appointment and must hand down a decision as quickly as possible, although there are no specific time limits. In the period between the date when a request is received and the date when the arbitration hearing is held, the Minister may appoint a mediator to help the parties find a mutually acceptable solution to their dispute (Carter 1981). These developments have reestablished the standards of speed and economy. In the process, however, arbitration has become less of a private and more of a public institution.

The public nature of grievance arbitration also is becoming more evident as a result of administrative, court, and other legislative decisions. For example, arbitral jurisprudence long held that disputes over the application of laws such as employment standards were beyond the mandate of arbitrators. Such disputes should be settled by the courts or by special purpose public tribunals. If arbitration was no more than an element of private self-government, its existence should be irrelevant to the settlement of disputes over rights based in statute. However, in Ontario the administrators of employment standards decided not to entertain complaints from unionized employees if the collective agreement contained a clause that would permit the employee (or, more precisely, his agent—the union) to submit the dispute to arbitration (Hess 1976). The regulation implicitly defines arbitration as an alternative to (and presumably the equivalent of) the public procedure available without restriction to those beyond collective bargaining.

A 1975 Supreme Court of Canada decision would seem to carry the same implication with regard to the resolution of disputes over dismissal. In that decision the Court held that common law rights do not survive the advent of collective bargaining. Thus, unionized employees apparently may not have wrongful dismissal allegations settled by the courts (Handman 1979, *Bourne* v. *Otis Elevator* 1984). Instead, if they allege that wrongful dismissal has taken place, their only recourse is arbitration. However, unlike the employment standards regulation mentioned above, the unionized employee is barred from the courts whether or not the collective agreement contains a clause regarding dismissal. Most Canadian agreements do, however, contain such clauses.

Another recent court decision also had the effect of expanding the role of the arbitrator from reader of a private agreement to adjudicator of the law. The court held that if a law impinges upon a collective agreement, not only may the arbitrator make reference to it, indeed he must do so (*McLeod* v. *Egan* 1974). In effect, that decision requires arbitrators, in certain situations, to resolve legal disputes.

A recent British Columbia law goes even further, Arbitrators must settle employment-standard disagreements even if the collective agreement is silent with regard to the issue in dispute. In effect the legislation turns certified unions into legislative compliance committees since they must fairly process reasonable grievances.

The slow transformation of arbitration from private to public process has been lamented by some as a decline in industrial self-government (Weiler 1980). On the other hand, overlaps and redundancies resulting from the proliferation of dispute-resolution procedures demanded rationalization. In fact, the process of rationalization has only just begun. If current trends persist, it is likely that the final product will be a system more similar to European labor courts than to private arbitration in the U.S.

Parting Ways?

In 1960 Canada and the United States could be referred to as a single system and few observers on either side of the border would disagree. During recent decades, however, the two countries have moved in much different directions.

If dominant trends continue, a Canadian system with the following attributes may emerge:[8]

1. In unionized companies the union will have co-decision powers with management in regard to a list of specified issues. Arbitration will be available to resolve disputes over those issues. In nonunion enterprises, statutory committees will have the same power to co-decide specific issues with arbitration available to resolve impasses. The following are likely candidates for co-

---

[8] By constructing this model I am not attempting to predict the future. Rather, the model will be, it seems to me, the likely result if current trends continue. Of course, trends do change.

determination issues: occupational health and safety, mass terminations, training, the pace and consequences of technological change, pension management, profit-sharing, and human rights at work.

2. In unionized companies the union will be responsible not only for overseeing the application of the collective agreement, but also for the entire range of employment law. Disputes over the implementation of either law or contract will be arbitrable. In nonunion companies, a statutory committee will be responsible for ensuring the proper application of all aspects of employment law, and it will be able to submit disputes to a neutral and binding procedure similar to grievance arbitration. Thus, in each enterprise there will be an employee representative agency responsible for ensuring the implementation of statutory rights and standards.

3. Only unions will be able to negotiate wage issues, and only unions will be legally permitted to strike. However, some form of arbitration will be available to settle impasses occurring during any bargaining round, not just the first agreement.[9]

4. Prior to initiating policies that affect the critical interests of the parties, governments will consult fully with representatives of labor and management. So long as the results are not seen to be seriously detrimental to the public, governments will not pursue policies vigorously opposed by management or labor. So long as the results are seen to be advantageous to the public as a whole, policies agreed to by labor and management will be put into effect.

The progression of Canadian industrial relations towards the model outlined above is by no means certain. Since the recession of 1981–1982, counter-trends more in line with U.S. developments have emerged. Conservative provincial governments, especially in Western Canada, have pursued policies strongly resisted by organized labor and have, therefore, exacerbated adversarialism. By legislating limits to the wage progression of federal employees instead of negotiating wage restraint, the federal government has raised serious questions about its commitment to collective bargaining. It has also provoked the ire of the unions and in doing

---

[9] During the Summer of 1984 the Manitoba government put forth such a proposal in a discussion paper on labor law reform. Although the government decided against proceeding with the proposal, the fact that it was put forth for discussion suggests that it has moved beyond the realm of academic speculation into the arena of serious political debate (see Dolan 1984).

so has substantially reduced their enthusiasm to be cooperative. Despite the conciliatory attitude of the BCNI, some employers have begun to pursue policies contrary to the fundamental interests of the unions. For example, double-breasting (a phenomenon whereby unionized employers set up nonunion companies in order to pay lower wage rates) which first appeared in the United States in the mid-1970s has begun to occur in Canada since the recession.

These developments may be minor deviations from the general trend towards participatory cooperation, or they may be ominous signs that Canada is about to follow the authoritarian nonunion road pursued by the U.S. in recent years. But the experience of many countries in the West is that the attempted suppression of the democratic right of working people to participate in employment-related decisions will surely produce conflict and misery for the entire population. After a decade or more of expanding rights, employee-citizens are unlikely to tolerate for long exclusion from policy-making at the enterprise and political levels. Suppression of participatory mechanisms now is almost certain to produce violent conflict in the future.

The authoritarian, nonunion strategy is generally justified on the basis that it is more efficient economically than is democratic participation by right. There is, however, little objective evidence to support that proposition. Indeed, a great deal of recent research on Wagner-Act-style collective bargaining suggests that it is not detrimental to economic efficiency (Freeman and Medoff 1984). Available research on the new participation procedures introduced in Canada during the past decade also indicates generally positive results.[10] At the national level labor and management have demonstrated an ability to address important policy issues constructively.

There is also an ethical issue involved in the choice. Most North Americans place very high intrinsic value on democracy. They would not trade political democracy even if it could be

---

[10] There has been a considerable movement, typically initiated unilaterally by management, to involve employees in decisions at the workplace level. This expansion of Quality of Worklife programs may be laudable, but it should not be confused with collective bargaining or other mechanisms designed to bring about a form of democracy in industry. Typically, QWL programs owe their continued existence to the benevolence of management. Employees do not participate by right, as do citizens of democracies. QWL is better thought of as a management technique than as a form of industrial democracy.

demonstrated that an authoritarian system would be more economically efficient. Historically, the relationship between economic and political democracy has been ambiguous. Many zealots for political democracy have accepted the anomaly of authoritarian decision-making in economic life. During the past few decades, however, the inconsistency between political democracy and economic authoritarianism has become increasingly obvious. From the perspective of the democrat, the issue can never be efficiency at the cost of democracy. Instead it can only be the pursuit of efficiency within the context of democracy. From the democratic perspective, the authoritarian strategy is unacceptable not only because it is unnecessary and likely to provoke strife, but also and more fundamentally because it is ethically repugnant.

References

Aaron, Benjamin. "Settlement of Disputes over Rights." In *Comparative Law and Industrial Relations*, eds. R. Blanpain and F. Millard. Deventer, The Netherlands: Kluwer, 1982.

Abella, R. *Equality in Enployment*. A Royal Commission Report. Ottawa: Supply and Services Canada, 1984.

Adams, Roy. J. "The Federal Government and Tripartism." *Relations Industrielles* 37, No. 3 (1982a): pp. 606–16.

_____. "Industrial Relations Systems in Europe and North America." In *Union-Management Relations in Canada*, eds. J. Anderson and M. Gunderson. Don Mills, Ont.: Addison-Wesley, 1982b.

_____. "The Unorganized: A Rising Force?" In *Jobs and Labor Peace—An Agenda for Action*, ed. Lisa R. Cohen. Proceedings of the 31st Annual Conference of the McGill IR Centre. Montreal: 1983.

_____. "Two Policy Approaches to Labor-Management Decision-Making at the Level of the Enterprise: A Comparison of the Wagner Model and Statutory Works Councils." Paper presented at the Symposium on Labor-Management Cooperation in Canada organized by the Royal Commission on the Economic Union and Development Prospects for Canada, Ottawa, June 22, 1984. Also *Faculty of Business Research Paper* No. 227. Hamilton: McMaster University, 1984a.

_____. "The Extent of Collective Bargaining in Canada." *Relations Industrielles* 39, No. 4 (1984b): pp. 655–67.

Archbold, W. D. "The Business Council on National Issues: A New Factor in Business Communication." *Canadian Business Review* (Summer 1977).

Arthurs, H. W., D. D. Carter, and H. J. Glasbeek. *Law and Industrial Relations in Canada*. Toronto: Butterworths, 1981.

Barbash, Jack. "The 1980's—A New Era in Industrial Relations." In *Les Relations des Travail en Periode de Crise Economique*, École de rélations industrielles, Université de Montréal, 1983.

Bourne v. Otis Elevator (1983). Supreme Court of Ontario, Toronto Motions Court, Southby, J., released March 7, 1984.

Canada Department of Finance. "Canadian Business Leaders Endorse Program." *6 + 5 Newsletter*, August 1, 1982.

Carter, D. D. "Grievance Arbitration: The Present Role of the Labor Relations Board." Address to a Conference on the Grievance Arbitration Process. In *Labor Relations Law*. Kingston: Queen's University IR Centre, 1981. Pp. 378–79.

Christie, Innis. *Employment Law in Canada*. Toronto: Butterworths, 1980.

Cordova, E. "Workers' Participation in Decisions Within Enterprises: Recent Trends and Problems." *International Labour Review* 121 (March-April 1982): pp. 125-40.

Craig, A. W. J. *The System of Industrial Relations in Canada.* Scarborough, Ont.: Prentice-Hall, 1983.

Dolan, Mary Beth. "Information Concerning Proposed Changes in Manitoba's Labour Legislation." Winnipeg: Manitoba Department of Labour, April, 1984.

Errington, G., and E. Finn. "Blood-bath in B.C." *The Facts* 5 (October 1983).

Frazee, R. C., and T. P. d'Aquino. "National Priorities, a Submission to the Royal Commission on The Economic Union and Development Prospects for Canada." Ottawa: Business Council on National Issues, December 1983.

Freeman, Richard B., and James L. Medoff. *What Do Unions Do?* New York: Basic Books, 1984.

Giles, Antony. "The Canadian Labour Congress and Tripartism." *Relations Industrielles* 37, No. 1 (1982): pp. 93-125.

Handman, S. "The Juridical Status of an Individual Work Contract in Relation to Collective Agreement and Recourses of an Employee." *Revue du Barreau de la Province de Quebec* 39 (1979): pp. 995-1017.

Hess, Paul. "Employment Standards in Ontario." Toronto: Law Society of Upper Canada Special Lectures, 1976.

Jain, Harish C. "Employment and Pay Discrimination in Canada: Theories, Evidence and Policies." In *Union-Management Relations in Canada,* eds. J. Anderson and M. Gunderson. Don Mills, Ont.: Addison-Wesley, 1982.

Kochan, Thomas, and Michael Piore. "Will the New Industrial Relations Last? Implications for the American Labor Movement." *Annals of the American Academy of Political and Social Science* 273 (May 1984): pp. 177-89.

Kwavnick, D. "Labour's Lobby in Ottawa: How the CLC Influences Government Policy." *Labour Gazette* (July 1973): pp. 433-41.

Lang, Ronald. "Labour's Manifesto for Canada: A New Independence?" *Proceedings* of the 29th Annual Meeting, Industrial Relations Research Association, 1976. Madison, Wis.: IRRA, 1977. Pp. 91-99.

List, W. "Strikebreaking Law Reflects Progressive Ontario Record." *Toronto Globe and Mail,* June 13, 1983.

_____. "National Bargaining in its Death Throes." *Toronto Globe and Mail,* August 7, 1984.

MacLaren, R. *How to Improve Business-Government Relations in Canada.* Ottawa: Department of Industry, Trade and Commerce, 1976.

Maital, S., and N. M. Meltz. "Labour and Management Attitudes Toward a New Social Contract: A Comparison of Canada and the United States." Paper presented to the 21st Annual Meeting, Canadian Industrial Relations Association, University of Guelph, May 30, 1984. In *Macroeconomic Conflict and Social Institutions,* eds. I. Lipnowsky and S. Maital. Cambridge, Mass.: Ballinger, 1985.

McLeon v. *Egan* (1974), 46 D.L.R. (3d) 150, per Laskin, C.J.C.

Meltz, Noah M. "Labour Movements in Canada and the United States." In *Challenges and Choices for American Labor,* ed. Thomas A. Kochan. Cambridge, Mass.: MIT Press, 1985.

Moye, W. T. "Presidential Labor-Management Committees: Productive Failures." *Industrial and Labor Relations Review* (October 1980): pp. 51-66.

Munro, John. "Notes for an Address on the Speech from the Throne." Ottawa: October 18, 1976.

OECD Economic Outlook, July 1984.

Perlman, Selig. *A Theory of the Labor Movement.* New York: Macmillan, 1928.

Ponak, Allen M. "Public-Sector Collective Bargaining." In *Union-Management Relations in Canada,* eds. J. Anderson and M. Gunderson. Don Mills, Ont.: Addison-Wesley, 1982.

Position Paper on the Practical Application of Labour's Manifesto for Canada. Ottawa: Canadian Labour Congress, 1976.

Rose, J. B. "Employer Accreditation: A Retrospective." Proceedings of the 20th Annual Meeting, Canadian Industrial Relations Association, Vancouver, June 1–2, 1983. Quebec: CIRA, 1984.

Rose, J. B., and G. N. Chaison. "The State of the Unions: United States and Canada." *Journal of Labor Research* 6 (Winter 1985): pp. 97–111.

Ross, A. M., and P. T. Hartman. *Changing Patterns of Industrial Conflict*. New York: Wiley, 1960

Sass, R. "An Assessment of the Saskatchewan Trade Union Amendment Act, 1983." *Saskatchewan Law Review* 48, No. 1 (1984): pp. 143–69.

Stone, T. H., and N. M. Meltz. *Personnel Management in Canada*. Toronto: Holt, Rinehart and Winston, 1983.

Srinivas, K.M. "Humanization of Worklife in Canada: Progress, Perspectives and Prospects." *Journal of Occupational Behavior* (1980): pp. 87–118.

Swimmer, Eugene. "Six and Five." In *How Ottawa Spends 1984: The New Agenda*, ed. Allan Maslove. Toronto: Methuen, 1984.

Tarnopolsky, Walter. *Discrimination and the Law in Canada*. Toronto: De Boo, 1982.

Thompson, Mark, and G. Swimmer. "Broken Bargaining." *Policy Options* (January 1984): pp. 56–60.

Thompson, Mark. "Anatomy of a Crisis in Labor Relations: Restraint Legislation and the Public Sector in British Columbia." Proceedings of the 32nd Annual Conference, Industrial Relations Centre, McGill University, *Managing Industrial Relations in an Era of Change*. Montreal: McGill University, 1984. Pp. 146–57.

Waldie, K. G. "The Evolution of Government Consultation on Economic Policy." Paper presented to a Conference on Labour-Management Cooperation in Canada, sponsored by the Royal Commission on The Economic Union and Development Prospects for Canada, Ottawa, June 22, 1984. Mimeo.

Walkom, Thomas. "Center Planned for Productivity." *Toronto Globe and Mail*, February 3, 1983.

Weiler, Paul. *Reconcilable Differences*. Toronto: Carswell, 1980.

_____. "Promises to Keep: Securing Workers' Rights to Self-Organization Under the NLRA." *Harvard Law Review* 96 (June 1983): pp. 1769–1827.

Wood, W. D. "An Overview of the Canadian Industrial Relations Scene." Paper presented to the Saskatoon Personnel Association, February 1984. Kingston, Ont.: Queen's University Industrial Relations Centre, 1984. Mimeo.

Wood, W. D., and Pradeep Kumar, eds. *Canadian Perspectives on Wage-Price Guidelines*. Kingston, Ont.: Queen's University Industrial Relations Centre, 1976.

_____. *The Current Industrial Relations Scene in Canada*. Kingston, Ont.: Queen's University Industrial Relations Centre, annual.

Woods, H. D. *Labor Policy in Canada*, 2d ed. Toronto: Macmillan, 1973.

_____. "Shadows Over Arbitration." In *Arbitration—1977*, Proceedings of the 30th Annual Meeting, National Academy of Arbitrators, eds. Barbara D. Dennis and Gerald G. Somers. Washington: Bureau of National Affairs, 1978.

Zoeteweij, Bert. "Anti-Inflation Policies in the Industrialized Market Economy Countries." *International Labour Review* 122 (September-October 1983).

Chapter 5

The Effect of Recent Changes in the World Economy on British Industrial Relations*

William Brown
University of Warwick

The 1980s have brought the most traumatic change experienced by British industrial relations in peacetime. An unprecedentedly large rise in unemployment coincided, in 1979, with the first government this century to be explicitly hostile to collective bargaining. At the same time Britain's rapid emergence as a major oil producer brought, through its effect on the country's rate of exchange, a competitive shock to all industries exposed to world trade. In fighting for their market shares, private-sector employers have adopted increasingly innovative policies towards their workforces. They have, in so doing, revealed substantial weaknesses in established trade union organization. For the public sector, government hostility has brought a series of defeats for trade unions, culminating in the bitter, year-long, coal-miners' strike.

The scale of the upheaval is best appreciated by a brief reminder of what preceded it. To an extent that is internationally exceptional, industrial relations in Britain has been allowed to develop with little legal intervention by the state. Governments had generally encouraged collective bargaining, especially in the public sector, and when they had felt forced to intervene, in wartime or in inflationary crises, their principal concern had been to win trade union cooperation. A peculiar feature of British collective bargaining has been its emphasis upon regulation at the place of work rather than through agreements at industry level. Under postwar full employment, this had become increasingly important, and its principal figure, the shop steward, had come to play an

---

* The author is grateful to Roy Lewis and Peter Nolan for helpful criticism.

important role not only throughout manufacturing but also in much of service industry. In this way trade unions had won a substantial influence over the conduct of work and, for many employers, workplace negotiation had become a necessary preliminary to change and innovation.

A central feature of the economic philosophy of the Conservative government that took office in 1979 was the belief that economic recovery required the freeing of markets; the reduction of the monopoly power of trade unions was seen as an essential part of this. It was to some extent fortuitous that a doubling in the level of unemployment greatly reduced the capacity of trade unions to resist the onslaught. This chapter will describe the radical developments in government policy and the extent to which employers were influenced by them. It will consider the implications for trade union organization and the longer-term development of industrial relations. The starting point is, however, the deepening difficulties of the British economy.

Economic Background

Since the Second World War, the growth rate of the British economy has lagged substantially behind those of its major competitors. The shallow growth experienced in the late 1970s was abruptly halted in 1979 and, though there was some recovery by 1983, forecasters do not expect any major expansion during the rest of the 1980s (IER 1983). A widespread pessimism as to the timing and extent of any recovery from the current recession, in contrast with its postwar predecessors, has exercised a strong underlying influence upon the conduct of industrial relations.

The recession has paradoxically coincided with the dramatic arrival of North Sea oil. From having to import all its oil only a decade earlier, by 1985 Britain had surged into the position of the world's fifth largest oil-producing nation. On the basis of probable reserves, however, 1985 is likely to be the year of maximum production, with the economy from then having to adjust to the consequences of a declining contribution from oil to both tax revenue and foreign exchange.

Exports have remained broadly level at about 30 percent of gross domestic product since 1979. But their composition has altered substantially, with petroleum emerging to make up 20 percent of total exports by 1983 and the share of manufactured

TABLE 1
U.K. Economic Indicators 1974–1984

	1974	1975	1976	1977	1978	1979	1980	1981	1982	1983	1984
Gross domestic product[a] (1975 = 100)	100.9	100.0	103.7	105.0	108.7	110.9	108.3	107.3	109.7	113.6	116.7
Effective exchange rate[a] (IMF Index)	108.3	100.0	85.6	81.2	81.5	87.2	96.1	94.9	90.5	83.2	78.5
Terms of trade[a] (1975 = 100)	93	100	98	100	106	110	114	115	113	112	110
Inflation rate[a] (Annual % change in RPI)	15.8	24.3	16.6	15.8	8.3	13.5	17.9	11.9	8.6	4.6	5.0
Output per person hour in mfg.[a] (1975 = 100)	102	100	105	106	108	109	108	112	116	123	128
Hourly earnings in mfg.[a] (1975 = 100)	78	100	116	128	148	171	206	235	258	281	302
Wage costs per unit of output in mfg.[a] (1975 = 100)	77	100	111	120	136	157	192	210	221	227	235
Total mfg. employment[a] (1975 = 100)	105	100	97	97	97	96	93	83	79	75	74
Unemployment as % of total labor force[b]	3.2	4.7	6.0	6.3	6.3	5.6	7.0	10.6	12.3	13.2	13.5
Trade union density[c] (%)	50.4	51.0	51.9	53.4	54.1	54.4	52.6	49.3	47.0	45.5	—
Number of strikes[d]	2922	2282	2016	2703	2471	2080	1330	1338	1528	1352	1154
Number of days lost in strikes[d] (thousands)	14750	6012	3284	10142	9405	29474	11964	4266	5313	3754	26564

[a] Source: National Institute for Economic and Social Research.
[b] Source: Organisation for Economic Co-operation and Development.
[c] Source: Bain and Price (1983).
[d] Source: Department of Employment Gazette.

goods falling to 66 percent. The volume of manufactured exports fell by 6 percent between 1979 and 1983, and the volume of manufactured imports into Britain rose by 18 percent. Over the same period Britain's share of total OECD trade fell from 9.7 to 8.0 percent; 30 years earlier it had been roughly 20 percent. While oil revenues have enabled the government to meet the enormous cost of unemployment pay relatively inconspicuously, the fluctuating price of oil on world markets has been an additional factor contributing to unemployment. The halving of the value of sterling in dollar terms between 1981 and 1985 was too dependent upon the fickleness of petroleum prices for British manufacturers to be able to gain full advantage from their apparent increase in competitive strength in world markets.

Britain's oil has, however, only been a recent contributor to the country's weakening position in world trade. Domestic inflation has consistently run ahead of that of most competitors for over 20 years. Output per person in manufacturing, handicapped by sustained low levels of investment, has risen more slowly than in other major OECD countries; hourly earnings have generally risen faster. Most recently this has meant that wage costs per unit of output rose 45 percent between 1979 and 1983, more than three times as much as in Japan, West Germany, or the United States.

The contribution of industrial relations factors to this poor economic performance has been a matter of controversy. It is likely that most strikes have relatively slight direct impact, although their indirect effects upon the confidence of overseas investors and customers may be more substantial. More important is the British tradition of workplace bargaining, with its implication that trade unions can influence the conduct of work and hence the productivity of labor. Most commentators have inferred that this has been to the detriment of efficiency and technological innovation. There is, however, as will be discussed later, substantial evidence that in the recession many employers have been able to take advantage of the relative autonomy of workplace union organization to achieve more substantial changes in working practices than would have been possible under industry-wide agreements. A more profound British problem, lying dormant so far in the 1980s after having been a major source of economic weakness in the previous 20 years, is the tendency of the bargaining system to exacerbate inflation through its fragmented and uncoordinated character. Stemming in large part from the traditional lack of solidarity among British employers—in marked contrast to their continental European counterparts—this is likely to handicap any move towards economic recovery.

The Labor Force

The population of working age in Britain, and also the proportion of them offering themselves for employment, has grown slowly over the past decade. Unemployment, having moved unevenly upwards during the 1970s, increased sharply in the early 1980s, and increasing with it were the proportion of those unemployed for long periods. The measurement of unemployment is inevitably imprecise. The figures given in Table 2 are of those eligible for and claiming state benefit. A higher level of economic activity would probably tempt up to a million more people out of early retirement, household tasks, and the like. As it is, unemployment is not expected to fall substantially during the rest of the 1980s (IER 1983).

The most dramatic shift in jobs has been out of manufacturing industry. The decline under way in the 1970s has turned into something approaching a collapse in the 1980s, with the combined effect of falling exports, increasing imports, labor-replacing technology, and the wholesale closure of less efficient plants. Particularly hard hit have been the metal-working industries and textiles. It is also evident from Table 2 that the long-term decline in employment in agriculture and fuel extraction (despite North Sea oil) has continued. Construction and transport have both suffered in the 1980s. The public services, despite a government committed to shedding work to the private sector, have held their numbers up surprisingly well. Growth has taken place most noticeably in the private services, and in particular in the various financial services despite, it should be added, the wholesale introduction of electronic automation. A statistical factor that gives a slightly misleading impression of the growth of services at the expense of manufacturing has been an increasing tendency for firms to subcontract out to specialists functions such as catering, security, transport, and cleaning.

There has been a longer-term tendency for the proportion of women in the workforce to rise and this has continued in the 1980s, assisted by the changing structure of industry. Much of the growth

TABLE 2

Labor Force in Great Britain 1974–1983 (June)

	1974	1975	1976	1977	1978	1979	1980	1981	1982	1983
Employed Labor Force (in thousands)										
Agriculture, fishing, etc.	404	388	382	378	373	359	352	343	345	339
Coal, oil, etc.	352	356	350	353	358	356	357	344	329	314
Gas, electricity, water	354	360	360	355	348	356	360	355	347	339
Manufacturing	7737	7365	7150	7200	7163	7127	6816	6109	5812	5548
Construction	1232	1217	1212	1177	1171	1216	1216	1112	1033	991
Transport	1031	1038	1012	1017	1036	1039	1034	974	926	890
Distrib., hotels	3879	3902	3891	3951	4009	4173	4237	4091	4102	4135
Post., telecomm.	434	439	422	411	406	413	428	429	428	424
Banks, fin., and insurance	1473	1468	1472	1496	1548	1638	1688	1714	1758	1811
Public admin.	1865	1941	1939	1938	1947	1947	1917	1849	1816	1834
Health and education	2478	2628	2704	2694	2721	2777	2783	2791	2815	2835
Other services	1057	1110	1163	1172	1209	1251	1282	1284	1298	1294
Total employed	22297	22213	22048	22126	22274	22639	22458	21386	21000	20744
Percent female	40.1	40.4	40.6	40.9	41.2	41.8	42.0	42.6	43.1	43.4
Percent of female part-time	38.3	39.6	40.1	40.0	40.2	n.a.	n.a.	41.6	43.0	44.5
Self-employed	1935	1933	1888	1843	1843	1842	1950	2057	2129	2199
Unemployed	502	803	1215	1303	1282	1175	1444	2299	2664	2871
Overtime Working in Manufacturing										
Percent male manuals working overtime	33.1	30.3	32.2	34.6	34.8	34.2	29.5	26.6	29.8	31.5
Average overtime hours worked by those working any overtime (annual averages)	8.4	8.3	8.4	8.7	8.6	8.7	8.3	8.2	8.3	8.5

Source: Department of Employment (1984).

in female employment has been part-time—under 30 hours a week—and, as Table 2 shows, this has tended to accelerate recently. While full-time male employment has fallen, married women have come into part-time employment in increasing numbers. Self-employment, having been fairly static during the 1970s when, for example, small retail shops were declining, has increased, partly as a result of increased subcontracting to individuals who were previously employees.

There has been some slight reduction in the length of the basic working week during the 1980s, with the engineering industry reducing standard hours for its manual workers from 40 to 39. But this has had relatively little impact upon actual hours worked. Britain remains exceptional among developed countries in the extent of overtime working by its male manual workers. As Table 2 shows, despite the massive job losses of manufacturing industry in recent years, almost a third of its male manual workers work overtime, most of which is regular, and on average they work the equivalent of an extra day's work per week. It should be added that the majority of these employees are members of trade unions whose national policies are strongly opposed to overtime working. It is difficult to generalize about the extent to which this overtime is worked at management's discretion and thus may be considered to increase, rather than restrict, labor market flexibility.

As in the depression of the 1930s, those in jobs have on average more than maintained the purchasing power of their pay. Since unemployment started to rise sharply in 1979, earnings have increased a quarter as fast again as the retail price index. The average is, however, misleading. Table 3 gives the dispersion of male and female earnings over the past decade. For both it is evident that the dispersion of pay increased substantially after 1980, with the upper end of the distribution most noticeably pulling ahead. Added to this growing inequality were more regressive changes in income taxation and in benefit payments. State benefits for the unemployed have deteriorated in real terms. Since 1981 the link between benefit and previous earnings was scrapped, the consequent flat-rate was linked to prices and not average wages, and benefits became taxable. At the level of individual occupations, the 1980s has been characterized by a general widening of skill differentials. The sex differential, which had narrowed somewhat in the early 1970s as a result of equal pay legislation, appears from Table 3 to have stabilized.

The sharp deterioration in the labor market in 1979 was accompanied by the arrival of a government whose attitude to collective bargaining was in marked contrast to that of any other this century. It was an attitude that grew out of a broader economic philosophy that places a somewhat unquestioning faith in the utility and existence of free market mechanisms, and also places considerable emphasis upon the role played by changes in the stock of money in determining the price level. Accompanying this is the desire to reduce the size of the public sector and to reduce the level of public expenditure, an objective thwarted by the growing requirement for payments for retirement pensions and the unemployed. In the short term, at least, the policy package has proved politically popular. With the assistance of the brief war in the South Atlantic and an ineffective parliamentary opposition, the government was able to increase its majority very substantially in 1983.

It is necessary to step back a little in order to put this policy change in perspective. Since the beginning of the century successive British governments have kept a stance of benign abstention towards collective bargaining. Legislation at that time had given trade unions and employers' associations immunity from civil proceedings. Collective bargaining had consequently continued to develop as a largely private affair between employers and trade unions, with little judicial involvement. Governments had, with varying degrees of enthusiasm, supported collective bargaining and encouraged trade unions, not least in the public sector. By the 1960s there was widespread dissatisfaction with various aspects of British industrial relations, but the main proposals for change involved the reform of collective bargaining rather than its reduction. Thus the Industrial Act introduced by the Conservative government in 1971 sought to utilize North American ideas by introducing a system of certification of recognized unions and legal enforceability of collective agreements. The Labour government that abolished the Act in 1974 instituted an independent Advisory, Conciliation and Arbitration Service with the facilitation of voluntary reform as one of its objectives.

The Conservative government that arrived in 1979 proposed to redress what it identified as an imbalance of power favoring trade

TABLE 3

Male and Female Pay Dispersion and the Sex Differential 1974-1984

	1974	1975	1976	1977	1978	1979	1980	1981	1982	1983	1984
Full-Time Men's Weekly Earnings, as Percentage of Median											
Lowest decile	66.8	67.0	67.6	68.1	66.8	66.0	65.9	65.6	64.5	64.1	63.0
Lower quartile	80.7	81.0	81.3	81.4	80.6	80.3	80.1	79.8	79.0	78.8	77.7
Upper quartile	124.6	125.3	125.6	125.6	125.1	125.1	126.5	129.5	129.8	129.8	130.1
Highest decile	157.0	157.6	159.5	157.7	157.9	156.9	161.6	167.7	168.1	169.7	170.7
Full-Time Women's Weekly Earnings, as Percentage of Median											
Lowest decile	67.7	67.4	66.1	68.6	69.1	69.4	68.4	68.0	66.9	66.4	66.1
Lower quartile	81.0	81.5	80.2	82.1	82.2	82.1	81.3	80.6	79.7	79.7	78.9
Upper quartile	126.4	125.2	125.9	124.7	125.3	124.7	126.1	129.8	129.4	129.9	130.1
Highest decile	159.1	164.5	165.9	162.1	161.4	158.6	161.3	172.6	169.0	168.3	167.2
Female Average Earnings as Percentage of Male Average Earnings											
	56	61	64	65	63	62	63	65	64	65	64

Source: Department of Employment, *New Earnings Survey* (1984 figures adjusted to allow for change in series).

unions. What has been unfolded in its "step by step" approach has been a succession of piecemeal measures—principally the Employment Acts of 1980 and 1982 and the Trade Union Act of 1984—which have been intended to attack what were seen as the worst abuses of trade union power. Prime Minister Thatcher has said that she is willing to continue to legislate every two years "until we get it right."

The 1980 and 1982 Acts restrict the legal freedom to strike by the reduction of immunities from civil actions for those engaged in picketing, secondary action, and action in support of closed shops, and also by making unions as such as well as individual members legally liable. Trade unions lose their immunities under the legislation if strike action is carried out against employers who are not party to the trade dispute in question. The definition of trade dispute has also been narrowed in an attempt to exclude from immunity strikes for political objectives. Lawful picketing can now only be conducted by individuals at their own place of work or by trade union officials who accompany them.

The closed shop covers approximately a half of trade union members in Britain, mostly in a "post-entry" form—that is, a union shop in North America. It is now unlawful to insist that subcontractors use only unionized labor, and unions lose immunity if they take action to enforce such requirements. The grounds on which individuals can refuse to join a union in a closed shop have been widened, and the compensation to which they are entitled if dismissed for refusing to join is very much greater than for normal unfair dismissal. Employers must have ballots on the continuation of closed shops if they are to avoid these penalties for dismissing an employee who refused to join any or a particular union; the necessary majority of 80 percent of those entitled or 85 percent of those voting is exceptionally high by international standards (Lewis 1983).

The 1984 law was directed at trade union government. It required balloting procedures to be followed for trade union executives and senior officers and also for strikes if they are to carry the immunities. In addition, balloting procedures are now necessary if trade unions are to be allowed to have provision for a levy of their members for political objectives, including contributions to party funds. These measures continue the process of shifting the emphasis of the law from collective rights to individual rights and, thereby,

they further undermine collective bargaining. More than any previous legislation of the 1980s, the Act poses a fundamental threat to
trade unions. They cannot be seen to be opposing it on principle
without appearing to oppose the democratic ideals upon which they
are themselves built. Nor can they realistically ignore it. Sooner or
later a disaffected group of members is likely to use the legislation
to challenge the union leadership's democratic legitimacy.
Moreover, employers are likely to take advantage of a union's lack
of legal immunities when a strike has been called without the
observance of the new balloting procedures.

The year 1984 is likely to prove a watershed in the legislative
experience of British trade unionism. Until then it was possible to
believe that the privacy of strong collective bargaining arrangements was relatively safe from legal intervention. The provision of
new rights on matters such as unfair dismissal and health and safety
did have important consequences, but employers and unions could
carry on their day-to-day relations much as before. By tacit consent,
measures to regulate picketing, the closed shop, disclosure of
information, and many other matters were quietly ignored in the
interest of maintaining the bargaining relationship. The type of
employer who might use legal powers to penalize trade unions was
generally a "cowboy" small businessman with a weakly organized
workforce and, it was generally felt, penalizing trade unions was
likely to be counterproductive, creating martyrs, widening
conflicts, and only bringing financial compensation with great
difficulty.

These widely held views were called into question in the 1980s.
For the reasons outlined, the Trade Union Act of 1984 poses a threat
that requires a major constitutional response from unions. Large
employers with well-established bargaining arrangements used it
quickly and effectively to curb strike action. The courts developed
ingenious ways of extracting fines for contempt of court from
unions without obliging their leaders with the martyrdom of
imprisonment. As a result, fines of many hundreds of thousands of
pounds were paid with little opportunity for polemics or protest.
The predisposition of the British judiciary to favor individual over
collective rights suggests that union finances are in severe jeopardy.
Moreover, it would be politically difficult for a future government
to repeal legislation so concerned with upholding democratic
procedures. Nor would trade unions necessarily welcome its repeal,

for with two of the largest unions now wanting to claim state funds to cover balloting costs, the financial implications could be serious.

The government's singular view of market forces has also affected employees without trade union protection. Rights not to be unfairly dismissed and to return to work after pregnancy leave have been weakened. Statutory provisions to ensure that government contractors follow established wage levels have been rescinded. Wages councils, which provide minimum terms and conditions for certain lightly unionized industries, and which have their own inspectorate and enforcement procedure, are under threat. It is felt that fresh employment will be created if real wages are allowed to fall without restraint. In the same spirit of faith in the capacity of market forces to meet strategic needs, statutory support has also been removed from the majority of industry-wide training arrangements. It remains to be seen whether companies will be able to anticipate the skill shortages that might accompany an economic revival and whether the labor market will operate more efficiently for having less external validation of skills.

It is difficult to imagine that so substantial a change in official policy towards collective bargaining and the labor market could have been effected in a more buoyant economy. Heavy unemployment has eased the inflationary pressures that previously would have obliged governments to maintain a dialogue with trade unions. It has suspended anxiety about skill shortages. It has cowed workforces that might otherwise have challenged the erosion of collective rights. More generally, economic recession has encouraged a political style remarkable in Britain for its degree of intolerance.

The Public Sector

The shock of the recession has been all the greater for the British public sector because it has been accompanied by a government with an unprecedented preference for private-sector solutions. The industrial relations consequences have been particularly traumatic because of the government's departure from its predecessors' policy of encouraging public-sector collective bargaining. There are almost seven million employees in the British public sector, approximately 29 percent of the employed workforce, spread across central and local government, education, health, fuel and power, transport, communications, and a number of nationalized manufacturing concerns. By the 1980s over 80 percent of these employees were unionized, and collective bargaining played a central part in the management of employment relations for all but the police and armed forces.

The 1970s had seen a growing challenge to the established practices of public-sector industrial relations. Financial stringency had come to almost every industry and service, bringing pressure on labor utilization and costs. Partly because of this, the public-sector workforce, traditionally docile other than in coal-mining, had become remarkably strike-prone. Throughout the 1970s successive governments had suffered serious political damage from such strikes. By adopting a robustly unconciliatory attitude to trade unions, the Conservative government that came into office in 1979 has been able to make considerable political advantage out of the disruption of public industries and services, successfully standing up to sustained strike action in the civil service, health service, railways, steel industry, and coal-mining, as well as more minor action elsewhere. Its only substantial reversal was in the historically surprising terrain of the water and sewage industry, where the unions' success in a pay claim was aided by an unusually maladroit group of employers.

The most extreme measure that the government took against public-sector trade unionism was its banning of existing unions from the large security, telecommunications, and intelligence headquarters at Cheltenham in 1984. The almost fully unionized staff were offered £1000 each to renounce their membership on penalty of dismissal or redeployment if they refused. The action soured industrial relations throughout the civil service, and it is unclear whether the new house union established by the authorities will behave very differently from its more independent predecessors. A more subtle measure was the government's weakening of the unity of the health service unions by giving preferential treatment on pay to those nurses whose union was unaffiliated to the Trades Union Congress (Winchester 1985). Specific new legal restrictions on bargaining in essential public services are in prospect.

This policy of withdrawal from previous governments' acceptance of collective bargaining has been closely associated with one of reducing the size of the public sector by selling off parts to private enterprise and by subcontracting particular functions where possible. The telecommunications industry has been the largest component to be "privatized" so far, but all or part of the nationalized aircraft, shipbuilding, air transport, sea ferry, car manufacturing, haulage, oil extraction, and oil refining industries have received, or are due to receive, similar treatment. The pressure to subcontract activities has been intensified throughout local authorities, the health service, education, and road and rail passenger transport, with catering, cleaning, laundry work, and the like being put out to often nonunionized private firms. Union opposition has had minimal impact upon these developments.

One of the more puzzling features of the government's policy towards the public sector has been its apparent willingness to precipitate open conflict with trade unions, at enormous cost, when the same managerial objectives could probably have been achieved through negotiation. In the railways, major stoppages resulted in 1982 when the government used its influence over funding to force a confrontation over a relatively minor question of working arrangements (Ferner 1985). In the steel industry in 1980, an unprecedentedly low wage offer was announced at the same time as a dramatically increased forecast of labor force reductions, triggering a bitter three-month strike in a hitherto peaceful industry (Hartley et al. 1983). The massive coal strike of 1984 and 1985 was precipitated against all the odds when the manager previously associated with cuts in the steel industry was placed in charge, crystallizing opposition to a program of pit closures that had been progressing uneventfully for years. Whatever their broader symbolic impact, it is not evident that these disputes will create more tractable unions, or improved day-to-day bargaining relationships, in the industries concerned.

Conflicts over labor force reductions are generally once-and-for-all matters, ending with the departure of the workers whose jobs have gone. Conflicts over pay, affecting those in work, are perennial. The coming of high unemployment and major public expenditure cuts has to some extent protected Mrs. Thatcher's government from public-sector pay disputes that plagued governments of the 1970s. It is unlikely that this circumstance will endure, particularly if inflation starts to rise with a recovery in the world economy or sustained deterioration in the exchange rate. So far, however, it has been possible to dismantle much of the formal machinery of public-sector pay policy in an attempt to create crude proxies for market forces.

The Conservative government abolished the short-lived attempt to have a standing commission to link pay throughout the public services to prevailing levels elsewhere. It also broke a similar, but more firmly established, comparability arrangement for the civil service. A linkage remains for the armed forces but is under threat for the police and fire services. Instead the government has tried to restrain bargaining in the public services by strict limits on their overall budgets, in the hope that this will also encourage increased labor productivity. But there is an unavoidable involvement of government in setting the assumed pay increases built into the overall budgets. Furthermore, productivity-increasing measures have been inhibited by the desire of the government, in its efforts to contain public expenditure, to centralize, rather than devolve, control. Even if fresh legislative powers are taken to inhibit strikes in essential services, public-sector pay is likely to become a major problem area, made worse by the disarray into which established bargaining arrangements have been thrown.

The Private Sector

It might have been expected that changes in legislation and in labor market circumstances that came with the 1980s would have been seized by private-sector employers as an opportunity to make a counterattack on trade unionism, and especially on the workplace trade union organizations that had developed so strongly in the previous two decades. In 1979 and 1980 a great deal of publicity was given to just such an attack on shop stewards at the largest factory of British Leyland, the state-owned car firm. But, as subsequent surveys have shown, this was unusual. Employers have tended to avoid direct attacks on their shop steward organizations, preferring to achieve changes in working practices through collective bargaining, although in a distinctly modified and diluted form.

There is substantial, and encouragingly consistent, evidence on recent developments in bargaining. Three studies have been made of manufacturing industry, the part of the private sector most seriously affected by the recession and overseas competition. In 1981 Chadwick studied ten factories in a local labor market, interviewing management and union representatives. In 1983 Batstone conducted a postal survey of industrial relations managers that yielded replies from 133 factories. In 1984 Edwards had the general managers interviewed at a stratified sample of 229 factories with 250 or more employees. Both the latter studies permitted comparisons with a survey of manufacturing industry that had been carried out in 1978 (Brown 1981); the strictness and similarity of their sampling techniques makes the comparison of the earlier survey with Edwards's particularly reliable.

The studies all make it abundantly clear that there have recently been widespread changes in working practices. Batstone found that 86 percent of managers reported major changes during the previous five years. Edwards found that 84 percent of factories had had at least one major change, and 43 percent had experienced at least three, and that these had been particularly common in larger factories where shopfloor union organization was stronger. The majority of factories reported that labor utilization had been improved through acceptance of new technologies and through increased efficiency in the use of existing equipment. Substantial minorities reported more flexible working, changed demarcation lines, and overtime reduction. These changes had generally not been imposed in the face of union opposition. Edwards found that the managers in 73 percent of those factories achieving changes experienced no resistance at all from the workforce. In only 2 percent of cases did managers report that resistance was sufficiently strong to prevent proposed changes being carried out.

The lack of effective opposition to what appears to have been a widespread rolling back of union control over the conduct of work raises the question of whether there was an accompanying rolling back of union organization. It is clear from the studies that there was not. Although the character of collective bargaining may have been modified, the structure of workplace unionism is remarkably unchanged. Both Batstone and Edwards found there to have been no significant change in the proportion of factories where trade unions were recognized, or where senior shop stewards were recognized, since 1978. Nor, despite the 1980 and 1982 Acts, was there any change in the percentage of factories with closed union shops. Edwards did find a reduction of a third in the proportion of factories with a shop steward who was paid to spend all his time on trade union duties, which is partially explained by the sharp decline in the size of British manufacturing establishments during the early 1980s. Although the proportion of factories reporting strikes in the two years up to 1984 had declined (reflecting the general fall in number of stoppages in Table 1), the proportion reporting industrial action of any sort (overtime bans, go slows, and the like) had not. Batstone detected a reduction in the regularity of shop steward meetings and in the range of bargaining, which Chadwick's case studies confirm. In broad terms, however, these findings support the assertion made by four out of five managers to both Batstone and Edwards: that they had made no attempt to change their bargaining arrangements or to reduce the role of their stewards.

The nature of bargaining has, however, changed substantially; more accurately, it has continued to develop in ways in which it was already showing signs of developing in 1978, with the recession possibly having a catalytic effect in accelerating change. This applies to employer strategy in the choice of bargaining units. The postwar period has seen the weakening, at first slowly but in the 1970s very rapidly, of industry-wide bargaining in the private sector, and consequently in the role of employers' associations. The collapse of the labor market might have been expected to stem these developments and to revive employer solidarity with the prospect of raising bargaining above the level of the individual company and out of the hands of shop stewards. This has not happened. There is no evidence of a revival of industry-wide bargaining. Although Batstone's data are less positive, Edwards's leave no doubt that the move towards single-employer bargaining, and especially the fixing of pay through establishment-level negotiations, has continued strongly in the 1980s. Bargaining at establishment level has fitted in with employers' efforts to increase labor efficiency and has not, as would have been the case in the 1970s, been held back by an apprehension that shop stewards could force through interplant pay comparisons.

A similar story of accelerating change is apparent with the use of joint consultative arrangements. Traditionally, there has been a sharp distinction drawn in British industrial relations between bargaining and consultation. The first implies the threat of collective sanctions and the consequent probability that management might have to modify its intended actions; consultation, by contrast, is concerned with the exchange of information and opinion, unsullied by threat or by the need to reach agreement. There is, in practice, considerable overlap between them. In the immediate postwar period, joint consultative arrangements tended to fade away, either ignored or usurped by the emerging unofficial shop steward organizations whose concern was with bargaining. During the 1970s, as stewards came to have a more secure place in the workplace bargaining procedure, and with a greater public interest in worker participation, joint consultative arrangements reemerged, often dominated by union activists but seen as having a distinct, nonbargaining function (Daniel and Millward 1983). Chadwick, Batstone, and Edwards all report strong continued development of joint consultation. Edwards, for example, found the proportion of factories with joint consultative committees in his 1984 sample had risen to 78 percent from 63 percent of the comparable 1978 sample. All studies report a substantial rise in management's desire to involve unions in the running of their enterprise in a nonbargaining way through devices such as quality circles, improved newsletters, and briefing sessions. Even if some of this development is the temporary consequence of unions' weak bargaining position, it is important that managements are seeking to facilitate change through, rather than outside, union channels of representation.

This more compliant form of collective bargaining has been facilitated by changes in employment practice which have also been hastened by the recession. The rise in the proportion of female employment, of part-time employment, of self-employment, and of subcontracting has already been described. It has increased the part of the labor force which is to varying extents peripheral to normal bargaining arrangements and harder to organize effectively in trade unions.

Substantial change in the ways in which labor acquires its skills is another contributory factor. Skills are becoming less industry- or occupation-specific and more related to the needs of individual companies and their current production processes. Occupational apprenticeship schemes have been in decline for many years, partly because of the decline of the more traditional technologies with which they have become associated. A more abrupt blow to industry-wide training arrangements has come with the abolition of 20 of the 27 statutory industrial Training Boards since 1980. These bipartite bodies laid down standards, defined modules, and monitored skill certification. In their place has come a mixture of more or less adequate arrangements for which the emphasis is generally on company-specific training with little or no union involvement. Skills are less acquired through a single course at the start of the employee's career and more on an incremental basis as the career develops. This leads to individuals having more idiosyncratic job descriptions and thus less opportunity and inclination to compare and identify themselves with employees outside their own firm. The weakening of the terminology of the labor market has the effect of weakening the basis of solidarity of the labor movement.

Alongside these developments in the ways in which labor is contracted and trained are complementary developments in the way in which it is motivated. For those in relatively secure full-time employment, the shift to some sort of variable, discretionary salary system continues, more codified where the employees are unionized but still more geared to the characteristics of the individual than where fixed wage rates prevail. Occupational pension schemes have developed rapidly in recent years and other nonpay fringe benefits, for long relatively neglected in Britain, have become important, contributing to the opacity of the labor market for those in less peripheral jobs. For them the means to improvement increasingly lie within the firm, rather than outside the firm within a defined occupational group. For those who are more likely to be unionized, there is thus the paradox that the means by which they are motivated are becoming increasingly individualistic.

Contributing to the more compliant form of collective bargaining that is accompanying these developments is a widespread experimentation with incentive payment schemes that seek, through profit-sharing, share ownership, factory bonuses, and similar devices, to inculcate in employees a sense of identity with the particular sphere of financial accountability defined by management. More generally, employers are increasingly defining bargaining units in ways that are geared more to the circumstances of their product markets and the internal structures of their firms, and less to the labor market circumstances of their employees. This presents trade unions with formidable problems of organization.

Trade Unions

Trade union membership has declined sharply with the rise of unemployment in the 1980s. Having risen steadily from 45 percent of the labor force in 1969 to 55 percent—nearly 13½ million members—in 1979, it tumbled back to 45 percent in 1983. Much of this decline can, however, be accounted for by the contraction of heavily unionized manufacturing and public-sector industries, rather than employer hostility or employee disaffection. With some form of closed union shop covering a half of union members, and with union dues deducted by check-off arrangements for over 80 percent, there is unlikely to be further substantial collapse in membership.

As important as the magnitude of trade unionism is, however, its character, in terms of its coherence as a movement, range of objectives, and capacity to modify undesired employer actions. This is strongly influenced by the way unions are organized. There is good reason to believe that developments in union organization, in combination with the developments just mentioned in employment practice, have contributed to the more compliant character of private-sector unionism suggested by the survey evidence. They are likely to make this compliance more than just a temporary response to the collapse of the labor market. The undue reliance placed by unions on shop stewards in the 1960s and 1970s appears to be producing a parochial, fragmented, and more managerially malleable form of unionism in the 1980s.

Although workplace organization has, to varying extents, long been a distinctive feature of much British private-sector trade unionism, it traditionally depended heavily upon union resources outside the individual workplace or company. Full-time officials and bodies such as district committees provided bargaining strategy and support with a perspective far broader than that of a single firm. Furthermore, industry-wide agreements, disputes procedures, apprenticeship schemes, and the like provided an authoritative set of standards to which shop stewards in difficulty could appeal.

These external supports became increasingly weakened and irrelevant during the 1960s and 1970s. Shop steward organizations gained confidence, and they were copied through much of the private sector, encouraged by left-wing union leaderships and growing management recognition. Industry-wide bargaining arrangements increasingly gave way to those based on individual employers. Union resources thus shifted to being heavily dependent upon sources located within the enterprise, usually within individual establishments, whether for finance, collective action, job control, or collective agreements. Despite growing membership, the number of officials employed by unions barely changed. Members' contributions, which provide over 80 percent of unions' income, fell from an annual average (already low in international terms) of 0.38 percent of average male annual earnings in 1960 to 0.30 percent in 1979. Bargaining resources external to individual firms were withering.

At least as significant as the growing isolation of shop steward organizations was their increasing dependence upon management. In the 1950s the stewards with whom junior managers dealt on a generally unofficial and covert basis relied on the voluntary contribution of time and money by union members. But, as management increased its recognition of stewards with the rapid development of formal factory and company bargaining, so it also increased the resources available to them. It became normal for stewards to be allowed to hold meetings on company time, to have access to office facilities, and, in larger workplaces, for one or more senior stewards to be allowed to spend their whole time on union business at the company's expense. The voluntary contributions of members became unnecessary; the records of one fairly typical powerful steward committee show the income raised from members declining from the mid-1960s. Many managements, on deciding to have factory or company agreements where there was no local bargaining tradition, established fully-resourced steward organizations for nothing. By the late 1970s, full-time shop stewards, who had been relatively unusual 20 years earlier, easily outnumbered the full-time officials employed by their unions. Equally important, for practical purposes both procedural and substantive agreements were, for the majority of private-sector union members, specific to their individual employers and were largely unwritten.

These emerging features of much private-sector union organization help explain the two puzzles that are presented by the survey findings. First, why it is that manufacturing industry has recently experienced such historically remarkable changes in working practices. Second, why managements have apparently achieved them through, rather than despite, workplace collective bargaining.

There is indeed ample evidence that, when shop stewards are up against poorly coordinated managements in relatively comfortable product market positions, they can achieve a substantial degree of control over both the conduct of work and the level of pay with little need for help from the union outside. This can be evident even when the level of unemployment in the local labor market is high. But where managements bring a sense of strategy to the conduct of industrial relations, which may or may not be associated with a competitive product market, they can make the relative isolation of the shop steward organization into a powerful force for change. In the first place, in multifactory companies it has proved possible to take advantage of the factory-based parochialism of steward organization. Secondly, shop stewards are immediately accountable to their electorates in ways that most union officials are not, and as a result they tend to be less concerned to preserve employment per se, and more willing to accept job losses arising from voluntary redundancy or natural wastage than full-time officials, especially if their remaining members believe that their pay or job security will benefit. Thirdly, the decline of industry-wide agreements and training arrangements has removed many of the constraints on staffing levels, job descriptions, and working practices that might previously have existed. Small wonder that trade union leaders of the 1950s, often portrayed as right-wing bureaucrats, viewed the acceleration of the shop steward bandwagon with dismay.

There is little sign of trade unions going against this tendency towards what, in its more extreme form, might be characterized as de facto enterprise or establishment unionism. On the contrary, shaken by technological change and the forces of international competition, they appear to see their future to depend upon successful adaptation to it. Increasingly unions are becoming more open in the membership they will accept, weakening their attachment to particular technologies, industries, or occupations. They are vying for the agreements requiring one union to cover the whole workforce that many newly arrived companies are asking for. There is, furthermore, little enthusiasm for the rebuilding of industry-wide agreements or the regaining of union influence over training.

This picture of growing fragmentation is reinforced by evidence from the wider labor movement. The proportion of voting trade unionists who have voted for the Labour Party in general elections has declined steadily, from 73 percent in 1964, to 55 percent in 1974, to 51 percent in 1979, and finally, with the big surge in unemployment, to as low as 39 percent in 1983. On the other hand, the ballots, required by the 1984 Act to permit unions to levy funds for political purposes, have been yielding powerfully affirmative results. Opinion polls suggest that, under the requirements of the 1984 Act, relatively few unions will be permitted by their members to contribute to the Labour Party, a source which hitherto has provided nearly 80 percent of the Party's funds. Trade unions' parliamentary channel of influence is in serious jeopardy.

Is the conclusion to be that Britain's trade union movement is becoming like that of the sort of Third World country which has a highly unionized and fractious public sector, and a private sector in which an elite of company unions stand aloof from the unorganized mass? Such a prediction is premature. A new generation of union leaders is taking over, well aware that it can no longer rely upon shop steward organizations largely taking care of themselves. Instead, full-time union officials will have to return to their prewar position as the front-line organizers, going out to recruit and bargain with particular emphasis on service industries (Edmonds 1984). Already average subscriptions have been raised from 0.30 percent of average male annual earnings in 1979 to 0.36 percent in 1983. The lessons of the Mineworkers' defeat, and the increased use of litigation against unions by both employers and members, are likely to force greater centralization of both funds and discipline. But the factor most likely to stem the fragmentation of trade unions is the 1984 Trade Union Act. Difficult to evade and difficult to repeal, the threat it poses to union finances, and the greater legitimacy it gives to approved strike action, will force a greater discipline in unions' internal politics. It is likely to encourage electoral 'party' organizations within unions, to strengthen the coordinating role of full-time officials, and to assist the reconciliation of inter-union rivalries. If trade unions can meet this challenge, history may judge that Mrs. Thatcher's government has provided the most important legislative support there has yet been to the unity of their movement.

Conclusion

The effect of the world recession of the 1980s upon Britain has been made distinctive by the country's emergence as a major oil producer and by the unprecedentedly uncomprising economic policy adopted by its government. Manufacturing industry and the public sector have been particularly severely hit. The shock to the collective bargaining practices that dominate them has probably come less as a result of the high prevailing levels of unemployment than of the pressures of competition and budgetary restraint which have forced their managements to strive for the improved utilization of labor. The evidence suggests that in manufacturing industry there have been substantial achievements in this respect. The trauma of international competition appears to have accelerated developments in collective bargaining already under way which are making it more responsive to companies' market needs than hitherto. There appears to be a strong preference among employers to achieve productivity improvements by working through trade union channels rather than by obliterating them.

It is, at present, harder to credit success to those areas where the government has had direct influence. Its withdrawal from the traditional forms of collective bargaining in the public sector has been marked by embittered relationships and costly stoppages which may outweigh any improvements in labor utilization. If and when inflation starts to rise, the problems of developing a public-sector pay policy are likely to be greater than before. The magnitude of the recession has, however, permitted the government to feel sufficiently free of the need for trade union support to pass some major acts of labor legislation. Those parts of them relating to trade union government and immunities are likely to have a lasting, and far from simple, impact upon British industrial relations.

References

Bain, G. S., and R. Price. "Union Growth: Dimensions, Determinants, and Destiny." In *Industrial Relations in Britain*, ed G. S. Bain. Oxford: Blackwell, 1983.

Batstone, E. V. *Working Order*. Oxford: Blackwell, 1984.

Brown, W. A., ed. *The Changing Contours of British Industrial Relations*. Oxford: Blackwell, 1981.

Chadwick, M. G. "The Recession and Industrial Relations." *Employee Relations* 5 (1983).

Daniel, W. W., and N. Millward. *Workplace Industrial Relations in Britain*. London: Heinemann, 1983.

Department of Employment. *New Earnings Survey, 1983*. London: HMSO, 1984.

————. *Employment Statistics: Historical Supplement* No. 1. London: HMSO, 1984.

Edmonds, J. "Decline of the Big Battalions." *Personnel Management* (March 1984).

Edwardes, M. *Back from the Brink*. London: Pan Books, 1983.

Edwards, P. K. "The Management of Productivity." IRRU Discussion Paper, 1984.

————. "Managing Labour Relations Through the Recession." *Employee Relations* (1985).

Ferner, A. "Political Constraints and Management Strategies." *British Journal of Industrial Relations* 23 (March 1985).

Hartley, J., J. Kelly, and N. Nicholson. *Steel Strike*. London: Batsford Academic, 1983.

Institute for Employment Research. *Review of the Economy and Employment.* Coventry: IER. University of Warwick, 1983.

Lewis, R. M. "Collective Labour Law." In *Industrial Relations in Britain*, ed. G. S. Bain. Oxford: Blackwell, 1983.

National Institute for Economic and Social Research. *Review.* London: NIESR, various issues.

Winchester, D. "Labour Relations and Disputes Settlements in the Public Services: United Kingdom." In *Labour Relations and Disputes Settlements in the Public Service*, ed. T. Treu. Geneva: International Labour Organisation, 1985.

Chapter 6

Economic Change and Industrial Relations in France

Francois Sellier
*Laboratoire d'Économie et de Sociologie
du Travail, Aix-en-Provence*
Emeritus Professor, University of Paris-Nanterre

To what extent has the economic change which began in France in 1974 influenced the industrial relations system? For an answer to this question it is necessary to present a historical panorama of the economic, social, and political scene.

Economic and Political Background

Social and economic events were occurring in a climate of strong economic expansion until 1974. Industrial production rose by about 50 percent from 1967 to 1974, continued to grow but at a slower rate until 1976 (after a slump in 1975), and remained rather stable thereafter until 1984. However, industrial employment decreased continuously, from 7.7 million in 1974 to 6.2 million in 1984, although at the same time tertiary private employment rose from 6 to 7.2 million. There has been net aggregate unemployment, resulting from both a lack of new jobs and a large increase in the labor force (active population)—from 20,400,000 in 1968 to 23,500,000 in 1982. The employed labor force numbered 20 million in 1968, rising to 21 million in 1975 and to 21,500,000 in 1982 (Institut National de la Statistique et des Etudes Economiques-INSEE 1984).

This great economic expansion in the 1960s and 1970s occurred at the same time the economy was undergoing important structural changes. Not only was it rapidly becoming internationalized, but trade within the European community was growing significantly. At the same time the rate of adjustment of imports to exports was much more favorable with underdeveloped and postcolonial countries than within the European Economic Community (EEC).

The regional structure of industry also was being greatly altered. Rather than highly concentrated development, there was movement towards a more balanced growth. The most developed regions showed a relative decline, although the general prosperity helped them hold or slightly increase their employment around a yearly rate of 1.5 percent (Paris and Lyon regions). But in less developed industrial regions (west, northwest, center), industrial employment grew 5 percent annually from 1968 to 1974. The increase in female employment in rural areas was especially important in these regions, although there was a greater percentage of women in the labor force everywhere and in all occupations.

Real gross national product (GNP) rose almost continuously during this period, as did real wages until 1981. Unemployment insurance compensated about 70 percent of individual wages, and the social security system covered health expenses for every employed and unemployed worker (70 percent of medical cases are compensated 100 percent).

Social and Political Evolution

The social and political evolution during the post-1974 period was largely determined by social and political events after 1968. The most important of them was the students' uprising of May 1968 when schools and universities closed for one month. This demonstration was accompanied by a two-week general strike among blue- and white-collar workers in the private and public sectors.

These events provided evidence of a deep feeling of uneasiness towards authoritarian and impersonal relations in schools as well as in plants and offices, which was further aggravated by the fact that unemployment had been rising slightly but continuously from 1965 onwards and rather rapidly in 1967, at a time when the mass of young people born during the baby boom were arriving at working age.

Charles de Gaulle succeeded in getting the situation in hand, dissolving the National Assembly which had been elected in 1967, and gaining a stronger majority in the newly elected one. However, his political authority had been unsettled, and when he failed to get a majority in a referendum aimed at changing the role of the Senate, he resigned. George Pompidou, elected president in June 1969, chose Jacques Chaban Delmas as prime minister; Jacques Delors, a future Socialist minister, was his adviser.

It would not be accurate to say that this was the beginning of a new era. When Pompidou was prime minister during the de Gaulle presidency, he had already successfully induced the social partners to bargain at the national level on illness compensation and on reduction of working hours (still 45 hours in 1965). More important in the 1960s was the government's role in solving the unemployment crisis in the coal mines and in the steel industry by providing compensation for wage losses as well as redundancy measures; these were used as models in the 1970s and 1980s when unemployment was widespread.

However, the 1968 "Grenelle protocol" between unions and managements had opened a period of bargaining that matured in 1969–1970 with several important agreements that substantially changed the industrial relations system. The most influential of these was the agreement of December 1968, soon followed by a law, giving unions the right to organize locals at the company level. Before that, only committees and representatives elected by *all* employees were compulsory. Management had always opposed the principle of a legal representation of unions inside the plant, although there were such locals in large plants.

This marked the beginning of a period of "consensus policy" which will be described in some detail below. It is important to get an overview of it now by listing the national agreements concluded between unions and management, always under government pressure.

March 1969: National agreement on employment security (compensating workers for loss of wages in new employment; improving the possibility of reemployment, especially through training; improving the right of committees to information on projected redundancies).

April 1970: General agreement to conclude branch agreements aimed at giving blue-collar workers the same rights as white-collar personnel concerning the payment of wages in case of illness, seniority premiums, etc. (*accords de mensualisation*).

July 1970: National agreement for providing training possibilities during employment.

March 1972: National agreement on preretirement wage compensation.

October 1974: National agreement on 100 percent wage compensation for certain unemployed workers.

March 1975: National agreement on the improvement of physical working conditions.

During the same period two laws were enacted that granted more procedural guarantees for workers in case of either individual or mass dismissals (1973, 1975).

Such measures helped to maintain social peace while unemployment was increasing; however, employers continued to complain of the rigidities these laws had introduced in the management of employment. This resistance culminated in 1984 with the opening of discussions between employers and unions on "flexibility." The first phase of these discussions, in December 1984, did not succeed, nor did their reopening in February 1985, but new laws allow employers to achieve some of the demanded flexibility (e.g., right to hire employees for longer fixed contracts).

It is clear that the government's consensus policy was rather successful well before the presidency of Francois Mitterand. Not only did President Pompidou convince employers to bargain with unions at industry and multi-industry levels, but after his death and the May 1974 election of Giscard d'Estaing as president with Jacques Chirac as prime minister, the same policy of cooperation with management for "continuous bargaining" with unions was pursued. Chirac launched a program of economic growth to reduce unemployment, but inflation and external deficits grew rapidly. Raymond Barre, nominated as prime minister in August 1976, reversed this policy. He insisted on the necessity of limiting wage growth.

The new economic policy improved the balance of trade, but did not improve the inflation rate nor the trend of unemployment (1,800,000 in 1981). An alliance between socialists and communists allowed Mitterand to win the 1981 presidential election. From June 1981 to June 1982, the Mauroy government (with four communist members) attempted to promote economic recovery by increasing low incomes, family allowances, and public employment; the number of unemployed stabilized, but the rise of prices and imports created a large trade deficit.

The policy was completely reversed in June 1982. Prices and wages were frozen for six months, and the government declared that the purchasing power of wages should now be reduced. In the social field, several laws were enacted to increase the power of unions and committees: imposing the duty to bargain once each year on wages and hours in branches and enterprises; limiting the right of employers to hire on short, fixed-duration contracts; allowing the committees to be informed in advance of any economic decision having an impact on personnel and allowing them to call in experts to assess the social consequences of introducing new technology; and establishing workshop consultation procedures, etc. (*lois Auroux*).

The new socialist economic policy succeeded in the areas of prices and trade balance, but unemployment increased again in 1983 and continued to rise dramatically in 1984—from 2 million in April 1983 to 2,400,000 in December 1984 (10 percent of the labor force, seasonally adjusted).

In the industrial relations field the most important change was the 1969 reorganization of the employers' confederation, Conseil National du Patronat Français (CNPF). It has evolved from a loose association without any clear right of representation of its members to an organization with strong rights of representation—one which is now enabled to underwrite agreements with national workers' unions. The unions maintained their division between the communist-led Confédération Générale du Travail (CGT, with around 2 million members in 1974, 1,600,000 in 1984),[1] the Confédération Française Démocratique du Travail (CFDT, 900,000 members); the Force Ouvrière (CGT-FO, with a rising membership of about 900,000); and the Confédération Française des Travailleurs Chrétiens (the Christian CFTC). Middle management and some engineers are members of the Confédération Générale des Cadres (CGC).

In the 1982 national elections of labor court representatives, the votes were as follows: CGT, 44.9 percent; CFDT, 23.5 percent; FO, 16.7 percent; CFTC, 6.8 percent; CGC, 5.6 percent (with an abstention rate of 32.4 percent and other union votes of 2.3 percent). Bargaining procedures are rather centralized, centralization having increased greatly since 1969 with the above-mentioned bargaining

---

[1] All numbers exclude retired members.

of interindustries' national agreements on special subjects. In addition, in each large industry (e.g., metals, chemicals, banks, insurance), and also in a number of small ones, collective agreements on wages and working conditions are signed either on a national or regional level. Traditionally, general agreements at the firm level have been the exception in some large companies.

Economic Restructuring and Evolution of Wages

Both attempts to promote economic recovery through direct credit or income expansion, in 1976 (Chirac) and 1981 (Mauroy), collapsed following increasing trade deficits primarily due to a structural weakness in the industrial system. But another factor should be added: Until 1982 it was politically impossible to lower the rate of earnings in order to adjust the purchasing power of wages to the higher costs prevailing because of the two oil shocks. These two factors will be developed in the following section.

International Trade

The unfavorable structure of France's international trade promptly produced heavy deficits in the balance of trade (see Table 1). As a whole, the value ratio of exports to imports improved

TABLE 1
Balance of Payments (billions of francs)

	1973	1974	1975	1976	1977	1978	1979	1980	1981	1982
Goods	−6.7	−35.5	−6.7	−39.0	−30.3	−15.9	−36.1	−89.3	−89.1	−138.2
Services	13.1	16.6	15.6	19.9	25.1	30.2	33.4	33.9	34.7	42.5
Surplus or deficit	6.4	−18.9	9.9	−19.1	−5.2	14.3	−2.7	−55.4	−54.4	−95.7
Nonfinancial operation (balance)	−2.6	−30.6	−1.6	−27.2	−14.2	−14.3	−1.5	−39.8	−43.9	−105.2

Source: Le mouvement économique de la France, 1949–1979, INSEE, p. 198, and Rapport sur les comptes de la nation (1982), Les Collections de i'INSEE, 108-109, p. 89.

between 1973 and 1981, but with a strong imbalance between industrial and developing countries—a decreasing ratio for industrial countries and an increasing ratio for developing countries (Delattre 1983, p. 15). The rate of penetration of external products in the internal market rose from 22 to 31 percent between 1973 and 1981.

External deficits can be seen during the whole period of 1973–1982, but they increase dramatically with the second oil shock of 1979–80 and in 1982, following the economic policy of the left. To this first constraint is added the rigidity of real incomes and wages over this same period.

Incomes and Consumption

With regard to incomes and consumption, a comparison of France and Germany illustrates the difference in management of the two crises which struck industrial, and especially European, economies from 1973 to 1983. Enterprises and government faced many more difficulties in France than in Germany in adjusting income and consumption to the new international conditions; on the other hand, efforts to reduce energy expenses—especially for oil—and investment for production and research on new energy sources were more important in France.

TABLE 2
Percent Increase of Average Hourly Real Earnings
of Workers in Industry (including mining and construction)

	1970/75	1975/76	1976/77	1977/78	1978/79	1979/80	1980/81	1981/82
France	5.6	5.8	2.8	2.4	0.7	2.4	0.9	3.3
Germany	2.9	2.9	3.1	3.3	0.2	2.3	0.9	0.6

Source: Chiffres significatifs de l'évolution sociale dans le C.E.E., Commission des Communautés Européennes, Direction Générale de l'Emploi et des Affaires Sociales, April 1983.

The difference is particularly marked for the period 1970–1975 when the rate of growth of real earnings in France was almost double that in Germany (Table 2). After 1979, in the two years following the second oil crisis, the behavior of the two economies was similar, but the political victory of the French left in June 1981 induced a strong increase in household consumption: GNP growth was 2.4 percent from April 1981 to July 1982, whereas household consumption increased 5 percent, with a compensating external deficit. This increase in consumption was mainly the result of the rise in nominal wages and a decline in household savings; it could not be totally attributed to the rise of family benefits under edicts of the new government, the effect of which is estimated to be only 0.4 percent of the 2.4 percent growth in GNP (Meunier 1983, pp. 12–13). However, the main cause of the rise in wages was the increase in the national minimum wage in 1981 and 1982, a factor already important in 1973 (see Table 3).

TABLE 3
Rising Purchasing Power of the Legal Minimum Wage (SMIC)

	1973	1974	1975	1976	1977	1978	1979	1980	1981	1982	1983
Yearly nominal rise of hourly SMIC (%)	18.1	23.3	19.2	14.7	12.7	12.8	12.5	15.6	18.1	17.6	10.1
Yearly rise of consumers' price index	7.3	13.7	11.7	9.6	9.3	9.0	10.7	13.5	13.4	11.8	9.4
Yearly rise of hourly SMIC purchasing power	10.8	9.5	7.5	5.1	3.4	3.9	1.8	2.1	4.7	5.8	0.7

Source: INSEE, Données Sociales 1983, SMIC, Fig. 5, p. 107; prices, Fig. 6, p. 107.

The disposable income of households depends not only on the evolution of wages and enterprises' incomes, but also on social benefits, taxes, and social contributions, the impact of which has been increasing (Table 4).

TABLE 4
Change in Structure of Disposable Income of Households
(percent)

	1975	1978	1982
Net wages (social contributions deducted)	50.4	50.2	47.7
Income of individual enterprise	16.6	15.3	13.8
Income of property	10.8	10.4	11.0
Direct income	77.8	75.9	72.5
Income tax	−7.0	−8.1	−8.9
Social benefits	+29.1	+31.9	+36.0
Other transfers	+0.1	+0.3	+0.4

Source: INSEE, Données Sociales 1984, p. 175.

Social benefits as a share of disposable income have increased, partly as a systematic government policy especially for pensions, but also as an involuntary consequence of the rise in health expenditures. The socialist government increased family allowances in 1982 to offset the wage freeze policy; however, in the long term the family allowance share of total social benefits has decreased significantly as benefits were more and more geared to low-income families with the introduction of means tests for some of them (Table 5). Family allowances, old age assistance benefits (as distinguished from pensions), and unemployment benefits as well as health benefits (reimbursement of costs and 50 to 100 percent of lost wages) have an important antipoverty effect: an average worker's family with three children and only one wage-earner receives half of its income from family allowances.

Rising unemployment has put pressure on the social security system and obliged the government to increase contributions. At the same time, the reduction in hours of work has decreased total labor earnings.

TABLE 5
Structure of Social Benefits

	1960	1970	1980	1982
Unemployment and workers' adaptation	1.2	2.0	6.9	9.7
Old age	33.7	39.8	42.8	41.4
Health	33.1	35.9	35.3	34.1
Family	31.0	21.2	14.7	14.5
Other and adjustment	1.0	1.1	0.3	0.3
Total	100	100	100	100

Source: INSEE, Données Sociales 1984, p. 179.

Unemployment and Earnings

As noted above, unemployment has been particularly significant for industrial employees, whereas until recently employment was increasing in the private- and public-tertiary sectors. The increase in the unemployment rate was greatest in 1974–1975, with a lower but continuous trend thereafter. The number of unemployed has risen from 400,000 in 1973 to 1 million at the end of 1975, to 2 million by December 1982, and to approximately 2,400,000 by the end of 1984 through the first half of 1985. It was mainly a movement of structural unemployment, but at the end of the period demand deficient unemployment increased as governmental measures to decelerate wages and increase taxes tended to decrease consumption. All these factors influence growth of the "net wage fund" (wage fund minus social contributions; see Table 6).

TABLE 6
Quarterly Rate of Growth of the Purchasing Power
of the "Net Wage Fund" (1982–1984)

1982-1	1982-2	1982-3	1982-4	1982/81	1983-1	1983-2	1983-3	1983-4	1983/82	1984-1	1984-2
+0.4	−0.2	−0.7	−0.3	+0.2	+0.5	−0.7	−0.3	+0.3	−0.8	−0.1	−0.2

Source: INSEE, Tendences de la conjoncture, note de synthèse, April 1983, pp. 40; July 1984, p. 20.

Even without taking account of rising social contributions, the reduced hours of work significantly influenced the rate of growth of effective money and real earnings at the end of the period, especially for higher wage and salary earners. As shown in Table 7,

TABLE 7
Rate of Growth of Monthly Money and Real Earnings
(Workers, Technicians, and Engineers)

					Workers					
Money	17.5	18.7	15.1	13.1	12.0	13.0	14.8	14.1	18.6	10.7
Real	3.8	7.0	5.5	3.8	3.0	2.3	1.3	0.7	6.8	1.3
					Technicians and Engineers					
Money	13.1	14.3	8.9	9.9	11.0	11.0	12.5	14.1	13.2	8.3
Real	−0.6	2.6	−0.7	0.6	2.0	0.3	−1.0	0.7	1.4	−1.1

Source: INSEE, Données Sociales 1984, p. 109, and Bulletin Mensuel du Ministere des Affaires Sociales, June 1984, p. 21.

pressure to hold down wages was always more effective for technicians and engineers than for workers, whose real monthly wages began to decline seriously only after 1979. This is surprising from a strictly economic standpoint since the unemployment rate is lower for technicians and engineers than for workers (Table 8).

TABLE 8
Registered Unemployment[a] and Labor Force
for Different Categories in the Private Economy

	Unemployed[b] (x)	Active Labor Force in Private Sector (y)	(x/y) x 100
"Cadres"	60,000	3,000,000	2.0%
White collar	950,000	4,000,000	23.7%
Workers	1,000,000	8,000,000	12.5%

Source: Unemployment: Ministere de l'Emploi, Service des Etudes et Statistiques, Données Mensuelles; active labor force: census.
[a] January 1983 (rounded)
[b] All demands of employment, including people looking for a first job or re-entering the labor market.

Conclusion

Adjustment to the new economic conditions that developed after 1973 was quite difficult in France. The response in wages and consumption to the 1973 and 1979 oil shocks was inadequate, the consequence being heavy trade deficits. It seemed that the government's main preoccupation was with maintaining a certain level of social peace; apparently it feared that any decision to cut purchasing power would provoke a reaction from the workers. This policy was pursued until 1979, then abandoned by the Barre government, reestablished with the first phase of the socialist administration, and abandoned again in June 1982.

This analysis is not in accord with the general view that French unions are weak. since such weakness—increased by growing unemployment—would have allowed the government as well as management to freeze wages as early as 1974. In fact, although total union membership is certainly rather low (and decreasing), it is the highest in some large corporations which may have the greatest influence on government decisions.

On the other hand, the unions' influence on government decisions is determined by their capacity to mobilize not only their members, but also every wage or salary earner whose interests are jeopardized. This capacity is not negligible, particularly considering that a number of political elections took place during this period. The policy of consensus was a response to this situation, and it is an interesting paradox that only the socialist government has been able to pursue, since 1982-1983, a policy of decreasing purchasing power.

The unions' weakness, however, is manifested by the fact that they give a higher priority to the interests of those employed, on whom they depend during elections for the business committees, than to the interests of the whole labor class. Only the CFDT proposed measures—such as reducing hours without full compensation—which were directly aimed—right or wrong—at sharing employment.

Government Policies

It has always been an important concern of French governments to use social policy as an element of economic policy. Anti-inflation programs regularly include the direct control of prices and wages as methods complementary to credit squeeze or regulation. As early as 1963, after the great coal miners' strike, the chief of the planning agency, Pierre Massé, organized a joint commission on incomes in order to discuss objectives and methods. The conference ended without concrete results as the social partners were suspicious of any incomes policy.

However, in the early 1960s Prime Minister Michel Debré insisted on the necessity of using government guidelines to limit the rise in wages to the rise in productivity. The government tried to induce employers, especially the large companies, to apply the wage policy by threatening to deny them their share of subsidies or public credits, or even of public contracts, if the wages of their employees rose more than those proposed by the guidelines. These methods were applied repeatedly during this period. At the same time, however, there were systematic efforts to obtain the consensus of workers as well as to encourage bargaining between unions and employers.

Consequently, it may be said that there was more continuity than change in the period following the two great oil crises, a continuity that was not denied by the socialist government from 1981 onward in either employment or income policies.

Employment and Training Policies

Until 1976 the unemployment policy consisted of a series of measures that rendered redundancies more difficult. From 1976 onward job-creation policies were added, especially for young people, aimed at improving their vocational education and training. First, the government of Raymond Barre tried to redevelop apprenticeship programs, which had been in decline since 1968. Three plans for young workers, called *pactes pour l'emploi des jeunes*, were organized between 1977 and 1981. Second, employers and government created a specific plan of action to increase the retraining of unskilled and unemployed young people at the plant level. That retraining effort was either through a single temporary contract (without any formal training obligation) between a firm and young workers *(stage pratique en enterprise)* or an employment training contract *(contrat emploi-formation)* without any obligation to hire the young workers at the end of the contract.

These policies had some positive results. About 1 million young workers received such contracts between 1975 and 1981 (62,000 in 1975 and 1976, 347,000 in 1978, 285,000 in 1979, and 372,000 in 1980). In addition, there was quite a strong development in apprenticeship during that period—120,000 apprentices in 1975 and double that number in 1981. Moreover, this type of action has the long-term consequence of improving firms' interest in training young people—interest that is still very low in France, especially in industry. Finally, youth unemployment as a percent of total unemployment stabilized between 1975 and 1982 at less than 40 percent.

Other results were more negative. The largest firms avoided these plans, preferring to utilize ordinary short-term contracts and temporary employment or to continue hiring more experienced workers. Small firms tend to have more efficient and selective hiring policies, and they in fact refuse to make contracts with the most unskilled and marginal young workers.

Organizing the training or retraining for these disadvantaged young workers was one of the original policies of the new socialist government. The goal was to provide minimum training assistance to young dropouts between ages 16 and 18 who were unemployed and without any vocational or even low-level general education. One of the unusual aspects of this plan was to provide part of the training in the schools and part in industrial plants *(formation en alternance)*. It is too soon for an evaluation, but no fewer than 150,000 young workers received this elementary training in 1982.

Another aspect of the socialist government's training policy is linked with industrial restructuring in the nationalized sector (steel, telecommunications, coal mining) or in the private sector (shipbuilding, motor vehicles). In the past, such restructuring plans were mainly social programs (preretirement opportunities, redundancy payments, high levels of unemployment compensation); subsidized periods of layoff with training, without the labor contract being cancelled, are the core of the new program, called *stage* or *congés de reconversion*. These plans will be negotiated between government, unions, and employers.

The most original policy of the socialist government is the institutionalization of solidarity contracts. One type of solidarity contract is for a firm, after negotiation with the Ministry of Labor, to recruit new workers at the same time they organize voluntary early retirement for older workers between the ages of 55 and 60. The second type, time-reducing, allows the firm to receive temporary monetary compensation for each new recruit hired as a result of at least a two-hour decrease in weekly working time.

The success of the early retirement solidarity contract has been rapid and general. Many older workers were impatiently waiting to be able to retire under customary financial arrangements (the pension was 70 percent of the last wage), and firms were interested in changing the demographic structure of their workforces. During 1982, 28,862 early retirement contracts were signed, involving 18,000 people. This type of action has been very efficient in the short term, but is too expensive as a long-term tool. The time-reducing solidarity contracts have been much less successful.

Because of continuing unemployment of young people, recent measures (1984–1985) offer 16- to 21-year-olds either new kinds of training or the possibility of part-time work on "collective utility jobs," with hourly compensation equal to about half the legal minimum wage.

Wage Policies

In December 1973 the government launched an anti-inflationary program. But after the death of President Pompidou and the May 1974 election of Giscard d'Estaing with Chirac as prime minister, the government stressed antiunemployment action, in their efforts to stimulate consumption and production. The failure of this policy was followed by the retreat of Chirac and the nomination of Barre as prime minister in August 1976, along with a new anti-inflationary program. This was a rather involuntary policy of stop and go, which was to be continued during the first and second phases of the socialist government.

Barre tried to combine a policy of limiting the money and budget deficit and controlling wages and prices, which included a price-freeze period in 1977. Guidelines to induce a decrease in the trend of rising wages were proposed to employers (see Tables 1 and 8). In another attempt to improve the control of wages, the government proposed to bargain on minimum annual earnings, including elements of wages not included in the national wage minimum.

At the same time the government limited increases in high wages (those more than 18,000 francs per month) to half the price rise and prohibited any increase in the highest wages (more than 20,000 francs per month); any excess above these norms was subject to a tax paid by the employers.

In the first period, the purchasing power of the total wage fund was raised in order to increase the lowest wages, especially those not far above the national minimum. In May 1978 the government invited the management confederation and unions to bargain in branches on the evolution of annual wage funds, a procedure similar to that being used in the nationalized industries.

Progressively, the principle of strictly maintaining the purchasing power of the wage fund—and at the same time relatively raising the lowest wages—takes the place of the principle of maintaining the purchasing power of middle wages but raising that of the wage fund. After a period of wage increase in 1981, the socialist government adopted the first principle; since June 1982, the principle of reducing purchasing power and abandonment of the de facto sliding scale has been considered a decisive rule. (The sliding scale has been illegal for all incomes except the national minimum since 1958.)

Consensus Policies

As discussed above, the Pompidou administration (1969–1974) encouraged the social partners to bargain on special matters (reducing hours, compensation of wages lost through illness, employment facilities), on the all-industries (*interprofessionnel*) level of either industries or companies; a 1971 law improved the possibilities of contracting at this particular level. We have already seen that several important national-level agreements for all industries were signed.

The propensity of governments to improve the status of workers is linked to the insertion of the industrial relations system into the political and economic systems. It is all the more important to obtain the goodwill of workers when the political equilibrium loses stability and when the economic situation deteriorates, as in May 1974 when, at the death of Pompidou, Giscard d'Estiang was elected president with only 50.8 percent of the vote (Mitterand received 49.2 percent) and unemployment was rising rapidly.

The new government launched a policy of austerity in 1974 and, in the interest of consensus, also a program to improve social relations within corporations. A commission was appointed to present a report on the subject (*rapport Pierre Sudreau* 1975). The report called for more recognition of the bargaining rights of unions in the plants and more recognition of the consultation rights of the enterprise committees to improve the conflict resolution process and generally effectuate the possibilities offered by the 1975 law on improving the quality of work.

The policy of austerity was followed in 1975 by one to promote economic growth; unfortunately, it had inflationary consequences and no salutary effect on the trend of unemployment.

Although the Barre government (August 1976) emphasized a new austerity policy rather than consensus, consensus was not completely lacking; there was an effort to increase low wages and to "reevaluate manual labor." However, the 1978 elections, which were won by the government, and the clash between the socialist and communist parties just before these elections, greatly discouraged the unions and allowed the government to strengthen the austerity policy and largely ignore consensus.

The results of this change in the political climate were increased taxes and social contributions, reduced unemployment benefits (in 1979), higher public tariffs, and flexible industrial prices. Budget equilibrium and balance of payment surpluses allowed the franc to stabilize versus the dollar, but not versus the mark. Unemployment continued to grow, and consumer prices rose.

After the 1981 elections were won by the left, the new government launched a series of nationalizations and, in the social field, raised the national minimum wage and some family allowances. The main effects, however, were the results of the passage of the numerous labor laws discussed above, the most important providing a yearly "duty to bargain" in plants, the right for a company's committee to designate experts to give evidence on its situation, and "a right of expression" for workers at the shop levels.

These "qualitative" laws probably cushioned the impact of the government's revised social policy of July 1982 which, for the first time since the 1950s, froze prices and wages for six months, maintained and then reduced the purchasing power of wages, increased social contributions paid by employees, and instituted a policy of industrial restructuring which increased unemployment to 2,400,000 by the end of 1984.

Management Policies

The financial position of enterprises deteriorated from 1974 to 1982: gross profits declined from 27.1 percent of the value added to 21.7 percent. The main cause of this deterioration was the rise of social contributions rather than of wages (see Table 9).

TABLE 9
Structure of Value Added, Investment Rate
(Private sector, in percentages)

	1974	1975	1976	1977	1978	1979	1980	1981	1982
Wages and social contributions	66.0	68.5	69.1	68.8	68.9	68.5	69.7	71.2	71.1
Direct wages	50.9	51.7	52.0	51.5	51.4	50.6	51.4	52.5	52.0
Social contributions	15.1	16.8	17.1	17.3	17.5	17.9	18.3	18.7	19.1
Taxes (net of subsidies)	6.9	6.8	6.4	6.8	7.0	7.5	7.3	7.0	7.2
Gross profits	27.1	24.7	24.5	24.4	24.1	24.0	23.0	21.8	21.7
	100	100	100	100	100	100	100	100	100
Investment rate	18.2	16.4	17.0	16.0	15.3	14.8	15.7	15.2	15.0

Source: Rapport sur les comptes de la Nation, vol. I, collection de l'INSEE, Nos. 108-109, p. 115.

The increase in employers' contributions to the social security system was an easy way for the government to restore its equilibrium, just as the passing of labor laws after 1973 was an easy way for it to buy some goodwill from the employee sector. Rising costs and economic uncertainty induced a decrease in the investment rate.

The task of the management association (CNPF) during this period was to increase its authority in its relations with individual enterprises and to restore its public image, exploiting the weakness of unions which was due mainly to their refusal to acknowledge the seriousness of the economic crisis.

Increasing the Authority Towards Enterprises

It is very important to governments that the social partners possess strong authority in relations with their members, an impossible task in view of the political divisions within unions, but easier with managements. However, until the end of the 1960s, CNPF was considered more as a forum than as a policy-maker. The situation changed in 1969 when the government asked CNPF to induce the unions to bargain at the national level and to bind their industries to agreements in such areas as redundancy, work hours, and recognition of unions in the plants.

At the same time, CNPF succeeded in changing its status, obtaining a general power to negotiate binding agreements for all member enterprises at the national level with the union confederations. This is perhaps the most important change in the French system of industrial relations. Such a change was facilitated by the growing influence of the Union of Metal and Mines Industries (UIMM) and to the declining influence of the Confederation of Small Enterprises (CGPME).

The government and management formed an efficient alliance to improve collective bargaining and control wages. Not only were various national agreements signed or improved, but the scope of collective bargaining was considerably broadened. The proportion of firms in which an industry collective agreement applied increased from 62 percent in 1972 to 86.2 percent in 1980. Ninety percent of employees were covered in 1980, up from only 74.8 percent in 1972 (Ministry of Labor "Notes," L'etat de la negociation collective 1980-81, May-June 1983, p. 2).

It is important to note, however, that collective bargaining applies mainly at the interindustry national level or for an industry as a whole at either the national or regional level. Collective bargaining at the company level is not the ordinary practice— hence, the importance of the national level association and of national unions.

In the area of wages, CNPF was an efficient mediary for the application of the governmental guidelines. However, the effort to rationalize the system of wage determination did not meet with success in every industry. When the CNPF and the UIMM tried to promote wage agreements through percentage increases in the wage fund but not in the absolute value of the minima, a number of enterprises refused to concur (Sellier 1983, p. 220ff). The new method would have helped to apply the governmental guidelines and to link the rise of wages more closely to that of prices. However, the management association helped to introduce the idea of managing wages through the notion of wage fund increases, a method that the government had introduced in the nationalized industries at the end of the 1960s.

The CNPF did succeed in stimulating the government's restructuring of vocational and continuing technical education. Apprenticeship had always been a very weak branch of the educational system with low participation from industry's training centers. This management interest in improving the training system dates back to the late 1950s, well before the beginning of the crisis; its goal was to increase the supply of skilled workers, a recurring objective of employers, as well as to increase flexibility of labor markets. The objective became one of progressively adapting workers to new jobs and new techniques.

Such was the case with the general collective agreement of July 1970, completed by a series of laws enacted before and after that date, to organize programs, to provide paid educational free time, and to make contributions by firms compulsory. Particularly relevant was a 1980 law under which a dual approach (*formation alternée*) was organized—a theory program administered in the educational establishments and a practical one given in firms. Such agreements and laws were all the more important for management, not only because of the practical results that could be obtained in the labor market, but also because the state and the unions officially recognized some management control of the training and retraining of employees. This recognition had previously been largely denied by the long-held monopoly of the Ministry of Public Education on all matters of technical education (Maurice, Sellier, and Silvestre 1983, p. 230), a situation management felt was responsible for the lack of fluidity of labor markets.

With the election of the socialist government in June 1981, the enactment of the new social laws (*lois Auroux*) was vehemently opposed by the CNPF, which stated that these laws would have a negative effect on employment. Employers were becoming more and more cautious about hiring new workers, a tendency that had already been observed after the passage of the 1973-1975 laws relating to the dismissal and redundancy procedure.

A number of laws (election of delegates or enterprise committees, dismissal procedures, timing of the consultation before a reduction in manpower, etc..) apply to firms with more than a certain number of employees (10, 50, etc.). Management officials asked for a change in these rules which, according to them, impeded the propensity to hire. Up until then the government had refused to comply; however, the socialist government admitted that in geographical zones seriously affected by unemployment, some of these rules could be put aside (*poles de conversion*).

Another management success related to the problem of taxes and the firms' social contributions. In 1984, the socialist government promised that compulsory levies would be reduced in the years to come.

A specific trait of the French industrial relations system had been the quasi-regular consultation between government, particularly the prime minister, and the social partners—unions, of course, but also the CNPF. The socialist government continued this practice. Since the oil crisis, CNPF can be defined as the official and practically the only representative of all enterprises in industry and commerce, which has significantly increased its authority in its relations with its members.

When the CNPF changed its status in 1969 in order to become the bargaining representative for all industries and member companies on social issues, it declared that from now on it no longer represented owners (*patrons*) but enterprises, a distinction which stressed its economic rather than political function. Bargaining with unions and the government became its main task. This was an important change, for French management had a long tradition of antiunionism.

Attitudes Towards Unions

In the 1950s and even the 1960s, management's attitude towards unions was that they were acceptable only at the industry level, not at the level of the firm. Many firms still hold this view, but in the larger ones there is no longer a question of eliminating unions.

The geographic decentralization of firms in the sixties and seventies, and the influence of large and dynamic companies in the CNPF, helped to promote this new orientation towards unions.

Even company agreements, which had been considered with much distrust, occurred more frequently, at least on special issues. In 1980–1981, 10 percent of the firms—but 25 percent of the employees—were covered by company agreements, notwithstanding the industry agreements signed by the industry association of which the firms were members.[2] But the main change was the generalization of national all-industries agreements, frequently signed by all unions and the CNPF. At the industry or company level, union divisions often impede such general agreements; frequently only one or two unions (branches of locals of national trade federations) underwrite an agreement which nevertheless applies to all employees. Because of this, it may be said that there is a functional division of labor between unions (Lozier 1979): the most radical unions put the pressure on employers, the less radical ones simply settle.

On the whole, management has become more tolerant of the union as a legitimate institution. This change was certainly fostered by the 1968 law which gave union locals the right to organize in the firms. But that was important only for small firms; locals were already well organized in most large firms. More importantly, the economic crisis and the increase in unemployment which weakened the unions gave management more opportunity to accept the principle and the fact of bargaining. It should also be said that the May 1968 strikes, "the 1968 events," made it easier for employers to appreciate the necessity of regular consultation as a way of improving communications within their firms, not only with unions but also with middle management and supervisory personnel.

These changes, even with exceptions, have helped transform the public image of French management from an anachronistic one to a modern one. Francois Ceyrac, president of CNPF in the seventies, played an important role in this transformation.

Management Attitude Towards Quality of Work and Promoting Flexibility of Employment

At the 1977 national meeting of the CNPF, its president emphasized how vital it was for employers to promote innovations in communications, information, consultation, and quality of work.

---

[2] "L'etat de la negociation collective," 1983, p. 2. Forty-five percent of firms with at least 500 employees have agreements of this type.

It was important, he stated, to meet the challenges of the oil crisis and of new technologies, of course; it was also necessary, however, to progress in the area of social responsibility to promote a consensus, particularly by meeting the demands of employees for improved quality of worklife (Ceyrac 1980, p. 5).

Of course, this declaration was a response to the demands of unions and a consequence of the 1973 law which created an agency for quality of work and of the 1975 collective agreement on this subject. But it is clear that the response of management, in large firms as well as in many others, has been rapid. Even as early as the beginning of the 1970s, new methods of work organization, such as autonomous workgroups, had been tested in a number of firms, and an effort had been made to introduce more multivalence in jobs, especially when new technologies were introduced. The Japanese pattern of "quality circles" was tried in many companies, and when the socialist government enacted a law in 1982 on the "right of expression" for workers, a number of managements could apply this new guideline under their control.

Because these approaches were initiated by management, unions generally opposed them, even when employees recognized their value. These exchanges were particularly useful in the area of worktime organization. For example, management was concerned with matching worktime to the distribution of orders. A possible solution was to ask employees to work irregular schedules, either part-time or with irregular hours matched to the company's needs— that is, firms were demanding more flexibility in worktime. Unions vehemently opposed these practices, arguing that it was an attempt to break the workers' collective. However, many employees— especially, but not only, women—approved of these new methods (part-time work is still relatively rare in France), so that unions often faced some hostility from workers, if not from their members. However, since management had initiated this popular solution, its image benefited at the expense of the unions.

Management Attitudes Towards Social Security

One of the most difficult industrial relations problems of this period was the financial balance of the social security system. Although management representatives held dominant positions on the social security boards from 1967 until 1983, the CNPF strongly criticized the centralization of the system and the fact that local boards had no actual responsibility for the management of health problems, especially for hospitals. The socialist government reorganized the boards, giving unions a dominant role. At the same time, however, management initiated some propositions for reforming the system, such as the decentralization of the health system management or differentiating compulsory from voluntary insurance according to the incomes of those insured ("Le debat," 1983). These proposed reforms were deemed reasonable by certain union leaders. In addition, the socialist government agreed to management's demand that family allowances be financed through general taxes rather than social contributions in the wage fund; this reform is slowly being implemented.

Conclusion

In all these areas, the CNPF not only reinforced its authority as a representative partner, but enhanced its public image as well. The oil crisis, considered a temporary phenomenon at the beginning of the period, helped everyone to recognize the importance of well-managed firms.

The stature of men like Francois Ceyrac was certainly decisive in this evolution; even more important was the progressive awareness that unenlightened management had been an important factor in French industry's lack of progress and that new management techniques critically influenced its economic and social modernization.

The Strategy of Unions

A series of decisive events in the past 15 years on the political and economic scene have produced profound changes in the relations among the unions, employees, management, and the political elite. Paradoxically, some of these events have reinforced the legitimacy of unions in society and at the company level, but others have weakened their legitimacy at both levels. Interestingly, at the same time that unions were losing members, they became more influential, especially after the 1981 electoral victory of the left.

Increased Legitimacy

Employers have constantly attempted to limit, even to oppose, the presence of unions in firms; usually they resist the outcome of bargaining at the company level. Governments, however, have tried to promote bargaining at all levels.

The permitted power of unions has increased significantly through a series of laws discussed earlier: the right to organize at the plant level (1968); interindustry and industry collective agreements on redundancies (1969); equalization of status of workers and white-collar employees (*mensualisation*) (1970); classification of jobs (1972–1978); compulsory consultation with the company's committee before redundancy measures and procedures for improving the quality of work (1975); and the right of the committee to appoint and consult with experts and its duty to bargain (1982). In fact, the number of organized firms has increased during this period, either directly through union locals or indirectly through the establishment of elected committees.

The 1968 and 1982 laws allowed national unions to organize locals, and employers are obliged to give them office space. In 1975 it was estimated that 46.3 percent of firms with more than 50 employees were organized; in 1980 the figure was 60.2 percent. The highest percentage is found in the chemical industry (72 percent), the lowest in construction (47 percent). The announcement of redundancies by employers was frequently an opportunity for unions to organize and increase their influence.

In firms with more than 50 employees, company committees should legally be elected by all personnel, whether or not they are union members. But, in fact, very frequently in the past no committee was organized. Since the oil crisis, unions have seized on problems of redundancies as an opportunity to force employers to organize and conduct committee elections. The percentage of firms (more than 50 employees) electing committees increased from around 60 percent in 1973 to 84 percent in 1982.

Employers' announcements of redundancies were frequently the direct cause of some very long strikes. Although some strikes developed spontaneously,[3] most of them were organized by unions. In this way, at least until 1978 or even 1979, the crisis has permitted unions to increase their influence, if not always their membership. Only since 1980 has a diminishing trend been observed for

---

[3] Labor law allows any group of workers to strike, whether or not they are unionized. Spontaneous strikes often are subsequently sustained by unions.

TABLE 10
Strikes, Workdays Lost, Participation Rate

	1973	1974	1975	1976	1977	1978	1979	1980	1981	1982
Registered strikes (monthly average)	310	374	323	440	333	267	351.4	252.8	254	3.5
Lost workdays (monthly average)		326.2	281.4	292.1	337.9	202.9	173.4	264.4	125.9	120.8	188.1
Participation rate	33.6	34.6	32.4	36.2	35.5	35.0	36.1	28.4	28.8	33.3

Source: INSEE, Annuaire Statistique de la France, 1983, p. 91.

registered strikes, for lost workdays, and for participation rate (see Table 10).

The data indicate that strikes were at their peak in 1976. This probably is related to the inflationary consequences of the economic upswing policy of Jacques Chirac, followed by the appointment of Raymond Barre as prime minister. The 1979 numbers relate to a temporary alliance of the two principal unions, CGT and CFDT, and to a long dispute in the steel industry; in 1982 numerous conflicts concerned the government decision to reduce the legal workweek to 39 hours. Most interesting perhaps is the diminishing rate of participation in the last three years which can be linked to a decrease in membership, particularly for CGT and CFDT. In this period—since 1976 for CGT and 1979 for CFDT—membership declined mainly as a consequence of decreasing industrial employment (1 million, 1973–1980), but also because of the rank-and-file's anger over growing unemployment.

Less Legitimacy: Decreasing Returns to Organizing Efforts

The great effort to organize more firms was followed by a rise and then a fall in membership. The first years after the 1968 strikes were ones of growing membership despite some opposition to the unions' policies among the rank and file. As the number of employees increased 13 percent between 1968 and 1974, CFDT membership rose 24 percent and CGT membership 18.5 percent. Beginning in 1976, membership began to decline. Part of this decline is certainly due to the decrease in industrial employment—from 7.6 million (1974) to 6.8 million (1980). However, this 10 percent decline in industrial employment might not fully explain an official decrease of 20 percent for CGT members in the same period.

CFDT membership continued to grow until 1976. This difference between the two union confederations might be explained by the fact that 60 percent of CGT members are workers as opposed to CFDT's 48 percent, that 29 percent of CGT members are white-collar versus CFDT's 44 percent,[4] and that CFDT recruits among teachers but CGT does not (it advises potential members to affiliate with another left-oriented teachers union, the Federation of National Education (FEN)).

The evolution in influence is shown by the results of elections of delegates to the enterprises' committee (Table 11). The elections of labor court representatives in 1979 and 1982, though providing only a statistic of influence and not of members, provides another image of this evolution (see Table 12).

The decline in membership for the CGT and CFDT, according to their own official statistics, is related to a decline of influence only for CGT. But FO, the third largest union, is gaining influence and probably membership (though it does not publish detailed statistics). It should be added that, in general, the average rate of membership in the private sector (20 percent) is far less than in the public sector (40 percent), where FO has the largest share of

TABLE 11
Evolution of Influence of Different Unions Through Elections
of Delegates to Enterprise Committees (Private Sector)[a]
(percent)

	1974	1976	1978	1980	1982
CGT	42.7	41.5	38.6	36.5	32.3
CFDT	18.6	19.1	20.4	21.3	22.8
CFTC	2.6	2.7	2.7	2.9	2.9
FO	8.3	9.3	10.0	11.0	11.7
CGC	5.3	5.3	6.6	6.0	7.0
CSL	3.5	2.5	1.6	1.9	1.5
Other unions	2.9	4.5	3.5	3.1	2.9
No union members	15.7	14.6	16.3	16.8	18.4

Source: INSEE, Annuaire Statistique de la France, 1983, p. 91.

[a] Comparable results are given every two years since this is the duration of delegates' mandates. The evolution shown by the table should be qualified by the fact that the rate of penetration of committees has been more important in small firms where CFDT has made great efforts to organize. Thus, the decline of the CGT is probably overestimated.

[4] The remainder being agricultural workers (CGT, 12 percent; CFDT, 8 percent). Cf. Louis Harris sample, in G. Adam, p. 56.

TABLE 12
Elections of Labor Court Representatives
(percent)

	1979		1982	
	Commerce	Private Sector	Commerce	Private Sector
Abstention	28.4	44.1	32.1	48.9
CGT	50.1	42.4	44.9	36.7
CFDT	22.4	23.2	23.5	23.4
FO	15.6	19.6	16.7	20.4
CFTC	5.8	7.4	6.8	9.4
CGC	1.7	1.6	5.6	5.7
Others	4.0	4.2	2.3	4.0

Source: Ministry of Labor.

members (more than 50 percent, compared to CGT's 30–40 percent and CFDT's 35 percent) (Froment-Meurice 1983, p. 73).

All unions probably maintain their affiliations in the public sector, so that total union membership is not declining as much in France as in other countries. However, there has been a transfer of membership among unions. In the period 1973–1976, a certain amount of transfer took place from CGT to CFDT, and between 1976 and 1982, from CFDT to FO.

Factors of Change in Membership of Radical Unions

These changes in membership among unions are related to a series of factors. First, the increase in the share and influence of women, young people, and migrant workers was not followed by a change in the representation structure on the union boards, especially in the CGT, in such a way that their demands would be fully taken into account. Many strikes by these groups in the low-paid industries were organized by independent groups of workers, though CFDT did cope rapidly with these problems; its gains in numbers and influence between 1974 and 1979 might be explained by this development. Second, the political crash of the "alliance of the left" (communist and socialist parties) just before the legislative elections of 1978, and the resulting loss of these elections by the left, seriously discouraged many members.[5]

_____
[5] A "common program" approved in 1972 by both socialist and communist parties, was the basis of this "union of the left." In 1977, when polls gave favorable results for the left, especially the socialists, the communist party declared that the socialist party had broken the pact (on a matter relative to the number of companies to be nationalized) and retired from the union.

However, factors more directly linked to the economic crisis and to changing attitudes of people should be added to this list, which explains how the more radical unions lost part of their legitimacy.

First, management had become more conscious of the changing attitudes of young workers towards industrial work and traditional authority in the plant. As shown above, in the early seventies the management confederation developed a series of initiatives to promote a new kind of growth as well as manpower management. The unions considered these initiatives as purely profit-motivated, but many people were aware of the advantages of these programs, particularly of flexible worktime.

The decline of membership of the two radical unions should also be attributed to their bargaining policy. From 1973 onward, union leaders refused to sign many agreements on wages at the industry level as well as agreements relating to the important matter of equalizing wage- and salary-earners' status (*mensualisation*). Those agreements, insufficient from the point of view of the two radical unions, were signed by the two other workers' unions (FO and CFTC) and by the "union of cadres" (CGC). To the extent that some of these agreements granted effective gains to workers (increased seniority bonus, improved illness compensation), FO and CFTC were considered more realistic by many people.

CGT's and CFDT's systematic refusal to sign agreements with management was in line with the political opposition of the communist and socialist parties. The danger of such a policy was distinctly felt by CFDT leaders after the leftist parties' failure in the 1978 elections. The leaders of this union declared that it was necessary to take a more purely syndicalist line (*recentrage*), that is, centering the policy more on unions' than on political parties' objectives and insisting on immediate action on specific subjects without waiting for political change. This new attitude was favorable to CFDT's public image but did not prevent a continuing decline of membership.

Conscious of its own declining position, the CGT, at its congress of 1980, decided on "a democratic opening" (increasing the number of socialist members at the Commission Executive) and adopted certain objectives similar to those of CFDT (workers' participation, quality of worklife).

No growth in union membership has been observed under the socialist government. On the contrary, the declining trend continued.

Change in the Industrial Relations System?

With regard to institutions and the institutional role of unions, there has been considerable progress in the part played by unions in the industrial relations system. Committees and locals are now unavoidable partners in most firms, though their presence is more frequent and effective depending on the size of the plants. Administrative support by labor inspectors[6] and by courts has improved; the number of inspectors increased from 1000 to 2000 between 1974 and 1981, and unions appealed to civil courts more often on matters relating to the right of consultation on industrial accidents. It is important to say in this connection that young judges were often more favorable than older ones to unions' or workers' demands, a result of the change of attitudes linked to the social movement of 1968.

In addition, collective bargaining at the national all-industries level between unions and the CNPF has incited unions to participate on joint boards such as those governing unemployment insurance and many old-age complementary schemes as well as on local employment-redundancy committees.

Finally, as it has been said above, government consultation with union leaders has been the rule on matters like the reduction in hours of work or increase of holidays, the reform of the company committee (creation of committees for groups of companies), social security, training, and continuing education.

---

[6] Labor inspectors are in charge of enforcing labor law at the company level. The increase in their number, their enlarged powers relating to the redundancy law of 1975, and above all the frequency of redundancy cases have increased the importance of these government officers in the resolution of labor disputes. However, this is practically the only method for public intervention (besides the role of labor or civil courts). It is characteristic of the French industrial relations system that there is no compulsory mediation before a strike. Arbitration has become obsolete. However, the mediation procedure allows one of the parties or the public authority to call upon a mediator, who has rather broad powers of investigation, to write his or her opinion on how the dispute should be resolved. Although such a decision is not binding on the parties, the moral authority of the mediator may help end the dispute. Recourse to mediation is exceptional, however, and takes place only when the government tries to put an end to a long strike in an important firm or industry.

Political Action or Collective Bargaining

Such institutional changes, however, have not necessarily increased the actual power of unions nor their effectiveness in the collective bargaining process. The change in relative influence between the radical unions (CGT and CFDT) and the more *syndicalist* ones (FO and CGC) has shown that the balance between political action and collective bargaining is now the main question for future union strategy.

CFDT's 1978 policy of *recentrage* was a consequence of a reconsideration. However, the electoral victory of the left in 1981 and CFDT support of the socialist government (CGT's opposition was renewed when the Fabius government was formed without communist ministers) questioned the *recentrage*, as many governmental measures were directly inspired by the CFDT leaders.

Before 1981 it appeared that when governments consulted with unions, it was merely to obtain the level of consensus that they needed to maintain their legitimacy. For instance, after consultation between the leader of FO and President Giscard d'Estaing in 1978–1979 in regard to the generalization of a fifth week holiday, instead of announcing this generalization as a result of these consultations, it became part of the president's campaign platform (Fouquet 1983, p. 7). Governments are often ready to deal with qualitative demands of unions or even to promote them in order to prevent the unions from pushing their quantitative demands. Again, this was obvious with the policy of the socialist government in 1981–1982 (production of a series of "social laws," hence, the insistence of FO on restoring collective bargaining).

Structure and Subjects of Bargaining

A characteristic of the French scene is the weight of the bargaining at the national all-industries level, a way of substituting general agreements for law or even of combining both, as in the case of continuing education. However, the growing importance of local unions and the increasing impact of the economic conditions on the crisis at the company level has incited workers to negotiate at this level over new rules of employment, without strictly obeying the principles of their national unions. This has been the case with the bargaining on reduction of hours. Although the CGT, not the CFDT, insisted upon maintaining weekly wages for every reduction in hours, a lot of agreements were concluded with clauses specifying only partial rather than full weekly wages.

Even some types of productivity agreements have been concluded, as in the example of establishing the five-shifts working week at the B.S.N. glass company; it was agreed that the new rule was dependent upon maintaining a level of labor productivity.

These examples are evidence that new types of behavior are penetrating union action at the company level, often in spite of criticism by the national leaders who insist on rejecting any agreement that tends to suppress vested interests (*avantages acquis*).

Another change has already been mentioned: the tendency towards a rationalization of wage bargaining, taking into account not so much individual wages as the whole wage fund of the business and its adjustment to guidelines. Such principles have been fully applied by the civil service in bargaining between government and unions, and similar devices have begun to be proposed in the private sector.

The tendency to apply collective bargaining at the level of firms as well as the tendency to take account of economic guidelines are perhaps symptoms of significant changes in the fields of industrial relations in France.

However, it seems necessary to point to the very special relations between governments and national unions, as a way for governments to reinforce their own legitimacy. Government efforts to issue laws or to raise low wages in order to encourage acceptance of their tentative austerity policies have been to the relative disadvantage of employees earning higher salaries, a category whose voting power has not been as appreciated as that of workers and ordinary employees. The political system appears in this perspective as an important element of the industrial relations system itself and as hindering its evolution towards more bipartisanship.

Conclusion

After a long period of continuous economic expansion and growth of real wages and of employment, the economic crisis of 1973–1983 was not easily accepted by the unions or by the people.

The industrial relations system that had been geared to generalized collective bargaining at the industry and interindustry levels, and whose goal was to facilitate modernization of industry, was no longer viable. For example, easing the lot of workers displaced by modernization through the collective agreement on unemployment compensation (signed in the late 1950s), which granted the unemployed person between 40 and 100 percent (1974 rider) of annual income from 1979 onward, eventually became an onerous burden. It was necessary to reduce benefits and to raise contributions, a solution the unions could accept.

However, the industrial relations system also had to solve the problem of the adequacy of the movement of wages in relation to movement of the GNP. In this area, French unions have always resisted the acceptance of any kind of incomes policy. For employers, too, raising wages has always been the surest means of obtaining social peace.

It is characteristic of the French situation during the crisis that real wages continued to rise until 1980. No government before Barre dared to propose a general reduction of real wages; even he spoke merely of maintaining the real wage fund by raising low wages at the expense of higher ones. Only the socialist government, since 1982, proposed a general reduction. Austerity policies, either of slow wage increases before 1976 or of stabilizing or even reducing wages, were offered in conjunction with qualitative measures favorable to unions (legalization of company locals, duty to bargain) or with measures improving the status of workers (illness compensation, quality of worklife)—what we have described as a "consensus policy." This is the way the industrial relations system has managed to get wage reductions accepted, if not by all unions (CGT always rejected such reductions), at least by most of them.

But has the change in economic conditions induced changes in the industrial relations system itself?

Two changes may be observed. The first is a change, which is only in the beginning stages, in the level of bargaining. Traditionally, collective bargaining in France has been centralized and has taken place at either a national interindustry level or at the industry level. The crisis has facilitated attempts to solve concrete problems (hours, quality of work, organization of work, flexible worktime) at the level of companies and plants. Wage bargaining, however, remains at the industry level.

The second change relates to the relative strength of various national unions. Although CGT remains the first, its membership has declined the most, mainly as a consequence of decreasing industrial employment. CFDT, the other radical union with a strong socialist bias, has lost members, too. On the other hand, FO is gaining influence in social elections (work committees, labor courts, social security) and probably is also gaining membership, in the goods and service industries. This is certainly an indirect consequence of the crisis, as the rank and file are becoming more and more convinced that the political programs of the left-wing parties and unions have been inadequate in coping with the economic problems.

References

Ceyrac, Francois. Preface in CODESE, "Amelioration des conditions de vie dans l'enterprise, experiences et realisations." Paris: Editions et Techniques, 1980.
Delattre, Michel. "Points forts et points faibles du commerce exterieur industriel." *Economie et Statistique*, INSEE, No. 157 (Juillet-Aout 1983).
Foquet, O. "Pouvoir syndical et democratie." *Pouvoirs, Quarterly Review*, No. 76 (1983).
Froment-Meurice, P. "Le pouvoir syndical dans la fonction publique." *Pouvoirs, Quarterly Review*, No. 26 (1973).
Harris, Louis. In "Le pouvoir syndical" by G.Adam. Paris: Dunod, 1983.
Institut National de la Statistique et des Etudes Economiques (INSEE). *La population de la France en 1982; population active*, premier resultats, No. 13 (Fevrier 1984).
"Le debat," entretien entre Edmond Maire et Simon Nora. *Quarterly Review* No. 26 (September 1983).
"L'etat de la negociation collective 1980-1981." *Travail-Informations*, Ministere des Affaires Sociales (Mai-Juin 1983).
Lozier, F. "Pour une approche fonctionelle du pluralisme syndical." *Project Monthly Review* No. 133 (1979): pp. 379-87.
Maurice, M., F. Sellier, and J. J. Silvestre. "Politique d'education et organisation industrielle en France et en Allemagne." Paris: PUF, 1982. Forthcoming in *The Social Foundations of Industrial Powers*. Cambridge, MA: MIT Press, Spring 1986.
_____. "The Search for a Societal Effect in the Production of Company Hierarchy: A Comparison of France and Germany." In *Internal Labor Markets*, ed. Paul Osterman. Cambridge, MA: MIT Press, 1983.
Meunier, F. "La France et ses face au second choc pétrolièr." *Economie et Statistique* (INSEE) N2755 (Mai 1993).
Sellier, Francois. *La confrontation sociale en France, 1936-1981*. Paris: Presses Universitaires de France, 1983.
Sudreau, P. "La reforme de l'enterprise." *La documentation francaise*. Paris: 1975.

CHAPTER 7

World Economic Changes and Industrial Relations in the Federal Republic of Germany

OTTO JACOBI

Johann Wolfgang Goethe University

The end of the long postwar boom, the displacement in the international division of labor, as well as the emergence of new labor-saving technologies have left their mark on the Federal Republic of Germany. The productive capacity of the German economy has shrunk and high rates of unemployment should continue well into the 1990s. However, neither these economic events, nor the political shift towards conservatism, nor the change of the social structure in favor of the employers should cause a dramatic change in German industrial relations. There are two major reasons for this conclusion.

Under the political leadership of the Social Democrats, a consensus was reached to promote international competitiveness through technological superiority and to overcome barriers to innovation by integrating the trade unions into the process of change. Labor has continued to support economic modernization in the 1980s.

Secondly, the West German system of industrial relations, with its key features of centralization, juridification, and participation, has functioned well, even in the face of changed socioeconomic conditions. The efficiency and legitimacy of collective bargaining has been maintained because the participants utilized the existing instruments of the system flexibly. Thus, in spite of recent developments, the traditional features of the industrial relations system, including a low level of conflict and a commitment to cooperation among the parties, has been maintained.

This general assessment has not been challenged by the difficult dispute in 1984 over the introduction of a 35-hour week. This particular conflict must rather be seen within the context of the German tradition of "exchange deals" between capital and labor. Periodically, industrial disputes are a test for unions committed to "social partnership." They demonstrate their militancy and ability to mobilize their members to produce viable solutions which, in turn, have always brought about longer periods of industrial peace.

Economic Development and World Economic Conditions

The economic boom in West Germany from the end of World War II until the mid-1970s was supported by a "beneficent circle" of high growth rates in the industrial sector and cooperative relations among interest groups (Bergmann, Jacobi, and Müller-Jentsch 1975, Bergmann and Müller-Jentsch 1975, Müller-Jentsch and Sperling 1978, Gourevitch et al. 1984). This cooperation secured the employees' participation in the economic success without undermining investment. The key element of the German economy has always been the manufacturing sector featuring highly competitive prices and quality, enabling producers to capture the ever increasing shares of international markets. The strong export orientation of the West German economy has been effectively supported by the state and the banks. Thus, the workers and their unions almost inevitably realized how much their employment and living standards depended on the growth of German exports. It is therefore hardly surprising that labor's efforts to improve wages and working conditions, reduce working time, and expand social security payments have considered the need to maintain international competitiveness. There is a general understanding that West Germany's extremely high dependence on exports, which is higher than that of any other developed nation of comparable size, and which heretofore has certainly promoted economic progress, also makes the economy highly vulnerable to external events.

The two foundations of the beneficent circle, an efficient export sector and a "concertation" of interests based on "social partnership," have determined the socioeconomic conditions in the Federal Republic. However, the beneficent circle has lost part of its efficiency and legitimacy. Both its early dominance and gradual erosion can be observed in the three postwar recessions as well as in the economic development since 1979.

The first recession in 1966–67, triggered by disinflation policies, was home-grown and showed all the signs of a potential crisis. But union wage restraint, an anticyclical economic policy of the state, and most of all a dynamic foreign demand assisted in the recovery. Although the subsequent boom assisted some branches of industry (mining, textile, clothing, and watch-making), there were nevertheless early signs of the structural problems and world economic "ruptures" developing in the 1970s.

The second West German recession of 1974–75, which was then part of a world-wide stagnation,was preceded by significant gains by unions in the redistribution of income. The slump was mainly a result of the collapse of the Bretton Woods monetary system and the emergence of the OPEC oil cartel. Underlying these developments were the erosion of American economic dominance in the face of a growing challenge from Europe and Japan, the weakening competitive position of the existing industrial nations vis-à-vis newly industrializing countries, and, above all, the end of the Keynesian prescriptions for economic policy. As a result, government policy sought to check the acceleration of inflation, while a trend towards saturation of world markets for manufactured goods and intensified cost competition made an expansive economic policy less effective. In these circumstances, the German reserve bank pursued the neo-monetarist doctrine of restricting the supply of money, and the government sought to improve corporate profits by reversing a trend in income distribution which had favored labor. Budgetary policy sought to promote innovation and investment. Thus, the recession in the mid-1970s has led to the creation of the "German Model" (*Modell Deutschland*), with the dual objectives of protecting international competitiveness by producing technologically advanced industrial goods and of overcoming the social barriers to innovation by incorporating the trade unions.

The outcome of these policies was a considerable growth in the second half of the 1970s. But in spite of the trade union cooperation in terms of wage policy and the external success of German industry, decline in employment could not be avoided. Since 1975 mass unemployment has been a constant feature of the West German economy, and the average number of people unemployed amounted to 1 million by the early 1980s (Brandt, Jacobi, and Müller-Jentsch 1982, Markovits 1982).

When the third West German recession of 1981–82 hit, unemployment figures rose to over 2 million. Foreign competition led to crises in certain sectors (steel, ship-building, and parts of the electrical engineering industry), causing unemployment to rise far above levels for the regions where these industries were located. The new Conservative-Liberal government maintained the export-oriented modernization strategy, but extended the scope of the policy by shifting emphasis away from the social welfare state and participation in favor of more market power, greater economic flexibility, and more innovation.

The remaining power of the "beneficent circle" has obviously contributed to the relatively strong economic situation of the Federal Republic by international standards. Recent economic developments suggest, however, that the balance of the "beneficent circle" has been threatened by the trade unions' loss of power and the economy's excessive dependence on exports. (See Table 1 for key economic variables.)

The shift of power relations in favor of employers can easily be demonstrated by employment trends. The loss of approximately 1 million jobs as a result of the recession of 1974–75 was largely made up in the subsequent recovery, but since 1980 the decline of employment has appeared permanent, in spite of the current pickup in economic activity. The trend towards growth in joblessness has been a major factor in labor's loss of power.

There has been a decline of employment throughout the manufacturing sector (plus the energy, mining, and construction industries) which has already led to a loss of 2 million manufacturing jobs. At least 1.5 million of these jobs were in the core industrial sector, representing a decline of 16 percent. In contrast, the industrial output in 1984 was 20 percent above the 1975 level. The decline of employment has almost exclusively affected blue-collar workers, which has affected unions' bargaining strength. Employers have pursued a selective personnel policy by dismissing first the less capable and unskilled workers. Thus, 50 percent of the unemployed are women or unskilled workers, and almost two-thirds of all those made redundant had jobs with low skill requirements. These changes were in addition to the "export of unemployment," that is, the reduction during the last ten years in the number of foreign employees by almost a million persons.

The result for trade unions was that either poorly unionized employees (women and unskilled), or those (like foreigners and semiskilled workers) who were inadequately represented within the industrial relations system, lost their jobs. In other words, the skilled workers, who have traditionally been well organized and who constitute the regular ("core") workforce, have largely been spared unemployment and still form the backbone of the labor movement. Consequently, union bargaining power and influence have not been weakened to the extent that might have been expected in the presence of high unemployment throughout the economy. This fact is of great consequence in that the IG Metall (the metal-workers' union)—with 2.5 million members (1983)—remains the largest individual union in the Western industrial countries and the dominant organization in the most important economic sector in West Germany (after the chemical industry). IG Metall is the traditional pacemaker in collective bargaining and sees itself as a pioneer of social progress.

Another aspect of the growth in joblessness is the dwindling capacity of economic sectors like services and public administration to create new jobs. Previously they had helped to absorb labor surpluses. By the beginning of the 1980s, the growing opportunities for labor-saving technology in these areas halted the expansion of employment. The changing occupational structure of the workforce implies a shift away from industrial manual work and in favor of nonindustrial white-collar work which threatens further weakening of the trade union movement. The sectors of the economy that are expanding are either nonunion (the private service sector) or, in the public sector, where the trade unions have no tradition of industrial action and are bound by no-strike clauses—the permanent civil service whose share of public-sector employees is 50 percent. It is likely that wages and working conditions will diversify along industrial or plant lines, corresponding to the bargaining strength of the trade unions concerned. The IG Metall is still the trail-blazer, setting the pattern for the weaker trade unions. But it is unlikely that this role will continue in the future.

Unions have been forced to make only limited "sacrifices" in wages and income distribution. This is due to the power of the "dual effect," in that IG Metall has a core membership which can be mobilized and whose capacity for engaging in industrial action remains strong. In addition, agreements reached by the IG Metall have been transferred to other sectors of the economy with only

TABLE 1
Key Economic Variables

Item	Unit	1979	1980	1981	1982	1983	1984
Production							
GNP at current prices	Percentage change from previous year	8.3	6.5	3.9	3.6	4.5	4.6
GNP at 1976 prices	Same	4.4	1.9	−0.3	−1.1	1.3	2.6
Output in the producing sector (excluding construction)	Same	5.2	0.3	−1.7	−2.8	0.9	3.4
Employment							
Employed wage and salary earners	Millions	22.7	23.0	22.8	22.4	22.0	21.7
	Percentage change from previous year	1.7	1.3	−0.6	−2.0	−1.9	−1.4
Unemployed persons	Millions	0.9	0.9	1.3	1.8	2.3	2.3
	Percentage of total labor force	3.3	3.3	4.8	6.7	8.1	8.5
	Percentage of dependent labor force	3.8	3.8	5.5	7.5	9.1	9.6
Distribution of income							
Entrepreneurial and property income	Percentage change from previous year	8.3	−0.9	−0.1	6.4	10.5	7.4
Wage and salary income	Percentage change from previous year	7.7	8.4	4.7	2.1	1.7	3.0
	Percentage of national income	63.4	64.7	65.6	65.1	63.7	63.0

TABLE 1 *(Continued)*
Key Economic Variables

Item	Unit	1979	1980	1981	1982	1983	1984
Prices							
Cost of living index for all households	Percentage change from previous year	4.1	5.5	6.3	5.3	3.3	2.4
Producer prices of industrial products	Same	4.8	2.5	7.8	5.8	1.5	2.8
Foreign trade							
Exports (f.o.b.)	DM billion	315	350	398	428	432	488
Imports (f.o.b.)	Same	283	331	357	365	378	421
Balance	Same	32	19	41	63	54	67
Long-term capital transactions							
German investment abroad	DM billion	21	29	28	28	37	39
Foreign investment in Germany	Same	33	35	36	14	29	25

Source: Report of the Deutsche Bundesbank for 1984.

minor modifications. Consequently, the nominal gross incomes of wage and salary earners have risen in each year, although the growth in nominal net incomes has proceeded more slowly, due to the policy of placing an increasing burden of tax and social security contributions on wage and salary earners.

After taking also into account the impact of inflation, there was a growth of real net incomes per employee after 1979; the trend since then, however, has been negative (see Table 2).

TABLE 2
Average Earnings of Wage and Salary Earners,
Percentage Changes from Previous Years

Year	Nominal Gross Income	Nominal Net Income	Real Net Income
1979	5.6	6.1	2.1
1980	6.6	5.0	−0.3
1981	4.9	4.5	−1.3
1982	4.2	2.9	−2.2
1983	3.4	2.3	−0.7
1984	3.1	2.2	−0.3

Sources: Welzmüller (1984), WSI-Mitteilungen des DGB, 6/1984.

In 1983 the average annual income of wage and salary earners amounted to DM 34,000. In terms of income distribution, men earn more than women, white-collar workers more than blue-collar workers, and qualified workers more than those less qualified. However, it is significant that income differentials, which are still rather modest by international standards, have not risen during the recession, contrary to normal expectations. This stability is due to the trade unions' successful opposition to the demands of government, the reserve bank, and the employers for increased differentiation.

Overall, wage and salary earners have suffered some losses, but the impact of these declines was diminished by the previous success of labor in the redistribution of incomes during the early 1970s. If the adjusted wage quota is an indicator (keeping constant the quota of wage and salary earners) which reflects the changes of the earnings' quota of the national income and, thus, the changes which are relevant in distributional terms, we get the following picture. The (adjusted) wage quota was 61 percent in 1968 and increased to 66 percent by 1975. Since then the general trend has been to reverse the redistribution of income achieved by the trade unions. This reversal of the trend in income distribution has not yet reached a magnitude which could have been expected in view of the high levels of unemployment and the efforts of the state, the employers, and the majority of economists. This points to certain rigidities or a degree of resistance based on the comparatively favorable labor market situation of the permanent ("core") workforces in the industry. Nevertheless, by 1984 income distribution had reverted to 1970 levels.

The material situation of the unemployed is, of course, much worse. In spite of attempts to limit the financial consequences of unemployment by measures promoting the return of immigrant workers, the return of women to household work, or preretirement schemes, there are increasing signs of a newly emerging poverty. An important reason for this is that the duration of unemployment benefits is one year at most, while the number of those who suffer longer unemployment is increasing.

Export Industries

The second foundation of the "beneficent circle," industrial exports, has become more and more important. Exports have risen each year, and the surplus in commodity trading has become enormous. The increasing importance of foreign trade for the German economy is due not only to the expansion of commerce, but is also the result of international long-term capital transactions and the acceleration of the transfer of technology. In response to these trends, there have been extensive efforts to encourage technological innovations in order to be able to offer highly advanced goods. The German Council of Economic Experts (an advisory body for the government) has summarized the objective of this modernization strategy as follows:

> The improvement of competitiveness must be achieved through the adoption of new products into the product-range, i.e., of those products whose production requires special technical knowledge available only to a few suppliers . . . . Such products are not competitive because they are particularly cheap, but because of their high utility for those who use them; in short, because they are particularly expensive. In other words: in a dynamic economy, competitiveness is the ability to develop new

specialty products and new technical solutions to an extent
that permits rising incomes under circumstances of a high
level of employment even though competitors who are
following-up are gradually acquiring the necessary
technical knowledge and organizing abilities to manufacture those products as well . . . . A high-wage country
cannot afford to fall back on the role of follow-up
competition. (SVR-Sachverständigenrat zur Begutechtung
der gesamtwirtschaftlichen Entwicklung (1981), Ziffer
459)

In examining the position of the German economy internationally, the success of this strategy is obvious. The long-term trend of
the volume of exports and imports and their proportion of real GNP
makes clear how much the importance of foreign trade has
increased (see Table 3).

TABLE 3
Exports and Imports: Share of Real GNP (in percent)

Year	Export	Import
1960	17.0	14.0
1965	17.8	17.2
1970	22.6	21.6
1975	26.6	24.1
1980	29.5	28.1
1984	33.0	30.0

Source: SVR, Jahresgutachten (1984).

With a third of the national product going into exports, export
ratios are quite high in some branches of industry. This is
particularly true in the case of four sectors that constitute the core of
German industry (see Table 4). With a share of 17 percent of the
world trade in industrial goods (1982), the Federal Republic is the

TABLE 4
Industrial Export Ratios, Core Sectors

Year	Electrical Engineering	Chemical Industry	Automobile Industry	Engineering Industry
1970	21.8	29.9	33.4	39.4
1982	34.1	38.1	49.6	50.6

Source: Schmidt et al. (1984).

industrial nation with the largest share of international markets (compared with the U.S. and Japan, each of whom has a 15-percent share).

This level of exports has been achieved because the whole country, with all its political, economic, and social resources, is in effect one big export lobby. A broad consensus exists that the German economy depends very much upon a prosperous and expanding world economy. This consensus is reflected in the policy of the government and the reserve bank, as well as of the organizations of capital and labor. Therefore, protectionist policies have been opposed vigorously at home and especially abroad. But there has been a lively debate on whether the innovative capacity of the German economy will be sufficient to maintain its position in the increasingly important market of high technology goods. In view of the high level of external dependence, promising economic success on the one hand and implying a high potential of external vulnerability on the other, many fear that in the event of a disruption of the world economy or of a technological lag of the industry, the economic repercussions for the Federal Republic could be devastating.

In the high technology debate, there is agreement that Americans are the best innovators, the Germans the best perfectionists, and the Japanese the best imitators. According to Nussbaum (1983), the Germans are the best in producing goods on the basis of an advanced "19th-century-technology" (cars, machines, electrical appliances), but have "missed the bus" with regard to future technological developments. This pessimistic view has not been supported by the findings of recent studies commissioned by the government, although all studies show that the Federal Republic has not improved its position in the high-technology market vis-à-vis its two main competitors, the U.S. and Japan. Depending on how high-technology industry is defined, it has been suggested that the German industry could either hold onto its market or suffer rather severe losses. If a more restricted definition of high technology is applied, the competitive position of the German industry appears weak, but if the definition is broadened, its position looks much better. The government study reported: ". . . the conclusion that the economy of the Federal

Republic has generally lost its competitiveness cannot be drawn. This does not preclude that German companies have difficulty in closing up" (BMWi 1984, p. 19). The expectation of overcoming a gap in innovation and thereby catching up with the technological lead of the U.S. in certain areas (biotechnology, office communications, computer technology, satellite technology) is based on the comparatively high levels of research and development expenditures in the Federal Republic. It ranks next to the U.S. and well ahead of Japan in patent applications. The advantage of the German economy over the U.S. lies in its higher investment rates, and over Japan it rests on the diversity and specialization of its industrial goods. German industry is particularly successful in the application of process engineering, especially in the capital goods sector, and its ability to resolve problems of individual customers.

A similar conclusion has been drawn by the electrical engineering group Siemens, the largest private company in the Federal Republic. Despite competition with the U.S. in innovation and the productivity competition with Japan, German industry could successfully stand its ground (Bechurts 1984). German industry could make use of its great experience in refining and applying new technology to mature industries to generate products with high value. When combined with the second strong point of German industry—the so-called "problem-solving business" (flexibility in the face of customers' demands)—this capacity has provided combined competitive advantages. To sum up: for Germany high technology offers a new challenge which can be met by taking advantage of the traditional strengths of German industry.

These optimistic expectations are reflected in a projection of the Federal Republic's economic development until the year 2000 by a well-known Swiss research institute (Hofer et al. 1983), summarized in Table 5. This forecast assumes an average annual growth rate of 3 percent of the GNP and of over 3.5 percent in productivity. A reduction of working time has been taken into account by assuming a trend toward a 30-hour workweek. The employment effect is relatively moderate. A substantial reduction in the unemployment rate will be mainly the result of a population decrease. If the economic development actually follows this prediction, the current decline in union power will end.

TABLE 5
Prospects for Economic Development

	1985–2000
Real national product	+51%
Productivity per work hour	+73
Employees	−2.5
Working time	−15
Unemployed	−22

Source: Hofer et al. (1983).

Government Policy

The old coalition of the Social Democrats (Sozialdemokratische Partei Deutschlands/SPD) and the Liberal Party (Freie Demokratische Partei/FDP), established in 1969, broke apart in October 1982. Since then there has been a coalition of the two Christian parties (Christlich Demokratische Union/CDU and Christlich Soziale Union/CSU) and the FDP. This change of government first took place at the parliamentary level where the FDP shifted allegiance to the CDU/CSU. In the 1983 elections the new Christian-Conservative-Liberal alliance scored a clear-cut victory (see Table 6).

TABLE 6
Bundestag Elections of 1980 and 1983

	1980		1983	
Parties	Votes (000)	Votes (Percent)	Votes (000)	Votes (Percent)
CDU	12,978	34.2	14,857	38.2
CSU	3,920	10.3	4,140	10.6
FDP	4,030	10.6	2,706	6.9
SPD	16,261	42.9	14,866	38.2
Grüne	569	1.5	2,165	5.6

Seats in Parliament

CDU	174 ⎫	191 ⎫
CSU	52 ⎬ 226 (opposition)	53 ⎬ 278 (government)
FDP	53 ⎫	34 ⎭
SPD	218 ⎬ 271 (government)	193 ⎫
Grüne		27 ⎬ 220 (opposition)

Source: Statistisches Bundesamt, *Statistisches Jahrbuch* (1983).

The significant aspects of the election were the losses of the FDP and the sudden growth of the Green Party. The decline of the FDP was due to its change of coalition partners. The radical Greens could upset the traditional three-party domination in West Germany and establish themselves as the fourth political party. The outcome of subsequent local and state elections underscored the difficulty the FDP faces in getting over the 5-percent vote threshold for parliamentary status, whereas the Greens find polling 5 percent easier. If this trend prevails, it implies that the political landscape of the Federal Republic will be altered significantly. The traditional three-party system, with the FDP furnishing the necessary majority for the Christian-Conservative or the Social Democratic–trade union power bloc, would no longer work. Instead, a four-party system (including the Greens) or a new three-party arrangement (without the FDP) might emerge. Thus a change in office of 1982 initiated a "conservative shift" (*Konservative Wende*), but the new government cannot rely on a stable majority among the electorate. The famous remark made by the chairman of the SPD, Willy Brandt (Chancellor from 1969 to 1974), that there is a majority "to the left of the centre" appears relevant again. The possibility of a "red-green alliance" is not out of the question; at present a coalition between the SPD and the Greens is being tried in one state.

The Socialist-Liberal coalition, which lasted 13 years, was an alliance of the reformist German labor movement with the enlightened liberal bourgeoisie. Most of its extra-parliamentary support came from the trade unions. The objectives of the Socialist-Liberal government were to extend the democratic participation of the citizens, to reduce discrimination, and to improve the welfare state. For wage and salary earners, the reform era entailed an increasing standard of living and improved social services; their plant-level and trade-union interest organizations were granted extended rights of consultation and a voice in policies at the micro- and macroeconomic levels as well as a constant share in political decision-making.

Helmut Schmidt's appointment as Chancellor during the recession of the mid-1970s signalled the end of the era of reform. His period in office lasted from 1974 until 1982. The *Konservative Wende* of the mid-1980s has not produced a change in general principles of economic policy, since a significant switch had already taken place during Schmidt's term of office. Although Keynesian elements in steering the economy were never abandoned completely, they increasingly receded into the background. The government policy of controlling the money supply, which had been pursued by the reserve bank since the switch to floating exchange rates in 1973, increasingly turned to a supply-side strategy of economic policy. Priority was given first to increasing investment in promising new technologies. Some employment and tax reduction programs aimed at the promotion of investment. The improvement of business profits was achieved by reducing overall costs—that is, by reducing relative labor costs above all. The formula of the period of prosperity, whereby wages were adjusted in line with both the increase in productivity and the rate of inflation (the so-called "dual adjustment"—*Doppelanpassung*) was thus revoked. There were a considerable number of social security cuts, although a substantial encroachment upon the structure of the welfare state was avoided.

The strained relations within the Socialist-Liberal alliance became increasingly complicated and fundamentally untenable in the late 1970s. Although there was also a growing trade union opposition to the government's policies, it was the faction within the Liberal Party supporting economic liberalism that brought about the collapse of the alliance. It rejected Schmidt's continuation of seeking trilateral agreements with the peak organizations of capital and labor as well as his economic policy objective to find "a middle path between the two extremes of Keynesian economics and monetarist policy" (Schmidt 1983). While the politically and intellectually dominating Chancellor Schmidt and the interest in continuing detente with Eastern Europe helped keep the Socialist-Liberal coalition in power, it was the Social Democrats' modernization that was seen as a promising perspective for the 1980s by all the established parties and interest groups.

This explains why the shift of political power to a Christian-Liberal government did not entail a change of policy. On the contrary, there have been clear continuities of economic and social policies. The cumulative effect of a more severe austerity policy, applied without any protective social or political compensation and employing a variety of separate measures over time, was a new strategy—the *Konservative Wende*. Although German conservatism is intellectually less ambitious and less rigid than the British variety, clearly a result of the less pressing political, economic, and social problems in the Federal Republic, the ideological affinity is nevertheless obvious. The Federal Republic too has witnessed the emergence of an alliance of *Wertkonservative* (referring to traditional conservative values) and *Strukturkonservative* (referring to doctrines of economic liberalism, laissez-faire policy, etc.) that differs fundamentally from the interventionist, integrating, and cooperative intentions of the Socialist-Liberal alliance.

The *Wertkonservative* seek a strong state that is able to keep the trade unions away from the political market. They argue that the growth of the public sector and the concurrent centralization of power during the past three decades has reduced the state's capacity to solve political, economic, and social problems. They wish to alter the widespread habit of making excessive demands on the state (Landesregierung von Baden-Wurttemberg 1983). They also seek to reverse the trend that had led to the erosion of traditional values such as "discipline," "obedience," "loyalty," and "honor" and had opened the way for new orientations such as "emancipation," "equal treatment," or "self-fulfillment." It would be important to create a synthesis of values such as the freedom of individuals to make the most of their talents along with such values as a "sense of duty" and "acceptance."

The *Strukturkonservative* favor restoring the rule of the market, and they want to oust trade unions—which they see as major obstacles to efficient markets—from the economic order. The extent of the state's economic intervention, the degree of social security provided by the welfare state, and the improvements of working conditions enforced by the unions have been identified as the main fetters on innovative forces of the market by seriously impairing both the entrepreneurs' willingness to take risks and employees' work ethic and efficiency. The conclusion drawn from these assumptions was that the entrepreneurs' readiness to invest in promising new technologies would be stimulated by reducing the labor costs, removing the obstacles to innovation in the form of state or collective bargaining regulations, and introducing more flexibility into labor relations.

Even if the alliance of *Wert- und Strukturkonservative* is not calling for an outright elimination of trade unions, they certainly favor a definite limitation of their power. As mediators of social interests, unions are expected to generate the legitimacy and stability required for the continued functioning of the system, but they are no longer to be allowed to interfere as political or economic powers or to exercise a veto.

In spite of many common interests of the Social Democratic and the conservative power blocs, there exists a fundamental difference in their respective assessments of the market and the role of trade unions. Whereas the former emphasized the inherent imperfections of the market and regard a confrontation between the government and the organizations of capital and labor as a grave obstacle to solving economic problems, the latter blame excessive union influence for the market's failure to secure prosperity and employment. Thus, in contrast to the Social Democrats' tendency towards intervention and corporatism, the conservatives tend to expel the trade unions from the political and economic market.

Trade Union Structures

To better understand trade union policies in recent years, it is useful to summarize briefly the basic principles and structures of German unions.

Because of their defeat at the hands of fascism in the 1930s, unions in the immediate postwar period rejected strong commitments to political parties. Since then, the German labor movement has consisted of unions with a unitary structure which is a synthesis of traditional elements of the socialist and the Catholic labor movements. Although labor is dominated by social democracy, the legacy of the Catholic teachings such as co-determination (*Mitbestimmung*), social partnership (*Sozialpartnerschaft*), or capital formation for employees (*Verm ögensbildung*) has become an integral part of the German trade unions' ideology. A second organizational principle of the trade unions is that they are organized on an industrial basis. Although there is a Christian trade union and some professional organizations, their influence on social matters is minimal.

The dominant labor organizations are 17 trade unions affiliated with the Deutscher Gewerkschaftsbund (DGB, Confederation of Trade Unions). The Deutscher Beamtenbund (DBB, Association of Civil Servants) cannot be regarded as a trade union because it has no bargaining rights and civil servants are not allowed to strike; wages and working conditions are unilaterally determined by the government, with the settlements negotiated by DGB unions for workers and white-collar employees in the public sector setting the pattern. Their small membership, plus the fact that it is distributed over the whole range of the economy, results in the DAG (Deutsche Angestellten-Gewerkschaft—white-collar association) and the Confederation of Christian Trade Unions (CGB) being unable to strike or even to be taken seriously by the employers, who therefore enter into collective bargaining agreements with them in only a few sectors (banking, insurance). (See Table 7 for data on membership in trade union organizations.)

In effect, therefore, the DGB unions are without competition. Employees who do not agree with the trade union policy have no alternative but to remain nonmembers or to leave the union; the scope for an internal opposition is limited by the high degree of centralization in the unions' organizational structure.

In the 1980s unionized employees who are members of DGB affiliates make up a third of the labor force (see Table 8). This density of union membership does not indicate the unions' power and influence, for two reasons. First, employees support for unions far exceeds their readiness for unionization; at the works council elections (election of workplace representatives, the works councillors—Betriebsrat), about 80 percent of all employees vote regularly for candidates who have been nominated by DGB unions. Secondly, as far as bargaining power and fighting strength are concerned, the decisive factor is the trade union density by industrial sectors; because the wage autonomy and the strike monopoly rests with the individual unions, they, and not the DGB, make key decisions.

Beyond these general measures of union density, three additional elements should be considered. About 50 percent of all manual workers and 25 percent of all white-collar workers are unionized; men (about 45 percent) are much better organized than women; and union density in industry (just under 60 percent) is almost 2.5 times higher than that in the nonindustrial private sector. The favorable conditions of recruitment for the unions in the metal-working industry (engineering, the electrical industry, the automobile industry) are also significant, since collective bargaining in this sector affects the whole economy. This explains why IG Metall shows a disproportionately high union density and why the organization of the male, highly qualified, industrial workforce has an undisputed monopoly of representation.

Another feature of the German unions is their centralized

TABLE 7
Level of Trade Union Organization of the Federal Republic of Germany, 1980

	Beamte[a]		White-Collar Workers		Manual Workers		Total	
Employed								
Total	2,261,000		10,002,000		11,372,000		23,635,000	
Percent	9.57		42.32		48.11		100.0	
	Number	Percent	Number	Percent	Number	Percent	Number	Percent
Unionized								
DGB	847,952	50.29	1,658,121	72.17	5,376,454	97.71	7,882,527	83.09
DBB	746,329	44.26	58,951	2.56	15,732	0.28	821,012	8.65
DAG	—	—	494,874	21.54	—	—	494,874	5.22
CGB	91,976	5.45	85,707	3.73	110,487	2.01	288,170	3.04
Total	1,686,257	100.00	2,297,653	100.00	5,502,673	100.0	9,486,583	100.0
Percentage unionized	74.58		22.97		48.39		40.13	

Source: Jacobi, Müller-Jentsch, and Schmidt (1981), p. 199.
[a] Permanent civil servants with life-long job security who have no right to strike.

TABLE 8

Deutscher Gewertschaftsbund—Membership, December 31, 1983

Union	Manual	White-Collar	Beamte[a]	Men	Women	Total	Shares (%)
Metal industries	2,148,262	387,382	—	2,173,663	361,981	2,535,644	32.7
Public service	575,443	510,693	87,389	837,655	335,870	1,173,525	15.1
Chemical industry	515,057	20,219	—	515,079	120,197	635,276	8.2
Construction	480,817	42,312	—	498,864	24,265	523,129	6.8
Post	142,881	44,979	270,069	321,099	136,830	457,929	5.9
Rail	189,434	7,990	182,110	360,795	18,739	379,534	4.9
Mining and energy	318,423	47,676	229	359,327	7,001	366,328	4.7
Trading, banking, insurance	48,234	312,138	—	156,744	203,628	360,372	4.7
Textile, clothing	238,103	25,817	—	110,739	153,181	263,920	3.4
Food, drink, tobacco	209,870	53,655	—	177,861	85,644	263,525	3.4
Education, science	—	46,749	138,741	88,714	95,776	185,490	2.4
Police	9,073	16,885	141,614	153,949	13,623	167,572	2.2
Wood processing, plastics	139,144	10,580	—	129,838	19,886	149,724	1.9
Printing	112,975	31,369	—	111,420	32,924	144,344	1.9
Leather	47,839	2,845	—	28,393	22,291	50,684	0.7
Arts	—	46,668	—	38,891	7,777	46,668	0.6
Agriculture	36,636	2,919	2,694	37,112	5,137	42,249	0.5
DGB 12/31/1983	5,212,191	1,710,876	822,846	6,101,143	1,644,770	7,745,913	100.0
DGB 12/31/1982	5,319,430	1,701,657	827,916	6,199,604	1,649,399	7,849,003	100.0

Source: DGB, *Mitgliederstastik.*

[a] Permanent civil servants with life-long job security who have no right to strike.

authority. Most of the internal decision-making takes place in the peak echelons of union bureaucracy, so that there is no countervailing power with the rank and file. Externally, the unions' strong position is based on their exclusive right to set wages and call strikes. Groups at the workplace level or the works councils have no such right.

It is surprising that German unions, whose structures correspond in various ways to a Marxist view of a united, disciplined, and firmly led class organization, have not remained organizations of class, but have developed, partly voluntarily and partly under compulsion, towards bodies of intermediary interest representation. In other words, unions have not exercised their potential for disruption or veto power to attack capitalism, but, on the contrary, have accepted responsibility for promoting the political and economic development of a capitalist democracy. During the long period of prosperity, their role as intermediaries was to secure social peace by continuously improving the living conditions of the working population without endangering stability and growth. In view of the current modernization and technological change, the trade unions' intermediate function is to mitigate the social consequences of this process and to provide a high level of acceptance among the employees (Brandt, Jacobi, and Müller-Jentsch 1982).

To appreciate fully labor's role in Germany, it is necessary to understand the system of co-determination and the industrial relations system. Each system has clearly defined tasks and functions. The industrial relations system is the collective bargaining system, whereas co-determination is a model for participation.

The foundation of the collective bargaining system is free collective bargaining, which implies that only the employers' associations and the unions are officially recognized parties in bargaining and are responsible for the regulation of all relations at work. In the Federal Republic there is a broad consensus on the need for such regulations. This includes both the mutual recognition and the regular negotiations covering all aspects of employment. Consequently a network of collective bargaining agreements exists. They include binding both sides on wage levels, wage differentials, and systems of wage determination as well as on the length and distribution of working time. They also cover a number of other specific regulations such as protection against dismissal, job security for older employees, security of wage levels in case of reallocations of labor or demotions, protection against rationalizations, preretirement, etc. The contracts are almost exclusively negotiated on a sectoral or industry-wide basis; the bargaining process is largely absent at the level of plants or individual companies. Thus, there are no trade union bargaining agents at the plant level, nor are there any shop stewards.

Not only the right to bargain, but also the right to engage in industrial disputes is exclusively reserved to the parties in collective bargaining. The right to strike rests with the unions and the right to lock out with the employers' associations. All industrial conciliation also falls within the sphere of collective bargaining and is based on regulations negotiated by the parties. There are no statutory provisions or state conciliation agencies. The conciliation system varies from industry to industry and normally comprises three elements: Arbitration committees with equal representation of both parties have seldom been successful in reaching agreements. More efficient are conciliation proceedings chaired by a neutral third party, appointed with the mutual consent of the parties to the dispute. The neutral is usually a judge, a professor, or the president of a state agency. In situations where industrial disputes are particularly significant, such as the 1984 dispute over the 35-hour week, "special" arbitration proceedings are chaired by highly placed politicians.

On the one hand, free collective bargaining provides the system of industrial relations with a broad area for regulation free of state interference. On the other hand, it is characterized by a high degree of institutionalization, juridification, and centralization leading to extensive regulation. There is a close relationship between the structural and organizational principles of the trade unions and this system.

By contrast, the system of co-determination is based on two foundations. The law (Works Constitution Act) states that a works council, representing the interests of the whole workforce, shall be elected in all establishments with more than five employees. The works council has a number of rights to information and consultation, and in personnel matters (recruitment, dismissal, reallocation of labor) the council and management have an equal number of votes. A works council is legally constrained in certain areas—that is, it has to consider the interest of the plant and company and may not strike. Beyond solving day-to-day workplace problems, it can negotiate with management only on subjects the parties to collective bargaining either have not negotiated at all or on those which the parties have ceded responsibility to the works council. The law requires that the workforce and its trade unions in large companies be represented on the supervisory board. With the shareholders having a guaranteed majority on the executive board and with company's management resting firmly with the board, the employees have only a marginal influence on the business policy (Markovits 1982).

Co-determination grants the trade unions and the mostly unionized members of the works councils extensive rights of information, but only limited rights of participation. These rights do not entail substantial limits on management authority. It is also clear that co-determination promotes the integration of workers and that it has contributed to social peace.

Trade Union Policy

In their three most important policy areas—wages, working conditions, and working time—trade unions have been relatively successful in balancing the representation of their members' interests and promoting German competitiveness in international markets.

Union objectives for wage and income distribution have largely been maintained, so labor is now aiming at increases that are neutral in distributional terms. Although demands for a redistribution of incomes are still on the unions' agenda, they have clearly receded into the background. However, labor opposes an extension of wage differentials. Since these objectives are at variance with government neo-monetarist policies and supply-side strategies, labor has proposed alternative Keynesian economic policies. Unions demand employment programs which stimulate growth and promote and advocate an expansion of public-sector employment. Their wage demands refer to the need for increased purchasing power.

There is, however, considerable discrepancy between these objectives and the actual practice of trade union wage policy. This is not so much a question of the unions' inability to enforce their claims; rather, they have not fought seriously to achieve what they have demanded. This reluctance is reflected in the unwillingness of

IG Metall, since 1975, to engage in industrial action in support of the implementation of their wage policy. Instead, the union compromises readily on wage policy demands. Moreover, there are indications that labor's stand against an extension of interindustry wage differentials is weakening. Although unions in the public service attack the earnings lag, other unions tacitly accept the gap. Public service unions themselves are relatively powerless. Judging from the collective bargaining agreements of some smaller trade unions favoring highly qualified employees, there are signs that the occupational wage differences also will expand.

Thus the contrast between government and employer economic and wage policies, on the one hand, and those of the trade unions, on the other, have not led to greater conflict over wage and distribution policy. In contrast with their former success in promoting income redistribution, the trade unions are now voluntarily suffering losses in real wages. Their cooperation with management and government on wage policy cannot be attributed to their weakened bargaining power, although it cannot be denied that such a general tendency exists (Esser 1982).

The decisive factor in the trade unions' wage policy is the inconsistency of their economic policy goals—a Keynesian macroeconomic policy combined with the belief that the modernization of the economy via structural change is inevitable. Whereas the economic policy prescriptions are based on the assumption of deficient demand, agreement to the modernization strategy recognizes the priority of investment. Obviously, the trade union policy assessment that wages should not block structural change has won increasing support. These facts explain union restraint in the pursuit of their collective bargaining objectives. They also are consistent with the belief that a contribution could be made to assuring the competitiveness of the West German economy through advance concessions to wage policy. Labor counts on the West German economy as being one of the winners in international competition. This expectation, and not only their weakened bargaining position, is responsible for the cooperative posture of the unions.

The unions have responded to stress resulting from technological change and reorganization in the factory or office by putting forward so-called qualitative demands. These demands are concerned with issues such as increased efficiency or intensified work effort as well as the threat to jobs, skills, and income. The linking of demands for protection against the social consequences of employer rationalization schemes with the traditional objectives concerning wages and working time marks an important new step in the development of collective bargaining. All in all, unions have become critical of the social effects of technological progress. The traditional confidence of organized workers in technical progress certainly has not given way to pessimism, but the concern over the application of modern production methods, administration, and "control" technologies has grown. However, this judgment must be qualified by noting that only two trade unions, the IG Druck (printers' union) and the IG Metall, were prepared to turn such new demands into negotiating issues. The explosiveness of such demands was manifested in two bitter disputes in 1978, involving both strikes and lockouts.

In the printing industry union demands concerned the introduction of the new technology, which replaced the traditional metal type with electronically directed "text systems." This development threatened the continued employment of a group of highly skilled workers who constituted the core of the printers' union. Demands for rules on manning, protection of earnings, rest periods, and reduction in working time for employees working on video display terminals were directed towards both job and income protection as well as organizational objectives. The jobs and income of the type-setters were threatened, as was the strength, or even the existence, of the union. At the same time, the demands implied far-reaching intervention in employers' personnel and investment policies. After a long strike, the IG Druck was able to achieve some new contract provisions (far-reaching provisions for earnings and temporary manning rules for work on terminals, and special protection for jobs and earnings of skilled employees). As it was waging a defensive struggle against the consequences of an inexorable development, the IG Druck had to concede any control over the application of modern technologies and the new jobs to which they give rise.

In the metal-working industry in 1978, the IG Metall demanded individual and collective safeguards against occupational "demotions" caused by changes in jobs brought about by rationalization. Technological change and the reorganization of work created jobs which, on the basis of existing job evaluation systems in collective agreements, were to be paid at a rate lower than that of the positions lost. Management could, therefore, demote the employees affected by such changes into lower categories. In order to prevent these losses, the IG Metall wanted to stop individual demotions. To prevent enterprises from reducing wages by the dismissal of higher paid employees and recruiting in the lower paid categories, the union demanded collective safeguards to preserve existing job categories. The individual, and especially the collective, safeguards against demotion would have involved extensive interventions in management rights over personnel policy and the determination of pay scales. The protection against demotion was a defensive measure, in contrast with the more far-reaching demands concerning changes in the wage structure. With the agreement that demotions may not exceed two job categories and, in a case where a demotion has been made, previous earnings are temporarily guaranteed, the IG Metall obtained a new set of collectively bargained regulations and therefore was partially successful. But it was not able to enforce a complete ban on individual demotions or even the rudiments of collective safeguards against demotions.

Unions clearly generated fresh bargaining demands in response to the new forms in which present rationalizations harm workers' interests. Such safeguarding provisions (which, after all, are not widespread) do not constitute obstacles or disincentives to technology and productivity; rather, they only serve as transitional arrangements and social protection (in trade union jargon, "a soft landing") for those who are currently affected. They do nothing for those who will be recruited in the future. Qualitative goals may become more significant in collective bargaining if the process of rationalization, with its negative consequences for employment and working conditions, affects not only unskilled employees, but also skilled workers more drastically than before.

With continuing high rates of unemployment, the traditional trade union demand for a reduction of working time has again come to the fore. The trade unions expected that a reduction of working time, particularly the introduction of a 35-hour workweek, would reduce unemployment and thus distribute existing work more evenly among all employees. Leisure, health, humanization, and leveling policies, which have also been pursued within the context of the trade unions' hours campaign, have been of only secondary importance. Since the end of the 1970s a number of agreements have been reached incorporating a wide range of measures. The hours initiative was attended by strikes and lockouts and led to escalating trials of strength in the major disputes of 1979 and 1984. The most important outcomes of these struggles will be briefly summarized.

In the early 1970s annual 20-day vacations (equal to four weeks) existed in almost all regions of the economy. Prior to 1979, repeated improvements of one or two days in vacation entitlements were negotiated. The most important agreements were reached in 1979. In the steel industry annual holidays for all employees were increased in stages to 30 days, and this provision was carried over into metal-working, chemicals, and printing. Similar agreements were later concluded in other areas of the economy. As a result, by the mid-1980s a holiday period of six weeks became normal for most employees. Additional paid holidays were granted to older workers and to shift workers in the steel and printing industries. Comparable agreements were reached in only a few areas—as, for example, for postal employees in 1980 after a short strike.

The IG Metall was able, through a limited strike in 1973, to gain selective reductions in working time for groups of employees with difficult working conditions. For the first time the unions obtained "minimum rest periods" of 5 minutes per hour within the framework of the prevailing 40-hour week for all assembly-line workers and those on incentive pay plans. Labor has succeeded only in exceptional cases in obtaining similar provisions in other sections of the IG Metall or the rest of the economy.

New ways to cut working time originated with the agreement on "preretirement sabbaticals" for older workers. The aim of such measures is to offer older workers a flexible transition into retirement. In 1978 older workers in the cigarette industry were given the opportunity to reduce their weekly working time up to 20 hours with full compensation, or to retire on 75 percent of their gross earnings. Subsequently, such benefits were extended to the foodstuffs industry.

In 1984 a voluntary early-retirement plan for employees ages 58 to 64 was introduced in some sectors of the economy. This scheme had been proposed by some trade unions and had government support. The regulations, based upon collective bargaining agreements, specify that employers pay a considerably reduced "wage" to their employees who are willing to retire—the wage being about 50 percent of former effective earnings plus pension and insurance contributions. Employers include the costs of such schemes in the total package of collective agreement revisions for all employees. Employers may also replace inefficient older workers with efficient younger employees. In addition, the government grants subsidies for filling jobs that have become vacant under these voluntary retirement plans. However, the effect on the employment situation is limited, as few employees are eligible for retirement and the majority of those who are will not make use of preretirement because it involves a considerable loss of income.

In some manufacturing plants the trade unions have accepted agreements for flexible working time. The normal workweek of 40 hours is distributed in such a way that working time in some weeks is greater than in others. This allows an extension of machine cycles by introducing additional shifts or weekend work. The trade unions accept such regulations because they are linked to increased employment.

The focus of trade union policy on hours of work, and also of two strikes, was a reduction in the workweek. In recent years almost all unions have declared that the introduction of the 35-hour week was one of their primary bargaining objectives. However, only the IG Metall and the IG Druck have made this demand a topic for negotiation and strike action. Other unions held back from pressing the issue, stating that it was a long-term objective or that they themselves could not set a pattern.

The issue of the 35-hour week led to a strike with widespread consequences in the steel industry in 1978–79. As the employers had stipulated in their so-called "taboo catalogue" that any movement to reduce the 40-hour week was to be flatly rejected, both bargaining parties were aware that the dispute could affect all unions and employers' associations. The strike ended after six weeks, with the IG Metall giving up its basic objective and settling instead for the progressive extension of annual holidays up to 30 days. This agreement could not stabilize employment; it must therefore be evaluated as a defeat not only for the IG Metall, but for the entire trade union movement. Perhaps as a consequence, no other union attempted to pursue the issue for five years.

In the beginning of 1984 the IG Metall launched a campaign for the 35-hour week, again seeking to create employment. This time it risked the conflict in the metal-working industry, the core of the West German economy, which employs 4 million people. (At the same time the printers' union also was on strike for a reduction in weekly working time.) The metal industry strike lasted for seven weeks and became the largest industrial dispute in West German history. There were 57,000 striking workers, another 155,000 who were locked out, and 315,000 who were laid off due to the conflict. The latter were subject to what is called in German trade union jargon "a cold lockout," as many companies stopped production on the grounds that supplies were either lacking or could not be delivered to the strike areas. The auto industry was most affected by the strike and almost came to a complete standstill. The loss of economic growth for the whole economy amounted to 1 percent per annum, although the major part of the production losses caused by the dispute could be made up. The IG Metall spend DM 600 million during the strike, largely on strike pay for members on strike or locked out, while employers spent DM 1,000 million, mostly on payments to companies suffering from the effects of the strike.

This confrontation was predictable for two reasons. On the one hand, the employers adhered to the positions laid down in their "taboo catalogue" which rejected any reduction of weekly working time. On the other hand, the Conservative-Liberal government interfered in the conflict in a manner that had been unknown in the Socialist-Liberal era. It exploited an internal split within the unions affiliated with the DGB, with one group advocating the 35-hour week and the other favoring a reduction in working time by a preretirement scheme. Chancellor Kohl and his government not only rejected the 35-hour week "as stupid and silly" and economically irresponsible, but also passed a law providing financial means for preretirement.

Since the union strike ballot found 80 percent of the members favored a strike and the stoppage had strong support, the union's action must be regarded as a success for IG Metall. Eventually the strike was settled by arbitration. A conservative Social Democrat and committed Catholic, who had also been a president of the construction union and a cabinet minister, was chosen as arbitrator. He awarded a wage increase over two years, a voluntary preretirement for workers age 58 and over, a reduction in the average workweek to 38.5 hours with no loss of income, and a plan to vary the workweek between 37 and 40 hours for particular individual groups of employees.

The essential part of the agreement was the compromise on working time. The 40-hour week, which was introduced as the standard in the mid-1960s, would be reduced to 38.5 hours. These arrangements clearly reflect the intermediary role of IG Metall—and thus of the whole German trade union movement. The sometimes militant representation of their members' interests contrasts with their obvious readiness for compromise; the trade unions are still able to combine a social agreement of interests with the imperatives of the modernization strategy.

When the cuts in working time are measured against the trade unions' aspirations, it is clear that the extension of the length of holidays took account of leisure-time and health considerations to a high degree. It has now become possible for the majority of wage and salary earners to benefit from dividing their annual holiday entitlements into two holidays of three weeks each. In view of the small number of wage and salary earners who benefited from selective measures to reduce working time, the trade unions cannot point to any notable success in terms of "humanizing" working life. But they experienced their greatest failure when they attempted to stabilize employment through cuts in working time.

Industrial Relations

Even in the past five years, industrial relations have not been greatly strained. The structure and the institutional framework of the collective bargaining system have remained unchanged. In terms of its capacity to settle social problems, the German industrial relations system provided efficient instruments that can be applied in a flexible way. It is especially notable that the employers have become stronger as a result of higher unemployment and technological change.

German employers are much more organized and centralized than their trade union counterparts. There are employers' associations in several industries, often dominated by large-scale enterprises, which negotiate legally binding agreements. Negotiations of these industrial federations are coordinated by the employers umbrella organization, Federation of German Employers' Associations (BDA). For example, in 1978 the BDA presented its so-called "taboo catalogue" containing rules for coordination within the association as well as guidelines on the limits of management compromise in bargaining. Among its instructions was one that Saturday, usually not a "working day," should remain a working day in order to maximize the use of labor and machinery. It was not until 1984 that employers had to yield on demands to reduce the 40-hour week, but in return they secured concessions to allow greater flexibility in the employment of labor.

Since more than 80 percent of all employers, including all large-scale enterprises (except Volkswagen), belong to employers' associations, these organizations can establish common policies. This enhances management's bargaining power by avoiding decentralized bargaining structures and fragmented bargaining positions. Thus labor is always faced with a central organization, which usually precludes reaching pattern-setting breakthroughs against companies willing to make concesssions.

Another source of employer strength is their considerable influence on government economic and social policy, even though there are no formal links with the government or any political party. Because of the traditionally close relationship between private enterprise and the Liberal and especially the two Christian-Conservative parties, the political influence of business has grown since the change of government in the fall of 1982.

Two other specific features of employer strength are the right to lock out and the dominant position within firms. As a response to trade union strike action, employers' associations have the right to lock out. This step creates a considerable burden on the trade unions' strike fund because union payments to striking or locked-out members are comparatively high. The right to lock out, which was established by judicial decisions, provides them with a powerful weapon in bargaining. A reassertion of their authority at the plant level, which was weakened during a period of prosperity, is a result of the modernization strategy. Employers are taking advantage of the technological reorganization to enhance their control over the discipline and efficiency of their workforces.

Given the continuing high unemployment rates and the change of government, it is not surprising that employers' readiness for cooperation has decreased. In their relations with the trade unions they are faced with the dilemma of having to choose between cooperation and conflict. Their problem is that social peace is important, though sometimes expensive. Attacking trade unions would mean losing them as social partners and running the risk of their subsequent radicalization. The development of the industrial dispute in 1984 over the introduction of the 35-hour week and the agreement reached subsequently illustrate that the parties need existing structures and institutions of the collective bargaining system, although the inevitable detour of the conflict was necessary before a return to their cooperative behavior.

Generally, industrial disputes are highly juridified—that is, regulated by judicial decisions. A number of legal barriers have been erected against strikes: political strikes are unlawful; the strike target has to be the employer; the right to strike lies with the union organization and not with the workforce or the trade union group within the firm; a strike is allowed only after all efforts of negotiations have failed. Trade unions have developed a wide range of graded actions to exert pressure on employers; the stage of an industry-wide stoppage is rare. Legally, the employers are allowed to take defensive lockout actions (*Abwehraussperrung*) but cannot lock out for offensive reasons (*Angriffsaussperrung*). In case of a lockout, there are restrictions on the employers that limit the scope of an industrial dispute. The limits and flexible use of industrial action have contributed to the relatively long duration of disputes and the small number of persons directly affected.

Since 1950, years in which there were major strikes have regularly been followed by periods of an almost total absence of labor disputes (see Table 9 for the recent record). The strike behavior can be attributed to the maintenance of trade unions' readiness for cooperation, which was developed in the long phase of economic expansion, despite 10 years of high unemployment. The strikes in the Federal Republic show the unions' ability to

TABLE 9
Strikes and Lockouts

Year	Workers Involved (Annual, in 000s)	Days Lost
1978	487	4,281
1979	77	483
1980	45	128
1981	253	58
1982	40	15
1983	94	41
1984 (estimate)[a]	600	6,000

Source: Statistisches Bundesamt, *Statistisches Jahrbuch*, 1984.
[a] Trade union figures.

withstand employer pressure by demonstrating their members' continued commitment and the militancy of their organizations. A survey of the major disputes since 1978 (Table 10) demonstrates two tendencies. First, it is remarkable that the major issues have been almost exclusively nonmonetary in character. Second, the table shows how extensively employers exercise their right to lock out and have thus adopted a strategy of industrial action that has effectively increased their resistance to trade union demands.

TABLE 10
Major Labor Disputes Since 1978

| Year | Economic Sector | Number of Workers Involved | | Demand |
		Strikers	Locked Out	
1978	Printing industry	20,000	50,000	Job and earnings protection
1978	Metal-working industry	90,000	145,000	Earnings protection
1978–79	Steel industry	45,000	35,000	35-hour week.
1980	Post office	25,000	—	Additional leisure time for shift-workers
1984	Printing industry	45,000	—	35-hour week
1984	Metal-working industry	57,000	55,000 315,000 (affected by "cold lockouts")	35-hour week

Sources: Information published by the trade unions and employer associations.

The labor disputes of 1984 were certainly consistent with the tradition of industrial relations in the Federal Republic. Since the employers and the government had believed they could soundly defeat labor, the IG Metall, as the traditional union pacemaker, first had to prove its fighting strength before all participants could agree to a compromise formula. The IG Metall's success thus paved the way for a renewal of cooperative relations. The ability of the IG Metall to maintain its position as the legitimate representative of a broad spectrum of employees and to continue as the major partner in bargaining will be an essential determinant for the development of industrial relations.

The great flexibility in the conduct of bargaining which is characteristic of both sides is based internally on their claim to leadership and authority and externally on their monopoly powers of representation. The peak organizations of both parties to collective bargaining are thus provided with the autonomy which makes possible a calculated combination of stubborness, readiness for compromise, and the intention to reach a settlement (Scharpf 1978). Membership support in conflict situations and the leadership's ability to bind the members to resulting agreements have always been decisive factors in reaching workable compromises. The processing of conflicts is encouraged by splitting the negotiating package and dealing with different issues separately. Whereas wage agreements have a term of 12 to 18 months, all other arrangements are normally valid for five years. An absolute ban on strikes exists during the life of these contracts; supplementary agreements are possible by mutual agreements, and industrial disputes are unlawful.

The root of economic flexibility lies in the dominance of industry-type collective agreements. The bargaining arena thus lies in the middle between the individual enterprise and the whole economy. This creates simultaneously an orientation towards macroeconomic issues and, as well, the possibility of reaching supplemental collective agreements embodying microeconomic conditions. The macroeconomic orientation of collective bargaining policies, which is not evident at first, is attributable to the dominant role of the industrial sector. The metal-working sector occupies an especially significant position in this process as, with the exception of the chemicals industry, it comprises the most important industrial branches: the machine-building, electrical engineering, and automobile industries. The market and production conditions to which these branches were subject are partly comparable, but differences predominate. When a single collective agreement for the whole metal-working industry is concluded, macroeconomic conditions come strongly to the fore.

The fine-tuning of industry-wide collective agreements with conditions specific to individual factories or enterprises is carried out via factory agreements between management and the works council. The legally prescribed superiority of the (sectoral) collective agreement, however, guarantees that developments in introductory collective bargaining cannot be reversed, but can merely be modified at the factory level. As collective agreements set minima, which can be improved only by factory agreements, working time and other general working conditions are subject in every branch to a basic regulation that is binding on all enterprises. The branch-differentiated and microeconomic regulations give the macroeconomic system as a whole the flexbility it needs to be able to cope with economic change.

The notable efficiency of the German system of industrial relations also explains why its structures and institutions have not been changed by legislation or jurisprudence. As free collective bargaining (*Tarifautonomie*), which is the exclusive domain of the social partners and is vigorously defended by both, implies a high degree of self-regulation, independent of any interference by the state, the demand for tripartite corporatist arrangements has never been particularly strong. Without doubt, there was a tendency in favor of tripartite regulation during the Socialist-Liberal era. Although the current Conservative reversal leads to a cooling of labor's relations with the government, it does not entail a political disaster for the trade unions because they can still take the initiative in their traditional area of free collective bargaining. But in terms of its export-oriented modernization strategy, the government does not run much risk because the trade unions are very much interested in its success and, for lack of alternatives, are forced to cooperate when they are no longer a courted participant in the modernization cartel. The outcome of the industrial dispute of 1984 confirms that the traditional policy of social partnership, cooperation, and the harmonization of interests will be continued despite the considerable loss of power on the trade union side.

References

Beckurts, Karl Heinz. "Die Schlacht kann gewonnen werden." *Die Zeit* 37 (September 1984): p. 44.

Bergmann, Joachim, Otto Jacobi, and Walther Müller-Jentsch. *Gewerkschaften in der Bundesrepublik. Gewerkschaftiche Lohnpolitik zwischen Mitgliederinteressen und Ökonomischen Systemzwägen*. Frankfurt and New York: Campus Verlag, 1979.

Bergmann, Joachim, and Walther Müller-Jentsch. "The Federal Republic of Germany: Cooperative Unionism and Dual Bargaining System Challenged." In *Worker Militancy and Its Consequences, 1965–1975*, ed. Solomon Barkin. New York: Praeger, 1975.

BDA-Bundesvereinigung Deutscher Arbeitgeberverbände. "'Katalog der zu koordinierenden lohn- und tarifpolitischen Fragen (Tabu-Katalog)." *Frankfurter Rundschau* (January 27, 1979): p. 28.

BMWI-Bundesministerium für Wirtschaft. *Hochtechnologien und internationale Wettbewerbsfähigkeit der deutschen Wirtschaft.* Bonn: BMWI-Dokumentation, 1984.

Brandt, Gerhard, Otto Jacobi, and Walther Müller-Jentsch. *Anpassung an die Krise: Gewerkschaften in den siebziger Jahren.* Frankfurt and New York: Campus Verlag, 1982.

Deutsche Bundesbank. *Report for the Year 1983.* Frankfurt: Deutsche Bundesbank, 1984.

Esser, Josef. *Gewerkschaften in der Krise.* Frankfurt: Suhrkamp Verlag, 1982.

Gourevitch, Peter, et al. *Unions and Economic Crisis: Britain, West Germany, and Sweden.* London: George Allen & Unwin, 1984.

Hofer, Peter, et al. *Die Bundesrepublik Deutschland 1985/1990/2000—Die Entwicklung von Wirtschaft und Gesellschaft in der Bundesrepublik un den Bundesländern bis 2000.* Stuttgart: Horst Poller-Verlag, 1983.

Jacobi, Otto, Walther Müller-Jentsch, and Eberhard Schmidt. *Starker Arm am kurzen Hebel. Kritisches Gewerkschaftsjahrbuch 1981/1982.* West Berlin: Rotbuch Berlag, 1981.

Landesregierung von Baden-Württemberg. *Zukunftsperspektiven gesellschaftlicher Entwicklungen.* Stuttgart: Kommissionsbericht im Auftrage der Landesregierung, 1983.

Markovits, Andrei S. *The Political Economy of West Germany.* New York: Praeger, 1982.

Müller-Jentsch, Walther, and Hans-Joachim Sperling. "Economic Development, Labor Conflicts and the Industrial Relations System in West Germany." In *The Resurgence of Class Conflict in Western Europe since 1968, Volume 1— National Studies,* eds. Colin Crouch and Alessandro Pizzorno. London: Macmillan, 1978.

Nussbaum, Bruce. *The World After Oil. The Shifting Axis of Power and Wealth.* New York: Simon and Schuster, 1983.

SVR-Sachverstandigenrat zur Begutachtung der gesamtwirtschaftlichen Entwicklung. *Jahresgutachten 1981/82.* Bonn: Deutscher Bundestag, Drucksache 9/1061, 1981.

————. *Jahresgutachten 1984/85.* Bonn: Deutscher Bundestag, Drucksache 10/2541, 1984.

Scharpf, Fritz W. *Autonome Gewerkschaften und staatliche Wirtschaftspolitik: Probleme einer Verbändegesetzgebung.* Köln-Frankfurt: Europaische Verlagsanstalt, 1978.

Schmidt, Helmut. "The World Economy at Stake." *The Economist* (February 26, 1983): pp. 21–32.

Schmidt, Klaus-Dieter, et al. *Im Anpassungspprozep zuruckgeworfen. Die deutsche Wirtschaft vor neuen Herausforderungen.* Tubingen: J.C.B. Mohr (Paul Siebeck), 1984.

Welzmüller, Rudi. "Einkommensentwicklung und Verteilung." *WSI Mitteilungen des Deutschen Gewerkschaftsbundes* 37 (June 1984): 342–52.

CHAPTER 8

Japan's Industrial Relations: A Social Compact Emerges

KOJI TAIRA
University of Illinois at Urbana-Champaign

SOLOMON B. LEVINE
University of Wisconsin-Madison

Since the early 1970s the Japanese economy has experienced a series of major external shocks and, as a result, has undergone extensive, though unanticipated, structural changes. In 1971 there were what the Japanese labeled the "Nixon shocks"—the U.S. economic policy which realigned and later abolished the fixed exchange rates that had been in effect for more than two decades. The result was a substantial appreciation of the yen and a high degree of economic uncertainty (Taira 1972). In 1973 the first oil shock brought about the sudden obsolescence of much of the economic and technological structure built on cheap oil. Japanese economic growth came to a sudden halt in 1974, and industrial production continued to decline for another year before recovery (Taira 1975, Levine 1975). The second oil shock struck Japan in 1979–1980. Although Japan weathered the crisis rather successfully, its delayed effects overlapped with ripples from the U.S. recession of 1981–1982 to result in a prolonged slowdown through the first quarter of 1983. Table 1 shows a few key economic indicators that suggest how drastically economic fundamentals have changed since 1970.

While these economic changes profoundly impacted the Japanese system of industrial relations, important trends already under way for several years before the external shocks hit appeared to intensify. While this era saw a halt in the growth of union membership for the first time in more than two decades,

TABLE 1

Selected Macroeconomic Indicators of Japan, 1970–1983:
Economic Growth, Unemployment, Prices, and Wages
(in percent)

Year	GNP Growth Rate	Unemployment Rate	Rate of Change in Consumer Price Index	Rate of Change in Money Wage Index	Rate of Change in Real Wage Index[a]
1970	9.9	1.1	7.7	16.9	8.7
1971	4.7	1.2	6.1	14.6	8.1
1972	9.0	1.4	4.5	16.0	11.0
1973	8.8	1.3	11.9	21.5	8.7
1974	−1.2	1.4	24.5	27.2	2.2
1975	2.4	1.9	11.8	14.8	2.7
1976	5.3	2.0	9.3	12.5	2.9
1977	5.3	2.0	8.1	8.5	0.5
1978	5.1	2.2	3.8	6.4	2.5
1979	5.2	2.1	3.6	6.0	2.3
1980	4.8	2.0	8.0	6.3	− 1.6
1981	4.0	2.2	4.9	5.3	0.4
1982	3.3	2.4	2.7	4.5	1.7
1983	3.4	2.6	1.9	3.5	1.6

Sources: Ministry of Labor, Rōdō hakusho (White Paper on Labor), 1983, statistical appendix, pp. 6-12, supplemented where necessary by Ministry of Labor, Rōdō tōkei yōran (Abstract of Labor Statistics), 1985, pp. 12-15.

[a] As given in the sources. Technically, this should be equal to the difference between rate of change in money wage index and rate of change in consumer price index.

nonetheless labor-management collective bargaining spread. In addition, the scope of collective bargaining widened, government social and labor welfare measures were strengthened, and trilateral and bilateral consultation at national, industrial, and enterprise levels seemed to flourish as never before. With these developments came a notable shift within organized labor toward economic concerns and away from political activism. There was also a precipitous decline in industrial disputes resulting in work stoppages. Each of these aspects is treated in the pages that follow.

Our conclusion is that collective bargaining, originally implanted by the labor reforms of the Occupation Era (1945-1952), in fact has become increasingly vigorous and widespread during the past 35 years. Moreover, despite the serious impact of the economic crises of the 1970s, and their ensuing recessions, upon industries where unionism and collective bargaining had become most firmly entrenched, so far there has been no dire threat to the viability of the institution. Collective bargaining has managed to cope with numerous adjustments required by the recent economic changes, and, while it is difficult to ascribe cause and effect, the outcome, compared to other market-oriented economies, has been avoidance of prolonged inflation, distorted income distribution, high-level unemployment, inadequate manpower skills, and sharpened overt conflict. In a sense, then, Japan may be seen as *the* case of compatibility between collective bargaining and economic and social change. Indeed, by all measurements, collective bargaining has become increasingly important as a principal institution for rule-making in industrial relations especially as national policy has come to rely more and more upon market mechanisms (Kōshiro 1983a, Shirai 1984).

Transformations in the Labor Economy

Controlling Inflation

With the exception of 1974 and 1975, Table 1 shows a rather steady decline in the growth rate from the "miracle growth" of the pre-oil shock years to moderate but sustainable growth of the 1980s. Along with the substantial deceleration in growth, the rate of unemployment of the labor force doubled between the early 1970s and early 1980s—to 2.6 percent by 1983. Despite the precipitous drop in the growth rate of GNP between 1973 and 1976, the transition in the unemployment rate to a higher level was far less dramatic. The avoidance of drastic changes in employment after the first oil shock may well be considered "miraculous" and can be attributed to special characteristics of labor market institutions and processes—to which we return later.

Table 1 also shows that the rate of change in real wages has been roughly consistent with the trends in economic growth and employment. The consistency is illustrated by changes in consumer prices and changes in money wages. Short of perfect stability in the level of consumer prices and perfect foresight and confidence in such stability, the usual way in which workers can ensure themselves of rising real earnings is by increases in money wages faster than those in consumer prices over which they have no control. Lack of confidence in the course of price movements and insistence on more and more money wages were the inclinations of Japanese workers and unions during the period of "miracle growth." These inclinations culminated in the crisis of 1974 and 1975 when workers had little difficulty in obtaining increases in real wages not justified by the then negative or very low rates of economic growth. These successes were quickly reversed by 1976, however, and as a consequence money wages have followed changes in consumer prices kept low since then by Japan's macroeconomic policy.

There was an implicit contract between the government, unions, and workers. If the government kept its promise to reduce the rate of increase in consumer prices and to maintain employment, workers would keep their promise not to demand a greater increase in money wages than could be justified by increases in productivity as reflected in real economic growth. And, since it was the employers who knew best whether real growth was actually taking place, they endeavored to make sure through their enterprise-level bargaining that wage increases were within the bounds of productivity increases. In this effort, individual employers were advised and assisted by the wage policies formulated by national and industry-level employer associations (Levine 1984). Enterprise unions were likewise advised and assisted by their national centers and industry-wide union federations. Government, employers, and labor leaders also had frequent meetings to discuss socioeconomic issues of national importance and to sound one another out as to how national affairs might be translated into decision and action at the everyday level. Thus arose what some observers have begun to call an informal incomes policy or the "corporatist state" of Japan (Evans undated, Taira 1978, Pempel 1982, Shimada 1983).

The lessons from the fiasco of a price-wage-price spiral in 1973–1974 under the first oil shock were put to good use under the second oil shock of 1979–1980. By then an increase in the oil price along with the induced worsening of the terms of trade for Japan was regarded as a "tax" that had to be borne equitably by all socioeconomic groups of Japan, especially the employers and workers. Workers or unions did not insist this time, as they did before, on preventing the loss of real wages. They absorbed a part of the "OPEC tax" burden, which the employers had almost exclusively borne in 1973–1975. How equitable the sharing of the OPEC tax burden was between employers and workers can be illustrated by the movement of labor's relative share in national income since 1976, as shown in Table 2. The crude share as shown in the first column of the table persistently rises throughout the period. At the same time the percentage of the labor force in paid employment also increases substantially. When the share of labor in national income is adjusted for the rise in the percentage of the labor force in paid employment, labor's adjusted share still rises dramatically between 1973 and 1977 and then roughly stabilizes—at almost 10 percentage points higher than that for 1970. This somewhat surprising redistribution of national income in favor of employees can be attributed in part to the well-known tendency of labor's share to rise during a recession (Ono 1983, Economic Planning Agency 1981, Ch. 1). But a major factor behind the change in labor's share in 1973–1977 may well have been the militancy of labor unions in 1974 and 1975 and the concessions made by

TABLE 2

Labor's Relative Share in National Income
and Labor Disputes in Japan, 1970–1983

Year	Share of Employee Compensation in National Income (%)	Labor Force in Paid Employment (%)	Adjusted Share of Employee Compensation in N.I. (%)[a]	Labor Disputes (Number)		Rate of Unionization (%)[b]
				Total	Strikes Lasting ½ Day or Longer	
1970	54.7	64.6	54.7	4,551	2,256	35.4
1971	57.3	66.0	56.1	6,861	3,515	34.8
1972	58.0	66.7	56.0	5,808	2,489	34.3
1973	59.2	68.1	56.2	9,459	2,320	33.1
1974	63.0	68.0	59.8	10,462	5,197	33.9
1975	66.3	68.7	62.4	8,435	3,385	34.4
1976	66.6	68.6	62.7	7,984	2,715	33.7
1977	68.0	68.1	64.5	6,960	1,707	33.2
1978	66.6	68.7	62.6	5,416	1,512	32.6
1979	67.0	69.8	62.0	4,026	1,151	31.6
1980	67.2	70.2	61.7	4,376	1,128	30.8
1981	68.9	70.4	63.2	7,660	950	30.8
1982	69.9	71.0	63.6	7,477	941	30.5
1983	71.0	71.4	64.3	5,562	889	29.7

Sources: Ministry of Labor, Rōdō tōkei yōran (Abstract of Labor Statistics), 1985, pp. 16, 22-23, 198-99, supplemented by earlier issues.

[a] First, the percentage of the labor force in paid employment is turned into an index with its 1970 value as the base (=100). Then the share of employee compensation in national income is deflated by this index to get the adjusted share.

[b] The numerator is the number of labor union members and the denominator is the number of paid employees (i.e., labor force participants in paid employment, as in the third column).

employers at the expense of profits and by the government in accepting a new, albeit implicit, social compact.[1]

The inflation induced by the second oil shock was short-lived thanks to workers' and unions' refusal to prolong it by demanding higher money wages. By 1983 Japan came to enjoy the world's lowest rate of inflation. With the cooling of inflation, real wages improved, seemingly proving the wisdom of workers' and unions' earlier decision not to demand money wage increases as much as the increases in prices. The essential lesson was apparently this: the best way to secure real wage increases is to help reduce the inflation rate. This means above all that the way of thinking that characterized earlier union policy—namely that higher real wages were secured only by consistently insisting on and obtaining money wage increases larger than price increases—had to be abandoned. This ability to discard outmoded habits and take on ones more appropriate to changing circumstances may well be the ultimate of the Japanese miracle.

Restructuring the Labor Economy

The first oil shock and the recession of 1973–1975 also marked the end of an era based on heavy industries and cheap energy. The next, based on energy-saving knowledge-intensive industries, would in due course be known as a "microelectronic revolution." These considerable shifts and changes within the economy led to a new set of economic fundamentals in which the economic growth rate was half as high as before, the unemployment rate twice as high, and changes in wages and prices contained within the bounds of price stability and productivity growth. When the second oil shock and its aftermath produced unprecedented dislocations and unemployment in other industrialized countries, Japan, which had already begun the transition, alone succeeded in maintaining socioeconomic stability and alone proceeded unwaveringly towards a future which other countries belatedly began to acknowledge as the right choice.

---

[1] While the role of militancy in the determination of labor's relative share in national income is not amenable to a statistical test on the basis of annual data on wages, incomes, employment, etc., annual wage increases can be explained to a statistically significant extent by the labor dispute indicators such as mandays lost due to work stoppages, percentages of workers participating in strikes, etc. For an econometric test of the latter type, see Kōshiro 1983a.

TABLE 3
Employment Index, Overall and by Major Class of Industry
(1980 = 100)

Industry	1970	1973	1975	1979	1983	1983/ 1970
Paid employment, total[a]	83.2	91.0	91.8	97.6	106.0	127.4
Regular employment, total[b]	93.4	96.8	95.4	98.5	103.4	110.8
Mining	257.9	153.2	121.0	102.0	92.0	35.7
Manufacturing[c]	112.1	111.1	104.8	99.0	101.7	90.7
Textiles	180.2	158.2	128.9	103.3	91.7	50.7
Iron & steel	123.8	119.8	120.9	100.7	95.2	77.2
Machinery	122.1	116.8	110.8	99.1	103.5	84.8
Electrical & electronic machinery	104.5	101.4	90.7	95.2	112.8	107.9
Transportation equipment	98.6	112.4	112.0	97.3	104.5	106.0
Precision instruments	87.8	93.5	86.3	95.5	108.1	123.1
Ordnance	107.5	98.8	93.9	101.0	105.6	98.2
Construction	86.4	98.7	93.8	102.3	102.4	118.5
Wholesale & retail trade	82.4	90.1	91.1	97.9	105.8	128.4
Finance & insurance	83.2	90.6	91.7	100.6	100.1	120.3
Transportation & communication	100.4	98.9	99.9	99.9	99.2	98.8
Utilities[d]	85.8	89.8	91.4	97.5	101.6	118.4
Services	67.0	74.5	79.2	95.3	108.8	162.4

Sources: Ministry of Labor, *Rōdō tōkei yōran* (Abstract of Labor Statistics), 1985, pp. 34–35, supplemented by earlier issues.

[a] From the labor force survey by the Bureau of Statistics, Prime Minister's Office.

[b] From the monthly labor survey (establishment-based) by the Ministry of Labor. This index and its components refer to regular employment in establishments with 30 or more regular employees.

[c] In this major industry class, there are 20 two-digit industries, seven of which are listed here for illustrative purposes regarding changes in the structure of employment.

[d] Electricity, gas, water, and heating.

The picture since 1976 is even more remarkable when it is seen as a dynamic equilibrium of conflicting structural changes at the microeconomic level. Table 3 shows an example of structural changes with emphasis on trends in employment in different industries. The years are chosen with reference to their historical significance. With the exception of the arbitrary beginning in 1970 and the arbitrary end in 1983, 1973 is the year of the first oil shock, 1975 the trough of industrial production, and 1979 the end of employment decline in manufacturing.

Throughout this period paid employment has increased

unabated. On the other hand, "regular employment" in nonagricultural establishments employing 30 or more regular employees has fluctuated over time. The difference between "regular" employment and paid employment is "nonregular employment." The latter apparently has increased steadily and substantially since 1970. Opinion may differ in interpreting the situation in which regular employment stagnates while nonregular jobs multiply. Regular employment has been declining in industry (mining and manufacturing) while the tertiary sector (wholesale and retail, etc.) has been absorbing regular employment by leaps and bounds.[2]

It is important to emphasize that "regular employment" is a statistical concept comprising workers with no specified term of employment (therefore expected to be in their jobs indefinitely or, more popularly, "permanently") as well as workers who, whatever their contractual periods of employment (a day, a month, three months, etc.), have been in continuous employment in the same establishments for more than a month. The latter type of "regular employment" refers, in common parlance, to day laborers and casual, temporary, part-time, and seasonal workers who just happen to be lucky enough to be working for the same employer for extended periods through successive renewals of contracts.

The size of establishment is another important factor in Japanese labor statistics: many labor market and employment characteristics are correlated with size. For example, labor turnover rates among "regular employees" decrease as establishment size increases—that is, they are higher in smaller than in larger establishments. Among establishments with fewer than 30 regular employees, turnover is high enough to render "regular employment" largely meaningless (Van Helvoort 1979, Levine 1983).

To understand how these various categories of employment stand quantitatively in relation to one another, nonagricultural paid employment in 1979 was somewhat less than 70 percent of the total labor force of almost 56 million. The remainder, somewhat more

---

[2] At this point it is useful to note certain distinct characteristics of Japanese statistical categories of employment. In Table 3, "paid employment," which includes everyone who works for wages and salaries, comes from the household-based labor force survey by the Bureau of Statistics of the Prime Minister's Office. "Regular employment," in the same table and throughout this chapter wherever the term is used, comes from the establishment-based monthly labor survey by the Ministry of Labor. The most widely used regular employment index is based on the survey results of establishments employing 30 or more regular employees (Ministry of Labor 1984).

than 30 percent in agriculture and nonagricultural self-employment, included unpaid family workers and some paid workers. Less than half of nonagricultural paid employment was in establishments with 30 or more regular employees. This means that more than half of nonagricultural paid employment was found in smaller workshops and stores where employment relationships are relatively unstable. The fabled "lifetime employment" of Japan, often cited as the source of the strength of Japan's competitive advantage and thus of the threat to American manufacturing employment, can at most be attributed to larger and more powerful firms, primarily in manufacturing. Statistically they are identified by manufacturing establishments employing at least 500 regular employees. Employment in these private-sector establishments is less than 5 percent of Japan's total labor force.

Thus, it is important to emphasize that "regular employment," a very important term in the lexicon of Japanese labor economics, has been shrinking relative to nonregular types of employment in recent years. In mining and manufacturing, regular employment has suffered a permanent absolute decline since the first oil shock. Table 3 shows that the traditional branches of manufacturing (textiles and iron and steel), which were standard-bearers of Japan's industrial revolutions at different historical times, have clearly done their job and receded into the history books. A technological revolution is now in full swing in branches of manufacturing like electric and electronic machinery, transportation equipment, precision instruments, and ordnance. In all industries, the universal mark of new technology is the use of microelectronic devices like integrated circuits.

It is ironic but conceivable that the prospect of unlimited labor productivity increases opened up by the wide diffusion of microelectronics is also the prospect of "de-industrialized" Japan. For example, blue-collar workers, the quintessential industrial class, are fast disappearing (Sadamoto 1981, OECD 1981, Sōgō Kenkyū Kaihatsu Kikō 1983). At the same time, white-collar workers are increasingly using machines based on microelectronics. The electronization of labor means the demise of both conventional blue collar and white collar. The pundits say that now everyone wears a gray collar. The computer, the most visible centerpiece of the new technological revolution, threatens to confiscate and absorb all the conventional skills, processes, and procedures by a complete codification of them in software. In the computer-integrated business and production systems, any useful skill can be coded and stored in the computer. This generates the need for a large army of software technicians, while automating much of the routine work in the factory and the office and reducing human labor to the position of a helper for robots. This bifurcation of labor into software technicians and semiskilled helpers of automation will destroy conventional crafts and office work alike and reorganize the workforce of an organization in ways radically different from current practices.

While the broad issue that this chapter could address is how Japan, at the epicenter of a new technological revolution, is managing its own "deindustrialization" together with a complete reorganization of its economy, that issue is too far-reaching. Its manageable subset is how Japan has dealt with the impact of the external shocks of the 1970s and how, in the course of coping, Japan has made institutional and technological innovations that have transformed her labor markets and industrial relations. In examining these changes, we deal first with the realms of government, management, and organized labor and then analyze developments in the collective bargaining and consultative activities among these realms.

Government Policy in the Era of Moderate Growth

In the area of industrial relations policy, the Japanese government dealt with the dramatic economic shifts of the 1970s by emphasizing increased labor-management-government consultation, nonintervention in private-sector collective bargaining, maintenance of employment security for the labor force, and equitable sharing of economic gains and losses among diverse sectors of the population. Especially following the "Nixon shock" of 1971 and the first oil crisis two years later, the incumbent conservative government, controlled by the Liberal Democratic Party (LDP), seemed to recognize that its survival in power depended as much on providing an enlarged role for organized labor and management in deliberations over economic planning and adjustment as on measures for strengthening social security, promoting equity in income distribution, and improving the quality of life for the populace as a whole.

As discussed above, the government offered an implicit "social compact" beginning midway through the 1970s. It should be noted, however, that this response did not rest upon any enactment such as a formal incomes or wages policy (which, in fact, after several investigations was officially rejected). Nor did it rest on amendments to certain key labor laws which were newly adopted, particularly in regard to social security, health and safety, and employment and wage maintenance. Rather, the new relationship that developed among the three major actors emerged from established practices that were then followed with increased intensity within the existing legal framework for industrial relations. It was a pragmatic response to the changing economic and social conditions of the times.

The Evolution of Pragmatism

This pragmatism seemingly grew from a realization by the LDP leadership and government bureaucracy that "production first" could no longer be the prime objective in an era of slowed economic growth, increased internationalization of the Japanese economy, industrial restructuring, and threat of stagflation. No longer could the conservative government depend upon a "fallout" from high-speed growth to provide rapid wage gains and improvements in working conditions and social welfare. Unless the government party could demonstrate, in both symbolic and real terms, a deliberate shift towards strengthening economic security and equity, it ran the risk of losing popular support and perhaps giving up the reins it had held continuously from the late 1940s. Throughout the 1960s, it should be noted, the LDP strength in the Diet had steadily eroded, and by the early 1970s it was holding but a bare majority of the seats. Only a malproportioned voting system that favored conservative-dominated rural areas and a sharp continuing rift among the opposition parties sustained the LDP, itself faction-ridden, throughout this period.

A threat to the precarious position of the LDP was a growing restiveness within organized labor during the 1960s and into the first half of the 1970s—primarily over sharing the gains of economic growth and improving the quality of working life. As indicated in Table 2, the incidence and extent of labor-management disputes had shown a steady increase from 1970 to 1975. This trend was a continuation of a rising tide of disputes and stoppages throughout the decade of the 1960s. From 1965 to 1975, the number of officially recorded labor-management disputes, with and without work stoppages, more than tripled from about 3000 to 10,000 per year. In the same period, strikes themselves rose from 1500 to 4000 annually, and workdays lost per year from 2 million to 8 million (Levine and Taira 1980).

From the point of view of government and employers, the spread of work stoppages, especially as they were bunched so closely together during the annual *shuntō* (spring labor offensive), contained an ominous threat of a general strike. Such a "big bang," if it were to occur, could readily bring the economy to a total halt and, more dangerously from the standpoint of the LDP, turn into a political challenge from the union-supported left-wing opposition parties that could bring down the conservative government. Undoubtedly for the LDP leadership it was wiser to step up joint consultative practices and to favor measures for increased social welfare and equity which, through sharing responsibility and economic gains, could head off such an eventuality. From the mid-1970s on, central government budget deficits soared with the expansion of welfare spending that resulted without a matching growth in tax revenues.

As also shown in Table 2, since 1975 the number of disputes and work stoppages fell precipitously, the latter reaching unprecedented lows by 1983. As the Japanese economy seemed to weather the second oil shock of 1979–1980 and the ensuing worldwide recession by maintaining near "full" employment, relative price stability, and labor's increased share in GNP, the LDP managed by the early 1980s to regain popular and Diet strength, although in the general elections of late 1983, as a reaction to the conviction of former Prime Minister Tanaka on bribery charges, the downward trend for the conservatives appeared once again. The LDP, now lacking a majority, had to join in a coalition with a minority group of conservative independents to form a government.

Joint Consultation

Since the mid-1970s, the degree of joint consultation, both bipartite and tripartite, has shown a notable rise. This trend, unlike the decline in disputes, was the culmination of earlier efforts to foster union-management consultation. Government promotion of joint consultation with organized labor on economic matters, including labor market policy, may be traced to the early 1960s. Up to that time the conservative government either had been hostile to much of the labor movement or had attempted to ignore union demands. Its position was that it was not inclined to deal with organized labor as long as many of the unions were emphasizing political radicalism.

A noticeable turnabout in governmental attitudes began to emerge following the year-long strike at the Mitsui Miike coal mines in 1960, which basically was fought over the government's policy to substitute petroleum for coal as a chief industrial energy source, thereby rather suddenly displacing several hundred thousand miners from employment. While this bitter conflict ended in defeat for the coal miners' union, it had come to involve most of organized labor and was a dramatic demonstration for political and industrial leaders of the need to prepare carefully for major labor force adjustments as Japan plunged ahead into a period of rapid industrial growth and drastic shifts in industrial structure. For many years, even to the present, the experience of Miike, although never repeated, remained a vivid reminder of the likelihood of forceful labor protest if significant changes were introduced without joint planning and consultation well in advance.

Throughout the 1960s, and for the first time since the Occupation, the government, including the Prime Minister and cabinet ministers, occasionally discussed economic policy matters and leading labor issues with labor leaders. Such steps were facilitated by a trend towards moderation within organized labor. As wages and benefits, working conditions, and employment security steadily improved during an era of rapid economic growth, union leaders increasingly turned their attention towards obtaining economic gains through rational collective bargaining, joint consultation, and legislative enactment and, at the same time, moderated their shrill ideological pronouncements and mass political demonstrations. Also, within the government bureaucracy (for example, the Ministry of Labor and the labor relations commissions), younger officials were emerging who were more aware of and better educated about modern industrial relations systems and the need to accommodate conflicting interests.

At the national level, a key development in the emergence of tripartite consultation came with the initiation in 1970 of the *Sanrōkon* (Sangyō Rōdō Konwakai), or Industry and Labor Conference, officially sponsored by the Ministry of Labor. Sanrōkon, for the first time since the Allied Occupation, brought together eminent employer, labor, and government leaders. While the participants did not engage in any formal negotiations, they began the practice of airing the most important economic and labor questions and hearing expert opinion and analysis of the issues on a regular basis. The conference has continued to the present, meeting as often as once a month, with the intent of gaining a clearer understanding of each party's perspective and narrowing differences among them. Usually the participants, who at times have included the Prime Minister and other important cabinet officers, have focused on long-run policy problems.

Much credit for the initiation and continued success of Sanrōkon is due to the late Dr. Nakayama Ichirō, who as President of the Japan Institute of Labor from 1961 to 1980, organized the conference with the assistance of the Institute's expert industrial relations staff. The Institute itself, a semidetached agency of the Ministry of Labor, was a major innovation when it was established in 1958 as an independent body for research and education in the field of labor-management relations, and it has continued to maintain its excellent reputation.

Formation and regularization of Sanrōkon seemed also to stimulate similar tripartite and bipartite meetings on a regular basis at industrial and regional levels. By the mid-1970s consultative mechanisms had been established in at least 19 of the major industries, again not expressly for purposes of collective bargaining but for information-sharing and mutual understanding. Also, the leaders of Nikkeiren, the Japan Federation of Employers' Associations, began meeting more frequently with leaders of the major national labor centers. No doubt such activities in turn nurtured the growing practice of joint union-management consultation within many of the large enterprises (Shimada 1983).

During this period, managements in the large private companies, often led by new younger executives more attentive to and better trained in personnel and industrial relations, accelerated joint consultation and information-sharing with their respective enterprise-level unions and introduced forms of worker participation and "humanization" techniques in the production process. Such a movement emerged without challenging the collective bargaining process, now increasingly institutionalized with each successive *shuntō*. There was increasing acceptance of the *shuntō* approach also as the means for equalizing wage and benefit gains among enterprises, industries, and sectors—thus removing the general wage issue from the industrial enterprise level.

The acid test for the developing network of joint consultation came in 1975 as Japan faced the aftermath of the first oil crisis. Despite the establishment of Sanrōkon five years earlier and the growing practice of joint consultation at all levels, there was an increase in worker participation in protest demonstrations in each successive *shuntō* and a rise in the incidence of work stoppages and the number of workers involved. Moreover, in each yearly settlement there were larger and larger wage increases in money terms, as the unions demanded a catch-up with European levels. Further, with the spread of industrial pollution, the aging of the labor force, and the rise in taxes as worker incomes increased, the organizers of *shuntō* began broadening the range of issues to be negotiated and by 1984 labeled the annual drive for improvements as "the people's *shuntō*." The near rampant inflation in 1973 and 1974, in which the cost of living rose more than 30 percent a year at one point, placed the government and the major employers on the defensive. The *shuntō* settlements in the Spring of 1974 averaged 32 percent, the highest ever. As the inflation showed no immediate signs of abating, the unions warned that they would aim to top even that figure the following year. To the conservative government, this spelled disaster, both economically and politically, as the spectre of a general strike loomed.

The Role of Joint Consultation in Crisis Management

In the months immediately following the 1974 *shuntō* settlements, the government launched rounds of intensive, national-level joint consultation with employers' associations and labor unions in hopes of achieving wage and price restraints that would halt the inflation and set the stage for an era of economic stability. As noted earlier, the consultation technique proved successful, although a number of trade-offs were made in the process. In view of the deleterious economic effects of the first oil crisis, the LDP leadership seemed compelled to demonstrate that it would restore stability in the economy in an equitable manner. While the conservative government admitted that the era of rapid growth was over, it wished to reassure the parties and the public that it was possible to have steady, moderate growth in which all elements of society would benefit equally and that, if there had to be sacrifices, they would be shared equally. Thus, rather than moving ahead unilaterally in developing fiscal, monetary, and industrial and trade policies, the government opted to step up the consultation on these matters and to provide "concessions" to workers that would secure the cooperation of organized labor.

From the political point of view, in all likelihood joint consultation was a preferred strategy, since, if the government failed to stem inflation and prevent a serious rise in unemployment, it could escape the stigma of being solely responsible for the failure. By emphasizing the achievement of consensus among government, business, and labor, all the actors would share equally in claiming success (or admitting failure). Given the precarious position of the LDP, especially on the heels of the Tanaka-Lockheed scandal, a conciliatory approach appeared to be the wisest for demonstrating skillful political leadership and restoring popular voting support.

Neither the representatives of the employers nor the mainstream of organized labor were willing to resist the invitation to participate in joint deliberations. The sense of crisis was so pervasive that no major group wished to be seen as uncooperative in efforts to rescue Japan from the greatest peril since the immediate postwar period. Memories of starvation, rampant inflation, and wholesale unemployment were still too vivid. Without the established machinery for regular joint consultation and information-sharing on a tripartite basis, the noninflationary *shuntō* settlements of 1975 and the years since may never have taken place.

The Policies of Moderation and Adjustment

The Japanese government adopted various policies in the mid-1970s to reverse the inflation, while minimizing its trade-off—rising unemployment. Inflation was controlled by restricting the growth of money supply, while the employment level was supported by a loose fiscal policy. Labor, in exchange, moderated its money wage demands.

The control of inflation was a brilliant success. Table 1 shows that the annual inflation rate fell from 24 percent in 1974 to less than 4 percent in 1979 (though the trend reversed somewhat with the second oil shock of 1979–80). Nor did success cost too much in terms of the unemployment trade-off. The unemployment rate rose by less than one percentage point and stabilized at somewhat above 2 percent. Even so, this represented a "doubling" of the unemployment rate.

The aggregate effect of such fiscal and monetary policies, helped by the changing environment of the labor sector, was the remarkable stabilization of the GNP growth rate at above 5 percent per annum. In a few years, however, the public debt had accumulated to the extent that it was at one of the highest levels among developed countries relative to current expenditures and GNP. This increasingly displeased the business community, which pressed for an "administrative reform" to reduce government expenditures.

In order to stabilize economic growth, the government also set in motion policies that would encourage a shift to newer, less energy-intensive, high-tech and information-processing enterprises, an expansion of exports and constraining of imports (especially oil), and a reduction or elimination of certain high cost and uncompetitive industries such as shipbuilding, iron and steel, petrochemical manufacturing, and aluminum refining. At the same time it strengthened pollution-control regulations.

As is characteristic for much of Japan's centralized governmental structure, the bureaucracy takes the primary responsibility for formulating and proposing policy for cabinet and Diet consideration and adoption. In this case, the Ministry of Labor played a key role. Much of the planning involved deliberations of the Ministry staff with the tripartite advisory commissions. The range of issues considered included minimum labor standards, manpower development and labor market strategy, wage and benefit policy, and industrial relations procedures such as mediation and conciliation. The process also included the participation and assent of the prefectural-level labor offices attached to each of the 47 prefectural governments. Throughout this period, the Ministry of Labor, on behalf of the government and ruling party, attempted to strike a balance between promoting "free" labor markets in keeping with the continual strengthening of the market sector in Japan's economic structure and achieving uniformity in improving wages, benefits, and working conditions across the economy. For the latter especially, the Ministry announced support for strengthening private collective bargaining, at least among the major industries and enterprises which could be expected to set economy- and industry-wide patterns. There is little to indicate that this dual approach has changed in any notable way in the years since 1975 except, as already discussed, giving greater encouragement to bilateral and trilateral consultation at national and industrial levels.

There were several specific changes in public policy that were of direct relevance to labor. Major improvements had already been made in the social security system in 1973, raising benefits and adopting indexation to guard against rises in the cost of living for the retired. These amendments, adopted in anticipation of the rapid aging of the Japanese population, essentially brought Japanese social security benefits for the fully eligible close to the levels of other advanced market economies. Of even more immediate importance were changes enacted in the Unemployment Insurance Law in 1975, which shifted the emphasis from unemployment compensation to the subsidizing of payrolls and prevention of layoffs and workforce reductions through additional taxes on employer payrolls. Significantly, the new act was entitled The Employment Insurance Law. It is estimated that the administration of this program, through its Employment Stabilization Fund, helped employers to keep workers on payrolls who otherwise might have been displaced. Especially pertinent for this program was the adoption of the Temporary Relief Law for Workers Displaced from Specific Depressed Industries and the Law for Temporary Measures for Workers Displaced from Specific Depressed Areas, both placed into effect in 1978. Still other legislative and administrative steps provided for income tax reductions in the lower brackets, for increased training and retraining activities, for maintaining older workers and handicapped persons on payrolls or for hiring them, for improving working conditions of construction workers and migrant and seasonal workers, for strengthening vocational guidance and placement services for new middle, high school, and college graduates, for raising minimum wage levels, and for reducing hours of work (Japan Institute of Labor 1982). Also under way was proposed legislation for fair employment opportunities for women and for establishing labor standards for part-time workers.

Along with these measures, all of which were subjects of discussion at the regularly scheduled meetings of Sanrōkon and other joint consultative bodies, the government engaged in "jawboning" for wage and price restraint. As mentioned, it had already rejected proposals for a formal incomes policy, for which no apparent consensus emerged especially in view of organized labor's strong objection. "Jawboning" was especially evident in the months following the 32 percent average settlements in the 1974 *shuntō*. At the Sanrōkon meetings at that time, for example, the government went to great lengths to present econometric analyses from the Economic Planning Agency (EPA) demonstrating that average settlements above 15 percent in the 1975 *shuntō* would not only result in further inflation but also wipe out any real wage gains for workers, and that lower settlements actually would allow an increase in real wages. Simultaneously, the government, with the backing of major employer groups, gave repeated assurances that it would follow fiscal, monetary, trade, and industrial policies that would hold inflation below that figure, even if they meant reduced profits or actual losses for business. As discussed later, the labor leadership eventually came to accept these arguments, albeit reluctantly, and settled for even less than the 15 percent target in the Spring of 1975. It was the first time since the early 1960s that the unions had accepted a money increase lower than in the preceding year.

In the years since 1975 it has remained government policy to foster and strengthen joint consultation and information-sharing for the purpose of constraining wages and prices. Compared to the preceding period, it has been an era of relative quiescence; yet, the sense of crisis has never ended. There are constant reminders, often issued by the government, that Japan's overall economic position remains highly precarious, despite the success in avoiding prolonged stagflation. Indeed, the sense of peril seemed to heighten as increasingly vociferous pressures from abroad demanded (and succeeded in) opening the Japanese economy for liberalized imports and investment. The urgency of the need for wage and price constraints was again argued in the face of the second oil crisis of 1979–80 and the ensuing world recession of 1980–83. Thus, in each succeeding *shuntō* round, settlements steadily dropped or leveled off although, as shown in Table 1, they resulted in relatively small average real wage increases in most of these years (except in 1980 when they were actually negative). While unemployment increased to double the level of the early 1970s, the government could claim credit for achieving a smooth transition, compared to other advanced industrial economies, from the era of high to moderate growth.

All of this does not imply that the conservative government has now fully embraced organized labor as a full and equal partner in national economic planning, on the same basis as it seems to accept employer groups. Formal consultation with union representatives still does not take place regularly in key bureaucracies such as the Ministry of Finance, the Bank of Japan, the Ministry of International Trade and Industry, and the Economic Planning Agency. It is still a far cry from the participation of organized labor in planning Japan's economic recovery of 1947 and 1948 when socialists predominated in the government. By and large, the government still perceives the union movement as part of an obstructive opposition even though that opposition is split among minority parties ranging from moderate to radical.

However, the industrial relations policies pursued by the government have acknowledged increased status for and acceptance of the unions and serious considerations of their perspectives in formulating national economic policy. In a sense, this recognition has occurred within the more general trend of a shift over the years from government predominance through administrative guidance to increasing reliance upon competitive market forces and private-sector institutions for economic decision-making. Within this context, it has signaled general willingness to rely on collective bargaining as a major mechanism for wage determination in labor markets. It may be that basically it is this acceptance that has been of prime importance in lowering labor-management tension and in reducing overt conflict in industrial relations—at least for the time being.

Industrial Relations in the Public Sector

As an employer itself, however, the government has had to face a series of difficult problems in its relationship with the public-sector labor movement. The government's policy over the past decade or more has been essentially to lessen or isolate the strong influence of collective bargaining procedures and outcomes in the public sector upon the entire industrial relations system. Although government employment, both central and local, has constituted less than 10 percent of the entire labor force (or about 12 percent of total wage and salary earners), this sector from the outset of the postwar period has been the most unionized, militant, and radical, especially in such national unions as the teachers, local government civil servants and workers, and the employees of the major national enterprises and public corporations (notably, the government-owned railway, telephone and telegraph, and postal operations). Compared to other advanced industrialized market economies, Japan's public sector has been of unusual importance in affecting the national industrial relations system. Since the English-language literature about industrial relations in Japan has not stressed this point, it is useful to focus on the role of the public sector in some detail.

First, it should be recalled that since the late 1940s, when the Allied Occupation began its "reverse course" policy aimed at rebuilding Japan as a major industrial ally, the law has differentiated the collective bargaining rights of government employees from those of private-sector employees. While civil servants (including public school teachers) may organize within their respective agencies, they may not engage in collective bargaining or strikes, and they are allowed only to petition the government in limited personnel matters. Instead, for the central government civil servants, the National Personnel Authority, which under the law is supposed to be politically neutral and must follow private-sector trends, recommends wage and benefit adjustments for the central government to adopt within the usual budgetary restraints (local governments usually follow suit). Yet, in 1982, as part of its austerity program, and disregarding NPA recommendations, the central government froze the pay of the national civil servants and in 1983 held their general increases to 2 percent.

Unions in national enterprises and public corporations, on the other hand, are free to organize within their firms and to carry on collective bargaining, but they are not allowed to strike. Strikers are subject to penalty. For this group, at both national and local levels, special tripartite labor relations commissions like their counterpart commissions for the private sector, rule on employer unfair labor practices and union qualifications, but unlike the private-sector commissions they are authorized by law to carry out compulsory mediation and arbitration of labor-management disputes.

As a result, over the years, *shuntō* demands for the public enterprises and national corporations have almost invariably been arbitrated by the neutral members of the central public-sector commission and, in turn, since the late 1950s the government has implemented these awards as virtually required by law. While, for the most part, the decisions of the commission have been in line with the general *shuntō* pattern for the private sector, the public-sector unions have constantly campaigned, including going on strike illegally, for restoration of the right to strike, and on several occasions they have filed complaints with the International Labor Organization that the government denies them full freedom of association and the right to bargain collectively. Often coupled with public-sector strikes have been various political demands as well as actions of questionable legality (such as mass demonstrations and slow-downs). A major instance of such a strike occurred in late 1975 when public-sector unions, notably the National Railway workers, conducted an 8-day walkout which resulted in adverse public reaction because of the inconvenience it created. There has been no repeat of such a stoppage since 1975 and, in fact, public-sector strikes seem to have become increasingly milder. Almost invariably when a strike has occurred in this sector, the government has taken punitive action against the strikers and their leaders.

Among the many issues that have arisen between the government and public-sector unions, probably the most conflictual, aside from wage and benefit increases, has been the continuing effort by the central government to streamline operations and reduce staff in its bureaucracies, corporations, and enterprises. While the number of central government civil servants (excluding Self-Defense Forces) rose steadily from about 675,000 to almost 900,000 between 1957 and 1967, the government since that time, as authorized by law, has succeeded in leveling off and slightly reducing that number. In contrast, civil service employment in local governments has risen by about 900,000 since 1967 and today numbers around 3.3 million (Kōshiro 1983b, 1984a, 1984b; Yamaguchi 1983).

Under recently revised central government plans for "administrative reforms," further legislated reductions in staffing are slated. So far, however, the government has relied almost entirely upon natural attrition and reduced recruitment rather than dismissal for holding down the number of employees. Even then, the public-sector unions, notably in the National Railways and Telephone and Telegraph, have continually protested reductions in force and, when they were inevitable, have sought to negotiate and delay changes. It is significant in this regard that the labor unions have succeeded in electing a vociferous minority of former labor leaders as opposition members of the Diet, among which the largest numbers are from public-sector unions.

Related to the issue of staff reductions have been union protest campaigns, especially within the national enterprises and public corporations, against "productivity drives" instituted by management, particularly when they entail worker displacement or transfer.

Because of these protests, managements have come to accept the slow process of close consultation in advance and have engaged in detailed negotiations with the unions in order to obtain acceptance of some personnel adjustments. The process has been complicated by deep ideological divisions and rivalry among the unions, and some managements themselves have been divided over the approach they should follow. A general view of most of the public corporations and national enterprises is that, compared to large companies in the private sector, they are overstaffed, their employees are overpaid, and their operations are highly inefficient and bureaucratic. Only now, for example, after many years of negotiations and frequent disputes, does it appear likely that a wholesale reduction of the workforce may finally take place in the deficit-ridden National Railways.

Throughout the period under review, the public sector in Japan, perhaps to the conservative government's embarrassment, continued to display labor-management tension and conflict visibly sharper than in the private sector. Shielded as it is from international economic forces, the public sector does not appear to reflect the strong sense of peril and crisis found among employers and unions in private-sector industries. Thus, the transition to a consensual and cooperative system of industrial relations in evidence in much of the private sector during the 1970s does not seem to have occurred in the public sector, and this difference appears to have driven a wedge between the private- and public-sector unions. As will be discussed more fully below, up to the early or mid-1970s, much of organized labor in the private sector, particularly the unions that regularly participated in the annual *shuntō* under the sponsorship of Sōhyō and Chūritsu Rōren, looked to an alliance with the militant public-sector unions to mount pressures for wage and benefit increases. Since 1975, however, when the joint consultation system was developing rapidly and the 8-day strike of the public employees caused adverse public reaction, the two sectors have been drifting apart. In the annual *shuntō* rounds, the private-sector unions have looked less and less to the likely outcome of compulsory mediation and arbitration for the public corporations and national enterprises as one of the major benchmarks for their own settlements.

The seemingly weakened role of the public-sector unions apparently has encouraged the government to proceed with plans to break up and transfer the national enterprises and public corporations to the private sector. While this idea has been around for at least a decade, no such transfer has actually as yet taken place other than adoption of legislation to begin to shift the government-owned monopolies of tobacco, salt, and camphor, and of domestic telephone and telegraph, to private companies, effective in 1985. However, while subject to considerable debate, the question of full labor rights for unions in these enterprises remains in abeyance at least until 1987. In view of the conservative regime's drive for "administrative reform" and "smaller government," it appears likely that more "privatization" will take place in the next several years, but the exact arrangements will depend on whether full private-sector labor rights, including the right to strike, will be granted.[3] Only then, it might be surmised, are industrial relations in the public sector, as now constituted, apt to evolve towards the bargaining and con-sultative system developed in recent years for the private sector.

Management Responses to Economic Crises and Technological Challenges

Japanese managers have long demonstrated their skills in adjusting labor input to reflect changes in labor costs relative to other factor costs. The persistent rise in labor costs during the period of rapid growth of the 1960s was met by equally determined shifts to more capital-intensive industrial techniques. Before the oil shock of 1973, for example, the ratio of wages to capital goods prices increased more than three-fold between 1960 and 1973 (Economic Planning Agency 1982, p. 597), while during this period the ratio of energy prices to capital goods prices decreased. The result was that

---

[3] Transfer of public corporations and national enterprises to the private sector is only one part of the conservative government's effort to reduce deficit financing. Since the early 1980s, the Nakasone government, like its predecessors, has pledged austerity in governmental operations, including capping or restraining rises in social security and other welfare benefits (notably health), even though willing to permit defense expenditures to rise. Many of the local government units, under pressure from the central government, also appear to be attempting to hold down budgetary rises. Much of this is quite reminiscent of parallel developments in other advanced market-oriented nations where conservatives have come into power. Thus far, in the case of Japan, the joint consultation and information-sharing approach that has emerged so strongly in the private sector has in general accommodated to the curtailment in the size of government-sponsored social welfare since the early 1980s. This ac-commodation could well be the result of the relative newness of the system with the apparent achievement of more equal status for the three major actors, including organized labor. Whether the system will continue may well depend on sharing gains equitably in the years ahead—provided there are significant gains to share as Japan proceeds further into the postindustrial age.

energy- and capital-using, that is, labor-saving, industries and technologies were favored in Japan. Between 1973 and 1981, the ratio of wages to capital goods prices about doubled, while the ratio of energy prices to capital goods prices rose two and a half times. This called for a shift to energy-saving and labor-saving industries and techniques. The giant operations of the heavy and the chemical industries have increasingly given way to R&D-intensive, high-value-added industries—machinery, instruments, and electronics. The expanding output of these industries has been absorbed by eager users and consumers in Japan and abroad, transforming production processes, labor markets, and life styles. Since the tightening of the labor market in the late 1960s, Japanese industries and Japanese firms have been coping as much as possible with the problem of how to minimize the labor costs subject to changes in other factor costs and social constraints arising from the human side of labor.

The Japanese approach to labor cost minimization emphasizes (1) level and structure of labor compensation, (2) hours of work, (3) number of persons employed, (4) social or contractual status of persons employed, and (5) quality of work effort and workers' participation. All of these aspects are in varying degrees interdependent, sometimes positively and sometimes not. Costs saved on one of them might thus affect the entire cost-effectiveness of workforce management negatively. For example, callous pay cuts might undermine work effort and cause labor costs to rise rather than fall.

Over the years, however, management of these issues has been quite distinct, especially the Japanese practice of labor compensation which is highly responsive to the profits of the firm. The nonwage labor costs (NWLC), which economists call "quasi-fixed," are not as large a proportion of labor compensation in Japanese firms as in American or European firms. Our best estimates for 1982 put the Japanese NWLC at 27.3 percent of total employee compensation, 10 percentage points lower than in the U.S. and Europe (Fujita 1984, Hart 1984). Within the wage costs, about a third are paid as bonuses twice or more times a year, bargainable each time. The bargaining over the base pay occurs once a year in the Spring.

Thus employers and workers in Japan are constantly bargaining over some component of annual earnings, adjusting them to the changing economic conditions that affect the firm's profitability. Changes in earnings are thus made flexible not only upward (which is no surprise), but also downward (which makes Japan somewhat unique). The particular characteristics of the Japanese compensation structure make the downward adjustment of labor costs possible before special action is required for the reduction of the number of persons employed.

Responding to Economic Change

When a sharp reduction of output occurred due to the first oil shock of 1973, Japanese labor input as total hours worked by employed persons declined as rapidly as output, but employment was cushioned and adjusted over a longer period, ending in 1979. According to Japan's official statistics, the labor input index (the index of employment multiplied by the monthly hours worked) for 1975 is 87 percent of the index for 1973. For the same period, the index of manufacturing output shows a decline of 15 percent. (The two-percentage-point difference between output and labor input suggests a slight decline in labor productivity—no novelty as a cyclical relationship between output and labor input.) Although labor input fell by 13 percent in 1973–75, employment fell by only 6 percent, the difference being accounted for by a cutback in hours worked. This may give the impression that it is hard to cut employment as required by decreasing output in Japan. But the essential thing is the adjustment of labor to output change, which can be accomplished without depending exclusively on the reduction in the number of persons employed.

Furthermore, employment can be reduced painlessly through employees' voluntary quits if replacements are not hired at the same time. Before the recession of 1973–75, the annual separation rates in Japan were nearly 30 percent, of which more than 80 percent was through voluntary quits. After the oil shock, the separation rates decreased to below 20 percent (Ministry of Labor 1983, statistical appendix, p. 27). However, even in larger manufacturing establishments, where labor turnover can be expected to be lower than average, more than 10 percent of employees quit voluntarily each year. This would afford the employer a 10-percent reduction of employment by a simple hiring freeze for a year. In addition, employment can be reduced by mandatory retirement of long-service employees and by not renewing the contracts of temporary workers. If a greater employment reduction is needed than can be brought about by these painless methods, justifiable economic reasons can be invoked for terminating an additional number of employees. Table 4 illustrates how Japanese manufacturing plants have been coping with the need for employment adjustment since 1974.

Table 4 first divides firms into those which took some special measures for employment reduction and those which did not. The movement of either percentage over time is consistent with the pattern of changes in economic conditions. The worst year for industrial production was 1975, and a majority of plants were taking measures to reduce employment or control labor input. After that point, the percentage of plants engaged in employment adjustment steadily decreased, but rose again, though very moderately, after 1979 under the second oil shock and the impact of the U.S. recession. In the inquiry that generated Table 4, the management of each manufacturing plant was asked to name all the measures it had taken, so that the sum of percentages of plants across all measures exceeds the percentage of plants engaged in employment adjustment. The last column (12) indicates the average number of measures taken by the plants which said they were engaged in employment adjustment.

In Table 4, various measures for employment adjustment are arranged from left to right (columns 1 to 9, followed by "Others" in column 10) in an ascending order of difficulties for managers who have to make tougher decisions and employees who have to face tougher adversities. The first measure for employment adjustment, freezing or cutting back the hiring of "mid-career workers," is painless to managers and workers alike. "Mid-career worker" is a status designation for anyone with job experience elsewhere and hired from the labor market. It contrasts with "standard regular worker" who is recruited upon graduation from school or college and meant to be retained in employment until retirement. The standard regular workers constitute the core workforce, to which mid-career workers are added as needs arise. For the same age, experience, and qualifications, the mid-career worker is expected to acquiesce with lower pay and privileges than the standard regular worker.

Temporary, seasonal, or part-time workers (column 2) are another group of expendable workers. Many of them are statistically "regular" by virtue of long service through renewals of their fixed-term contracts. But no one (except for the affected workers who suffer from frustrated expectations) would question the legitimacy of the employer decision to terminate them under understandably difficult economic conditions. Reduction of overtime (column 3) is

TABLE 4
Proportions of Manufacturing Plants Practicing Specified Measures for
Employment Adjustment, 1974-1980 (percent; all plants = 100)

Year and Month	Plants Not Practicing Employment Adjustment At All	Plants Practicing Employment Adjustment	Plants Practicing Employment Adjustment by Measure Practiced											
			(1) Reducing or Freezing Hiring of Mid-Career Workers	(2) Nonrenewals of Contracts with Temporary, Seasonal, Part-Time Workers	(3) Reduction of Overtime Work	(4) Increases in Holidays, Days Off	(5) Introduction or Extension of 2-Day Weekends	(6) Increases in Vacations	(7) Reassignments and Transfers, Intra- and Inter-firm	(8) Temporary Layoffs	(9) Request for Voluntary Resignation or Dismissal	(10) Others	(11) Total	(12) Number of Measures Per Plant
1974														
1-6	74	26	14	3	13	1	3		3	3	1	1	42	1.6
7-9	57	43	28	6	25	4	2		6	7	1	1	80	1.9
10-12	35	65	45	19	46	5	2		18	17	6	2	160	2.5
1975														
1-3	26	74	44	21	51	7	5	4	22	21	7	2	184	2.5
4-6	29	71	50	16	54	5	6	3	23	20	5	1	183	2.6
7-9	33	67	46	9	47	3	3	4	21	11	3	1	146	2.2
10-12	41	59	44	11	41	3	1	2	21	7	3	1	134	2.3
1976														
1-3	49	51	37	7	35	2	2	2	19	4	3	1	112	2.2
4-6	67	33	21	3	19	1	1	0	12	2	2	0	61	1.8
7-9	69	31	21	4	16	1	1	1	11	1	1	1	58	1.9
10-12	68	32	21	3	18	0	1	1	12	1	1	0	58	1.8
1977														
1-3	67	30	20	5	17	1	1	0	12	1	1	1	59	2.0
4-6	70	34	19	3	18	1	1	0	12	1	1	1	57	1.7
7-9	66	39	23	3	19	1	0	1	14	1	2	1	65	1.7
10-12	61	36	25	5	21	1	1	1	15	2	3	1	74	2.1
1978														
1-3	64	36	22	6	21	1	0	1	15	2	3	1	72	2.0
4-6	71	29	19	4	17	1	1	0	13	2	2	1	60	2.1
7-9	72	28	18	3	15	1	1	0	12	1	1	1	53	1.9
10-12	71	29	18	3	16	1	1	1	12	1	2	1	56	1.9

TABLE 4 (continued)

Year and Month	Plants Not Practicing Employment Adjustment At All	Plants Practicing Employment Adjustment	Plants Practicing Employment Adjustment by Measure Practiced											
			(1) Reducing or Freezing Hiring of Mid-Career Workers	(2) Nonrenewals of Contracts with Temporary, Seasonal, Part-Time Workers	(3) Reduction of Overtime Work	(4) Increases in Holidays, Days Off	(5) Introduction or Extension of 2-Day Weekends	(6) Increases in Vacations	(7) Reassignments and Transfers, Intra- and Inter-firm	(8) Temporary Layoffs	(9) Request for Voluntary Resignation or Dismissal	(10) Others	(11) Total	(12) Number of Measures Per Plant
1979														
1-3	75	25	15	3	13	1	0	0	11	1	3	0	47	1.9
4-6	81	19	10	2	10	1	1	0	8	0	1	0	33	1.7
7-9	85	15	8	1	7	1	1	1	7	0	1	0	25	1.7
10-12	85	15	7	2	6	1	0	1	5	0	0	1	23	1.5
1980														
1-3	85	15	7	1	7	1	0	0	6	0	0	1	23	1.5
4-6	87	13	4	1	6	1	1	0	5	0	0	1	19	1.5
7-9	86	14	5	1	7	2	0	1	4	0	0	1	21	1.5
10-12	84	16	6	3	8	1	0	1	5	1	0	0	25	1.6
1981														
1-3	80	20	7	3	10	1	1	0	6	1	1	1	31	1.5
4-6	84	16	6	1	8	1	1	0	5	1	0	1	24	1.5
7-9	85	15	5	1	7	1	0	2	4	1	1	1	23	1.5
10-12	82	18	7	3	8	1	0	1	5	1	1	1	28	1.5
1982														
1-3	79	21	9	4	11	2	0	0	6	1	1	1	35	1.7
4-6	74	26	11	4	14	3	1	0	8	1	1	1	44	1.7
7-9	71	29	13	3	17	2	1	1	7	1	1	1	47	1.6
10-12	69	21	14	5	19	2	0	1	9	1	1	2	54	2.6
1983														
1-3	71	29	12	4	17	1	0	0	10	2	1	2	49	1.7
4-6	75	25	10	3	15	2	0	0	9	1	1	2	43	1.7
7-9	78	22	9	2	11	2	0	1	9	1	1	2	37	1.7
10-12	80	20	8	2	10	1	0	0	7	1	1	2	32	1.6

Sources: Ministry of Labor, *Rōdō tōkei yōran* (Abstract of Labor Statistics), 1981, pp. 54-55, and 1984, p. 48. The specified measures for employment adjustment are arranged from left to right in the increasing order of difficulty in implementation in the context of Japanese industrial relations.

a popular means of labor input adjustment. Its cost to the employees is a reduction of earnings, but base pay remains intact. Other ways to reduce working hours are covered in columns 4–6. The next most popular measure, the use of transfers inside or between plants (column 7), requires careful planning on the part of management and negotiation with unions and employees likely to be affected by this measure.

After these easier ways of adjusting employment are exhausted, management faces the prospects of the most difficult measures, layoffs and dismissals (columns 8 and 9). The temporary layoff mentioned here was a new institutional invention under the emergency of 1973–75. It was almost alien to Japanese managers and workers. Layoffs meant staying home for a fixed period of time with pay and the employment relationship guaranteed. Under the Employment Insurance Law, adopted in 1975, employers laying off employees could ask for government subsidies to cover the cost of uninterrupted payments to the laid-off workers. The last measure, termination for good, though disguised as voluntary resignation, was truly the last resort, although it was more in line with conventional Japanese employment practices than temporary layoff.

The relative importance of various measures for employment adjustment illustrated by Table 4 suggests some distinct strategy, procedures, and consequences which are popularly called "Japanese-style" employment adjustment (Taira 1980, Japan Institute of Labor 1980, Valli 1983, Inagami 1984). Statistical data alone do not account for human and organizational problems that have to be attended to in the course of or as a consequence of various measures of employment retrenchment. The personnel structure of a firm must maintain a dynamic equilibrium among people who are differentiated by age, sex, education, position, responsibility, authority, privileges, etc. Precisely because vitality and efficiency are more prized under adversity, an equitable distribution of the burden of adjustment is required as a condition for a leaner but stronger workforce.

Some consistency has been observed in Japanese firms' efforts to ensure equity in retrenchment and renewed vitality at the same time. In the name of equity, sacrifice starts with the high and mighty: shareholders and executives, who show leadership and responsibility by a dividend freeze, a pay cut, a reduction of perquisites, etc. Then the organizational chart of the firm is redrawn. All middle managers are reshuffled, some positions are eliminated, and some managers are retired. During the period of rapid growth before 1973, middle management expanded greatly and layers of positions multiplied. Many firms also indulged in the luxury of granting high nonfunctional status to please long-service employees whose number exceeded the number of functional managerial positions. All such "excess fat" in management had to be sliced out after 1973. Generous, and considerate, outplacement services were provided to redundant managers, although senior employees sitting by the window reading newspapers (*madogiwazoku*) became a standard joke everywhere.

After everything was done, the last resort was the solicitation of voluntary resignations from older, expensive managers with some years before retirement (*teinen*). These cases were few, but horror stories were many. When the need for this measure was proved, the first thing to do was to announce the number of persons desired for resignation within an appropriate age bracket. If a sufficient number came forward before the deadline, that finished the business for the time being. If there were not enough volunteers, another round of solicitation was made. If the second round failed, specific individuals were picked ("tapped on the shoulder") and asked to volunteer for the honor. The honor came with generous severance pay far exceeding what was expected for the *teinen* lump sum.

After share-holders, executives, and managers were dealt with, a fair share of the burden of adjustment was allocated to unionized regular employees. Traditionally, union posture is that of "unconditional objection" (*zettai hantai*) to any kind of employment insecurity affecting the membership. In earlier postwar years, violent strikes against "rationalization" were frequent and widespread. As already noted in the case of coal mining, the memory of this period was very much alive in the minds of employers and employees in the 1970s and obviously both sides were anxious to avoid similar conflicts. Joint labor-management consultation councils, which were alter egos of Japanese enterprise unions, and most of which came into being in earlier postwar years, proved serviceable for the discussion of the impending problem and for the exploration of (and leading to agreements on) the best ways to deal with them. In the Japanese industrial relations system, almost all of the nonwage issues are discussed and acted upon through consultations. But when consultations do not resolve the issues, unions may declare that these be shifted to collective bargaining, a step not liked by either managements or unions (Kawahara 1982, Shimada 1983, Nitta 1984). Since job security (broadly interpreted as the security of the employment relationship) is uppermost in the union's concern, attention first turns to intraplant or intrafirm transfers so that the current employees are utilized at a uniform rate throughout the firm. In a large diversified enterprise, external shocks hit different products or different sections unevenly, giving rise to the desirability of well-planned manpower deployment. The same logic could be extended to cover temporary interfirm transfers between friendly firms. Depending on the dynamics of consultation, temporary transfers may become permanent.

Consultations also could cover voluntary resignations. The union could help determine the number, age, sex, and other characteristics of workers eligible for resignation and the terms of termination for them. Several hundreds or thousands of regular employees could be terminated in this way without damaging labor-management relations. Although much depends upon the art of management and the quality of industrial relations, it is noteworthy that the Japanese employment system, despite being generally called a system of lifetime employment, allows for preretirement job terminations. In addition, the attrition of standard regular employees at different stages between recruitment from school or college and the time of mandatory retirement generally amounts to two-thirds of the initial cohorts as may be seen from statistics on distribution of workers by age and length of service (Okunishi 1983).[4]

A rough quantitative test of how unions cooperated with employment adjustment is the change in the rate of unionization during the period of employment retrenchment. Most Japanese unions are enterprise-based, and unionization is correlated with the size of the plant or firm—high in large plants or firms and low in small. A constant rate of unionization among employees of firms which down-sized their workforces, such as larger firms during the 1970s, indicated that unionized regular workers had an equal share in job losses with nonregular workers who were the first to go, as discussed in connection with Table 4. The Japan Productivity

---

[4] Not every case, however, was resolved smoothly. One seeming failure is well known: the case of Oki Electric which was unable to maintain industrial peace when it terminated about 2000 employees by the mechanism of voluntary resignations and the employer's own initiative to reach the target level of terminations.

TABLE 5
Unionization Rates by Size of Enterprise, 1972 and 1980

Enterprise Size	1972	1980
500 or more employees	63.6%	62.0%
100–499 employees	31.5	28.8
30–99 employees	9.0	8.1
29 or fewer employees	3.4	3.1
Average	28.0	24.7

Source: Japan Productivity Center 1981, p. 149.

Center's estimates of unionization rates by size of enterprise in the private sector are shown in Table 5.

In smaller enterprises, employment generally increased during this period. As elaborated below, much of the employment expansion in these enterprises was in the ranks of nonregular workers impervious to unionization. Here one might expect to see a decrease in the unionization rate. But among larger enterprises which reduced employment, the implications of the figures in Table 5 is surprising: that is, union members lost their jobs faster than other kinds of workers, possibly because employment decreased faster in unionized firms than in nonunion firms or the number of permanent workers who are union members decreased faster than the number of nonpermanent workers. Since it is commonly believed that, as described earlier, firms took utmost care in reducing the number of regular employees (who tend to be union members), faster decreases in their ranks as shown by Table 5 figures must be considered enigmatic. They may even imply that the generalized version of "Japanese-style employment adjustment" presented earlier may not be true. However, with no more knowledge of estimates of unionization rates by size of enterprise than those presented, this question cannot be pursued.

Effect of Adjustment Policies on Hiring Practices

All of the above notwithstanding, in general it should be easier to get rid of casual, temporary, seasonal, or part-time workers than to reduce the ranks of regular workers. From the employment adjustment experience of the 1970s, the Japanese firms apparently learned the usefulness of nonregular workers for flexible workforce management. Japanese firms have always been ingenious in manipulating social and personal attributes of individuals (age, sex, education, social origin, etc.) and inventing ranks and statuses other than functional positions as instruments of workforce management. In recent years new job titles and contractual statuses have been created to disguise the basic characteristics of nonregular employment as low-cost expendable labor for dead-end specific jobs. Transliteration of foreign loan words (often mutilated to fit Japanese speech habits) are liberally used to advertise "modern" jobs for women (Shinotsuka 1984). Since the middle of the 1970s jobs generally called "part-time" or "arbeit" have been increasing, in addition to conventional day labor, temporary, or seasonal employment. The Special Labor Force Survey of 1981 found that 12.7 percent of paid employment was accounted for by nonregular employees, most of them called "part-timers" or "arbeiters." Japanese women obviously fall in the category hired for such "European jobs."

The proportion of nonregulars was particularly high among women workers, 26.1 percent, as compared with 6.9 percent among males. The Labor Ministry's Employment Trend Survey of 1982 found that workers hired as "part-timers" or "arbeiters" were 14.4 percent of all accessions—4.7 percent for males and 23.2 percent for females. A rising trend of these nonregulars' share in new hires was also clear in the time series. The turnover rates among them were high: nearly 30 percent were separated from their jobs in 1982 (Minister of Labor 1984, pp. 58–59).

Among reasons for hiring part-time workers, a great majority of employers said that there were jobs in their firms that could be filled adequately by part-time workers. About a third mentioned the labor cost advantage gained from the use of part-timers. A fifth pointed to the advantage of being able to adjust their workforces easily to hourly, daily, seasonal, or cyclical fluctuations in workload (Ministry of Labor 1984, p. 62). The most frequently mentioned reason—the availability of jobs for part-time workers—is extremely important when taken in conjunction with the recent rapid proportionate increase in the number of part-time workers in the labor force. It appears that firms are creating part-time jobs or redesigning work to permit an increased use of part-timers.

One of the factors responsible for this increasing casualization of work may be the on-going microelectronic revolution—the rapid diffusion of programmable automated equipment, machines, and systems embodying microelectronic devices such as integrated circuits. Machines do the work. It is widely believed that workers are becoming increasingly split into two classes: semiskilled helpers of the well-programmed machines, and technicians and engineers who lay out and program the machines. In many cases the conventional skilled workers who use machines to make things are no longer needed. These workers either upgrade their skills to become technicians or join the ranks of the semiskilled helpers of machines that are much more capable than they are. With the universalization of microelectronics, firm-specific technology disappears and with it goes the need for a lifetime of firm-specific on-the-job training along the lines of progression in the internal labor market. The mobile operators and technicians of microelectronics begin to dominate the labor market.

The Effect of the Microelectronic Revolution

In Japan, factory automation based on microelectronics is proceeding at a very rapid pace, and office automation is not far behind. Among manufacturing establishments experiencing the microelectronic revolution, the proportion of those cutting back their workforces is found to be higher than the proportion expanding: 30.1 percent versus 4.6 percent, with the remainder reporting no change. The negative employment effects are particularly marked among large establishments that have almost completed the adaptation of electronics to work. Among establishments with 1000 or more employees, 40.2 percent report a workforce reduction due to microelectronics, while only 3.5 percent report an expansion of employment (Ministry of Labor 1984, pp. 78–83). In another Labor Ministry inquiry which has to do with the employment effects of industrial robots in eight manufacturing industries, a great majority of the establishments reported that robots introduced to reduce the workforce and to cut production costs have had the desired effect. Among establishments that introduced industrial robots in 1981, about 70 percent of them obtained a reduction of the workforce on the robotized lines, with the remaining 30 percent either maintaining the same workforce or expanding it. However, true to "Japanese-style employment adjustment," no layoffs or terminations have occurred because the displaced regular workers have been transferred to other lines or units of the same firm (Ministry of Labor 1983, pp. 117–32).

Until very recently the Japanese labor unions were as favorable to the microelectronic revolution as was management—perhaps because reductions in employment mainly affected new hires rather than employed workers. Now, as a result of careful studies and actual adverse experience, a number of union federations have revised their basic policies to give priority to employment security and to reserve the right to refuse technological change perceived to have adverse employment effects (Fujino 1982, Inagami 1983, Japan Institute of Labor 1984, Kuwahara 1984).

Not only does the introduction of microelectronics reduce the numbers of employees required, it also changes the skill mix and has a profound psychological impact on the employees. Workers displaced by electronics are often asked to move from the factory floor to the control room to watch the entire process on monitoring devices. Many fail to understand or meaningfully relate to the atmosphere of the control room with its unfamiliar signals and noises. The "hands" which knew what they were doing with firm grips on products and tools are suddenly rendered useless or even stupid. These feelings of stupidity and powerlessness can be much more galling to the worker than the feeling of uselessness.

When robots take over the assembly line, some workers remain employed as the robots' "assistants" or "gophers," arranging the materials so the robot-masters can work, but many are transferred further back in the job stream to unload and unpackage materials and inputs for assembly, or are assigned further downstream to pack, carry, and sell the robots' products.

In the office, an educated man with the ability to use thousands of Chinese and Japanese characters is replaced by a less educated worker equipped with a word-processor capable of storing and recalling those very same characters. Clerical work, formerly an integral part of upwardly mobile managerial personnel, is now split between a dead-end typing job and genuine managerial work without the clerical interludes.

Thus, in the office as well as in the factory, the microelectronic revolution destroys the well-established internal labor market based on continuous gradations of jobs "learnable" by rotations and experience under pre-electronic technologies and deprives many workers of the formerly hoped-for opportunities for promotion. Workers are now boxed in narrower job categories based on qualifications they brought with them when hired. External labor markets become proportionally more important. The technological revolution implies a thorough reorganization of ability, aptitude, attitude, motivation, qualifications, etc., in close alignment with the new production and business processes. The transition involves considerable chaos as the job structure is adjusted and psychological trauma for workers.

Since the microelectronic revolution destroys the conventional structure of the internal labor market and makes job-specific hiring more rational than firm-specific recruitment of young workers for a lifetime of in-house training and promotions, employers and unions may be in for a rude awakening one day. But for the time being, employers, employees, and unions generally agree on the desirability of technological progress and the limitless willingness and ability of everyone concerned to keep adapting to required changes in production and labor processes.

The Restructuring of Organized Labor

Current Status of the Labor Movement

Union membership in Japan failed to increase after the mid-1970s for the first time in more than two decades. In 1975 the Ministry of Labor reported a total union membership of almost 12.6 million; in 1983 membership was slightly over 12.5 million. Unions actually lost members between 1975 and 1979, with membership declining to about 12.3 million. Most of the loss was recovered by 1982. With the expansion of the paid labor force, the ratio of wage and salary earners therefore declined from an estimated 34.4 percent in 1975 to 29.7 percent in 1983 (*Japan Labor Bulletin*, April 1984, pp. 4–8). This slippage was the first of its kind since the 1950s when membership declined from almost half the wage and salary earners to the one-third figure which remained stable until the decline of the mid-1970s (Shirai and Shimada 1979).

While membership did not grow, the number of basic union organizations, at the grass-roots level, actually increased from the 69,333 reported in 1975 to the 74,486 reported in 1983 (Ministry of Labor 1983, p. 198). Further, only slight shifts occurred in the distribution of members among the national union centers, with a small gain for unions unaffiliated with those centers (Ministry of Labor 1984, p. 195). The relative decline of Sōhyō's position and the relative gains by Dōmei, Chūritsu Rōren, and the unaffiliated unions, which occurred in the 1960s and had come to a halt by 1970. Since then, each group has remained quite steady to the present. The failure of organized labor to grow as a percent of the labor force during the period under review no doubt chiefly reflected the relative decline of manufacturing employment, the relative rise of employment in the service sector, and the increasing employment of women and part-time workers who are difficult to unionize. By size of union (and size of firm) there was scarcely any notable shift of membership (Ministry of Labor 1984, p. 196). The prevalence of union-shop provisions in collective bargaining agreements probably served to maintain membership. Only marginal changes occurred in the distribution of union membership between the private and public sectors, with the former continuing to account for 72 percent and more than 9 million union members (Ministry of Labor 1984, p. 197).

Overall, despite the notable slowdown in Japan's economic growth, the sudden changes in the economic structure, and the gradual decline in the proportion of workers unionized, the major contours of organized labor remained quite stable after 1975. The chief contrast with the preceding period, then, was the halt in membership growth and proportion of workers organized that had been advancing steadily from the early 1960s to 1975.

Emergence of a New National Center

Yet, by the end of 1982, the organized labor movement in Japan for the first time in three decades, succeeded in formally restructuring itself—or at least establishing the basis for doing so. In December of that year came the inauguration of *Zenmin Rōkyō* (Zennihōn Minkan Rōdōkumiai Kyōgikai), or Japanese Private Sector Trade Union Council (JPTUC), which brought together most of the major unions in the private sector, comprising close to 5 million members. It is the declared aim of this organization eventually to embrace the public-sector unions also and to establish a single national center for the first time in Japanese labor history. The road to labor unification in Japan has been a long one, and even now full unity remains elusive and may never be attained. However, in view of the changing economic, political, and social environment, Zenmin Rōkyō, while still in its infancy, evidences a greater chance for successful unification than any previous attempt. It should be recalled that the history of the Japanese labor

movement, going back to its origins in the late 19th century, has
been replete with divisions and splits, often characterized by
irreconcilable ideological, philosophical, and organizational
differences (Large 1972 and 1981, Levine 1958, Ayusawa 1966,
Ōkōchi 1958, Shirai and Shimada 1979). The record of the postwar
period has been no better. In the year following Japan's surrender to
the Allied Powers in 1945, when sweeping Occupation reforms
granted full rights to labor, the burgeoning union movement
immediately broke into rival camps of socialists, communists,
business unionists, and neutrals, with several national centers
competing intensely with one another for memberships. Following
legal, political, and economic setbacks in the late 1940s, the
movement made an initial attempt at unification with the formation
of *Sōhyō* (Nihon Rōdō Kumiai Sōhyōgikai), or General Council of
Trade Unions of Japan; but this effort soon failed with the 1952
breaking away of the right-wing socialists who later became
Dōmei (Zennihon Rōdō Sōdōmei), or Japanese Confederation of
Labor. Also, there remained a sizable bloc of neutral unions which
evidenced little interest in affiliation with any national center.

Sōhyō, however, with a membership in 1983 of 4.5 million in 35
affiliated industrial federations and left-socialist in orientation, has
managed to remain the largest single national center to the present.
It accounts for 36 percent of all organized labor. Although Sōhyō's
composition has long been dominated by the two-thirds of its
affiliates which are from the public sector, it still embraces some of
Japan's most important private-sector unions—in steel, private
railways, metalworking, and synthetic chemicals.

Sōhyō's chief rival, Dōmei, as a right-socialist confederation
took its present form in 1964 and today has about 2.2 million
members, or about 17.5 percent of the total, in 18 major federations.
It has been almost entirely a national private-sector center, although
with a few public-sector affiliates that compete with Sōhyō unions.
Also exclusively in the private sector have been the politically
neutral *Chūritsu Rōren* (Chūritsu Rōdōkumiai Renraku Kaigi), or
Federation of Independent Unions of Japan, established in 1957 as
a loose organization and today claiming 1.5 million members (about
11.8 percent of the total in nine industrial federations) and
Shinsanbetsu (Zenkoku Sangyōbetsu Rōdōkumiai Rengō), or National Federation of Industrial Organizations, dating from the early
1950s, a small group of about 65,000 members in five affiliates,

also politically neutral and devoted to the principle of industrial unionism. All four centers are still fully active today even though the new private-sector council has now been launched. Unaffiliated with any of the national centers is a large number of unions, ranging from large-scale industrial federations to tiny enterprise and shop-level bodies, which altogether account for about 38.7 percent of the total 12.5 million wage and salary workers who are union members. Among these unaffiliated independents are large union organizations in the auto, electric power, banking, insurance, and transport industries.

The Process of Unification

In view of these divisions, how did Zenmin Rōkyō finally succeed in achieving even a limited amount of labor unity across ideological, political, and organizational lines when all previous efforts ended in failure? Talk of unification had been going on and off since the days of the Allied Occupation, but until 1983 all attempts to form a single national center foundered over the deep-seated differences among the competing groups, especially as each became more and more institutionalized and led by rival personalities. Furthermore, with the basic structure of the Japanese labor movement largely characterized by enterprise-type rather than industrial, regional, or occupational organizations, there has often been considerable indifference or reluctance regarding upper-level affiliation.

On the other hand, even despite profound divisions within the Japanese labor movement, from the late 1950s on there was a steady growth of cooperative and coordinative activities, often informal, which brought rival groupings together. Most of these joint actions reflected a common need for developing union strength and pressure in the collective bargaining and political arenas. As Japan's economic, industrial, and social environment underwent dramatic transformation in the 1960s and 1970s, the tendency for unified activity grew. In the interim a new generation of labor leadership emerged, more and more directed toward economic gains within the established political framework and, therefore, increasingly amenable to working together for purposes of collective negotiations.

This long process probably began with the initiation of *shuntō* in 1955 as the principal strategy of the unions for obtaining general wage increases in postwar Japan. Originated by the Sōhyō leadership of that time, a central *shuntō* committee served to bring together key industrial union federations for the purpose of coordinating wage demands and settlements that otherwise might have been highly disparate had the enterprise-level unions been left to themselves to negotiate individually with employers. By that time, union efforts to establish or maintain a network of industry-wide bargaining had been defeated by government and management resistance. *Shuntō* at first was a defensive strategy, initially for the private sector, which emerged on the heels of legal and organizational reverses suffered by organized labor in the late 1940s and early 1950s and of the failure of radical mass movements to overcome the inherent separateness of enterprise-level unions. In the early years of *shuntō*, it was not at all certain that this new union strategy would work. Only a few union groups participated. The Dōmei confederation of unions originally scorned the *shuntō* approach. Employers and government resisted *shuntō* demands.

However, once it was apparent that Japan's economy was undergoing rapid growth and structural change which brought about labor "shortages," *shuntō* became the chief focal point for formulating wage demands and, to a growing degree after 1960, for reaching actual settlements. By the late 1950s both Chūritsu Rōren and Shinsanbetsu, as well as increasing numbers of public-sector unions, had joined the Sōhyō-sponsored joint council in mounting the annual wage drives. By the end of the 1960s, although still ideologically opposed because of the joint council's tendency to ignore differences among industries and to mix political with economic objectives, most Dōmei affiliates were articulating their collective bargaining demands with those of the Spring Struggle. As *shuntō* became more regularized over the years, all four national centers began to issue increasingly similar goals for *shuntō*. In 1981, for the first time, they jointly pronounced a unified set of demands. Since then, probably because of the difficulty of achieving uniformity with so many diverse groups participating in the planning of *shuntō*, the central *shuntō* committee actually has left it up to each industrial union federation to decide on its wage position. Still, with a few exceptions, there has been close similarity of union demands (*Japan Labor Bulletin*, February 1982 and February 1983).

Of perhaps even greater importance in this slow process of

unification was the formation in the early 1960s, after several years of preparatory negotiations, of the Japan Council of Metalworkers Unions (*Zennihon Kinzoku Sangyō Rōdō Kumiai Kyōgikai*), commonly referred to as the IMF-JC because of its affiliation with the International Trade Secretariat. IMF-JC primarily aimed at unifying and coordinating collective bargaining activities of the most important industrial union federations in metalworking (steel, auto, shipbuilding, electrical equipment, and metal manufacturing). These were, of course, the union organizations in the high growth and chief export industries of the then rapidly growing industrial economy. For the first time, affiliates of the four centers had joined together as a formal body on a continuing basis. The IMF-JC shunned political campaigning and concentrated on formulating issues for collective bargaining. Indeed, within a few years of its founding, IMF-JC affiliates came to predominate in the annual *shuntō* negotiations, no doubt as the result of the overwhelming importance of the industries represented. With this, the IMF-JC group began to override the influence of the public-sector unions and even that of the private railways and the synthetic chemical union federation, which had often been the pace-setters for *shuntō* and other economy-wide wage negotiation movements such as the semiannual bonuses.

Following the path of the IMF-JC, still other private industrial sector union councils formed in the 1960s and 1970s, also cutting across national center lines and focusing primarily on economic issues. Each such group affiliated with an international trade secretariat in due time. Prominent among them are councils for food manufacturing workers, chemical and energy workers, and commercial, clerical, and technical employees. While none of these has attained the stature and influence of the IMF-JC, together they have contributed to the increasing unification of labor demands and settlements.

The unification efforts which resulted in the recent inauguration of Zenmin Rōkyō began in a serious way in early 1970 following several years of discussion (*Japan Labor Bulletin*, March 1970, Kōshiro 1970), especially at the regional level. It was about that time when the chairmen of the largest private-sector industrial federations (iron and steel, electrical machinery, textiles, auto, and chemicals) first established a formal council, then called *Zenmin Rōkon*, to prepare for labor unification with the aim of reducing union ties to political parties, deemphasizing class-struggle ideology, and devising a new and broader approach to *shuntō* negotiations. Interestingly, this took place about the same time as the establishment of the tripartite Sanrōkon (see p. 259–60) under the auspices of the Ministry of Labor. While the new private-sector union council met on several occasions, it faced heavy criticism especially from Sōhyō, which accused the council of being too close to management and favoring the right wing. In fact, Zenmin Rōkon was immediately threatened both by attempts of Sōhyō and Dōmei to form their own separate and rival conferences for achieving labor unity in the private sector and by demands by each for increased representation in the new council itself (*Japan Labor Bulletin*, July 1970). Paralyzed by a lack of cooperation, if not hostility, from the major centers, the new council was essentially dead within a year.

While discussions regarding unification soon resumed, the chief stumbling blocks remained the rival claims by Dōmei and Sōhyō over which federation's representatives would predominate in the new center and whether and how soon public-sector unions should be included. Behind these conflicts, of course, were the sharp ideological and philosophical differences between the two centers, although within Sōhyō itself and even within its affiliates there were further such divisions. For example, the steelworkers federation, affiliated with Sōhyō, favored a private-sector-only approach and even withheld dues payments to Sōhyō for several years because of the latter's insistence on an all-inclusive council (*Japan Labor Bulletin*, October 1972).

Although the deadlock over unification continued until well past the oil crisis· of 1973-75, as already noted, the labor centers did mutually agree to restrain their wage demands following the series of intensified national and industrial-level joint consultations of that period. Thus, in the *shuntō* of 1976 the four national centers joined together in a common front for the first time by transmitting their wage demands together to the Ministry of Labor on the condition that steps be taken.to maintain employment (*Japan Labor Bulletin*, January 1976). The threat of rapid economic deterioration and unemployment, it appears, spurred this joint action and opened the way for new interunion negotiations for unification. For the 1977 *shuntō*, in fact, the president of Sōhyō proposed that all four centers join together in unifying their wage demands (*Japan Labor Bulletin*,

December 1976). With the continuing emphasis on employment security rather than wage gains, and buttressed by the new Employment Insurance Act of 1975, interunion discussions for unification were under way once again. Dōmei, Chūritsu Rōren, the steelworkers of Sōhyō, and several large unaffiliated private-sector industrial federations now joined together in a joint council for the 1977 *shuntō* without waiting for further agreement on unification among the national centers (*Japan Labor Bulletin*, March 1980).

Formation of the Zenmin Rōkyō

A turning point in the unification movement came early in 1979 with the formation by Chūritsu Rōren and Shinsanbetsu of a new national confederation for private-sector unions (*Japan Labor Bulletin*, May 1979). Both of these "neutral" centers had long been active behind the scenes in promoting labor unity and hoped that they could now serve together as "honest brokers" in reconciling the differences between Sōhyō and Dōmei. By that time the second oil crisis had struck, again arousing fears among the unionists of ravaging effects on employment and wage and benefit levels. Although the new talks made little headway toward unification, for the first time all four centers presented the same demands, in preparation for the 1980 *shuntō*. Yet wide disagreement continued over which unions would play a prominent role in unification. The member unions of the joint council originally formed for the 1977 *shuntō* themselves split over the admission of additional industrial federations. Specifically, while the unions of steelworkers, electric equipment workers, autoworkers, and electric power workers were reported in favor of admitting the private railway workers, Sōhyō's express delivery workers and Dōmei's metalworkers and textile workers remained adamantly opposed. Indeed, each rival group had developed alternative plans and strategies for achieving unification of the private-sector unions. This took the form of competing bodies, one called the Council for Promoting Unification, which favored more extensive membership, and the other, the Trade Union Council for Policy Promotion, which opposed admitting the three private-sector Sōhyō unions (*Japan Labor Bulletin*, March 1980).

The 1980 *shuntō* concluded again with cooperation among the four centers in announcing demands for uniform increases and in devising common positions on national economic and welfare policies. In September of that year the four centers finally achieved basic agreement for proceeding with unification. In this development, Chūritsu Rōren appeared to be the key go-between (*Japan Labor Bulletin*, November 1980). Undoubtedly the threat of world recession had spurred the four centers to work together and bury their differences. Increasingly, all had come to focus far more on economic issues than they had in the past. The decline in manufacturing employment and the rise of the microchip revolution were paramount. While implementation of the new unification agreement proceeded very slowly, for the 1981 *shuntō* the four centers again issued identical demands, noted for the first time in a joint announcement (*Japan Labor Bulletin*, February 1981).

For the next year and a half, under the leadership of the Council for Promoting Unification, meetings and conferences were organized primarily to attract new adherents to the unity movement and to ward off continuing opposition of the communist-led and other left-wing union groups, especially within Sōhyō. In December 1981, a unification preparatory conference brought together 39 private-sector industrial union federations, representing almost 4 million workers, from all four centers and from independents, and it was announced that a formal unification council would be established by the following Fall (*Japan Labor Bulletin*, February 1982). The ensuing months saw the addition of a number of key unions to the conference, including the private railway workers, the metal and engineering workers, and the general workers of Sōhyō (*Japan Labor Bulletin*, April 1982), virtually assuring the successful formation of the new organization. Inauguration of Zenmin Rōkyō took place on December 14, 1982, although the other unification groups were not dissolved. At its founding, Zenmin Rōkyō included 41 industrial federations, representing 4.2 million members.

While the long and tortuous journey toward achieving private-sector union unification seems to be almost at an end, there remains the large task of converting Zenmin Rōkyō into a true national center replacing Sōhyō, Dōmei, Chūritsu Rōren, and Shinsanbetsu, and gathering in the unaffiliated. To date only small progress has been recorded towards that goal. Zenmin Rōkyō at best remains a loose coordinating council or forum for joint discussions and planning. Its staff is small and its finances meager. However, it has continued to gain affiliates, with an additional 13 industrial federations joining in

1983. By April 1984 the council counted 58 industrial union affiliates with almost 5 million members, nearly half of all unionists in the private sector and more than in any of the national centers. Even though Zenmin Rōkyō now seems to be a going concern, much remains to be accomplished. It is the hope of the council leadership to become *the* Japanese member of the International Confederation of Free Trade Unions (ICFTU), thereby displacing Dōmei and a number of separately affiliated Sōhyō unions. Its basic organizational principle is to build only upon union federations, first in the private sector. Its avowed policy is to permit only industrial union federations as affiliates and to bring about their merger into a relatively small number of broad industrial federations somewhat reminiscent of the West German DGB. Here, the council must wait upon the willingness of numerous enterprise-level unions to grant authority to (and in many cases actually join) industry-wide federations. There also remains the problem of merging rival federations in the same industrial groups, particularly overcoming the fierce antipathy of the communist-led organizations. Organizing the unorganized, too, is a distant hope, especially since union membership as a proportion of wage and salary earners has shown a steady decline. Finally, there is the eventual goal of bringing in the public-sector unions, possibly first through a unification movement among themselves, still only infrequently discussed and likely to be most difficult. This step, however, could be facilitated as large units such as the telephone and telegraph workers shift to the private sector as part of the conservative government's plan for administrative reform. For the time being, however, the Japanese labor movement has now been divided formally into two separate groups according to sector for the first time in postwar history.

Should the new council succeed in its objectives, especially the consolidation of various industrial federations into a limited number of large affiliates, it would concentrate primarily on industry-wide collective bargaining, joint consultation, and worker participation on a comprehensive basis. Also, while seeking legislative improvements for labor and social welfare, it would avoid close ties with any political party—a matter to be left to the individual affiliates (JPTUC 1983). If successful, these achievements would be almost without precedent in the history of Japanese industrial relations. Given the established institutions and the record of past attempts at unification, they are not apt to be accomplished easily.

Collective Bargaining with Joint Consultation

Irrespective of the changes discussed above, formal collective bargaining in Japan during the past decade has shown no perceptible trend toward greater or lesser decentralization. As a legal matter, collective bargaining authority has remained primarily at the workshop and enterprise level because it is there that unions have typically formed and obtained approval of their qualifications under the examination procedures of the tripartite labor relations commissions, as the law requires. Accordingly, unions and management in overwhelming proportions execute formal collective bargaining agreements only at the enterprise level, reinforcing the impression that collective bargaining has remained a highly decentralized process. Thus, in 1983 almost 85 percent of the 65,805 unions, with 90 percent of the 10.15 million members eligible by law to conclude labor-management agreements, had achieved collective bargaining coverage.

This seemingly decentralized structure of collective bargaining coverage has broadened steadily over the years. The number of unions with agreements in the early 1980s was double the number in the 1960s, and the percentage of unions eligible for coverage rose in the two decades from less than 65 percent to almost 85 percent. Similarly, in the same period, union members covered by agreements rose from fewer than 5 million to more than 9 million, or from less than 80 percent to more than 90 percent of those eligible for coverage. While this spread of formal collective bargaining agreements, especially at the enterprise level, was slowed by the economic crises and downturns, by 1983 more unionists were covered by collective bargaining agreements than at any previous time (Ministry of Labor 1984, p. 196). In this development there is little evidence that employers have seriously resisted or avoided unionization of their workers although, as already noted, unionism is far more prevalent in large-scale enterprises than in small and medium firms.

To this growth might be added a large amount of informal agreement-making at the enterprise level that does not get into the official statistics. The extent of this practice is not known, but it is believed to be widespread, since under the Labor Standards law employers with at least 10 employees must seek the opinion of the majority of their workers, even in the absence of a union, in order to issue rules of employment for their shops and plants, subject to the approval of the Labor Standards Office of the Ministry of Labor. It appears that this requirement is reasonably well enforced, and that negotiations over such workrules are often the equivalent of collective bargaining, even though no union seeks registration from a labor relations commission. Undoubtedly, if these informal bodies petitioned for approval, many of them would be registered. One observer claims that a very large number of informal worker organizations have appropriate union qualifications, especially in the small and medium sectors, and actually engage in something like collective bargaining and joint employee-employer consultation. He estimates that, if the membership of these organizations were added to that of the formally recognized unions, the organizational rate in Japan would rise to more than 50 percent (Koike 1983, pp. 103–104). Thus, it is tempting to conclude that the officially reported percentages of unionists and of collective bargaining coverage in Japan actually are serious underestimates of the negotiating process between labor and management. We can only speculate why so many qualified bodies fail to seek registration, but the best guess is that they do not feel it necessary to do so, or possibly they prefer to avoid real or anticipated employer resistance.

All is not what it appears. It would not be correct to conclude that collective bargaining in Japan, whatever its content, is totally decentralized. The great majority of enterprise-level unions affiliate with industrial union federations and/or national centers and, while direct participation of the latter in formal procedures for negotiating collective bargaining agreements and participating in joint consultation is very limited, their influence has been important and no doubt is growing. Much the same may be said of employer associations (Levine 1984). The supra-enterprise bodies, at a minimum, play a role in coordinating bargaining through advice, information, and education and through staging union political campaigns. They are also important in lobbying and discussing union policies and demands with government officials, politicians, and business leaders. Moreover, formal industry-wide and multienter-prise collective bargaining *does* exist in several key industries such as maritime shipping, textiles, private railways, mining, chemicals, breweries, machinery, and glassmaking and, at the regional level, for taxi drivers, store clerks, and salesmen. None of these structural arrangements was undone by the economic downturn following the first oil crisis.

At the informal level, there also appears to be extensive coordination of bargaining positions, especially during *shuntō* and bonus negotiations, among the leading enterprises in the iron and steel, auto, shipbuilding, electric equipment, and other major industries. It is noteworthy that, since the mid-1970s, the response of major employers in these industries to *shuntō* demands has been almost identical and simultaneous, even though they maintain the form of enterprise-level negotiations. In the public sector as well, informal centralization of negotiations emerges from the government's attempt to set a uniform wage policy and from the compulsory mediation and arbitration procedures utilized to settle union-management differences under the law.

This tendency towards informal centralization in collective bargaining seems to have intensified at the same time that the subject matter dealt with has expanded, now cutting across enterprises, industries, and sectors. As Shirai notes (1984, pp. 312-13), there always were few limitations on items relating to employment conditions that could be bargained at the enterprise level, even though wages have always received primary and, in the earlier years, almost exclusive attention. With the critical changes in the level of economic growth and the industrial structure since the mid-1970s, the bargaining parties have broadened the scope of their negotiations to include employment security, workforce adjustment (transfer, recruitment, retirement, retraining), wage structure, hours of work, pensions, and similar matters. At the same time there has been notably less emphasis on fringe benefits, which have been left largely to social welfare legislation.

This expansion of subject matter has spilled increasingly into areas long considered management prerogatives, such as technological change and productivity measures, investment and production planning, company organization, plant relocation, and contracting-out. A prevalent union response to this expansion has been an increased use of joint union-management consultation, accompanied by stepped-up sharing of information often considered confidential and by joint consideration and discussion of management's plans—in hopes of modifying the latter without resort to bargaining. A majority of the collective bargaining agreements, most notably in the large enterprises, already included provisions for joint consultation committees, so that this mechanism was in place as the number of subjects for discussion began to increase. Such was the case in a recent dispute between Nissan and its autoworkers union regarding installation of technological change. Since the same union and management officials participate in both joint consultation and bargaining, the line between the two activities tends to blur, and the unions resort to collective bargaining (and perhaps to work stoppages) only when consultation fails to bring about mutual understanding.

It is believed that the spread of joint consultation and the increase in information-sharing over the years also established the foundation for worker participation schemes such as the quality control circles that are now found in virtually all major enterprises. On the other hand, except in a few isolated instances, these activities have not led to codetermination, where employee representatives become members of company boards of directors. While the broadening of subject matter for collective bargaining and joint consultation appears to be largely enterprise-centered, the result of the process has been an increased awareness by the parties of the interrelationship between the enterprises and the overall economy and the need to develop policies that go far beyond the enterprise itself, either through legislation or more centralized bargaining and consultative bodies. It remains to be seen, however, whether such a shift will become formalized on a permanent basis.

The Future of Labor-Management Tensions

In our effort to explain the recent transition of the Japanese industrial relations system, it has been necessary to stress events leading up to and surrounding the first oil crisis. During the 1960s the rate of economic growth was unusually high, with goods and services being turned out at rates that compelled radical changes in standards of living and life styles. The sustainability of economic growth at this rate, which in hindsight appears to have been assured, was full of uncertainties while it was going on. At the same time, the rate of inflation was high and accelerating. The labor market was rapidly tightening, opening up better job opportunities in unexpected places and revising previously established wage structures. Opportunities for a better life expanded, but the sociopsychological costs of failing to grab the best opportunities also increased. Band-wagon psychology and inflated expectations entirely engulfed Japan, inducing an escalation of wage demands and disputes over them. This culminated in the near "big bang" of 1974 with unprecedented rates of money wage increases and inflation. Since then, economic growth and inflation have quieted down, while opportunities for well-paid jobs have diminished. From the workers' standpoint, the scope for maneuver for higher wages has shrunk considerably, raising the costs of disputes in proportion. Under the circumstances, Japanese employers could have seen a golden opportunity to demand "give-backs" even at the risk of provoking labor disputes. Had employers behaved that way, labor disputes would not have decreased as remarkably as previously observed during the 1970s and early 1980s. Instead of seizing upon that golden opportunity to avenge the 1960s, employers, with the support of government, have wooed workers' participation in joint efforts to face and overcome what everyone was apparently willing to perceive as "national crises" bred of external shocks. By the logic of collective action, a national crisis called for national unity. The responsible behavior on the part of employers and government in taking a national-level view of economic problems, which, if confined within the narrow frame of labor-management relations, would have wrecked the employment system, was a remarkable feat when compared with the experience of other countries where problems still remained at the enterprise or industry level perpetuating the usual, adversarial style of industrial relations. Thus one might say that as long as the sense of national crisis and the need for unity across class lines last as conditioning factors in the Japanese employment system, there will continue to be industrial peace as it is observed in today's Japan.

But there is a danger that the scenario of national crisis and national unity may become untenable. Organized labor has already begun to question the nature of the employment effects of the ongoing microelectronic revolution. To cope with this potentially enormous impact, it has embarked on restructuring itself. The changes in the job structure and the extent of retraining called for by these changes are beginning to be felt as burdensome among some groups of workers, especially those over 40 years of age who have been the paragon of lifetime employees in the conventional internal labor markets and now are exposed to the risks of falling behind in adaptability to the rapid pace of technological changes.

On the other hand, younger workers who may even have had their childhood amid electronic toys and gadgets are thriving in the jungles of microelectronics. Premature retirement or stepping aside increasingly forced upon over-40s coupled with technological supersophistication of youth may tear the fabric of Japanese society at its seams. It will be difficult to resort to the national crisis/national unity theme under these circumstances where the pace of change in technology is internally generated and self-imposed. Anxieties and uncertainties about a proper share in changing opportunities may spread far and wide. Should this come to pass, worker protest against the burden of adjustment would intensify and rise to a new height. Japan's leaders may try to defuse social unrest by the well-known patriotic appeal in the name of Japan as a technological Number One. For a while they may succeed in inducing Japanese workers to keep adapting to relentless changes. But whether the Japanese, alone among peoples of the world, are endowed with aptitude and ability for Faustian perfectibility remains a question.

References

Ara Kenjiro, et al., eds. *Sengo keizai seisakuron no sōten* (Controversies in Economic Policy Studies of Postwar Japan). Tokyo: Keisō Shobō, 1980.

Ayusawa, Iwao F. *A History of Labor in Modern Japan.* Honolulu: East-West Center Press, 1966.

Dunlop, John T., and Walter Galenson, eds. *Labor in the Twentieth Century.* New York: Academic Press, 1979.

Economic Planning Agency (Keizai Kikakuchō). *Keizai hakusho* (White Paper on the Economy). Tokyo: Keizai Kikakuchō, 1981, 1982.

Evans, Robert Jr. "A Structural Incomes Policy for the United States: Lessons from Japan." Mimeo, undated.

Fujino, Masaru. "Response of Labor Unions to Technological Progress." *Japan Labor Bulletin* 21 (July 1982): pp. 5–8.

Fujita, Yoshitaka. *Employee Benefits and Industrial Relations.* Japanese Industrial Relations Series 12. Tokyo: Japan Institute of Labor, 1984.

Hanami, T., and R. Blanpain, eds. *Industrial Conflict Resolution in Market Economies: A Study of Australia, the Federal Republic of Germany, Italy, Japan and the U.S.A.* Deventer, Netherlands: Kluwer Law and Taxation Publishers, 1984.

Hancock, Keith, Yoko Sano, Bruce Chapman, and Pamela Fayle, eds. *Japanese and Australian Labour Markets: A Comparative Study.* Canberra and Tokyo: Australia-Japan Research Center, 1983.

Harari, Ehud. "Unemployment in Japan: Policy and Politics." *Asian Survey* 18 (October 1978): pp. 1013–28.

Hart, Roger A. *The Economics of Non-Wage Labour Costs.* London: George Allen and Unwin, 1984.

Inagami, Takeshi. "Employment Adjustments in Japan." *Japan Labor Bulletin* 23 (July 1984): pp. 5–8.

_____. "New Technology and Trade Unions" (in Japanese). *Nihon Rōdō Kyōkai Zassi* (Monthly Journal of the Japan Institute of Labor) 25 (October 1983): pp. 48–64.

Japan Institute of Labor. *Employment and Employment Policy.* Japan Industrial Relations Series 1. Tokyo: Japan Institute of Labor, 1982.

_____. *Microelectronics and the Response of Labor Unions: Results of a Questionnaire Survey of Labor Unions.* Tokyo: Japan Institute of Labor, 1984.

_____. (Nihon Rōdō Kyōkai). *Koyō chōsei no jisshi ni saishiteno rōshi kyōgi tō no jittai ni kansuru chōsa* (Inquiries into the Realities of Labor-Management

Consultation and Assimilated Practices in Relation to Employment Adjustment).
    Tokyo: Nihon Rōdō Kyōkai, 1980.
Japan Labor Bulletin. March 1970, July 1970, October 1972, January 1976, December
    1976, May 1979, February 1980, March 1980, November 1980, February 1981,
    February 1982, April 1982, February 1983, April 1984.
Japan Productivity Center (Nihon Seisansei Honbu). *Katsuyō rōdō tōkei* (Practical
    Labor Statistics). Tokyo: Nihon Seisansei Honbu, 1981.
Japan Private Sector Trade Union Council (JPTUC). *Zenmin rōkyō.* Tokyo: Zenmin
    Rōkyō, 1983.
Koike, Kazuo. "Workers in Small Firms and Women in Industry." In *Contemporary
    Industrial Relations in Japan,* ed. Taishiro Shirai. Madison: University of
    Wisconsin Press, 1983.
Kōshiro, Kazutoshi. "The Labor Unification Movement: Past and Future." *Japan
    Labor Bulletin* 9 (December 1970): pp. 4–10.
_____. "Development of Collective Bargaining in Postwar Japan." In
    Contemporary Industrial Relations in Japan, ed. Taishiro Shirai. Madison:
    University of Wisconsin Press, 1983a.
_____. "Labor Relations in Public Enterprises." In *Contemporary Industrial
    Relations in Japan,* ed. Taishiro Shirai. Madison: University of Wisconsin Press,
    1983b.
_____. "Labor Dispute Settlement in the Japanese Postal Service." In *Industrial
    Conflict Resolution in Market Economies: A Study of Australia, the Federal
    Republic of Germany, Italy, Japan and the U.S.A.,* eds. T. Hanami and R.
    Blanpain. Deventer, Netherlands: Kluwer Law and Taxation Publishers, 1984a.
_____. "Labor Relations and Disputes Settlement in the Public Service: Japan."
    Mimeo, 1984b.
Kuwahara, Masahiro Ken. "Worker Participation in Discussions Within Undertakings
    in Japan." *Comparative Labor Law* 5 (Winter 1982): pp. 51–64.
Kuwahara, Yasuo. "From 'Adaptation' to 'Control'—Labor and Management
    Response to Technological Innovations in Japan." *Japan Labor Bulletin* 23
    (March 1984): pp. 5–8.
Large, Stephen S. *Organized Workers and Socialist Politics in Interwar Japan.*
    Cambridge: Cambridge University Press, 1981.
_____. *The Rise of Labor in Japan: The Yuaikai, 1912–1919.* Tokyo: Sophia
    University Press, 1972.
Levine, Solomon B. *Industrial Relations in Postwar Japan.* Urbana, University of
    Illinois Press, 1958.
_____. "Japan's Economy: End of the Miracle?" *Current History* 68 (April 1975):
    pp. 149–53, 181.
_____. "Careers and Mobility in Japan's Labor Markets." In *Work and Lifecourse
    in Japan,* ed. David W. Plath. Albany: State University of New York Press, 1983,
    pp. 18-33.
_____. "Employers Associations in Japan." In *Employers Associations and
    Industrial Relations: A Comparative Study,* eds. John P. Windmuller and Alan
    Gladstone. Oxford: Clarendon Press, 1984.
Levine, Solomon B., and Koji Taira. "Interpreting Industrial Conflict: The Case of
    Japan." In *Labor Relations in Advanced Industrial Societies: Issues and Problems,*
    eds. Benjamin Martin and Everett M. Kassalow. Washington: Carnegie
    Endowment for International Peace, 1980.
Martin, Benjamin, and Everett M. Kassalow, eds. *Labor Relations in Advanced
    Industrial Societies: Issues and Problems.* Washington: Carnegie Endowment for
    International Peace, 1980.
Ministry of Labor (Rōdōsho) *Rōdō hakusho* (White Paper on Labor). Tokyo: 1983.
_____. *Rōdō tōkei yōran* (Handbook of Labor Statistics). Tokyo: 1981, 1984.
_____. *Yearbook of Labor Statistics.* Tokyo: Ministry of Labor, annual, various
    years.
Nitta, M. "Conflict Resolution in the Steel Industry—Collective Bargaining and
    Workers' Consultation in a Steel Plant." In *Industrial Conflict Resolution in
    Market Economies: A Study of Australia, the Federal Republic of Germany, Italy,*

Japan and the U.S.A., eds. T. Hanami and R. Blanpain. Deventer, Netherlands: Kluwer Law and Taxation Publishers, 1984.

Ōkōchi, Kazuo. *Labor in Modern Japan*. Tokyo: The Science Council of Japan, 1958.

Okunishi Yoshio. "Employment by Firm Size and Labor Market" (in Japanese). *Nihon Rōdō Kyōkai Zassi* (Monthly Journal of the Japan Institute of Labor) 25 (November 1983): pp. 14–26.

Ono, Akira. "Relative Wage Shares in Japan." In *Japanese and Australian Labour Markets: A Comparative Study*, eds. Keith Hancock et al. Canberra and Tokyo: Australia-Japan Research Center, 1983.

Organization for Economic Cooperation and Development (OECD). *Microelectronics, Productivity and Employment*. Paris: OECD, 1981.

Pempel, T. J. *Policy and Politics in Japan: Creative Conservatism*. Philadelphia: Temple University Press, 1982.

Plath, David W., ed. *Work and Lifecourse in Japan*. Albany: State University of New York Press, 1983.

Sadamoto, Kuni, ed. *Robots in the Japanese Economy*. Tokyo: Survey Japan, 1981.

Shimada, Haruo. "Wage Determination and Information Sharing: An Alternative Approach to Incomes Policy?" *Journal of Industrial Relations* 25 (June 1983): pp. 177–200.

Shinotsuka Eiko. *Nihon no joshi rōdō* (Female Workers in Japan). Chapter 9, translated and published in *Japanese Economic Studies* 12 (Spring 1984): pp. 3–20.

Shirai, Taishiro, ed. *Contemporary Industrial Relations in Japan*. Madison: University of Wisconsin Press, 1983.

Shirai, Taishiro. "Recent Trends in Collective Bargaining in Japan." *International Labour Review* 123 (May-June 1984): pp. 307–18.

Shirai, Taishiro, and Haruo Shimada. "Japan." In *Labor in the Twentieth Century*, eds. John T. Dunlop and Walter Galenson. New York: Academic Press, 1979.

Sōgō Kenkyū Kaihatsu Kikō. *Erekutoronikusu no shakaiteki inpakuto ni kansuru kenkyū* (Studies in the Social Impact of Electronics). Tokyo: Sōgō Kenkyū Kaihatsu Kikō, 1983.

Taira, Koji. "Power and Trade in U.S.-Japanese Relations." *Asian Survey* 12 (November 1972): 980–98.

_____. "Japan After the 'Oil Shock': An International Resource Pauper." *Current History* 68 (April 1975): pp. 145–48, 179–80, 184.

_____. "The 1973–78 Stagflation in Japan: A Watershed." *Current History* 71 (November 1978): pp. 170–73, 184.

_____. "Hitoberashi ni okeru nihonrashisa to keizai gōrisei" (Japaneseness in Manpower Reduction and Economic Rationality). In *Sengo keizai seisakuron no sōten* (Controversies in Economic Policy Studies in Postwar Japan), eds. Ara Kenjiro et al. Tokyo: Keisō Shobō, 1980.

Valli, Vittorio. "The Rise of Unemployment and Employment Adjustment Policies in Japan, Italy and West Germany." *International Review of Economics and Business* 30 (August 1983): pp. 716–34.

Van Helvoort, Ernest. *The Japanese Working Man: What Choice? What Reward?* Vancouver: University of British Columbia Press, 1979.

Windmuller, John P., and Alan Gladstone, eds. *Employers Associations and Industrial Relations: A Comparative Study*. Oxford: Clarendon Press, 1984.

Yamaguchi, Koichiro. "The Public Sector: Civil Servants." In *Contemporary Industrial Relations in Japan*, ed. Taishiro Shirai. Madison: University of Wisconsin Press, 1983.

Chapter 9

Economic and Political Impacts on the Swedish Model of Industrial Relations

Richard B. Peterson
University of Washington

In this chapter we will concentrate primarily on the developments that have taken place in Swedish labor-management relations since the "oil crisis" in 1973. In particular, we shall look at the role of economic and political developments as they have impacted the Swedish collective bargaining system in recent years.

The Swedish Model

The foundations of labor-management relations in Sweden, which emphasized centralized bargaining and industrial unionism, were laid in the first decade of this century in early agreements between the Swedish Employers' Confederation (SAF) and the Swedish Confederation of Trade Unions (LO). This bargaining structure was largely initiated by the employer side (Jackson and Sisson 1976).

Government played a very minor role in regulating Swedish labor-management relations prior to 1920. After that date, key labor legislation, enacted in 1920, 1928, and 1936, provided the legal ground rules under which collective bargaining would take place, although economic and political realities generally favored the employers until after World War II. Since labor-management relations in the 1930s were not particularly peaceful (Peterson 1966, pp. 29–39), leaders of both SAF and LO recognized the need to change the nature of this adversarial relationship if they wished to remain free of further government interference. In 1936 key representatives of SAF and LO met at Saltsjöbaden, outside

Stockholm, to hammer out a Basic Agreement recognizing the rights and responsibilities of each side. This agreement was signed in 1938, with both parties taking the position that labor peace could best be accomplished by compromise through the collective bargaining process rather than by government intervention.

The new spirit of Saltsjöbaden did not take root immediately. As late as 1945 there was a five-month strike and lockout in the metal industry that affected a substantial part of the labor force. The spirit behind the Basic Agreement, however, was eventually to carry over into the relationship between SAF and the union confederations representing clerical and professional employees—the Swedish Central Association of Salaried Employees (TCO) and the Swedish Central Organization of Academics (SACO). During the 1950s and 1960s labor market parties were highly successful in maintaining labor peace. In fact, Sweden was identified as one of the truly successful systems of labor-management relations in the world. Study groups came from most of the industrialized nations to learn how the system worked.

What were the basic features of the Swedish Model? H. G. Myrdal (1980, p. 57) identified eight distinguishing characteristics: (1) a properly functioning free market economy, (2) independent and freely competing enterprises, (3) a fully organized labor market with both sides being entirely independent of each other and of the state, (4) a highly developed, well-functioning system of consultation and participation for employees in the company, (5) practical reform in stages, (6) a general atmosphere of pragmatism, (7) friendly cooperation, and (8) a peaceful climate with reasonable compromises. Ideological conflict was rare.

Lundberg (1981) mentions two other basic features of the Swedish Model: a common social outlook regarding the value of free negotiations, and a desire for freedom from government interference, but not from the responsibility for the country's economic development.

The economic policy assumption underlying this model was contained in the EFO Report, "The Scandinavian Economic Model," prepared by Faxén (SAF), Odhner (LO), and Edgren (TCO). The basic premise of the report was that wage policy should be consistent with the central national economic aims of full employment, rapid economic growth, reasonable price stability, more equal income distribution, and foreign payments balance (Forsebäck 1976). There was general agreement that the sector most exposed to international competition should be the wage leader.

Consistent with these goals was the development of centralized collective bargaining, begun by SAF and LO in 1952. SAF and LO would reach a "frame" agreement on wages and other key economic issues. This would be followed by agreements at the national federation level and finally by company- and plant-level agreements, where they applied. Similar negotiations would follow between SAF and the other trade union confederations or cartels. Thus, a considerable degree of discipline was exerted by the key parties, with only minimal arm-twisting by government officials. The result was fairly reasonable settlements and a minimum number of labor disputes.

It is well to keep in mind that the Swedish Model was not perfect. For example, inflationary pressures could not be totally contained since the tight labor market led to wage-drift pressures. These pressures resulted in total wage and salary increases that exceeded productivity increases. However, since a number of other West European countries were also experiencing the same pressures, the demand for Swedish products remained high. Johnston (1962) and Schmidt (1962) provide in-depth analyses of the collective bargaining system at that time.

Why did the Swedish Model work so well through the 1950s and 1960s? Myrdal (1980) attributes its success to several factors. First, the labor and employer organizations were strong and centralized. Second, pay and working conditions were regulated through central basic and supplementary agreements. Third, there were very few legal strikes and few working hours lost through offensive actions. And finally, since LO and TCO represented almost all employees in Sweden, the central labor organizations could not make demands that excessively favored specific small groups at the expense of others. However, by the late 1960s there were hints of emerging forces that would weaken the model over the next 15 years.

The Changing Economic Situation in Sweden Before and After 1975[1]

Sweden prospered throughout most of the 20-year period prior to 1975. The population grew from approximately 7.3 million to

---

[1] Unless indicated, the figures in this section are drawn from various annual volumes of the *Statistical Yearbook for Sweden* and other reports published by the Swedish Central Bureau of Statistics.

almost 8.2 million. The gross national product increased from around Swedish KR45 billion to Swedish KR249 billion (in market prices). The consumer price index moved from 133 to 316, or an increase of 238 percent, during the 20-year period. The year-to-year increases in inflation were more moderate in the years prior to 1970. The labor force grew moderately (from 3,099,000 to 3,375,000) between 1950 and 1970. The major employment shifts during the period, in percentage terms, involved increases in building construction, commerce, and the public sector, while agricultural and forestry employment dropped by almost two-thirds. Public sector employment growth was 43.5 percent—an indication of later trends. The government budget deficit in 1954–55 was KR789 million. By 1974–75 the deficit had increased to KR10.697 billion.

Average hourly earnings for all workers in mining and manufacturing were KR4.26 in 1955 and KR20.36 by 1974. Even when we adjust for inflation, the average Swedish worker had clearly improved his or her real income; by the end of the period the Swedish worker was the best paid in the world. In addition, job security was very high, with annual unemployment rates running less than 2 percent of the labor force for most years.

The principal actors in the industrial relations system were also growing over the period. In 1955 SAF represented more than 15,600 employers who employed some 778,000 workers and salaried personnel; by 1975 these figures had increased to 30,683 and 1,307,000, respectively. LO showed gains of some 533,000 (from 1,384,456 to 1,918,085) and TCO grew almost 28 percent (from 337,513 to 431,947).

Labor relations were relatively strike-free. However, a number of legal and illegal strikes took place between 1969 and 1971, many of them directed against LO by the high-skilled union workers (e.g., miners) because of discontent over LO's wage solidarity policy that would result in diminishing wage differences between higher and lower paid workers.

A number of factors caused the rather dramatic downward shift in the economy after 1975. One of the most obvious ones was the oil crisis in 1973. Since Sweden imports 100 percent of its oil, the impact of the price increases was considerable. Like many other industrialized nations, Sweden was not in a position to absorb this level of shock without costs to economic performance.

The continued development of the welfare state also had its impact on the economy. Criticisms were being voiced that the labor force had weaker commitments to the work ethic than had been true in earlier years. Too, by 1974, labor costs in Sweden were the highest in the world (Childs 1980, Swedish Institute 1984).

Now let us turn our attention to the various national economic indicators in order to gain insight into what took place in the Swedish economy beginning in 1975 and continuing almost to the present. We will compare the Swedish experiences with those of other Organization for Economic Cooperation and Development (OECD) countries.

Gross National Product

The Swedish GNP was KR695.4 million in 1983. However, during the 1970s real growth in GNP had decreased to a yearly rate of 2.0 percent which represented a considerable drop from the 1960s when the comparable figure had been 4.5 percent (Lundberg 1981). Sweden also experienced a slower growth in GNP than the average for all OECD nations. Using 1960 = 100, between 1975 and 1982 the Swedish index moved from 179.4 to 190.3 (6.2 percent), while the OECD nations overall moved from 189.2 to 225.6 (19.2 percent) (Svenska Arbetsgivareforening 1983). By comparison, the Swedish index had increased more than 75 percent between 1960 and 1975.

We find that the gross domestic product (GDP) performed even more poorly than the GNP during the 1970s. The GDP grew at only a 1.75 percent annual rate during this period, which was quite a drop from the 3.5 and 4.5 percent annual rates in the 1950s and 1960s (Jakobsson 1983). Faxén (in Rydén and Bergström 1982) argues that the recent slowdown in economic growth was almost entirely at the expense of the private sector.

Consumer Prices

Table 1 shows the increase in the consumer price index (CPI) between 1960 and 1980 broken down into five-year periods. It indicates that inflation was not a real problem through 1970, but that it increased rather rapidly during the 1970s such that between 1975 and 1980 the average yearly increase in the CPI was 10.6 percent.

Between 1980 and 1983 the CPI increased by another 33 percent (*Sweden 1984*). These figures are similar to those of other OECD countries before 1983. However, the OECD rate was falling in 1983 while Sweden was experiencing an increase in the CPI (Svenska Arbetsgivareforening 1983).

TABLE 1
Average Annual Percentage Rise in Swedish Consumer Price Index
By Five-Year Periods, 1960–1980

Years	Annual Percentage Increase in CPI
1960–1965	3.6%
1965–1970	4.4
1970–1975	8.0
1975–1980	10.6

Source: Svenska Arbetsgivareforening (Swedish Employers' Confederation), *Fakta om Sveriges Ekonomi* (Stockholm: 1983).

Growth of the Public Sector

One of the most startling changes in Sweden during the postwar period has been the rapid growth of the public sector. The public share of GNP in 1950 was approximately 25 percent (Lundberg 1981). By 1982 the public sector represented 67 percent of the GNP (Bernstein 1983). Jakobsson (1983) reports that in 1970 public-sector expenditures represented 45 percent of GDP, while in 1982 the comparable figure was close to 70 percent. The growth of the public sector has been due in large part to an increase in transfer payments and in activities of local government. The result of this rapid growth is that Sweden has the largest public sector of any of the OECD nations (Halvarsson 1981).

Dependence on Exports

For many years Sweden has depended heavily upon her ability to export a considerable amount of her products. Between 1978 and 1982 exports of goods and services represented 30.69 percent of GDP (Svenska Handelsbanken 1983). During the 1950s and 1960s Sweden was quite successful in increasing her market share in the world economy. However, the period 1970–1982 saw her share of the world economy drop from 2.2 to 1.4 percent (Svenska Handelsbanken 1983). She had trade deficits for all but one year between 1975 and 1982 (Svenska Arbetsgivareforening 1983) such that by the end of 1982 Sweden had accumulated foreign debt of $28.5 million (U.S. Department of Commerce 1982). The effect of the weakening export market on labor-management relations was that the economy was not sufficiently strong to absorb the demand for high wage settlements.

Budget Deficit

The government had been able to operate with only modest budget deficits for many years. However, beginning in 1977–78 the deficit accelerated rapidly from KR25.2 million to KR91.8 million in 1982–83 (Svenska Arbetsgivareforening 1983), which represented 13 percent of GNP (Siven 1984). The budget deficit for 1983–84 was projected at 15 percent of GDP (U.S. Department of Commerce 1982). The demand for government services and subsidies was exceeding the ability of the national government to generate new revenues to cover them.

Industrial Production

Industrial production dropped 2.6 percent per year between 1974 and 1977 (Halvarsson 1981), and by 1980 industrial production was lower than in 1974 (Rydén and Bergström 1982); in fact, the 1982 index was only 8 percent above what it had been in 1970. The result was a general stagnation in industrial production over the entire period brought about by the declining demand for Swedish products.

Other Economic Indicators

Industrial investments slowed during the 1967–1982 period and dropped significantly during the late 1970s and early 1980s. The savings rate actually decreased by 25 percent during that period (Soderstrom in Rydén and Bergström 1982). Net profits of manufacturing firms with more than 50 employees did not exceed 4.4 percent in any year between 1975 and 1982. The figures for 1977 and 1978 were 0.0 and 0.2 percent (Svenska Arbetsgivareforening 1983).

What explains the crisis in the Swedish economy since the mid-1970s? Siven identifies five major factors that help us to understand what happened: (1) stagnation of industrial production; (2) loss of 25 percent of its market share in international trade; (3) growth of the public sector to two-thirds of GNP; (4) rapid growth in the central government budget after 1976; and (5) high taxation in combination with marginal effects of income-dependent transfers. Our conclusion must be that almost all of the economic indicators showed that Sweden experienced difficult times from 1975 to 1983, whether comparisons are made with other nations or with the domestic economic situation in the earlier postwar period. Now we turn our attention to the recent economic record as it relates to the labor force.

Labor Force

Table 2 shows figures for the Swedish labor force by sex and by full-time employment. Over 50 percent of the population are labor force participants, either full time or part time. Women today represent about 45 percent of the workforce. There has been a steady increase in their labor force participation, while the participation rate of men has decreased slightly (Statistisk Årsbok 1984). Approximately 25 percent of the labor force works part time, or fewer than 35 hours a week (Swedish Institute 1984). Women are far more likely than men to be employed on a part-time basis.

TABLE 2
Swedish Labor Force, 1976–1982 (in thousands)

Year	Employed			Employed Full-Time (Over 35 Hours per Week)
	Men	Women	Total	
1976	2337	1971	4088	3239
1977	2314	1785	4099	3191
1978	2297	1818	4115	3152
1979	2315	1865	4180	3169
1980	2327	1903	4230	3108
1981	2286	1938	4224	3161
1982	2272	1947	4219	3140

Source: Data are from the Central Bureau of Statistics in Stockholm, published in *The Swedish Economy April 1983—Revised National Budget for 1983* (Stockholm: Ministry of Finance and National Institute of Economic Research, 1983).

The most noticeable shift in the labor force in recent years has been in the direction of public employment. In 1970 there were 876,203 government employees; that figure had jumped to 1,131,055 by 1975. The comparable figure seven years later was 1,580,000 (Statistisk Årsbok 1984). Thus, in a 12-year period public-sector employment had grown by approximately 80 percent to account for

37 percent of the labor force (Swedish Institute, April 1984). Most of the growth was at the county and municipal level. Employment in manufacturing and mining declined by approximately 10 percent between 1975 and 1980 and has continued to decrease in the early 1980s (Statistisk Årsbok 1982–83, 1984). By 1982, industrial employment had declined to 25 percent of the labor force (Swedish Institute, April 1984).

Table 3 reports employment by labor force sector for 1970 and 1981, indicating that most of the private-sector categories decreased in percent of the total labor force over the period. On the other hand, local government employment increased from 14.1 to 23.3 percent of the total labor force.

TABLE 3
Employment by Sector, as Percent of Labor Force

Sector	1970	1981
Agriculture, fishing, and forestry	8.2	5.3
Mining and manufacturing	26.6	22.0
Electricity, gas, and water works	0.7	0.7
Construction	9.3	7.2
Wholesaling, retailing, restaurants	14.5	13.3
Other private and business services[a]	18.9	18.4
National government	6.2	7.3
Local governments	14.1	23.3
Unemployed	1.5	2.5
Total labor force (in thousands)	3910	4330

[a] Transport, communications, banking, insurance, property management, etc.

Productivity

The Swedish labor force had a solid record of improved productivity during the early postwar years. Forsebäck (1976) reports that productivity increased 4.1 percent annually between 1950 and 1975. Productivity growth was only 2.4 percent between 1973 and 1982 (Svenska Handelsbanken 1983), and the overall productivity record was even less impressive between 1976 and 1982 when the annual rate averaged 1.4 percent (Swedish Institute 1983). In every year from 1976 to 1982 productivity in public services lagged the record in the private sector.

Unemployment

For most of the postwar period Sweden was noted as having one of the lowest levels of unemployment in the industrialized world.

Table 4 shows the annual unemployment rate for the years 1975–1983. It should be noted that the figures were quite low during the early years, but had doubled by 1982 and 1983. These figures are somewhat misleading. For example, Childs (1980) noted that while 1976 unemployment was less than 2.0 percent, if trainees and other public works people were covered, the total figure would be anywhere from 4–6 percent of the labor force. Jakobsson (1983) estimated that if you add the 3.5 percent of the labor force involved in publicly financed relief work, job retraining, and other sheltered activities to those officially unemployed, the total would be close to 7.0 percent. More recently the government has subsidized employers for hiring younger workers, given the lower demand for labor since 1975. The trade union movement has not been entirely satisfied with the unemployment situation and has called for a more active labor market policy.

Labor Costs

Table 5 shows negotiated rates, wage drift, and total labor costs for all Swedish workers for the years 1974–1983. Not counting the predictions for 1983, the average annual increase in labor costs was almost 10.4 percent, which was considerably higher than the average increase in productivity for those years. Faxén (1982) reports figures for wage drift in Sweden from the Nordic Employers' organizations that are quite a bit higher than these official rates. Labor costs for Sweden declined noticeably in 1982 and 1983 due to pressure by the government for wage restraint because of the weak economic situation.

TABLE 4
Unemployment Rate, Sweden, 1975–1983

Year	Percent of Labor Force
1975	1.6
1976	1.6
1977	1.8
1978	2.2
1979	2.1
1980	2.0
1981	2.5
1982	3.1
1983 (October)	3.4

Source: Sweden 84 (Stockholm: Norstedts Tryckcei, 1984).

Labor costs rose dramatically during 1975 and 1976 in response to the oil price shock and employees' awareness of the record "excess profits" realized by some Swedish companies at that time. Halvarsson (1981) believes that total labor costs in Sweden increased by 44 percent for these two years, while Lundberg (1982) cites labor cost increases of 20 and 17 percent for the two years.

TABLE 5
Negotiated Wages, Wage Drift, and Total Labor Costs,
Industrial Wage-Earners, 1974–1983 (in percentages)

Year	Negotiated	Wage Drift	Total
1974	7.4	3.0	10.4
1975	13.0	1.9	14.9
1976	10.2	2.1	12.3
1977	7.3	3.8	11.1
1978	8.1	2.7	10.8
1979	6.7	2.5	9.2
1980	7.3	1.8	9.1
1981	6.2	2.8	9.0
1982	4.6	1.8	6.4
1983 (forecast)	4.0	2.5	6.5

Source: Data are from the Central Bureau of Statistics in Stockholm and the National Institute of Economic Research, published in *The Swedish Economy April 1983—Revised National Budget for 1983* (Stockholm: Ministry of Finance and National Institute of Economic Research, 1983).

Average hourly earnings of manufacturing workers increased from KR23.89 in 1975 to KR39.49 in 1982 (Statistisk Årsbok 1984). The annual wage in 1982 was KR83,000 for industrial employees (Swedish Institute 1983). Even so, Soderstrom (in Rydén and Bergström 1982) stated that real wages had decreased since 1976. Childs (1980) estimates that in 1975 alone Swedish labor costs averaged about $8.50 per hour. The comparable rates in the U.S. and Japan at that time were $7.00 and approximately $4.25. From 1973 to 1979 unit labor costs increased at an annual rate of 12.2 percent in Sweden, 5.5 percent in Japan, and 7.9 percent in the United States (Bernstein 1982).

Other Labor Force Statistics

There were other developments during this period that impacted Sweden's competitive position. Legislation enacted in 1978 specified a minimum of five weeks vacation for all Swedish employees (Halvarsson 1981). Average hours worked per year declined from approximately 1800 in 1965 to 1500 by 1980. Absentee rates in Sweden in 1979 were 15.8 days per year, significantly higher than in either West Germany or Japan where the comparable figures were 9.5 and 1.9 days (Bernstein 1982). Sweden has experienced a continuing stagflation problem during most years since 1975, not unlike that of many other industrial nations. The leading economic indicators showed consistently negative results until 1983. Sweden's economic situation has improved since 1983, however. GNP increased 2.3 percent in real terms and the forecast was 2.5 percent for 1984. Government consumption has been showing a steady moderate growth path of 1.0 percent. Gross fixed investment was expected to increase for the first time since 1980, spurred by an economic growth of no less than 8–10 percent in industrial investment. Industrial production is set to rise by 4–5 percent in both 1984 and 1985. Inflation was expected to decline to 8.0 percent for 1984, and unemployment for all of 1984 was estimated at 3.0 percent, a drop from the 4.0 percent figure earlier in the year. It was also expected that the current account deficit would be eliminated by late 1984 (*Business Europe*, April 27, 1984, p. 136). Pretax profits of Sweden's 500 largest firms increased from 3.6 to 7.4 percent between late 1982 and late 1983 (Sweden, *EIRR*, December 1983).

The Social Democrats' first and, as it proved, very successful measure after taking office in 1982 was to devalue the Swedish krona by 16 percent. This decision aroused strong criticism in other Scandinavian countries and within the European Economic Community (EEC). However, the devaluation took place just before a strong upswing in the international economy.

The rise of the U.S. dollar gave an extra push, not only to Volvo and Saab, but also to the Swedish pulp industry. Industrial production as a whole increased considerably; so did industry profits and, as a consequence, industry investments. Deficits in the balance of trade and balance of current payments were changed into surpluses.

But there were also some negative features. The general increase in costs within Sweden is higher than in most other OECD countries, and at the end of 1984 it seems that the main positive effects of the devaluation decision in 1982 have been used up. The unemployment rate is another negative item. Although the *official* figure shows a decline to 3.1 percent, the rate has actually increased from 7.3 to 7.6 percent. These latter figures also include those who are employed in publicly financed relief work, job retraining, and other sheltered work. As to government budget deficits, it is true that they have declined during 1983-84. However, critics of the government feel that it ought to have been possible to reduce them even more, namely when the prosperous economic development during the period is taken into account.

Political Developments Since 1975

From 1932 to 1976 the Social Democratic Party (SAP) ruled Sweden either by itself or in coalition with one of the other parties. The partner during the early years was the Agrarian or Center Party. However, in later years the Social Democrats periodically have required support from the Swedish Communist Party in order to hold their majority in the Parliament.

The major backer of the Social Democrats was, and still is, the LO. The Confederation provides financial support to the Party through a share of dues collected from union members covered by LO. Members who do not wish to support the Social Democrats must write a letter to their union saying that they do not wish to have money allotments sent to the Party. The number of union members who do so has been very small over the years.

The leadership of the Social Democrats during the early postwar years was considered fairly moderate as long as the legitimacy of its social welfare platform was recognized. However, in the late 1960s some people within the Party called for more radical changes in Swedish society—towards a corporatist state and away from a market economy—and some trade union leaders shared this opinion. There was a distrust of big business and the continuing growth of corporate concentration. The Prime Minister, Olof Palme, was considered less moderate than his two predecessors. The leadership of LO, on the other hand, was generally viewed as a moderating force on the Party during much of the 1960s, but this situation began to change in the late 1960s and early 1970s as LO proposed more far-reaching agendas for democratizing Swedish society. Olsen (1984) provides an insightful treatment of the problems facing the Swedish Social Democratic Party in the late 1970s and early 1980s.

One such proposal called for the establishment of wage-earner funds by which ownership shares in Swedish firms would be transferred, over a number of years, to boards with majority representation by the trade unions. The initial plan was developed in August 1975 by Rudolf Meidner, at that time an economist with LO. The so-called Meidner Plan became a very controversial issue prior to the 1976 national elections. Some observers, in fact, attributed the Social Democratic Party's defeat in large part to the controversy over this proposal.

The non-socialist coalition, made up of Liberals, Conservatives, and the Center Party, ran the government from 1976 to 1978 when Falldin's Center Party withdrew over the nuclear energy issue. The Liberals then took over the prime ministerial position in 1978. The non-socialists once again won the election in 1979. The Conservatives dropped out of the coalition in 1981 when the Liberal and Center Parties made an agreement with the Social Democrats on taxation reforms behind the back of the Conservatives.

As expected, the non-socialists found it difficult to unite on a common government policy for most of the period they were in office. Some voters could not identify much in the way of major differences in directions from the policies earlier advocated by the Social Democrats. Boalt and Bergryd (1981) reported the results of a mail questionnaire polling 1948 Swedish adults taken shortly before the 1979 election. The respondents were concerned with the need to curb the power of both employers and unions.

The non-socialist coalition was unable to agree upon a set of policies to counteract the deteriorating economic situation. In addition, it found itself bailing out a number of Swedish companies through nationalization and subsidies. The government was forced to take over firms in three major industries: it took over additional private firms in the shipbuilding industry; it became half-owner of three large firms that were merged into Svensk Stål (Swedish Steel Corporation); and a number of unprofitable textile firms merged under a state-controlled company called EISER (see Childs 1980, Halvarsson 1981). Childs (p. 169) concludes that between 1976 and 1979 the three bourgeoisie parties socialized more of the economy than the Social Democrats ever did. The inability of the non-socialist parties to improve the economy led to a victory for the Social Democratic Party in 1982. They also won the Fall 1985 election.

The Swedish government's political orientation did not change significantly after 1976 even though the non-socialist parties were in power for six years. Bernstein (1983) argues that the coalition was not able to decide whether to be an exponent of the free market or a pale imitation of the socialists. Their principal impact was in the direction of moderating the political course rather than redirecting the political orientation towards a more conservative course. On the other hand, economic problems had the effect of slowing the implementation of controversial political platforms by the Social Democrats. It is clear that both the socialist and non-socialist governments have tried to hold down unemployment as much as possible by encouraging private investment and the expansion of public labor market programs. The government has been reluctant to implement an incomes policy, though the Social Democrats did clamp down on price increases beginning in April 1984.

The government has not played a direct role in collective bargaining during the past ten years, although government leaders have put indirect pressure on the negotiating parties to exercise moderation in wage settlements. The track record generally has been that the trade unions have been more willing listeners when the Social Democrats were in power.

Some writers believe that an informal industrial policy has emerged in recent years. The political parties have been reluctant to allow companies to go out of business, with the resulting loss of jobs. This largely explains the active role of the non-socialist governments in providing state subsidies to some firms as well as establishing state corporations to oversee the operation of firms in those industries that are experiencing major economic problems.

Finally, the government has devalued the Swedish krona on several occasions since 1975 in response to the need for making Swedish products more price competitive in the world market. The non-socialist government devalued the krona by 10 percent in 1977 and again, by 6 percent, in 1981. Finally, the krona was devalued by an additional 16 percent shortly after the Social Democrats took office in the Fall of 1982 (Siven 1984). The Swedish krona, which traded at a 4:1–5:1 ratio to the American dollar through the 1960s and early 1970s, was at a 9:1 exchange rate in January 1985. These devaluations moved trade in the desired direction by 1983–84.

From the legislative perspective it should be noted that the government has been clearly reluctant to add any significant new legislation to the body of labor laws that were enacted in the mid-seventies. Some small changes were introduced in 1984, but more noteworthy is that the government at the same time established a study group to investigate possible ways of simplifying existing labor laws. No matter how fruitful this initiative will be in the end, it may well be interpreted as an acknowledgement of the too massive and complicated nature of the 1974–1977 legislation.

The Changing Nature of Swedish Collective Bargaining

We address a number of issues in this section. First, we briefly describe the major labor market parties, and then we show how LO and the Social Democrats were forging a new relationship in which the trade unions would take a more "activist" stand on political and economic issues beginning in the late 1960s. Next we focus on five major issues that have caused conflict between employers and trade unions in recent years, and finally we identify some trends that are discernible, based upon our analysis.

The Key Labor Market Parties

It is well to keep in mind that Sweden has the highest percentage of unionization in the free world (Faxén 1982). Approximately 85 percent of eligible employees are trade union members (Swedish Institute 1984). Union penetration is particularly high in the traditional LO section of blue-collar workers in the private sector; 90–95 percent of that workforce is organized.

SAF, now the dominant employer organization in the private sector, was formed in 1902 by some 40 Swedish employers for the purpose of representing employer interests in industrial relations. In 1982 SAF consisted of 33 employer federations in a considerable variety of industries. The organization represented 40,406 firms employing 725,406 workers and 522,001 salaried employees in 1983 (Statistisk Årsbok 1984). Thus, SAF firms employed approximately 30 percent of the entire Swedish labor force at that time. Small employer confederations exist in the banking, publishing, and co-operative fields (Halvarsson 1981).

Public-sector labor relations was not really an issue until the postwar period. Government employees gained the right to strike in 1965. The National Swedish Agency for Government Employers (SAV) is the principal state body bargaining with some 535,000 employees. The Swedish Association of Local Authorities and the

Federation of Swedish County Councils cover 465,000 and 340,000 employees, respectively. Finally, the Negotiation Organization of National Enterprises (SFO) is the employer organization for state-owned enterprises (Halvarsson 1981, Swedish Employers' Confederation 1981).

The unions are represented by three principal confederations. LO, by far the largest, was founded in 1898 by 16 national unions for the purpose of increasing their power relative to that of the employers. Between 1900 and 1980, membership grew from 40,000 to over 2 million (Swedish Institute 1984). Forsebäck (1976) states that in 1975 LO had 25 trade union federations with almost 2 million members. Eight years later the comparable statistics showed one less union federation and a total of 2,160,982 members (Statistisk Årsbok 1984). LO operates on the principle of industrial unionism. Slightly less than two-thirds of the membership was employed in the nonpublic sector; some 770,000 members were state and municipal sector employees (Labour Market Parties 1983). Approximately 850,000 members were covered by collective bargaining agreements with SAF-affiliated firms (Bratt 1982). LO membership has plateaued in the past few years.

The Central Organization of Salaried Employees (TCO) was organized in 1944, and by 1983 it had 20 trade union federation affiliates and some 1,080,000 individual members, of whom 500,000 were employed in the nonpublic sector (Labour Market Parties 1983). The TCO itself is not a bargaining party—rather, bargaining rests with cartels. The Swedish Union of Foremen and Supervisors (SALF) left TCO in 1980, taking with it 72,000 members, and formed its own trade union confederation (Bratt 1982). TCO represents approximately 80 percent of all covered employees, gaining close to 130,000 members between 1975 and 1983. Probably the largest growth was in the public sector where employment was expanding at the time.

The Swedish Confederation of Professional Associations (SACO), organized in 1947, was created to represent employees with a university education who were working in both the private and public sectors. In 1974 it merged with the National Federation of Government Employees (SR) to form SACO-SR, with a membership of approximately 165,000 (Forsebäck 1976). By 1983 SACO-SR was composed of 26 union federations with an estimated membership of 246,000 (Statistisk Årsbok 1984) in the following employment sectors: 53,000 in municipal government, 40,000 in nonpublic enterprises, 90,000 in state service, and 6500 self-employed professionals. There are important differences in how collective bargaining operates. Beginning in the mid-1950s, LO and SAF negotiated "frame" agreements covering the major economic issues. TCO and SACO-SR have never negotiated directly with SAF. Rather, over the years the highest level of bargaining has been between SAF and PTK, the latter a cartel of 14 TCO-affiliated unions, six unions affiliated with SACO-SR, and the Swedish Union of Foremen and Supervisors (SALF).

The big issue on the collective bargaining front in 1984 was wage bargaining under a new decentralized process whereby LO would merely seek to coordinate the claims of its affiliated unions. The first major agreement, covering 600,000 manual employees at the county and municipal level, was reached in March 1984. It provided wage increases for 1984 and 1985 and improvements in age-related annual leaves. For the first time, public employees would receive guaranteed compensation linked to wage drift movement in the private sector. Finally, the parties agreed to provide a reopener clause if subsequent contracts in other sectors proved more generous (Sweden, *EIRR*, April 1984). In the private sector, subsequent one-year agreements in the metalworking and steel industries provided for wage increases, a "kitty" for low-income groups, and the wage drift factor.

In general, these agreements so far have provided overall pay increases that exceed the 6-percent target that the socialist government had established in order to meet the 4-percent target inflation rate for 1984. There is fear that higher inflation rates would weaken the recent improvements in the economy (Sweden, *EIRR*, May 1984).

During October 1984 the Social Democratic government reached a verbal accord with the major labor market parties to hold 1984 wage settlements to no more than 5 percent. The Spring 1985 negotiations would determine if the anti-inflation agreement would hold.

Changing Values and Priorities of the Trade Unions

It is necessary to go back to the late 1960s if we are to understand the origins of the changing labor relations scene. Most writers agree that the harmonious relationship between unions and employers began breaking up at that time. H. G. Myrdal (1981) argues that until the late 1960s the unions were principally concerned with wages, employment, and working conditions. The union confederations recognized the general right of employers to make business and staffing decisions after completing consultations with union representatives. The trade union leaders accepted the idea of private property. The union leadership was also generally aligned with the conservative side of the Social Democratic Party. However, by the late 1960s there was less support for capitalism.

There is some evidence that the shift within both the LO and the Social Democratic Party was in part a response to the growing militance of the "left" in the unions and in the party. Younger members of the party in particular were becoming less satisfied with the state of Swedish society. Socialism clearly had its adherents.

Bernstein (1983) and others believe that the increasing demand for a better worklife led to expectations that employers could not easily meet. In fact, several years earlier the LO leadership had voiced discontent over the operation of the works councils, and during this period it was increasing its demand for more union and employee influence in the workplace. The joint LO-SAF Quality of Worklife experiments, established in 1969 in a number of Swedish companies, addressed some of these issues. However, by the mid-1970s LO had withdrawn from these projects.

The wildcat strikes of 1969–70 were further evidence of discontent in Swedish labor-management relations. The first strike was at the LKAB iron ore mines in Kiruna and was directed against both degrading working conditions and the new LO policy of wage solidarity (Ruth 1984). These highly paid miners were protesting the LO policy that provided additional compensation through bargaining for employees in low-paying industries and occupations that would, over time, reduce the differential between their pay and that of workers in those other sectors. The LO leadership would not back down on the wage solidarity policy.

Another important shift in LO thinking concerned the use of piece-rate wage systems. During the early postwar period, LO and SAF were in harmony regarding the advantages of piece-work pay and were encouraging the expansion of these systems wherever possible. Two-thirds of the industrial workforce (production and construction workers) were paid under some type of individual or group incentive plan in the mid-1960s, about the time that LO shifted away from its earlier position regarding piece-work incentives. Increasingly, the LO leadership came to view Taylor-inspired work practices as undesirable for workers' health and at odds with the trade union policy of solidarity. Between 1965 and 1980, the percentage of workers on piece-rates declined from 46 to 14 percent, the percentage on straight-time hourly rates increased from 30 to 47 percent, and the percentage on payment-by-results systems increased from 24 to 39 percent (Bratt 1982).

There was also a growing debate about whether or not Sweden was becoming a "corporatist" state. In addition, critics of the wage-earner fund proposal feared that such legislation would shift Sweden from a capital-based economy to one that was labor-based and managed by the trade unions.

Korpi (in Rydén and Bergström 1982) identified three other forces for change that were affecting the Swedish Model: (1) the international economic crisis beginning in the 1970s, (2) the negative political consequences of the 1976 election outcome for the trade unions, and (3) the feeling that workers were still in a subordinate position vis-à-vis their employers. There was growing pressure and agitation for greater industrial and economic democracy.

Moreover, Myrdal, writing in 1981, believed that the orientation of the LO leadership had changed considerably over the years. He viewed it as increasingly anticapitalist and prosocialist and as more representative of the left wing of the Social Democratic Party than it had been in earlier years. However, he did not see the leadership as wishing to nationalize Swedish industry.

The dynamics for change were to intensify during the 1970s and early 1980s, with pressures evidencing themselves in several ways. First, the trade union movement increasingly turned to legislation rather than collective bargaining in efforts to achieve its objectives. Second, codetermination was advocated as a means of realizing industrial democracy in a real sense. Third, industrial conflict was manifested through more lawful and unlawful industrial actions, culminating in the 1980 strike and lockout. Finally, the wage-earner funds debate culminated in 1983 legislation designed to provide tangible evidence of economic democracy in Sweden. We can best understand the changing collective bargaining scene by addressing each of these factors in turn rather than reporting chronologically the events in Swedish collective bargaining since 1975.

Shifts Toward a Legislative Approach

Perhaps the most obvious trend in recent years has been towards attempting to achieve trade union objectives through legislation rather than collective bargaining. Prior to 1970, both collective bargaining parties had, with few exceptions, worked out their differences through a host of supplementary collaborative agreements dealing with many facets of the employer-employee relationship. Korpi (in Rydén and Bergström 1982) writes that in the 1970s the trade unions abandoned the idea that employers and unions should regulate the process free of government interference. A major reason for this change was the view that SAF was unwilling to broaden worker participation, even though, at the time, LO had never asked SAF for specific changes in the basic or Works Council agreements. These differences were most evident in the private sector; therefore, the following discussion will center on LO and SAF, although the other trade union confederations had clear interests in most of the issues.

The shift really began in 1972 with legislation establishing employee representation on company boards of directors. Such representation was made permanent in 1976 in laws specifying that trade union organizations could appoint two members and two deputies to the board in limited liability companies or economic associations with at least 25 employees. Similar legislation took effect in the public sector in 1974.

Three other significant laws were enacted in 1974. The Employment Security Act governed the commencement and termination of employment and required that dismissals be only for objective grounds. It also provided for reinstatement and payment of damages in cases of employer violations. The act was amended in 1982 to allow employers to hire people on a trial basis of up to six months as a means of encouraging the creation of new jobs. Such temporary employment had been restricted under the earlier Act.

The rights of shop stewards were addressed in the second piece of legislation, which provided that such trade union representatives could perform their union duties on company-paid time. The local union controlled who would qualify as a union official and the time required for union business.

The third law enacted in 1974, the Work Environment Act, was designed to improve general working conditions and safety at the workplace. The Working Environment Act of 1978 expanded the coverage to include health risks and psychological aspects. The new legislation also allowed safety delegates the right to halt dangerous work under certain circumstances.

The Act on Employee Participation in Decision Making, passed in 1976, was the most controversial legislation on the labor market enacted during the 1970s. The legislative intent was to expand the participation of employees and their unions in the decision-making process. This legislation will be discussed in greater depth in the next section (Swedish Employers' Confederation 1978, Swedish Institute 1984).

Other labor legislation covered the right of employees to take leaves of absence for educational studies, child care, holidays, and training as well as equality between men and women at work.

Some of the legislation was all-encompassing, while other acts provided the framework for collaborative agreements between the principal collective bargaining parties. Some of these agreements are limited to SAF or LO or PTK; others, like that involving the working environment, cover SAF, LO, and PTK. The clear intent of the new legislation was to increase the power and influence of unions and employees generally.

It can be seen that a definite break had been made with the past when LO, and to some extent the other trade union confederations, increasingly turned to legislation to accomplish their objectives. It is doubtful that this step would have been taken had LO leaders been able to gain employer support for this new agenda through the collective bargaining process. However, the SAF leadership was not willing to accept the trade unions' new political platform. This goal incongruity was quite evident in the battle over codetermination.

Codetermination

LO and SAF reached an agreement in 1946 to establish a system of works councils. They were to be organized only for discussion and exchange of information between the parties, not to negotiate or to make decisions. Initially, this conformed to the wishes of both parties, as SAF did not want to delegate decision-making power to the councils and LO had no desire to establish a forum that would compete with their regular bargaining mechanisms. Both sides perceived benefits in terms of improving productivity and employee satisfaction. The 1958 amendments to the agreement included a separate provision for works council representatives from TCO.

LO commissioned a Report on Industrial Democracy that was generally accepted by delegates to the 1961 convention. The purpose of the report was to delineate LO objectives in this area for the coming years and to identify specific action steps. SAF also established a reference group to study industrial democracy, and this group published two reports regarding the organization and operation of works councils. Both sides were dissatisfied with the works councils system, but for very different reasons. By the mid-1960s the LO leadership had concluded that SAF was reluctant to agree to any major modification in their agreement that would lead to a significantly greater union voice. SAF's major concern was management prerogatives. (For more details on this debate, see Peterson 1966, 1968.)

During the late 1960s and early 1970s it became increasingly clear to LO leaders that SAF was not willing to go as far as LO desired on the issue of worker participation in decision-making. This agenda was more radical than SAF was prepared to negotiate. Schmidt (1977) also believes that LO realized that codetermination could be achieved more quickly through legislation. The fact that most of the Social Democratic members of Parliament came from labor unions would also increase the likelihood that such legislation would eventually pass.

The Act on Codetermination at Work, or Act on Employee Participation in Decision-Making (MBL), was passed by the Swedish Parliament in 1976, to become effective January 1, 1977. Schmidt (1977, pp. 225–28) provides a detailed background on the steps leading to the passage of this legislation. Controversy centered upon the proposals to extend greater employee and trade union influence in the work setting. SAF and individual employers spoke against the proposed legislation. TCO, for the most part, went along with LO in endorsing it.

The Codetermination Act superseded acts of 1920 (Act on Mediation of Industrial Disputes), of 1928 (Collective Agreements Act), and of 1936 (Act on Right of Association and Negotiation) in providing the framework for negotiation between the parties. The law had the effect of weakening Article 32 of the Basic Agreement, which provided broad interpretation of management rights in exchange for workers' right of association. That clause, which had its origins in the 1906 SAF-LO agreement, had been a source of dissatisfaction with LO for many years. There are a number of key features in the 1976 act. First, priority of interpretation of an agreement no longer rests only with the employer—employees may grieve certain actions through the trade unions. Second, the employer has a primary obligation to negotiate with trade union representatives prior to decisions on major changes in management or supervision of work. Third, new language provides the right of the unions to information on the company's production plans, economic status, personnel policy, and so forth. Finally, the framework for joint regulation is outlined (Forsebäck 1976). Schmidt (1977) and Bouvin (1977) provide considerable detail regarding the legislation.

In almost all respects the union confederations supported the new legislation advanced by the Social Democrats; however, the law did not respond to their demands for trade union rights of decision-making in certain matters. The main concerns of SAF and the employers included: (1) their desire that the basic policy of firms be excluded from collective bargaining agreements; (2) skepticism regarding the value of centralized negotiations due to resulting time delays in implementing decisions; (3) the onerous obligation of employers to provide certain information to the unions; and (4) the unions' power to veto subcontracting agreements (Mazzolini 1978).

This legislation, plus the Public Employment Act, applied to all parts of the private and public sectors. Negotiations developed separately in the two sectors. The first joint regulation agreement covered state-owned enterprises (SFO). A subsequent agreement between the unions and the State Bargaining Office covered 400,000 state-sector employees. Eiger (1981) expects joint regulation to succeed in the public sector because of the pragmatism of public-sector managers, the influence of Social Democratic ideology, and the quality of the educational effort by public-sector unions to prepare all levels for participation. Joint regulation agreements were reached subsequently for small groups of employees in state-owned firms, banking, insurance, and cooperatives (Eiger 1981). It took SAF, LO, and PTK until 1982 to reach a joint regulation agreement on efficiency and participation. The time-lapse provides some indication of the difficulty the parties had in reaching an understanding. Quite a few of the problems could be traced to policy differences between LO and the other trade union confederations.

The 1982 SAF-LO-PTK joint regulation agreement identified efficiency, profitability, and competitiveness as major goals. It encourages employers to use the full range of employee talents such that long-range planning, group work, and job enrichment are encouraged in the workplace. New technology is encouraged, but union representatives are to be consulted during the planning stages if major changes are expected. Unions are to be provided with information on the company's financial and economic situation as well as its planning, budgeting, and monitoring activities. Employee consultants, paid by the firm, are entitled to evaluate the firm's financial and economic data (Bernstein 1983). An Efficiency and Participation Board is established to promote these activities, and an Arbitration Board is provided to interpret the Joint Regulation Agreement.

The first major joint regulation agreement at the company level was reached by A.B. Volvo with its relevant trade unions. The new agreement provides, in particular: (1) guaranteed union involvement in projected changes in work organization and content, (2) guarantees of greater employee access to paid training needed as a result of the introduction of new technology, and (3) the appointment of paid "worker consultants" who can keep unionized company employees apprised of the firm's financial affairs, but are pledged to maintain secrecy with regard to such information disclosed to them (Sweden, *EIRR*, March 1984).

Is the Act on Codetermination at Work as radical as envisaged by some people both before and after the legislation was passed? It is too early to attempt an answer since the economic climate has not been favorable for the unions to press for complete adoption. What is clear is that industrial democracy has moved beyond the framework provided by the old works council agreement of 1946. Previously, some employers would notify the employee representatives on the councils of company actions that had, in many cases, already been taken. The 1976 act provides that the trade unions be consulted prior to management decisions, so the potential is there for the unions to have a real impact. How the unions use the information or influence joint regulation will determine whether Swedish codetermination will represent a modest extension of industrial democracy or a definite shift towards joint decision-making. So far no voices are being heard in favor of joint decision-making today. No further legislation on codetermination has been proposed; in fact, interviews indicated that it has been put on the back burner because of recent economic difficulties.

Wildcat Strikes and the 1980 Strike-Lockout

Table 6 shows Sweden's strike record from 1975 to 1982. The number of strikes ranged from a low of 66 in 1981 to a high of 289 in 1975. Of interest is the fact that more working days were lost and more employees were involved in unlawful, compared to lawful, strikes in 1975, 1976, 1979, and 1982. In contrast, strike activity in the earlier postwar years had been quite low, with the notable exceptions of 1945, 1953, and 1969–70.

TABLE 6
Strike Experience, Sweden, 1975–1982

Year	Number of Strikes	Working Days Lost		Number of Employees Involved	
		Lawful	Unlawful	Lawful	Unlawful
1975	289	14,795	343,161	2,280	35,231
1976	123	6,910	18,693	709	9,755
1977	105	105,041	13,750	9,282	9,076
1978	171	28,035	18,964	1,999	15,775
1979	207	890	27,824	263	32,052
1980	204	4,452,350	38,442	718,494	26,354
1981	66	201,964	7,173	88,354	10,357
1982	46	—	1,761	—	5,136

Source: Statistisk Årsbok 1982–83 and 1984. Stockholm: Statistiska Central-byron, 1982, 1984.

How does one explain the existence of unofficial (unlawful) strikes in Sweden? Korpi (1981) concludes that the increase between 1969 and 1975 was due largely to economic factors such as stagflation rather than being a reflection of a revolt of the rank-and-file against the wage policies of the union leadership or extremist political agitators.

The most dramatic abandonment of labor-management peace was the 1980 strike-lockout. Table 6 indicates that it directly affected some 718,000 employees during April and May of that year. Strikes began on April 24 in the public sector and then spread to the private sector when SAF-affiliated firms locked out their workers. Bernstein (1983) states that the conflict idled 20 percent of the labor force, while Halvarsson (1981) believes that at one time or another a quarter of the labor force was affected. The lockout affected 600,000 LO members alone (Swedish Institute 1984). Economic differences between the parties were at the root of the dispute. However, these differences were compounded because some of the wage proposals required government action on tax reductions and other changes. The non-socialist government's position was that a noninflationary settlement was necessary to make Sweden more competitive internationally. Negotiators from LO, PTK, and SAF met during the early months of 1980. On March 17 LO broke off bargaining and announced a ban on overtime. The public-sector unions followed with their own overtime bans. The public-sector strike began on April 24. Two mediation commissions were established. The conflict spread to the private sector on May 2 with simultaneous strikes and lockouts. By May 11 the key labor market parties had reached agreement (Faxén 1980).

Wage Earner Funds

For decades the LO leadership had been committed to expanding the role of democracy in the workplace, and they saw the Act on Codetermination at Work (1976) as an important step in that direction. However, LO and the Social Democratic Party also sought economic democracy. A report of an early LO-SAP joint committee headed by Ernst Wigforss and Gunnar Myrdal has stated:

> The goal of social democracy is to reformulate the economic organization of bourgeois society so that the right to determine production is placed in the hands of all its citizens; so that the majority is forced from its dependence on a minority of capitalists; and so that a social order built on economic classes gives way to a community of free and equal citizens. (Childs 1980, pp. 43–44)

How might "the right for economic democracy" be realized? Rudolf Meidner, then an economist with LO, developed a proposal on wage-earner funds in the early 1970s. In August 1975 the LO-appointed committee released a report calling for a system combining profit-sharing with collective ownership of stock capital in private firms. The revised report was then submitted to the 1976 LO Congress where it received general support (Albrecht 1980, Meidner 1981). The goals of the LO proposal were:

> (1) complement the policy of wage solidarity in such a way that the owners of highly profitable firms would not be enriched; (2) counteract the growing concentration of capital, and hence of power, which is the concomitant of self-financing in a highly industrial economy; and (3) reinforce wage earners' influence at the workplace through participation in ownership. (Meidner 1981, pp. 309–10)

The underlying principles behind the Meidner Plan submitted to the 1976 LO convention were:

> 1. Wage earner funds should be established out of capital accumulated out of company profits.
>
> 2. Benefits should accrue to all employees, even if they are not contributing to the funds.
>
> 3. The capital of the funds is not to be withdrawn from firms, and individuals cannot own shares.
>
> 4. There must be guarantees of strong influence by local members over the administration of the fund capital. (p. 311)

In September 1976, LO and the Social Democratic Party jointly appointed a working committee to reconsider the issue of wage-earner funds and to submit a report to the 1978 Party Congress. By 1978 a fourth fund goal was added: to provide collective savings and capital accumulation to strengthen the Swedish economy (Albrecht 1980).

There is general agreement that the controversy engendered by the Meidner Plan played a role in the defeat of the Social Democrats in the 1976 general elections. SAF and many industrialists spoke out against the plan. The then head of the Conservative Party called it "garbage, fit only to be thrown out" (Childs 1980, p. 62). SAF published a report that year proposing a program for individual profit-sharing instead.

H. G. Myrdal (1981) of SAF foresaw the wage-earner funds as a road to socialism that would result over time in the abolition of private ownership except for very small firms. He stated that all the non-socialist parties rejected the LO and LO-SAP schemes in favor a fund system with individual participation. The then chairman of LO, Gunnar Nilsson, was also having some reservations:

> But there is no doubt that if we transfer economic power over the firm to the employees we will eventually reach a limit where the economic responsibility is so great that we will be forced to take upon ourselves the role of company managers. We will then risk ending up with a Trade Union movement of the Eastern European model—we will be transformed from an offensive mass movement into a movement which administers the means of production and fulfills a supervisory function in relation to its members, making sure they meet their production targets. (1980, p. 68)

The Swedish public too was deeply divided on this and similar issues. For example, Boalt and Bergryd (1981) reported the results of a mail survey conducted just before the 1979 general election. They divided part of their sample into four groups of which "very convinced socialists" and "very convinced anti-socialists" were the two extremes. The results for four questions are reported below:

Statement	Very Convinced Socialists (% Yes)	Very Convinced Anti-Socialists (% No)
1. Employees have equal rights to profits as stockholders.	83	89
2. It is workers who produce profits of companies.	76	90
3. Conditions will not improve until workers take power.	85	75
4. Workers and employees are oppressed in this country.	95	71

Clearly, these respondents represented only the strongest dichotomies, but such results highlight the lack of consensus on the desired state of employees and employers in Swedish society at that time.

Three principal alternatives had been suggested by the early 1980s (Meidner 1981). The first proposal was submitted to the National Commission by LO and the Social Democratic Party. The regional funds would consist of 20 percent of the pretax profits of firms, paid in cash or shares and a payroll levy, the money to be invested in the stock market. Voting shares would be held jointly by the firms' employees and the regional funds. When the fund owned in excess of 40 percent of the stock in an individual company, the excess amount would be exercised by regional electoral colleges.

Business and the Conservative Party advocated a voluntary savings scheme that would be subsidized by tax deductions or savings. Individuals would be free to invest their savings as they wished. The savings could be disposed of after a certain period.

The Liberal and Center Parties offered a compulsory savings scheme. Parliament would decide each year the proportion of incomes that should be transferred to a number of economic associations. The assets would be invested in stock capital with access to the contribution after, say, five years. The latter proposals clearly offered moderate alternatives to the controversial wage-earner funds.

The Social Democratic government presented a proposal on wage-earner funds in June 1983, and throughout the Summer and early Fall various interest groups spoke out for and against it. SAF continued its strong opposition to wage-earner schemes. On October 4, between 75,000 and 100,000 people rallied in Stockholm to protest the need for such legislation. The demonstration was organized by concerned employers, but the protesters represented a broad cross-section of the Swedish population. The major complaint focused on the fact that semiannual public opinion polls from 1975 through 1981 showed that the vast majority of respondents favored individual rather than trade union ownership if employees were to be given a larger portion of ownership in companies (Larsson 1984).

The government was undaunted. Parliament passed the wage-earner fund legislation in December 1983 (Swedish Institute, March 1984). The English translation of the title of the act is "employee investment funds," which makes it clear that the funds apply to all employees, not just workers. The Swedish Finance Ministry views the legislation as aimed at avoiding increased profits that would give rise to a future concentration of power and ownership in trade and industry (Sweden, *EIRR*, December 1983). The new legislation established a system of regional funds, each with a nine-member board of directors of which at least five will represent employee (union) interests.

The act provides that a maximum of KR2 billion will be collected yearly from joint stock companies, unincorporated associations, savings banks, and insurance companies. The funds come from two sources: the 20 percent of net profits which exceed a certain level after adjustment for inflation, and a .2 percent increase in the employers' contribution to the state pension system. An initial kitty for the plan was set aside in 1983. The new system is scheduled to be in effect for seven years, from 1984 through 1990. Interestingly, experts in the Finance Ministry estimate that only 3300 of the 73,000 limited companies in Sweden will pay the tax on "surplus" profits (Sweden, *EIRR*, December 1983, p. 23).

It is too early to assess the impact of the new legislation in terms of either its financial effect on Swedish companies or bringing economic democracy to the labor force. The individual funds will be restricted to 8 percent of the voting shares in a listed company, or a total of 40 percent of voting shares for the five combined funds (Sweden, *EIRR*, December 1983). Hence, the funds will not be able to gain majority control of a given company's stock by 1990. The new legislation makes it possible for the local branch of a trade union to hold up to 20 percent of the company's voting shares. The act seemed to be clearly aimed at the major companies rather than at industry in general. What happens after 1990 will be the real test of whether or not the trade unions will be operating co-owners of major Swedish firms. Based upon the track record to date, we doubt that the Swedish trade union movement would really want this to occur because it could create a conflict of interest for them. What is clear is that the wage-earner fund debate was the most controversial issue in Swedish labor relations in the postwar period.

The Decline of the Swedish Model

Most experts agree that today the labor market parties are not as willing to compromise as they were in the years prior to 1970. After the 1980 strike/lockout, Gunnar Nilsson, then chairman of LO, was quoted as saying, "The Swedish Model is dead. Labor and capital can no longer cooperate in the old spirit." Olof Ljungren, managing director of SAF, was also pessimistic at that time (Bernstein 1983, p. 475). In the same year, H. G. Myrdal had this to say about the Swedish Model: "Something which, on the other hand, has not been observed, particularly abroad, is that the Swedish Model is now rocking on its very foundations. Its main components are now being questioned by the trade union movement. Its prospects for survival are precarious" (1980, p. 57).

Many reasons have been advanced for the loss of "the golden age of industrial relations" in Sweden. Lundberg (1981) asserts that forces were already at work during the 1950s and 1960s that would undermine the functioning of the model. First, he believes that the general view was that rapid and steady economic growth was evident and inexorable. The uninterrupted rise in GNP had led to attitude changes and new demands on the part of workers, employees, and their unions. Security and equity aims had taken precedence over sustaining economic growth. The abundant society mentality was well in place. The EFO or Scandinavian economic model could not withstand the inflationary upswing in the international markets after the oil price shock in late 1973 nor the increasing political dichotomy that emerged. The excess corporate profits in 1973 and 1974, as LO called them, provided additional fuel for the fire (Childs 1980). Bernstein (1982) believes that the old trust between the labor market parties eroded due to the desire of the Social Democratic Party and the trade unions to enlarge their workplace power and to the flood of labor legislation that weakened the entrepreneurial position of many Swedish employers.

Bratt (1982, 1983) attributes the cracking of the Swedish Model to other forces. First, there was a change in union ideology that resulted in severe ideological friction between the social partners. Second, a new generation of political leaders emerged who had different values and goals than their predecessors. Third, there was the glut of innovative but quite controversial labor legislation. Fourth, the very rapid growth of public expenditures created excessive pressures while, at the same time, weakening the influence of the private-sector organization in the labor market. Finally, the fairly deep and long-lasting economic recession was unlike anything that had ever been experienced earlier in the postwar period. Lundberg (1981) saw the parties' lack of consensus on mutual values as the foremost obstacle to a new Swedish Model.

If we return to H. G. Myrdal's distinguishing features of that model, we can draw some conclusions as to the reasons for its demise:

1. The free market economy was not functioning properly during most years after 1975.

2. Subsidies and governmental action make for less independent, less free competing enterprises.

3. Government played a less laissez-faire role in the collective bargaining system.

4. There was not as much emphasis on practical reforms than there had been prior to the 1970s.

5. Politics and ideology took precedence over pragmatism.

6. There was significantly less cooperation between the major trade union and the employer confederations.

7. Strike activity accelerated during the post-1975 period.

The only positive element was that the system of consultation and participation by employees in the firm was still functioning fairly well, even if some employers were not particularly supportive of the legislated participation structures. In general, it can be said that both economic and political forces played significant roles in shaping Swedish collective bargaining after 1975.

It is not clear that centralized bargaining will serve as a major element of Swedish collective bargaining in the coming years. Centralized bargaining between the principal organizations in the private sector was the common approach between 1952 and the early 1980s (Swedish Confederation of Trade Unions 1983). In 1983, however, the Engineering Employers' Association signed a separate agreement with the Metal Workers' Union. The impetus for decentralized bargaining came from manufacturing industry employer members of SAF. LO and SAF leaders agreed that there would be no centralized negotiations in 1984. Whether or not this is a temporary agreement is unknown as yet. Decentralized bargaining may well result in less discipline by the union and employer confederations. On the other hand, through decentralized bargaining the parties may be better able to address special needs of employers and all their employees in specific industries as they face different competitive situations. It is clear from interview responses that the employer demand for decentralized bargaining had its origins in their weak economic positions.

We have said very little about public-sector bargaining or the role of professional employees represented by SACO-SR. The major issues we have discussed primarily concerned the relations between SAF, LO, and TCO in the private sector. Since the public sector has been relatively protected from international competition and from some of the controversial issues presented here, writers and commentators have devoted little in-depth attention to public-sector industrial relations.

References

Agreement on Efficiency and Participation SAF-LO-PTK. Stockholm: Adrian and Holm, 1982.
Albrecht, Sandra. "Politics, Bureaucracy, and Worker Participation: The Swedish Case." *Journal of Applied Behavioral Science* 16 (July-August-September 1980): pp. 299–316.
Basic Agreement of 1938 Between the Swedish Employers' Confederation and the Confederation of Swedish Trade Unions, amended in 1947, 1958, 1964, 1974, and 1976.
Bernstein, Paul. "Work in Sweden: Trouble in Paradise." *The Wharton Magazine* 6 (Summer 1982): pp. 46–52.
_____. "The Unraveling of Labor-Management Relations in Sweden." *Personnel Journal* 62 (June 1983): pp. 468–77.
Boalt, Gunnar, and Ulla Bergryd. *Political Value Patterns and Parties in Sweden.* Stockholm: Almquist and Wiksell International, 1981.
Bouvin, Åke. "New Swedish Legislation on Democracy of the Workplace." *International Labour Review* 115 (March-April 1977): pp. 131–42.
Bratt, Christian. *Labor Relations in 17 Countries.* Stockholm: Swedish Employers' Confederation, 1982.
_____. *Workers' Participation in Sweden.* Stockholm: Swedish Employers' Confederation, January 1982.
_____. *Workers' Participation in Sweden.* Stockholm: Swedish Employers' Confederation, Document No, 139, October 1983.
"Business Outlook: Sweden." *Business Europe,* April 27, 1984, p. 136.
Childs, Marquis. *Sweden: The Middle Way on Trial.* New Haven, CT: Yale University Press, 1980.
Coulombe, Gilles. "Relations du travail dans le secteur public." *Relations Industrielles* 31 (1976): pp. 448–65.
Eiger, Norman. "The Expanding Scope of Public Bargaining in Sweden." *Industrial Relations* 20 (Fall 1981): pp. 335–41.
Faxén, Karl-Olof. "Calendar of Main Events." SAF Internal Memo, June 12, 1980.
_____. *Incomes Policy and Centralized Wage Formation.* Stockholm: Swedish Employers' Confederation, 1982.
Forsebäck, Lennart. *Industrial Relations and Employment in Sweden.* Stockholm: The Swedish Institute, 1976.
Francis, David R. "Pension-Fund Socialism Grows Quietly, But It's Gathering Clout." *Christian Science Monitor,* January 26, 1984, p. 15.
Halvarsson, Mats. *Swedish Industry Faces the 80s.* Stockholm: Federation of Swedish Industries/The Swedish Institute, 1981.
Hedlund, Gunnar, and Lars Otterbeck. *The Multinational Corporation, the Nation State, and the Trade Unions: An European Perspective.* Kent, OH: Comparative Administration Research Institute, Kent State University, 1977.
Jackson, Peter, and Keith Sisson. "Employers' Confederations in Sweden and the U.K. and the Significance of Industrial Infrastructure." *British Journal of Industrial Relations* 14 (November 1976): pp. 306-23.
Jakobsson, Ulf. "Economic Growth in Sweden." Paper delivered at Conference on World Economic Growth Problems, Mexico City, April 1983.
Johnston, Thomas L. *Collective Bargaining in Sweden.* Cambridge, MA: Harvard University Press, 1962.
Korpi, Walter. "Sweden: Conflict, Power and Politics in Industrial Relations." In *Industrial Relations in International Perspective,* ed. Peter Doeringer. New York: Holmes and Meier Publishers, Inc., 1981, Pp. 185–217.

_____. "Unofficial Strikes in Sweden." *British Journal of Industrial Relations* 19 (March 1981): pp. 66–86.
_____. *The Working Class Welfare Capitalism, Work, Unions and Politics in Sweden.* London: Routledge and Kegan Paul, 1978.
Korpi, Walter, and Michael Shalev. "Strikes, Industrial Relations, and Class Conflict in Capitalist Societies." *British Journal of Sociology* 30 (June 1979): pp. 164–87.
Landsorganizationen i Sverige. *De centrala overenskom mellan LO ach SAF 1952–1983.* Stockholm: 1983.
Larsson, Janerik. *Turning Point.* Orebro, Sweden: Timbro Forlag, 1984.
Lundberg, Erik. "The Rise and Fall of the 'Swedish Model.'" *Skandinaviska Enskilda Banken Quarterly Review* (1-2/1981): pp. 12–19.
Mazzolini, Renato. "The Influence of European Workers Over Corporate Strategy." *Sloan Management Review* 19 (Spring 1978): pp. 59–81.
Meidner, Rudolph. "Collective Asset Formation Through Wage Earner Funds." *International Labour Review* 120 (May-June 1981): 303–18.
Meyerson, Per-Martin. *The Welfare State in Crisis—The Case of Sweden.* Stockholm: Federation of Swedish Industries, 1982.
Ministry of Finance and the National Institute of Economic Research. *The Swedish Economy April 1983—Revised National Budget for 1983.* Stockholm: 1983.
Ministry of Labour. *Swedish Legislation on the Working Environment.* Stockholm: July 1978.
Myers, Charles A. *Industrial Relations in Sweden.* Boston: The Technological Press—MIT, 1951.
Myrdal, Hans-Göran. "The Swedish Model—Will It Survive?" *British Journal of Industrial Relations* 18 (March 1980): pp. 57–69.
_____. "Collective Wage-Earner Funds in Sweden: A Road to Socialism and the End of Freedom." *International Labour Review* 120 (May-June 1981): pp. 319–34.
Olsen, Erling. "The Dilemma of the Social-Democratic Labor Parties." *Daedalus* 113 (Spring 1984): pp. 169-94.
Organization for Economic Cooperation and Development. *OECD Economic Surveys 1981-1982: Sweden.* Paris: July 1982.
Peterson, Richard B. "The Status of Managerial Rights in Swedish Collective Bargaining." Ph.D. dissertation, University of Wisconsin, 1966.
_____. "The Swedish Experience with Industrial Democracy." *British Journal of Industrial Relations* 6 (July 1968): pp. 185-203.
Prais, S. J. "Strike Frequencies and Plant Size;: A Comment on Sweden and UK Experience." *British Journal of Industrial Relations* 20 (March 1981): pp. 101-104.
Rehn, Gosta. "The Wages of Success." *Daedalus* 113 (Spring 1984): pp. 137-68.
Ruth, Arne. "The Second New Nation: The Mythology of Modern Sweden." *Daedalus* 113 (Spring 1984): pp. 53-96.
Rydén, Bengt, and Villy Bergström, eds. *Sweden: Choices for Economic and Social Policy in the 1980s.* London: George Allen and Unwin, 1982.
Schmidt, Folke. *The Law of Labour Relations in Sweden.* Cambridge, MA: Harvard University Press, 1962.
_____. *Law and Industrial Relations in Sweden.* Stockholm: Almquist and Wiksell International, 1977.
Schwartz, Eli. *Trouble in Eden: A Comparison of British and Swedish Economies.* New York: Praeger, 1980.
Siven, Claes-Henric. "The Political Economy of Sweden in the 1970s." Department of Economics/University of Stockholm, Research Papers in Economics #1, 1984.
"Start Again, Sweden." *The Economist,* May 17, 1980, p. 12.
Statistisk Årsbok 1982-83. Stockholm: Statistiska Centralbyran, 1982.
Statistisk Årsbok 1984. Stockholm: Statistiska Centralbyran, 1984.
"Struck." *The Economist,* May 10, 1980, p. 58.
Svenska Arbetsgivareforening. *Fakta om Sveriges Ekonomi.* Stockholm: SAF, 1983.
Svenska Handelsbanken. *Sweden in the World Economy.* Stockholm: June 1981.
_____. *Sweden in the World Economy.* Stockholm: October 1983.

_____. *Sweden's Economy in Figures 1983*. Stockholm: 1983.
"Sweden: Bargaining Latest." *European Industrial Relations Review*, No. 124, May 1984.
"Sweden: Employee Investment Funds." *European Industrial Relations Review*, No. 119, December 1983.
"Sweden: First 1984 Agreement." *European Industrial Relations Review*, No. 123, April 1984.
"Sweden Freezes Prices in a Stab at Inflation." *Christian Science Monitor*, April 13, 1984, p. 2.
"Sweden—Joint Regulation Agreement at Value." *European Industrial Relations Review*, No. 122, March 1984.
"Sweden—Joint Regulation in Perspective." *European Industrial Relations Review* 71 (December 1979): pp. 12–13.
Sweden 84. Stockholm: Norstedts Tryckeri, 1984.
Swedish Confederation of Trade Unions. *News*, November 1983, March 1984.
_____. *The Unions and the Party—A Team*. Stockholm: March 1984.
Swedish Employers' Confederation. *Fundamental Principles of Labour Law Regulation*. Stockholm: Labour Law Section of SAF, November 1978.
_____. *This is SAF*. Stockholm: 1981.
The Swedish Institute. *Fact Sheets on Sweden—General Facts on Sweden*. Stockholm: April 1984.
_____. *Fact Sheets on Sweden—Labor Relations in Sweden*. Stockholm: March 1984.
_____. *Fact Sheets on Sweden—The Swedish Economy*. Stockholm: April 1982.
_____. *The Swedish Economy—Facts and Figures*. Stockholm: June 1983.
U.S. Department of Commerce. *Foreign Economic Trends and Their Implications for the United States*. Washington: International Trade Administration, June 1982.

CHAPTER 10

Structural Economic Change and Industrial Relations in the United States' Manufacturing and Transportation Sectors Since 1973*

RICHARD N. BLOCK
Michigan State University

KENNETH MCLENNAN
Committee for Economic Development

All businesses must adjust to continuous economic change. Fluctuations in demand over the business cycle require short-run adjustments, such as layoffs and recall or adjustments in hours worked. In contrast to these short-run adjustments, businesses are also required to make adjustments to longer-run secular changes in demand and more fundamental changes in production methods. These structural changes are usually continuous and occur over the long run. A gradual change in consumer preferences, or loss of competitiveness as foreign and other domestic competitors equal or surpass the firm's level of productivity, can enlarge the scope of market competition and reduce demand for the firm's product. If the firm fails to respond to consumer demand or to compete successfully in the new environment, some workers will become structurally unemployed as jobs are lost permanently.

* The analyses and views expressed in this chapter are solely the responsibility of the authors. The comments of the volume editors,and the participants in a seminar at the Wharton School, University of Pennsylvania, were invaluable. The authors wish to thank Nancy Bredhoff, Lorraine M. Brooker, Pamela Clausen, and Ruth Varner for their research assistance. Appreciation is extended to Daniel H. Kruger and David E. Mitchell for their help in data acquisition. Jerome Mark, Arthur Neef, and Pamela Capdevielle provided access to unpublished data from the U.S. Bureau of Labor Statistics. Thanks are also due to John Lien of the U.S. Department of Commerce and to George Ruben, Sandra King, and Harriet Weinstein of the U.S. Bureau of Labor Statistics.

Structural economic change in the United States since 1973 has resulted in markets becoming more competitive, especially in those sectors of the economy in which unionism was most strongly entrenched. For example, deregulation of previously regulated markets changed the competitive environment in the airline and trucking industries. Similarly, significant import penetration in basic steel and automobile manufacturing increased competitive pressures in those industries, while the textile and apparel industries continued to feel the import pressure that had characterized those industries prior to 1973. In the rubber tire industry, product and then process innovation led to structural change, while in the agricultural implement industry there has been a decrease in demand that appears to be relatively permanent.

From the end of World War II through the early 1970s, collective bargaining had flourished in these industries, primarily because of the ability of the companies to use their positions in largely sheltered markets either to absorb wage and benefit increases through increasing productivity and sales, or to shift the burden of the wage increases to customers through price increases. This chapter will analyze how structural change increased competitiveness in these previously sheltered markets and affected collective bargaining in much of the U.S. private sector.[1]

Symptoms and Sources of Structural Change: 1973-1983

Increasing Importance of Global Markets

For the United States, the 1970s was a period of rapidly expanding imports and exports. By the end of the decade most industries, and especially manufacturing industries, were competing directly or indirectly in international rather than domestic markets. The U.S. share of world trade declined as trade expanded rapidly, with a number of newly industrialized nations becoming important competitors in some U.S. markets.

Despite a decline in the U.S. share of world trade, there was a substantial growth in U.S. exports of manufactures, agricultural products, and services as the overall amount of world trade

---

[1] For a discussion of the development of collective bargaining in several of the industries discussed in this chapter, see Levinson (1980), Stieber (1980), and Kahn (1980). See also Katz (1984). For a comparison of collective bargaining in periods of structural economic change and bargaining in periods of cyclical downturn, see Gay (1984).

increased. The net overall employment effect of increased trade was positive, as more jobs were created in the expanding export sector than were lost from import penetration (see Committee for Economic Development 1984, Ch. 2). During the 1970s the contribution of manufacturing exports compared to imports, in terms of value added to output and unemployment, was positive and rising. According to one study, between 1973 and 1980 trade resulted in a net increase of 280,000 jobs in manufacturing. Since total manufacturing employment increased by 130,000 jobs during this period, the increase in jobs from trade was more than offsetting a decline in jobs attributable to changes in domestic consumption. Except for a few industries, such as motor vehicles, footwear, and apparel, increased trade was not the reason for employment loss in industries where employment declined (Lawrence 1984, p. 42).

In some industries, the newly industrializing countries, with hourly compensation rates of 10 to 20 percent of U.S. rates, became the leading suppliers in some U.S. markets. For example, in 1983 Hong Kong, Taiwan, South Korea, and China accounted for two-thirds of all imports of apparel and related products. Industrializing countries also accounted for a major share of imports of leather products, and Taiwan and South Korea became significant suppliers of fabricated metal products, electrical machinery, and, to a lesser extent, transportation equipment.[2]

As exports expanded over the 1972–1981 period, import penetration (imports as a proportion of the new supply of goods produced by U.S. manufacturers plus the value of imports) developed in many product markets. The import penetration ratio increased slightly for most of the 320 four-digit SIC code industries.[3] In about 55 percent of these markets, however, imports still account for less than 5 percent of the supply of goods produced in the United States and imports from abroad.

[2] U.S. Department of Labor (1984b). The employment effect of increasing foreign competition also depends on the performance of U.S. business in "third" markets. If import penetration continues in U.S. domestic markets, it is likely that U.S. industry will also experience loss of comparative advantage in the same product markets throughout the world.

[3] Unless otherwise noted, estimates of import penetration ratios and the data on specific 4-digit industries are based on U.S. Department of Labor (1984d). Import penetration rates are based on sampling estimates of an annual survey of the value of product shipments. The rate is calculated by dividing the value of imports by all new supply of the product (imports plus U.S. produced goods for domestic consumption or export).

Import penetration in some industries did not increase during the 1970s and remained at between 20 and 25 percent of the supply of new products. This occurred in cane and beet sugar, chocolate and cocoa products, wines and liquor, canned fish, and tobacco. The penetration rate remained high but stable in sewing machines (51 percent). The rate for calculating machines remained high (42 percent) even though it had declined since 1972.

Import penetration continued to increase significantly in a wide variety of apparel products, and by the end of the decade import penetration was between 15 and 30 percent, depending on the product. A similar upward trend occurred in phonograph and television equipment imports, accounting for 50 percent of new supply by the end of the decade.

Since the 1970s rapid increases in imports occurred in a number of industries with high rates of unionization. Import penetration doubled for such industries as motor vehicles and steel products, both of which increased to between 20 and 25 percent. The aircraft engine industry also experienced a significant increase, with imports accounting for about 12 percent of the supply of imports and U.S. production. The most dramatic penetration among the highly unionized industries occurred in the rubber and plastic footwear industry, which increased from 33 to more than 70 percent during the decade.

Technological transfer and comparatively high productivity growth have permitted foreign competitors to produce manufactured products requiring moderate skills. In the 1970s import penetration increased in semiconductors (25 percent), electrometallurgical products (40 percent), watches (48 percent), and metal cutting tools (over 20 percent), with the penetration rate for more sophisticated computer-assisted machine tools closer to 50 percent.

Poor Productivity Performance

The single most important source of structural change in the United States since 1973 has been the gradual narrowing of productivity levels among industrialized and industrializing economies. The U.S. productivity growth rate started to weaken before the first oil shock. After 1973, the decline became much more precipitous, with productivity growth coming to a virtual halt by the end of the decade. This decline was a widespread phenomenon affecting about 80 percent of U.S. manufacturing industries.[4] Since a consistent increase in productivity is the major determinant of improvements in real wages, the productivity decline reduced the ability of management and labor to negotiate improved wages and fringe benefits without reducing the competitiveness of U.S. industries.

On average, U.S. productivity growth rates have been lower—and in some industries significantly lower—than in most industrialized countries for at least 20 years. This has led to a convergence of productivity levels for a wide range of manufacturing industries, with an increasing number of U.S. jobs being threatened by import penetration. By the end of the decade, complete convergence occurred between the U.S. and Japanese levels for manufacturing (Baumol and McLennan 1985, Ch. 1).

In automobile production, Japan surpassed the U.S. level of productivity by the mid-1970s. In steel production, the United States, on average, was surpassed by Japan in the late 1970s and by West Germany by the mid-1970s. While the U.S. steel industry has, on average, lost its competitiveness, some plants can still compete and do not need to experience the adverse labor relations climate associated with industrial restructuring. Other firms in the industry, using older plants and technology, bear the brunt of structural change. This dispersion of productivity performance is especially significant for U.S. collective bargaining since the rate of unionization tends to be higher in older plants within many U.S. industries (Kochan, McKersie, and Cappelli 1984, pp. 17–18).

The introduction of process innovations to improve productivity results in structural unemployment, but innovation also generates more jobs in other parts of the firm, the industry, and the economy. Since innovation is the single most important determinant of productivity growth, more jobs were almost certainly lost through insufficient innovation than were lost by displacement of workers through technological change.[5]

Comparative Compensation Levels

The combination of productivity rates and compensation rates determine the unit labor costs of production. Labor costs represent between 25 and 30 percent of production costs in most manufactur-

---

[4] See U.S. Department of Labor (1982) and Baily (1982).

[5] See Doyle and McLennan (1984) and McLennan (1984a).

ing industries, with the labor cost ratios being significantly higher in less capital-intensive industries such as apparel. As a result, changes in the intercountry rates of compensation have altered the competitiveness of U.S. industry. In some industries this proved to be an important source of industrial restructuring in the latter part of the decade.

During the 1970s, declining competitiveness associated with adverse movement of comparative productivity rates was made worse by the double-digit inflation at the end of the decade. Prior to 1973 comparatively low rates of compensation increases offset relatively low productivity growth and kept most U.S. manufacturing products highly competitive in world trade. Table 1 shows, however, that since 1973 our relative unit labor cost advantage over all countries disappeared. In the late 1970s, the U.S. unit cost position deteriorated seriously compared to Japan and Germany. In 1980 U.S. manufacturing unit labor costs rose to over 11 percent before moderating. Between 1980 and 1983, Japan's extremely low

TABLE 1

Average Annual Percentage Increase
in Unit Labor Costs in Manufacturing
of Major U.S. Trading Partners, 1960–1983

	United States	Canada	Japan	France	West Germany	United Kingdom
1960-1973						
Country currency	1.9	1.8	3.5	2.6	3.7	4.1
U.S. $	1.9	1.9	4.9	2.4	6.1	2.6
1973-1982						
Country currency	7.7	9.8	2.3	10.4	4.7	17.1
U.S. $	7.7	6.7	6.8	9.7	9.2	15.5
1980						
Country currency	11.5	12.9	1.9	12.9	5.2	7.6
U.S. $	11.5	13.1	−5.2	13.3	8.3	32.6
1981						
Country currency	6.1	13.7	1.8	12.9	5.2	7.6
U.S. $	6.1	10.9	4.1	−12.4	−15.3	−6.4
1982						
Country currency	6.6	13.5	−2.8	11.7	4.1	4.6
U.S. $	6.6	10.2	13.9	−7.7	−3.4	−9.6
1983						
Country currency	−0.8	0.3	−2.0	6.6	−1.0	0.7
U.S. $	−0.8	0.5	2.8	−8.0	−5.9	−12.7

Source: U.S. Department of Labor, Bureau of Labor Statistics, *News* (December 1984), and Capdevielle, Alvaraz, and Cooper (1982).

growth in unit labor costs in producing manufactured goods gave them a considerable advantage in international markets. As shown in Table 1, in the 1980–1983 period the U.S. increase in hourly unit labor costs was at least three times more rapid than the increase in Japan and above the increase in West Germany. Moreover, the growing strength of the dollar made the loss of U.S. competitiveness in terms of unit labor costs much worse than it would otherwise have been.[6] As a result, since 1979 the differential in the *levels* of hourly compensation declined from 67 to 49 percent of the U.S. level. In 1978 the level of hourly compensation for West Germany was higher than the U.S. level, but by 1982 compensation in West Germany had dropped to 88 percent of hourly compensation in U.S. manufacturing (Committee for Economic Development 1984, Ch. 2).

Throughout most of the 1970s, Japanese labor costs in producing iron and steel gradually increased relative to labor costs in the U.S. steel industry. Rapid productivity growth provided foreign steel workers with an increase in real wages; this gradual convergence was produced by the strengthening of foreign currencies relative to the U.S. dollar. Japanese hourly compensation in iron and steel production in 1979 was 61 percent of U.S. compensation, compared to 51 percent in 1975. Hourly compensation costs in West Germany's steel industry were 84 percent of U.S. costs in 1979, compared to 70 percent in 1975. By 1982, however, the combination of rapid wage growth in U.S. industry and the strengthening of the U.S. dollar lowered the Japanese hourly compensation costs to 44 percent, and West Germany's to 51 percent, of the U.S. costs of production (U.S. Department of Labor 1984a).

---

[6] The net effects of exchange rate trends on the overall competitiveness of U.S. products has to take into account the composition of trade between the United States and other major trading partners and also the effect of competition in third markets. On this "trade weighted" basis, during the 1970–1977 period, the U.S. dollar depreciated against all major currencies, increasing the international competitiveness of United States goods and services. Between 1977 and 1983 the dollar appreciated about 20 percent, making it more difficult for the U.S. to compete in international markets. The Japanese yen continued to strengthen against other currencies until 1978. Since 1978 the yen has weakened against the U.S. dollar although its value in terms of U.S. dollars is higher than it was in the mid-1970s. Indeed, on a trade-weighted basis, the yen, like the dollar, has also appreciated compared to currencies of all other major trading countries. This is because the currencies of many European countries have depreciated substantially since 1978, giving them a relative advantage against both U.S. and Japanese goods traded internationally. For trends in exchange rates and an index of these effects on competitiveness, see U.S. Department of Labor (1984e).

As in the case of the steel industry, hourly compensation costs in Japan's automobile industry rose from 38 percent of U.S. auto industry compensation in 1975 to 54 percent in 1978. By 1982, however, the differential in hourly compensation had widened again to 38 percent of U.S. costs. For West Germany, hourly compensation costs in automobile manufacturing rose from 81 percent in 1975 to 103 percent of U.S. costs in 1979, but fell to 71 percent in 1982 (U.S. Department of Labor 1984a).

Redirection of U.S. Regulatory Policies

The latter part of the 1960s and the early 1970s was a period of enormous growth in government regulation designed to achieve widely supported social goals. The benefits of these regulations were usually associated with increased costs, which in some cases had indirect effects on the labor market. If the increased costs were passed on in the form of higher prices, this could reduce the demand for labor. The increased costs associated with environmental regulations were probably an important influence in several basic industries, such as steel, rubber, and paper, which accounted for a substantial amount of environmental pollution. Consumer protection regulation in other industries may have had a similar effect on the cost structure.

Studies of the decline in U.S. productivity attribute a small portion of the decline to increased regulation (Denison 1979). For most industries, however, this did not reduce U.S. international competitiveness, since most foreign competitors were also faced with similar cost increases from their own regulatory programs. The environmental standards, however, may have weakened the competitive position of the U.S. steel industry since a high proportion of the large existing steel plants had to be retrofitted to meet the new regulatory standards. Countries that built new plants were able to include pollution control in the original construction at lower cost, and achieve additional cost advantage over U.S. steel production (Barnett and Schorsch 1984, pp. 249–51).

Changes in economic regulations, affecting the government's role in controlling the entry and exit of firms from the industry and in approving prices in markets, have had a more dramatic effect on the industrial relations environment. The deregulation of the airline, railroad, and trucking industries substantially increased the degree of competition in an important segment of the U.S. market and signaled an entirely new type of industrial relations environment for both management and labor.

New approaches to economic regulation created serious disruptions for businesses and workers as former monopoly power was gradually diminished. Greater market competition from new nonunion entrants made it more difficult to maintain a bargaining system that provided for automatic percentage wage increases; job rights were challenged as employers began to demand more flexibility in worker assignments in order to meet the competition from other U.S. businesses.

Labor Market and Industrial Relations Implications

The weak demand for labor in manufacturing industries during the recession reduced union bargaining power. In addition, the corporate response to increased international competition in product markets had a significant influence on the industrial relations environment in the most heavily unionized sectors of the economy. Industries in manufacturing, construction, mining, transportation, and public utilities account for about 82 percent of the unionized workers in the private sector, but only 53 percent of private-sector employment.[7] The new competitive environment represented a serious challenge to the viability of the content of existing collective agreements and the bargaining structure that had produced them.

For a high-wage economy like the United States, restoring competitiveness requires increased innovation and greater capital per worker; otherwise real wages will decline. In some cases, restoring competitiveness requires that labor resources must gradually move out of industries in which the United States no longer has a comparative advantage.

Traditionally, the industrial relations system has provided the flexibility required to permit this adjustment to occur. But in some industries the actions of both management and labor throughout the 1970s contributed to labor market rigidities, poor productivity, and increased cost-pressures—all detrimental to the restoration of competitiveness.

How the U.S. collective bargaining system in manufacturing and

---

[7] U.S. Department of Labor (1979), U.S. Department of Labor (1973), *Employment and Earnings Supplement* (1983), and Troy (1965).

transportation responded to recent structural change depended importantly on the nature of the change and on the industrial relations environment within the industries most affected. The variations in response can be illustrated by reviewing bargaining trends in selected industries according to the major type of structural change affecting those industries.

Collective Bargaining Response to Loss of International Competitiveness

Competitiveness is constantly changing with comparative unit costs of production, fluctuations in exchange rates, and modifications of trade policy. The automobile and basic steel industries are illustrations of important U.S. manufacturing industries which were highly profitable, technologically advanced, and relatively protected from imports prior to 1970. Both are also high-paying industries and have relatively good productivity records compared to other U.S. industries, but have poor productivity performance compared to major foreign competitors. The emergence of higher levels of productivity performance of foreign competitors and the failure of the U.S. industry to respond to changes in consumer demand were the main sources of structural change affecting the basic steel and automobile industries by the mid-1970s.

Basic Steel

In the 1950s, management decision-makers elected to invest in large, open-hearth plants to achieve economies of scale rather than adopt the emerging but still unproven basic oxygen technique for melting raw materials. They chose to decrease costs through economies of scale rather than through technological innovation in steel-making. This technological disadvantage and the absence of continuous casting in the United States was compounded by high employment costs, world overcapacity in basic steel, and the development of steel substitutes such as plastics and aluminum (Barnett and Schorsch 1984, pp. 17–58; AISI 1983).

The large unionized, integrated producers suffered the most. Imports were taking an increasingly larger share of the market. In 1973, imports accounted for 12.4 percent of the U.S. steel market; by the end of the decade import penetration had risen to about 20 percent. Domestically, minimills which employed the latest technology and were generally nonunion increased their market share from 3 percent in 1960 to 18 percent in 1982, with the most rapid growth occurring after 1974 (Barnett and Schorsch 1984, pp. 26–30).

Output and employment consistently declined throughout the 1970s and early 1980s. Steel producers in the United States shipped approximately 150,800,000 tons of steel in 1973. Tonnage shipped declined to 139,341,000 tons by 1979, and to 74,600,000 tons in 1982, the trough of the recession. Hourly (unionized) employment showed a similar trend. It went from 509,000 in 1973, to 456,150 in 1979, and to just 292,000 in 1982 (AISI 1983, p. 8).

Despite the long-term decline in domestic output, the industry remained profitable during the middle and late 1970s. The generally strong, inflationary economy provided a hospitable environment for an industry strategy that was designed to extract profits from price increases, but was slow to adopt the basic oxygen furnace and continuous casting. This respite ended in 1980 with the deep, worldwide recession and an excess world supply of steel. It was during the early 1980s that the basic structural problems of the industry—high labor costs and a reliance on inefficient ingot casting—began to take effect.

In response to stiff foreign competition, excess world capacity in steel, and a large stock of outmoded but fully depreciated open-hearth capacity, firms with basic steel capacity began to alter their asset structures. This was accomplished in three ways: diversification out of steel, plant closings, and consolidation within the industry, primarily by mergers between steel-making companies.

Diversification. The American Iron and Steel Institute (AISI) reported that in 1979 steel accounted for 68 percent of the identifiable assets of its members. By 1982 this percentage had dropped to 52 percent (AISI 1980, 1983). The most vivid example of diversification was the 1982 U.S. Steel purchase of the Marathon Oil Company for $5.9 million.[8] The diversification strategy demonstrated that the scope of competition for the United Steelworkers (USW) was not only with workers in competing firms and more productive capital stock, but also with all other uses of

---

[8] See *Moody's Industrials*, 1983 edition, entries on Armco, Bethlehem Steel, Inland Steel, Jones and Laughlin Steel, National Steel, Republic Steel, and U.S. Steel; and O'Boyle (1984).

funds that could conceivably be allocated to wages and benefits. The USW was bargaining with the corporation while, at the same time, competing with alternative corporate asset structures.

U.S. Steel's purchase of Marathon was the catalyst for the inclusion in the 1983 basic steel collective agreement of a clause that required the steel company signatories to invest all savings from the wage concessions in the modernization of the industry (United Steelworkers, undated). A clause such as this, which attempted to restrict the company's right to deploy its resources, is rare in the United States.

Plant Closings. Many steel plants were closed to reduce excess steel-making capacity.[9] Some companies sold facilities, producing uncertainty as to the future terms and conditions of employment under the new ownership.[10] Employees of companies who were signatories to the basic steel agreement relied on the approach in the 1977 income security agreement in which laid-off steel workers (with at least 20 years of company service and whose age combined with service equalled 65) were entitled to a monthly payment of $300 until they became eligible for social security (at age 62) or until they found suitable long-term employment. In the 1983 negotiations, a retirement option was added to the agreement for all workers 60 years of age and older with at least 30 years seniority. The payment would last for a period of from 12 to 21 months (United Steelworkers, undated).

Capacity Consolidation. A third strategy being used by the industry in response to economic pressures is consolidation of facilities and reduction of capacity through mergers or joint ventures. For example, in 1984 Republic Steel Corporation and Jones and Laughlin Steel Corporation, a wholly-owned subsidiary of LTV, Inc., were merged ("The New LTV," 1984).

The acquisition of 50 percent of the shares of National Steel Corporation by Nippon Kokan is another form of consolidation. The new enterprise, jointly controlled by Nippon Kokan and National Intergroup Inc., announced that it had withdrawn from the multiemployer coalition of basic steel companies that bargains

---

[9] See, for example, "Big Steel vs. the USW" (1983) and "Why Johnstown's Steel Workers" (1984).

[10] *Moody's Industrials*, 1983 edition, entry on National Steel Company, p. 3208; "Plan to Purchase" (1984); *NLRB* v. *Burns International Security Services*, 406 U.S. 272 (1972); and *Howard Johnson Company* v. *Detroit Local Joint Executive Board, Hotel Employees International Union*, 471 U.S. 249 (1974).

with the USW ("Steel Forges," 1984). Such mergers encouraged the continued decline of multiemployer bargaining in the industry as corporations attempted to adapt the bargaining system to the changing economics of the industry.

Industrial Relations Response. Collective bargaining produced several innovative responses to structural change in the steel industry. These included the 1973 Experimental Negotiating Agreement to reduce hedging against strikes, the income security program for long-service workers, and the negotiation of an agreement to invest cost savings from wage concessions in modernization of plant. The most significant response was the series of 1983 reductions in basic pay, the COLA modification, and the termination of the savings and vacation plan (Carlson 1984, p. 29). These wage and benefit reductions represent a dramatic shift in the bargaining outcome necessitated by the industry's loss of competitiveness. The parties anticipated that the change would be a short-run phenomenon since the contract called for a restoration of most of the cuts by the end of 1986.

The 1986 negotiations will be the first in 30 years to be carried out on something other than a multiemployer basis as the Steel Companies Coordinating Committee was dissolved in May 1985 ("Steel Companies" 1985). As noted, different asset structures and corporate strategies imply different corporate options. All steel companies no longer found a common agreement acceptable.

Also important was the December 1984 agreement between the United States and seven steel-producing nations to limit their exports to specific shares of the steel market in the U.S. The policy of the United States over the next several years is to limit imports of steel to 18.5 percent of the U.S. market. In 1983, imports accounted for 20.5 percent of the U.S. market, increasing to 26.6 percent in 1984. This agreement, by easing competitive pressure in the industry, should make it easier than it otherwise would have been for the parties to adjust to declining steel demand and industry employment.[11]

Automobiles

Like the basic steel industry, the U.S. automobile industry has been adversely affected by loss of international competitiveness.

---

[11]AISI (1984); "Steel Imports Fell" (1985)

The market penetration of imports doubled during the 1973–1983 period to between 20 and 25 percent. The adverse effect of import penetration was compounded by the severity of the recession of 1981–1982. Hourly employment in the auto industry dropped dramatically in a short period of time. Production-worker employment in the industry, which was 755,000 in 1973 and 782,000 in 1978, had dropped to 516,000 by 1982 (Katz 1984, pp. 29–35).

Although production in the industry was adversely affected in the short run by the business cycle, the trend in automobile production throughout the 1950s and 1960s was consistently upward. Domestic car and truck production was 8 million units in 1950, 9.2 million units in 1955, 11.2 million in 1965, 12.75 million in 1973, and 12.9 million in 1978 (Katz 1984, pp. 38–61).

Collective Bargaining Prior to 1979. According to Katz, collective bargaining among the big three auto companies had been characterized by three distinctive features: wage rules augmented by increases in fringe benefits, wage standardization through pattern bargaining, and job control. The wage rules tied wage increases to the COLA plus an "annual improvement factor" (AIF) that was supposed to reflect annual productivity increases in the economy. This relatively rigid wage determination criterion operating in an environment of rising auto industry production and high inflation in the 1970s was successful in keeping auto industry wages at a premium about 50 percent above average manufacturing wages, with the premium rising throughout the decade (Katz 1984, pp. 17–38). Fringe benefits and rules designed to protect workers' incomes from the cyclical nature of the industry were also implemented during the postwar era. Importantly, a highly structured system of recall rights and the establishment of Supplemental Unemployment Benefits (SUBs) protected workers' incomes during the recurring periods of layoff (Katz 1984, pp. 38–66).

Under the wage standardization principle, all workers in the industry doing the same job received the same wages. The UAW and the auto companies negotiated standardization of wages and fringe benefits across the three major manufacturers. Intracompany wage variation across plants was avoided by the elimination of piece rates and the national standardization of job classification across plants.

The third feature of auto industry bargaining was job control, characterized by: (1) formal, detailed, written, legalistic procedures governing daily plant operations; (2) a detailed classification system that provided requirements for each job; and (3) limited worker and union participation in production and corporate decision-making (Katz 1984, pp. 17–67). Intercompany standardization, supported by both management and labor, eliminated the possibility that one company would obtain a competitive advantage in labor costs. The success of the bargaining strategy depended, however, on market domination by General Motors, Ford, and Chrysler, the major domestic automakers, and on the production employment growth to support wage increases and maintain wage rigidity (Katz 1984, pp. 82–84).

Collective Bargaining from 1979 Through 1983. By 1979, soon after negotiation of a new collective agreement, it became obvious that foreign auto manufacturers had taken a significant percentage of the U.S. market. This eliminated the relatively sheltered product market which was the basis of previous bargaining strategies.

Modification of some key features of the "big three" auto bargaining system occurred in bargaining with the Chrysler Corporation in 1979, 1980, and 1981, and with Ford and General Motors in 1982. Wage concessions to Chrysler compromised the principle of wage standardization among the big three. The institution of profit-sharing as a replacement for the AIF was a modification of the principle of wage rules. A small proportion of total auto worker earnings would be determined by the performance of the individual company. Some modification was made in the rigid job classifications and legalistic procedures of job control. Workrules were modified to permit plants to obtain work that might otherwise be outsourced. Quality-of-worklife programs were introduced on an experimental basis as an effort to give workers more participation in the production process and to avoid time-consuming dispute-settlement procedures (Katz 1984, pp. 67–82; "Contractual Highlights" 1982).

Chrysler's financial situation had improved by 1982. In September of that year the United Auto Workers (UAW) and Chrysler negotiated a one-year agreement which restored some of the concessions that had been negotiated since 1979. At the same time, profit-sharing was eliminated. A two-year agreement with similar provisions was negotiated in 1983 (Katz 1984, pp. 82–84).

As Katz points out, even under the "concessions" there was

unwillingness by both management and labor to modify the principle of wage rules. AIF and COLA increases were only deferred. The parties even removed profit-sharing at Chrysler, preferring to revert to a 3 percent annual increase and cost-of-living as a criterion for determining workers' pay. The UAW was unwilling to make wage or workrule concessions without some concessions by the company on job security. Modification of the principle of uniformity of work practices in situations where a local union was faced with the possibility of loss of jobs through contracting out was one of the few signs of some flexibility compared to past bargaining practices (Katz 1984, pp. 84–96).

The 1984 Response to Loss of International Competitiveness. In 1984, General Motors and the UAW negotiated an agreement that seems to go further in attempting to facilitate adjustment to change than did previous agreements. The key feature is the creation of a Job Opportunity Bank Security Program (JOBS Program). The program, which began in March 1985, is administered by a national JOB Security Program committee, consisting of three representatives each from GM and the UAW. There are also local JOB Security Program committees, composed of representatives of local plant management and the local union.[12]

Under the program, any worker with at least one year of seniority who loses his or her job because of the introduction of new technology, outsourcing of work, negotiated productivity improvements, transfer or consolidation of work, or because of a seniority-based bump from another employee due to the above reasons, is entitled to be placed in the GM-funded Bank. While in the Bank, the employee draws the wages earned in the last position. An employee in the Bank may be placed in a training program, replace another worker to facilitate training of that worker, appropriately transfer to an opening in another GM plant, be placed in an assignment outside the bargaining unit, or take an assignment otherwise consistent with the program. The Bank will be funded by a six-year $1 billion commitment from GM. It does not apply to employees laid off for cyclical reasons.

---

[12] Unless otherwise noted, the factual material included between this point and the end of the discussion of auto industry industrial relations was obtained from Orr, Fogel, and Bowles (1984), "UAW Summary" (1984), "Details of Wage and Benefit Changes" (1984), Bowles and Orr (1984), and "Summary of United Auto Workers-Ford Agreement" (1984).

The agreement also created a $100 million venture fund to be jointly administered by GM and the UAW. The purpose of the fund is to develop and implement new business ventures that will provide jobs for UAW members. GM will make available up to $100 million in venture funds.

The wage package in the agreement represented an improvement for the UAW membership, with the base wage being augmented by increases of 9 to 50 cents per hours plus a COLA add-in of $2.99. The continuation of the profit-sharing plan plus the payment to workers of bonuses of $180, and an additional 2.25 percent of year's hours in October 1985, indicates an attempt by the parties to increase the earnings of workers while avoiding increases in the base wage. Improvements were also made in the pension and the Guaranteed Income Security Program, which covers employees with at least ten years seniority.

The only provision in the agreement that could be described as a concession is the diversion of 13 cents in COLA adjustments over the life of the agreement to help pay for fringe benefits. In October 1984 Ford and the UAW signed an agreement almost identical to the GM agreement except that Ford agreement included a moratorium on plant closings.

The GM and Ford agreements represent some change in bargaining strategy. To restore competitiveness, management has negotiated more freedom to introduce state-of-the-art technology rapidly and require individual plants to compete with outside firms as suppliers of parts. This will reduce labor requirements in the long run. In return, management has agreed to a flexible approach to job security, including retraining, job reassignment, and relocation, as well as income maintenance for those laid off because of industrial restructuring.

Since the GM and Ford job security programs contain income/job guarantees rather than short-term income supplements for structurally unemployed workers, they represent an innovation in industrial relations[13] More generally, they seem to reflect a more cooperative spirit between the UAW, on the one hand, and GM and Ford on the other. Whether this new cooperation can survive a downturn in the auto industry, with its attendant difficulty in

---

[13] For a review of traditional collective bargaining approaches to job displacement caused by technological change, see Roberts (1984) and Somers, Cushman, and Weinberg, eds. (1963).

distinguishing between structural and cyclical unemployment, is unknown.

Despite the economic hardship for the industry, the economic package did not change appreciably. The COLA concept remains intact, there is virtually no reduction in the cost of fringe benefits, and while the sizes of settlements were smaller than in previous auto agreements, they remained high relative to settlements in other industries. Apart from the temporary deviation of Chrysler from the industry pattern, wage standardization was maintained. Industrial restructuring does not appear to have weakened pattern bargaining in the industry.[14]

The industrial relations response to structural change in the automobile industry occurred within a partially protected market under the four-year Voluntary Restraint Agreement (VRA), which limited foreign imports (and which expired in the Spring of 1985). The VRA has provided limited short-term protection to permit the industry to regain its competitiveness. The industry has made significant progress towards this goal, but without the VRA competitive advantage, the size of the negotiated basic wage and benefit package might have been significantly smaller.

Collective Bargaining and Economic Deregulation

For many decades several industries in the United States have been subject to extensive economic regulations, primarily because it was believed that, if left unattended, the market system was unlikely to produce a sufficient rate of return to provide adequate service and/or the market was likely to permit business to exercise considerable monopoly power in some market segments. For many years, microeconomists had questioned the validity of these assumptions, and by the mid-1970s government policies were eventually developed to substantially reduce government regulation of prices, the ability of businesses to enter and leave certain

---

[14] In all major areas, including job security, the 1985 Chrysler-UAW agreement brought terms and conditions of employment at Chrysler to levels comparable to those in the 1984 GM-UAW and Ford-UAW agreements. The UAW-Chrysler agreement also provides employees with a bonus of $2120, compensation for past concessions. The Chrysler agreement expires in 1988, while the GM and Ford Agreements expire in 1987. (See Job and Fogel (1985) and Fogel, Job, and Saunders (1985).) Thus, under the assumptions of no midcontract changes in any of the three agreements and wage and benefit increases in 1987 agreements between Ford and the UAW and GM and the UAW, there will be a one-year period during which Chrysler will enjoy a labor cost advantage over GM and Ford.

industries, and the ability of government to determine the type of service provided.

Deregulation of the For-Hire Trucking Industry

The Motor Carrier Act of 1935 created the Interstate Commerce Commission (ICC) and authorized it to restrict entry into the over-the-road trucking industry, approve all mergers and consolidations, and approve rates (prices) which were not unduly discriminatory or below cost.

In 1974 there were approximately 14,600 regulated firms engaged in interstate operations and over 100,000 owner-operated small trucking firms not subject to ICC regulation. This owner-operated small-firm sector was estimated to account for between 25 and 40 percent of all intercity truck transportation.[15] While such a large number of firms might imply a decentralized bargaining structure, the International Brotherhood of Teamsters had centralized bargaining, negotiating their first National Master Freight Agreement in 1964. Centralized bargaining led to quite large settlements in the early and mid-1970s, although differentials reflecting variations in regional markets have persisted (Levinson 1980, pp. 114-18).

These large settlements played an important role in changing the structure of the industry, bringing about a decline in union membership in trucking. The high-cost collective bargaining settlements of the 1970s encouraged buyers of trucking services to seek lower-cost means of freight transportation. In some cases larger employers switched to their own trucking companies, which were either nonunion or operated under collective agreements with relatively low wage scales. The growth in the owner-operated sector and the expansion of nonunion firms in the South provided shippers with additional options to control the rise in costs. It is estimated that, over the 1967-1977 period, the volume of freight handled by the union had declined substantially and that union membership had declined about 20 percent (Levinson 1980, p. 135).

The most important source of structural change affecting industrial relations in the industry was the gradual trend towards economic deregulation of the industry. This started in 1976 when

---

[15] For a review of the economics of the industry and the development of collective bargaining, see Levinson (1980), p. 101.

the ICC expanded the commercial trucking zones (not subject to ICC control) around major cities. In 1978 the ICC ruled that companies hauling their own goods could also apply for interstate trucking authority to ship goods of others. It also expanded commercial zones around airports and removed restrictions preventing contract truckers from serving more than eight shippers. Entry into the trucking industry was also eased as deregulation became a major policy debate. The trend towards deregulation culminated in the Motor Carrier Act of 1980, although it has been argued that this act was passed with the support of some of those who wanted to limit the amount of deregulation that was already under way (see Moore 1983, p. 37). The act made it significantly easier to get a license from the ICC by requiring protestors to prove why such a license would be inconsistent with "public convenience and necessity."

The structural changes brought about by the deregulation of trucking have been dramatic. Between 1975 and 1979 there was a gradual rise in the number of licenses issued, with a "series of sharp jumps of 1,000 in 1980, more than 4,000 in 1981, and 3,400 in 1983" (Moore 1983, p. 337). The value of licenses and trucking rates have declined significantly. The rate of return from investment in the industry has declined as the revenue per ton-mile dropped under the pressure of increasing competition. While some of this decline in costs and prices is attributable to the 1981–1982 recession, it is clear that under the previous regulatory arrangements some businesses and their workers were operating in protected markets, permitting some employers to earn monopoly profits, some of which were captured by unions in the form of significant wage and benefit increases.

Deregulation does not seem to have had significant adverse employment consequences for the industry as a whole. Marginal producers and their employees did suffer as bankruptcies increased following deregulation. Employment in the industry also declined, but this is probably due to the 1981–1982 recession. Indeed, since the employment decline in this recession was less than in the 1975 recession, it suggests that deregulation may result in a long-term rise in the industry, even though a larger number of workers in specific firms are likely to experience structural unemployment. Between 1977 and 1981, the real rate of compensation of all workers in the industry declined; for drivers and helpers, who are mostly union members, the decline was larger than for all workers (Moore 1983, p. 39).

The 1982 National Master Freight Agreement was the first agreement since the enormous growth of new entrants into the industry after deregulation. According to the union president, Jackie Presser, the goal of the 1982 negotiations was "to preserve the jobs of those now employed and . . . help them regain the thousands of jobs lost through lay-offs and business failures"; for the president of the employers' association it was "to enhance our companies' ability to compete in a deregulated marketplace" (Ruben 1982a, p. 64).

The terms of the Master Agreement clearly reflected the erosion of bargaining power of the union due to deregulation. There was *no* guaranteed wage increase throughout the three-year term of the contract. Indeed, in some of the regional supplemental agreements, wage reductions were negotiated in return for a share in profits. These supplemental agreements generally provided for new employees to start at 70 percent of the current pay rate for their jobs and gradually move to full rate after three years of service (Ruben 1982a, p. 64).

The COLA was retained but its cost to employers was reduced through less frequent adjustments. In order to maintain current health and welfare benefits, it was agreed to divert part or all of any future COLAs if this was necessary to finance increases in the cost of maintaining health and welfare benefits (Ruben 1982a, p. 64).

The 1982 contract contained a number of changes in workrules which provide employers with the opportunity to improve productivity and efficiency of operations. Employers are now able to require over-the-road drivers to make one pick-up and delivery in a city en route to another destination, and work scheduling can now be arranged to avoid some overtime. In an attempt to preserve jobs and compete in the more deregulated market, there was more flexibility in negotiating special provisions with employers experiencing financial difficulties.

Structural change in the industry, especially during the second half of the 1970s, had produced a dramatic change in collective bargaining. The bargaining structure had become less centralized, workrules were modified, the relative wage of unionized workers in the industry had declined, and real wages for new hires were reduced significantly below previous entry-level rates.

Deregulation in the Airline Industry

The airline industry was among the most heavily regulated in the United States until 1978.[16] Entry into the industry, the routes carriers were permitted to fly, and the fares they were permitted to charge were all regulated by the Civil Aeronautics Board (CAB). In practice, this meant no price competition for the airlines and little new airline entry into existing markets since the CAB limited the number of carriers on any particular route to a maximum of five (Kahn 1980, p. 322).

During the 1970s the increasing demand for the industry's product and the generally upward trend in employment levels, along with regulation, strengthened the bargaining power of unions relative to an unregulated market. Econometric evidence supports the proposition that during the 1970s unionized airline employees received higher wages and benefits compared to employees in most other industries (Hendricks, Feuille, and Szerson 1980; Graham and Kaplan 1982).

Despite increasing passenger traffic, the major trunk carriers were unable to attain consistently high levels of profitability during the middle and late 1970s. Return on equity for the trunk carriers averaged 9 percent for the 1973–1979 period, but there was substantial variation around this mean. In 1978, trunk carriers' return on equity was 17.7 percent, the high for that period. Two years earlier the trunk carriers had reached a low point, earning a return on equity of −2.1 percent. This profit performance on the part of the carriers may be compared with the profit performance of the smaller local carriers, who averaged a return on equity of 13.4 percent for the 1973–1979 period, and the rate of return on equity in manufacturing, which averaged 14.1 percent for this period (Graham and Kaplan 1982, p. 28). Even with high revenues under regulation, the industry was often operating on a narrow margin.

The Airline Deregulation Act of 1978 (ADA) deregulated the airline industry in the United States with respect to routes, fares, and entry into the industry. Since February 1979 air carriers have been free to serve or not to serve routes they choose, subject only to the availability of airport landing slots. The CAB's authority finally expired January 1, 1985, with its remaining functions being transferred to the U.S. Department of Transportation (Graham and Kaplan 1982, pp. 20–24.)

---

[16] For a thorough discussion of bargaining at each carrier, see Northrup (1983).

Industrial Relations Since Airline Deregulation. Deregulation has influenced airline industrial relations principally through the entrance of new, primarily nonunion carriers and the corporate response to deregulation of the established carriers. The new entrants into the industry (Midway, New York Air, and People Express) have established lower fares to compete with the major trunk lines on heavily travelled routes between major cities. The lower fares are supported by such techniques as contracting for ground services, efficient marketing of routes and equipment, and scheduling of most flights through one airport. In addition, since the new airlines were nonunion, management paid wages substantially lower than those paid by established carriers for employees in comparable occupations. The absence of collectively bargained job classifications also gave the new carriers the ability to assign employees to different tasks as needed (Northrup 1983).

Mergers in search of efficiency (the creation of Republic Airlines, the Pan American takeover of National Airlines), growth of routes, heavy debt to finance these steps, and a major downturn in revenue associated with the 1981–1983 recession, along with competition from the newcomers, created economic turmoil in the established sector of the industry in the post-deregulatory period, placing pressure on the industrial relations systems, especially for increased efficiency. Since increased competition reduced the degree of market power available to both management and labor under the former regulatory environment, the real income and/or employment of workers in the established operators declined after deregulation. Collective bargaining in the industry played an important role in determining how these losses were distributed.

Establishment of Two-Tiered Wage Systems. The most common industrial relations response to the deregulated environment in the airline industry has been the establishment of two-tiered wage systems. In such systems, unions and corporations agree to establish low starting salaries for newly hired employees, with these employees reaching the salary level of senior employees after a specified period of time (typically five years). As of mid-August 1984, airlines that had negotiated two-tiered wage systems with the pilots' union were Piedmont, Frontier, and Republic.[17] Northwest

---

[17] Telephone conversation with Ms. Jill Kastris, Supervisor, Representation, Air Line Pilots Association, August 20, 1984 (hereinafter cited as Kastris conversation). See also "Republic Airlines: One Union Down and One to Go" (1984) and Salpukas (1984b).

has negotiated a two-tiered wage system with its ground employees and flight attendants; Piedmont has also negotiated one with its flight attendants ("Dual Pay Rates," 1984, and "Flight Attendants," 1984). United, the largest carrier and industry leader, has obtained a two-tiered wage contract in negotiations with the unions representing its mechanics ("United Gets a Break," 1984). Taken together, these airlines accounted for 44.4 percent of the domestic revenue passenger miles flown by U.S. certified carriers in 1983 (U.S. Civil Aeronautics Board 1983).

The lower tier of these contracts is intended to be a temporary phase through which employees progress as they reach the higher salary tier of senior employees. It is a way of lengthening the salary structure and at the same time reducing wage costs. An exception to this pattern is American Airlines, which negotiated a two-tiered system with no merging of salaries of old and new employees. Once all current employees retire or quit, American will have a much lower salary structure.[18]

The popularity of the two-tiered wage system results from the assumption that it addresses the immediate efficiency needs of the affected carriers while doing minimal *short-term* harm to the interests of the union. The income loss of current workers is minimized, and prospective employees are required to adjust to the new economic environment and receive wages and benefits more in line with wages paid by the new entrants to the industry.

It is not certain, however, whether the system can withstand the test of time. Unions traditionally oppose systems that provide unequal pay for equal work. Although the Air Line Pilots Association (ALPA) has agreed to two-tiered systems for pilots at Republic, Piedmont, and Frontier, the union is opposed to them in principle (Betit 1984). It is possible that dissatisfaction will increase as employees are asked to do the same work as other employees but receive lower pay. This, in turn, could result in divisions within the union, destabilizing industrial relations in the industry.[19]

---

[18] See, for example, Salpukas (1984b), "A Labor Package" (1984), "How Frontier Airlines" (1984), Byrne (1984), Kastris conversation, and "Pilot Group Negotiates" (1983). The pilots at American are the only pilots of any unionized major airline that are not represented by the Air Line Pilots Association. American pilots are represented by the Allied Pilots Association.

[19] The negotiation of two-tiered wage systems has not been limited to airlines. Data published by the Bureau of National Affairs indicate that two-tier wage systems have been negotiated by firms and unions in food retailing, aerospace manufacturing, building construction, and electric utilities. This compilation of data is available from the authors upon request.

Employee Stock Ownership. Several airlines modified their wage systems through the introduction of employee stock ownership plans. Two major carriers, Eastern and Western, negotiated stock ownership plans with their unionized employees in 1983. This was followed by a 1984 agreement between Republic and its employees which also provided for employee stock ownership. In all three instances the unions were also able to obtain representation on the carriers' boards of directors.

Of the three agreements, the one negotiated at Eastern is the most radical. The agreement reduced wages between 4 and 18 percent of salaries, with the highest paid classification "contributing" the greatest percentage to decline. In return, union members received stock amounting to 25 percent of the outstanding shares of the company and substantial union involvement in corporate decision-making. Unions received the right to appoint four of the 21 members of the company's board of directors and had access to the company's financial statements and plans, with the right to appeal to the board's business decisions that union officials believe are unsound. Union officials are also permitted to attend, with voice, the carrier's private business meetings, providing the union with the same information available to corporate executives.[20]

Although the agreements at Western and Republic did not contain provisions for regular union involvement in corporate decision-making to the same extent as the Eastern agreement, those agreements did call for employee ownership of substantial proportions of the company's stock. Employees own roughly one-third of the company's stock at Western Airlines, and about 15 percent at Republic. Both airlines also have union representatives on their respective boards of directors, with two union representatives on the Western board and one on the Republic board.[21]

---

[20] See, for example, "Eastern's Revolutionary Treaty" (1983) and Salpukas (1984a).

[21] "Western Airlines Seeks Further Cuts" (1984), "A Labor Package" (1984), and "Republic Airlines, Unions" (1984). Two other strategies used by airlines also deserve to be mentioned. In September 1983, Continental Airlines filed for bankruptcy, whereupon it unilaterally altered the terms and conditions of employment contained in the collective bargaining agreements between the airline and various unions. Although Continental's actions withstood a legal challenge, bankruptcy reform legislation enacted by Congress in 1984 may make it difficult for another corporation to adopt the strategy used by Continental. See, for example, "Continental Is Coming Out a Winner" (1984), "The Trying Times" (1984), Witkin (1984), and "President Reagan Signs" (1984). In addition, the Frontier Airlines' strategy of establishing a nonunion subsidiary also appears to have been discontinued by the airline. See, for example, "How Frontier Airlines Is Getting Outgunned" (1984).

As in the case of the trucking industry, bargaining in the airline industry was forced to respond to changes in the industry structure. While there were some differences in the way management in each industry adapted their bargaining strategy, all parties were primarily concerned with minimizing the employment cost to current workers, increasing flexibility in compensation, and reducing rigidity in workrules.

Chronic Comparative Disadvantage and Collective Bargaining

Differences in the price and cost structures of domestic products in relation to the price and cost structures for the same products in other countries determine an industry's comparative advantage. During the 1970s the relative structure of costs and prices in industries within the U.S. textile and apparel sectors continued the deterioration that started in the 1960s. This led to the constant threat of import penetration as newly industrializing countries increased their comparative advantage.

Import Penetration in the Textile and Apparel Industries

Between 1972 and 1981, imports of most textile products accounted for less than 14 percent of the new supply (domestic production plus imports). In some industries, such as silk, hosiery, and knit fabrics of textile materials, the penetration rates were extremely low and remained constant. In most other industries, such as cotton fabrics and wool yarn, the rate increased but was still relatively low. The product lines which experienced the largest and most rapidly growing penetration rate were floor coverings (between 40 and 50 percent by 1981) and lace goods (about 30 percent by 1981) (*Employment and Earnings Supplement*, July 1984).

Most apparel industries experienced a similar increase in import penetration throughout the 1970s. In 1981, imports accounted for over 20 percent of the new supply of men's shirts, 15 percent of men's suits, over 13 percent of women's dresses and blouses, and 18 percent of women's coats and skirts (U.S. Department of Labor 1984d). In some products, such as rainwear, the rate of penetration moderated during the 1970s, but still remained high (about 30 percent).

For both the textile and apparel industries the growing strength of the U.S. dollar has accelerated the growth of imports since 1981.

In addition, penetration in apparel markets has reduced the domestic demand for U.S. textile manufacturers who were the major suppliers of raw material for the U.S. apparel industry. In response, some textile manufacturers have engaged in offshore production.

Economic and Industrial Relations Implications

Much of the response to the threat of foreign imports occurred in the 1960s, when both sectors went through extensive industrial restructuring which took the form of geographic redeployment of each industry's assets (Orr and Orr 1984).

Management in textiles has responded to chronic foreign competition by increasing the capital intensity of production. Despite union opposition, management has also relocated facilities to lower labor-cost regions of the United States. While this strategy has resulted in a gradual loss of jobs at least in the cotton mills, it has permitted the industry to compete in the international market and improve the generally low wages in the industry. On average, between 1975 and 1980 wages increased about 10 percent per year, a rate higher than the average increase in nondurable manufacturing industries (U.S. Department of Labor 1975, p. 1).

Industrial relations in the industry has been extremely confrontational since 1960, as the large nonunion plants in the Southeast strongly resisted unionization. Wage and benefit increases in the industry are heavily influenced by increases at nonunion plants, which amounted to about 8.5 percent per year in the late 1970s. Nonunion employers tend to make annual wage and benefit modifications, but the amounts are usually not disclosed. There is, however, some evidence that nonunion increases slowed down to less than 6 percent per year in 1982, with a delay in the effective date of the increase because of "poor economic conditions" (Ruben 1982c).

The increase in import penetration of the 1970s has had much more serious economic implications for the apparel industry than for the textile industry. The apparel industry, like the textile industry, had already undertaken industrial restructuring in the 1950s and 1960s. Employment distribution shifted towards the Southeast and Southwest, where labor costs were lower (Orr and Orr 1984). The heavily unionized industry employed mostly women and paid very low wages. A significant proportion of wages has always been at or near the minimum wage level, with many of the plants automatically adjusting wages with changes in the legal minimum wage. With such a low wage structure, modification of wages and benefits in response to foreign competition simply was not feasible. In addition, the labor-intensive nature of many segments of the apparel industry made it difficult to adopt the textile industry's strategy of innovation and increased capital investment to meet foreign competition. Declining employment, especially in New England, has been a major implication of chronic loss of comparative advantage.[22] In response to loss of comparative advantage, the industry has engaged in offshore production, where part of the final product is processed in another country and imported for final production in the United States. This has helped U.S. manufacturers reduce costs and remain in business, but it has done little for the employees who formerly made the entire garment.

Despite the decline in employment, wages in the industry have risen from their very low level at a rate equal to the average for nondurable manufacturing. The high rate of unionization has contributed to this wage performance, and significant improvements were negotiated in 1982.[23]

In the apparel and textile industries, both management and labor have sought protection to moderate the flow of foreign imports. This has largely taken the form of working successfully for the extension of the Multifibre Agreement. Under this agreement, the United States and other industrialized countries negotiate bilateral agreements with the textile and apparel exporters to determine the amount of imports that will be permitted to enter markets in industrialized countries. The intention of the agreement is to permit a gradual increase of imports from newly industrializing nations. The apparel industry has also successfully lobbied for federal legislation that requires all U.S. produced garments to carry a "Made in United States" label. This requirement was enacted in

---

[22] See U.S. Department of Labor (1981), p. 2. There is some evidence that the U.S. fashion apparel industry has been innovative in response to rapidly changing consumer demand. This claim is the reason for the first increase in employment in the New York City garment industry in eight years. Union spokesmen have claimed that this was only a temporary development. See "Study Finds Garment Jobs Up" (1984).

[23] See, for example, Ruben (1982b). Between 1979 and 1984 employment in men's and boys' suit and coat manufacturing rose 28 percent, largely as a result of contracts negotiated in 1982. Also see U.S. Department of Labor (1984c), p. 1.

1984 (P.L. 94-417) as an amendment to several existing textile labeling laws and the 1930 Tariff Act. These actions outside the industrial relations system have assisted in the restructuring of the textile industry, but it is unlikely that the long-term decline of employment in much of the apparel industry can be halted.

Structural Changes in Supply and Demand and Collective Bargaining

During the 1970s several U.S. industries experienced structural shifts in their product markets that had a significant effect on the industrial relations environment. In the rubber industry there was a major product innovation in the manufacture of automobile tires. This occurred at about the same time as a change in the U.S. share of the domestic demand for automobiles, which also affected the demand for original equipment tires. In the manufacture of farm equipment, the industry failed to recover from a deep cyclical recession, partially because of structural changes in demand. These changes had dramatic implications for labor markets in both rubber and farm equipment manufacturing.

Rubber Industry

The primary source of structural economic change in the U.S. rubber tire industry since 1973 has been the rapid increase in market share taken by steel-belted radial tires.[24] Radials accounted for about 28 percent of the passenger car market in 1974, but by 1983 they accounted for about 77 percent of the market.[25] Thus, unlike the steel, auto, and airline industries, in which the major factors causing structural change emanated from outside the country or outside the industry, structural change in the rubber industry was attributable primarily to product innovation.

The rubber tire industry produces an essentially undifferentiated product that is sold in multiple distribution channels (i.e., retail stores, service stations, department stores) under many brand names.[26] The industry has always been characterized by severe

---

[24] Telephone conversation with Mr. John Serringard, Vice-President, Industrial Relations, and Treasurer, Rubber Manufacturers Association, January 14, 1985 (hereinafter cited as Serringard conversation).

[25] *Modern Tire Dealer*, January issue of various years, obtained through telephone conversation with Mr. Greg Smith, Editor, *Modern Tire Dealer*, January 16, 1985 (hereinafter cited as Smith conversation).

[26] Serringard conversation.

price competition,[27] and unlike the steel, airline, and automobile industries, it has always been difficult to pass on labor cost increases in the form of higher prices.

Historically, the industry has experienced significant industrial relations conflict. Between 1959 and 1979, five of the seven targeted negotiations resulted in strikes. The bargaining relationship reached its nadir in 1976 with a 115-day United Rubber Workers (URW) strike against Firestone, Goodrich, and Uniroyal.[28]

The fact that the production of radial tires required additional capital investment and an entirely new and different production process made job insecurity a crucial labor relations issue. In 1974, 173 million passenger car tires were sold, of which 28 percent were radials. In 1983, 188 million passenger car tires were sold, of which 77 percent were radials.[29] Employment of production workers declined from 100,900 in 1974 to 69,200 in 1983 (*Employment and Earnings Supplement*, 1983).

The tire companies elected to build new plants rather than convert old bias-ply plants to radial production. From the companies' point of view, these plants had the benefits of efficient layout and a nonunion workforce (Kochan, McKersie, and Cappelli 1984). By 1982, it was estimated that only 45 percent of the industry's capacity was covered by the pattern agreement with the URW ("The Rubber Talks," 1982).

The demand for U.S. tires was also dependent on the demand for U.S. manufactured automobiles. As imports increased their share of the U.S. automobile market, the potential demand for U.S. tires was diverted to imported original equipment tires. The reduced share of the U.S. original equipment tire market held by U.S. tire manufacturers had an additional adverse effect on the bargaining power of the URW.

By 1977, these changes in the product market were instrumental in stimulating both management and labor to initiate new approaches to labor-management relations. That was the year when Peter Pestillo, then Vice President of B.F. Goodrich, called for a strike ban and contract arbitration in the rubber industry, and

---

[27] Serringard conversation. See also, for example, "Rubber: Short-run Prosperity Ahead" (1976), Kamm (1984).

[28] See, for example, "BLS Report on Collective Bargaining" (1982), "URW Accepts Firestone Accord" (1976), and Kochan, McKersie, and Cappelli (1984).

[29] Smith conversation.

Goodrich and the URW formed joint committees to address mutual problems. Although the union rejected Goodrich's no-strike proposal in 1978, Firestone and the URW did agree on a no-strike pact in February 1979. On the basis of deliberations of a labor-management committee formed in 1978, Firestone agreed to accept the URW-designated industry-wide pattern if it was unable to reach an agreement with the URW.[30] Despite these steps toward accommodation, the 1979 negotiations were not resolved without a five-week URW strike against Uniroyal, centered around the reluctance of the company to risk the loss of federal contracts that might result from negotiating agreements that exceeded the 22.5 percent three-year guideline promulgated by the Council on Wage and Price Stability.[31]

The continuing decline in demand for bias-ply tires after the 1979 agreement resulted in the closing of plants producing these types of tires.[32] The poor economic position of the industry produced numerous concessions following the 1979 agreement, and both parties appear to have moved toward less confrontational industrial relations. Negotiations in 1982 and 1985 were concluded without strikes.[33] While bargaining power has shifted away from the union, in some instances management has placed greater emphasis on human resource management as an industrial relations strategy.[34]

Farm Equipment and Machinery

Output and employment in farm equipment manufacturing increased dramatically during the first half of the 1970s. Employment expanded at an annual rate of 5.1 percent during the 1972–1975 period, and by 1979 an additional 14,000 workers had been added to the industry's workforce.[35] Output in the industry rose at an annual rate of 14.2 percent between 1972 and 1979, and the average hourly earnings of workers increased 7.4 percent per

---

[30] See, for example, "BLS Report on Collective Bargaining" (1982), "Address by Peter Pestillo" (1978), and "Rubber Workers, Firestone" (1979).

[31] "BLS Report on Collective Bargaining" (1982), "Rubber Workers, Goodrich" (1979), and "Firestone's Pricing Actions" (1979).

[32] See, for example, "Rubber Workers at Uniroyal" (1980), "Revisions in Firestone URW Agreement" (1980), "General Tire Announces" (1982), and Serringard conversation.

[33] See for example, "Tentative Accord" (1982), "National Rubber Bargaining" (1985).

[34] Kochan, McKersie, and Cappelli (1984).

[35] Based on *Employment and Earnings* 31 (January 1984).

annum. Exports grew six-fold and imports were four times the value in 1972.[36]

Most of the 1970s was a period of unprecedented expansion as sales for the domestic and export markets boomed. The outlook for the future of the industry was optimistic, and this probably affected expectations over the outcome of collective bargaining.

However, the industry was in a severe recession in 1979. Between 1979 and 1983, output declined at an annual rate of 4.6 percent and employment dropped from 150,000 to 88,000. This industry did not benefit from the economic recovery. Employment ranged from 85,000 to 95,000 between early 1984 and mid-1985 (*Employment and Earnings* 1984, 1985). During most of this period the average hourly earnings continued to increase, but for 1982–1983 average hourly earnings declined 2.1 percent.

The causes of the economic problems of the industry are partially attributable to changes in the worldwide capacity to produce farm equipment and partially to cyclical and structural changes in demand. Some U.S. manufacturers concentrated production on technologically advanced, large-scale, high-cost equipment. This strategy was successful during the worldwide boom in sales. The use of machinery is only viable, however, in farming in a limited number of countries outside North America. In addition, foreign producers entered the market and concentrated on smaller equipment, such as tractors, which were more adaptable to small-scale agriculture.

The growing strength of the dollar reduced farm equipment machinery exports, but not as much as the decline in domestic sales. Exports continued to exceed imports, as exports as a proportion of industry output rose from 13.4 percent in 1979 to a high of 22.7 percent in 1981.[37] The major problem facing the industry can be traced to the decline in domestic demand, due primarily to the declining competitiveness of U.S. agriculture and to the 1979 grain embargo. This was followed by a decline in farm incomes, an increasing rate of farm failures, high rates of interest, and a drop in the value of farm land. The grain embargo reduced U.S. agriculture's share of the grain market, which has not been recaptured since the embargo was lifted. Some former customers have switched to grain from

---

[36] Based on unpublished data from U.S. Department of Commerce (supplied by John A. Lien, January 1985).

[37] Based on unpublished data from the U.S. Department of Commerce.

Brazil and Argentina. The worldwide recession also reduced the demand for U.S. grain from third-world markets. Farmers were unable to continue investing heavily in modern farm equipment, and many switched to the used equipment market.

Industrial Relations Response in Farm Equipment Manufacturing. Traditionally, the UAW—representative for most of the unionized workers in the industry—has attempted to negotiate agreements with the major farm equipment manufacturers that follow the pattern agreements in the auto industry. During the rapid output and employment growth of the early 1970s, the UAW was able to negotiate agreements similar to those in auto, with most of the cost of improvements in wages and benefits passed on to customers. In addition, even when the auto industry pattern was not followed, the union was relatively successful in maintaining pattern bargaining within the farm equipment industry. By 1976, however, management began to resist accepting the auto industry pattern, and industrial relations within the industry entered a turbulent period.

In 1976 and 1979, Deere & Company experienced strikes prior to signing agreements, and in 1979 International Harvester took a 5½-month strike. In 1981, International Harvester requested that the three-year contract be reopened in order to negotiate for concessions, including forgoing future wage increases and about ten days of paid vacations. Caterpillar and Deere did not reopen negotiations but elected to negotiate at the expiration of the contract in 1982.

Since 1982 the agricultural equipment industry has seen a further relaxation of pattern bargaining. The UAW has been willing to grant concessions to International Harvester and Fiat-Allis, firms that are in serious financial difficulty.[38] But the drop in farm equipment sales since 1979 (Greenhouse 1984b) has not encouraged the UAW to grant industry-wide concessions without regard to the financial health of the firm ("Auto Workers Avoid Strike," 1983).

Overall, it appears that the industry has just begun to adjust to the five-year decline in demand for farm equipment, no doubt under the assumption that it represents a structural decline in the demand for the industry's product rather than a cyclical shift

---

[38] Based on unpublished U.S. Department of Commerce data; see also "Auto Workers Avoid Strike at Deere" (1983).

downward along the demand curve. International Harvester's sale of its farm equipment business to Tenneco, owner of rival J.I. Case Company, is likely to be the beginning of a capacity reduction in the industry,[39] as Case will presumably eliminate duplicative and inefficient facilities. In anticipation of this capacity reduction, the UAW and Harvester have negotiated a new job security program which will maintain a minimum level of labor input (hours of work) per unit of production for the six-year life of the agreement ("New Job Security Concepts," 1985). This agreement is an accommodation to the corporate strategy of consolidation that will be implemented by Harvester and its new owner, Case.

The Role of Government and Politics in Adjusting to Change

Legislation

During the 1970s, government enacted a series of adjustment assistance programs designed to assist workers adversely affected by changes in public policy. These programs were part of the government's employment and retraining policy and had little to do with labor relations.[40]

The most extensive labor market adjustment program was introduced in the Trade Act of 1974. The program goal was to encourage the mobility of workers who were permanently displaced because of increased imports of foreign-made goods. Title III of the Job Training Partnership Act of 1983 (JTPA) was another attempt to aid the adjustment of laid-off workers. The JTPA provided resources and a new joint public-private partnership approach to assist these experienced workers adjust to new jobs. While in some instances management and labor have participated in JTPA programs, these activities remain quite separate from traditional industrial relations practices.

In addition to policies addressing labor market adjustment, government trade policies may also have an effect on industrial relations by erecting shelters from foreign competition that would not otherwise exist. The agreement between Japan and the United States, under which Japan agreed to limit exports of automobiles to

---

[39] See, for example, Petzinger and Morris (1984), "The Radical Surgery" (1984), and Zieman and Kotlowitz (1985).

[40] For a review of government adjustment assistance policies, see McLennan (1984b).

the U.S., may have aided the industry in attaining high profits in 1983 and through much of 1984.[42] Similarly, negotiated agreements with other countries to limit steel exports to the United States may have moderated the declining economic position of the basic steel manufacturers.[43] These government actions have probably reduced the adverse effects of increased competition on collectively negotiated wages and benefits.

NLRB and Court Decisions

In the 1960s and 1970s, the National Labor Relations Board (NLRB) and court decisions established the legal basis for collective bargaining over corporate decisions resulting from structural economic change. Although there have been exceptions, in general the courts (often overruling the NLRB) established the basic principle that management need not negotiate over corporate decisions on the capital structure of the firm, even though such decisions may affect wages and jobs of employees covered by collective agreements.[44] While these cases did not necessarily deal directly with adjustments to structural and economic change, they have permitted corporations to exercise unilateral control over such matters as plant closings and capacity consolidations that are traditional corporate responses to structural economic change—that is, to shift capital resources in response to structural economic change.[45] The rights of unions are limited to negotiating over the effects of the corporate decision on the employees.[46]

Government Policies and the Collective Bargaining Environment

In the United States, the labor movement's emphasis on improving the narrow interest of union members is complemented by political action to support government wage and hour regulations, which indirectly affect collective bargaining and the

---

[42] See "Investment Outlook Scoreboard (1984), "Chrysler Posts Record Quarter" (1984), Stepanek (1984a and 1984b), and Holusha (1984).

[43] See, for example, "Reagan Seeks Cut" (1984).

[44] For a thorough discussion of Board and court decisions on this issue, see Sockell (1984).

[45] See, for example, First National Maintenance Corporation v. NLRB, 452 U.S. 666 (1981), and United Technologies, Inc., 269 NLRB 162 (1984).

[46] See, for example, First National Maintenance Corporation (note 44) and Ozark Trailers, Inc., 161 NLRB 561 (1966).

economic position of workers generally. Support for and the improvement of minimum wage legislation (Fair Labor Standards Act), regulations determining basic wage rates for companies with government contracts (Davis-Bacon Act and the Service Contract Act), and unemployment insurance have long been linked indirectly to union bargaining strategy. Since these wage standards tend to raise labor costs, management has been equally active in opposing changes that raise wage standards and in some cases have worked for their repeal.

During the late 1960s and the 1970s, collective bargaining and human resource management were also influenced by the passage of legislation with social as well as economic roots. This legislation included efforts to prohibit discrimination based on age, sex, race, or ethnic origin, legislation to improve occupational health and safety, and legislation to protect employees' rights in pension plans. Some environmental and consumer protection legislation also affected labor relations.

Neither business nor labor was in the vanguard initiating much of this legislation, but once it was proposed, both parties attempted to influence specific provisions to their own ends. In some cases management and labor had similar interests and concerns about the effects of the legislation; in others, such as pension reform, their response diverged dramatically.

Two particular legislative initiatives were noteworthy. In 1975, labor unions sought new legislation to increase union bargaining power and enhance their ability to organize construction workers by allowing unions to picket *all* employers working on a construction site, even though some of these employers had no labor dispute with the union. This proposed change in current law, known as the "common situs" issue, was defeated twice: first by presidential veto in 1975, and again by Congress when it was reintroduced in 1977. In the same year the labor movement strongly supported broader labor law reforms, most of which would have increased their ability to organize workers and strengthen their ability to secure new collective agreements. After a long and bitter lobbying fight between unions and employer organizations, the bill failed to have sufficient support in Congress—a sign that the political influence of U.S. labor unions had eroded during the 1970s (Levitan and Cooper 1984, Ch. 7). This decline in influence has been attributed by some to a reversion by labor to serving their own immediate constituency and a deemphasis of the coalition building which had been supportive of progressive legislation between the end of World War II and the mid-1960s (Piore 1982). Part of the decline, however, may also be attributable to reforms made in the Democratic Party following the 1968 convention. These reforms opened participation in party decision-making to groups based on demographic considerations, thus seriously diluting organized labor's informal interest-group role in the direction of the party.[46]

Conclusions

During the 1970s an increasing proportion of U.S. industries were competing either directly or indirectly in international markets. More industries experienced increased competition as productivity levels among industrialized countries began to converge, and several newly industrialized countries developed significant manufacturing capability. In most U.S. industries, management responded by attempting to introduce new technology and make their costs of production competitive. In the long run, these structural changes, involving the redistribution of capital and labor resources within and among industries, are crucial in determining the level of employment and the level of real earnings. At the same time the prospect of increasing structural change became a major issue in the debate over general economic policies and was an important influence in shaping industrial relations issues in many industries.

In the United States, the necessity of adapting to economic change has always had a profound effect on the industrial relations system. John R. Commons's theory of the U.S. labor movement accurately explained early unionization and bargaining strategy in the United States (Commons 1976 [originally published in 1909]). In the late 19th century, as specialization and growth of trade expanded the geographic boundaries of local product markets, labor unions sought to organize workers and negotiate similar wages and conditions of employment in all labor markets within a geographic area. This eventually led to the rapid development of craft unions in the United States. Between World Wars I and II, structural change brought about by innovation and the introduction of large scale production made the rapidly expanding occupational

---

[46] See, for example, Greenstone (1969) and Wilson (1979).

group of operatives a source of unionization, which culminated in a more centralized bargaining structure within mass production manufacturing industries.

In the 1970s, however, much of the structural change was significantly different from the type of changes that enlarged the scope of markets during the earlier part of the century. Much of the increased competition was from foreign competitors, and it proved impossible for U.S. labor unions to expand the concept of similar conditions of employment beyond national boundaries.

Industrial Relations: Response to Structural Change in the 1970s

The role of industrial relations in adapting to structural change varied by industry. The industrial relations system played only a minor role in the steel industry's adjustment to economic change. In the emerging global market for steel, the failure of the industry to innovate in the 1950s and 1960s proved a fatal weakness to much of the U.S. industry. While the small "minimills" were able to adjust and increase their share of U.S. production, the large integrated producers were unable to offset their cost disadvantage by investing sufficient resources in more efficient plants and equipment.

The locational disadvantage of many plants in the industry and the existence of overcapacity in world production in steel made diversification out of steel production, plant closings, and capacity consolidation through mergers the dominant adjustment techniques. For resources remaining in steel production, collective bargaining permitted increased efficiency and attempted to minimize the downward trend in wages and benefit levels, with the recognition that employment in the industry would decline permanently. For those workers who were displaced, collective bargaining provided an adjustment process based on traditional "effects" bargaining.

Unlike the situation in the steel industry, flexibility in industrial relations proved to be an integral part of the airline carriers' strategic response to deregulation. Among the major problems for the established carriers in the deregulated environment were the high wage levels and strict workrules negotiated during the regulated era. These wage levels contributed to placing the established carriers at a competitive disadvantage vis-à-vis new entrants into the industry. The new entrants were generally nonunion, paying lower wages, and burdened with less restrictive workrules than their established counterparts.

The industrial relations response in airlines included wage concessions, the relaxation of workrules, and the establishment of two-tiered wage systems to help the unionized carriers compete with the new entrants in the industry. The industrial relations response for some carriers included innovations in the form of substantial union participation in corporate decision-making and compensation systems linked to profitability of the company. The unionized sector of the trucking industry was also seriously influenced by deregulation. The scope of market competition increased substantially as both management and labor lost their ability to continue to pass on to consumers the cost of significant across-the-board wage increases and benefit improvements. The growth of the nonunion sector and the decline in employment among unionized workers contributed importantly to changes in the outcome of collective bargaining in trucking during the latter part of the 1970s.

In the automobile industry, many of the traditional features of bargaining in the industry were maintained; the concept of wage standardization throughout the industry, maintenance of extensive fringe benefits, and continuation of the COLA all remained central to industrial relations. On the other hand, both parties recognized that in order for a high-wage industry to remain competitive internationally, the U.S. industry had to produce process innovations rapidly. The bargaining agreements permitted management to follow this strategy, with both parties accepting the likelihood of a gradual decline in employment in the industry. At the same time workers were provided with some employment protection, especially if they were laid off because of new technology. Management and labor agreed on a new approach to assisting workers adjust to structural change. In addition to income maintenance assistance, displaced workers are in many cases now eligible for relocation and retraining assistance. In the automobile industry, industrial relations are much more central in the development of adjustment techniques for industrial restructuring than was the case in the steel industry.

The industrial relations system has also been an important factor in the rubber tire industry's adjustment to structural change caused by the acceptance of the radial tire. Unlike the auto industry, however, the strategy of the rubber tire industry has been one of shifting resources away from older unionized plants by making the necessary capital investment in new, radial capacity plants in new geographic locations where there is less likely to be an obligation to hire URW-represented employees. Innovation and geographic relocation of productive facilities within the United States was the most common adjustment technique used in the industry, although some companies also diversified out of tire manufacturing.

Over the past two decades the textile industry, and to a lesser extent the apparel industry, has used geographic relocation, both within the United States and offshore, as a response to structural change. Domestically, much of textile production has moved to new plants in the southwestern part of the country; in the apparel industry the relocation was to the Pacific and southern states. In both industries, offshore production to take advantage of low-cost labor has also been common. Management and labor had little leeway to modify wages and benefits as an adjustment technique. Instead, where possible, resources were shifted to high value-added types of production in the industries in an attempt to maintain or improve relative wage levels for a declining workforce.

In the agricultural equipment industry, an apparent cyclical decline in the quantity of agricultural equipment demanded in the early 1980s had become a structural shift downward in the industry's demand curve by the mid-1980s. Thus, the situation in agricultural equipment appears to be similar to that in basic steel; the industry must adjust to a decline in output and employment, with a consolidation of capacity and a shift of resources away from agricultural equipment by some of the firms currently in the market. The role of industrial relations will likely be the traditional one of easing the transition for laid-off workers.

Implications for Future Collective Bargaining

The collective bargaining response to structural change resulted in a reduction in the rate of wage increases and, in some cases, wage levels. In 1984 average increases in negotiated wages and benefits declined to less than half the average increase in contracts negotiated in the previous three years (Gay 1984). For the first time in 20 years, average hourly earnings declined in many industries, including steel, farm equipment machinery, and, for some workers, in trucking. Compensation flexibility was introduced, especially in the airline, trucking, and farm equipment industries.

The traditional bargaining practice of determining wages and benefits, primarily by comparability with wage and benefit outcomes in other unionized industries, and by inflation, was seriously challenged in some industries, and some have predicted the demise of pattern bargaining (Freedman and Fuller 1982, p. 30). How the adjustment to structural change of the 1970s will affect future industrial relations in the United States is uncertain. Employers are currently the dominant actors in industrial relations in most industries, and the reallocation of capital and labor resources is likely to continue to be a more important method of adjustment than are steps to protect the job security of existing workers.

Strategic management decisions about the reallocation of corporate assets are considered a management prerogative. Pattern bargaining and wage comparability did constrain management's reallocation decisions for a while, but the growth of the nonunion sector, the emergence of global markets, the convergence of productivity levels among industrialized nations, and existing labor relations law have limited the unions' ability to influence the resource reallocation.

Productivity growth and the competitiveness of industry require that capital and labor resources from time to time be reallocated to their most productive use. While legislative proposals to moderate the rate of structural change will continue to emerge from both management and labor, collective bargaining is likely to become an increasingly important forum for assisting workers in adapting to structural change.

Since the traditional bargaining approach of providing income maintenance and recall rights will be only partially effective in protecting workers, both management and labor are likely to experiment with innovative approaches to assist workers in adapting to structural change.[47] Experience in some European countries suggests that job protection, through either legislated or collectively negotiated benefits and protection against imports, provides only short-run employment security for current workers and increases the potential for long-term unemployment among laid-off workers and new entrants in the labor market. The only genuine protection against the long-run effects of a structural

---

[47] See Norsworthy and Zabala (1985) and McKersie and Klein (1985).

change is to increase the ability of workers to be more flexible within the enterprise and within the labor market. In the United States, labor and management in some industries appear to be moving towards this type of adjustment strategy.

References

"Address by Peter Pestillo, Vice President of B.F. Goodrich Company, on His Experience During 1976 Rubber Industry Strike and Negotiations." *BNA Daily Labor Report*, No. 48, March 10, 1979, p. A1.
American Iron and Steel Institute (AISI). *Annual Statistical Report, 1979.* Washington: AISI, 1980.
_____. *Annual Statistical Report. 1982.* Washington: AISI, 1983.
"Auto Workers Avoid Strike at Deere: Members to Vote on Three-Year Pact." *BNA Daily Labor Report*, No. 108, June 3, 1983, p. A5.
Baily, Martin Neil. "The Productivity Slowdown by Industry." Washington: Brookings Institution, 1982. Photocopy.
Barnett, Donald F., and Louis Schorsch. *Steel Upheaval in a Basic Industry.* Cambridge, MA: Ballinger, 1984.
Baumol, William F., and Kenneth McLennan, eds. *Productivity Growth and U.S. Competitiveness.* New York: Oxford University Press, 1985.
Betit, Eileen. "The Industry in Crisis Part V: Impact on Employees." *Air Line Pilot* 53 (April 1984): pp. 21–25.
"Big Steel vs. the USW: It's Showdown Time." *Business Week*, December 26, 1983, p. 23.
"BLS Report on Collective Bargaining in the Rubber Industry." *BNA Daily Labor Report*, No. 67, April 7, 1982, pp. E1–E9.
Bowles, Billy, and Ralph Orr. "UAW Council Approves Contract with Ford." *The Detroit Free Press*, October 18, 1984, p 1A.
Byrne, Harlan S. "United Air's New Tactics Bring Success." *The Wall Street Journal*, October 10, 1984, p. 35.
Capdevielle, Patricia, Donato Alvarez, and Brian Cooper. "International Trends in Productivity and Labor Costs." *Monthly Labor Review* 105 (December 1982): pp. 3–14.
Carlson, Norma W. "Pay Gains Tempered in Basic Steel Mills." *Monthly Labor Review* 107 (August 1984):: pp. 28–32.
Committee for Economic Development. *Strategy for U.S. Industrial Competitiveness.* New York: Committee for Economic Development, 1984.
Commons, John R. "American Shoemakers, 1648–1895." In *Readings in Labor Economics and Labor Relations*, ed. Richard L. Rowen. Homewood, IL: Richard D. Irwin, 1976. Pp. 88–100.
"Continental Is Coming Out a Winner." *Business Week*, January 30, 1984, p. 21.
"Contract Highlights." *The Detroit Free Press*, March 23, 1982, p. 15A.
Denison, Edward F. *Accounting for Slower Economic Growth.* Washington: Brookings Institution, 1979.
"Details of Wage and Benefit Changes in Proposed GM Settlement." *The Detroit Free Press*, September 27, 1984, p. 11B.
Doyle, Frank P. and Kenneth McLennan. "Labor Market Policies and Industrial Competitiveness." Paper prepared for conference on Employment Growth in the Context of Structural Change, Manpower and Social Affairs Committee, Organization for Economic Cooperation and Development, Paris, October 6–8, 1984.
"Dual Pay Rates Fly at Northwest Air." *Business Week*, April 30, 1984, p. 20.
"Eastern's Revolutionary 'Treaty' with Its Unions." *Business Week*, December 26, 1983, p. 22.
Employment and Earnings 31 (January 1984 and January-September 1985).
Employment and Earnings Supplement (1983 and July 1984).

"Firestone's Pricing Actions to Compensate for Noncompliant URW Pact, CWPS Announces." *BNA Daily Labor Report*, No. 213, November 1, 1979, pp. A17-A18.

"Flight Attendants Ratify Pact at Piedmont." *BNA Daily Labor Report*, No. 249, August 2, 1984, p. A2.

Fogel, Helen, Ann M. Job, and William Saunders. "UAW's Chrysler Council OK's Contract." *The Detroit Free Press*, October 25, 1985, p. 1A.

Freedman, Audrey, and William E. Fuller. "Last Rights for Pattern Bargaining." *Harvard Business Review* 60 (March/April 1982).

Freeman, Richard B., and James L. Medoff. "The Impact of Collective Bargaining: Illusion or Reality?" In *U.S. Industrial Relations 1960-1980: A Critical Assessment*, eds. Jack Stieber, Robert B. McKersie, and D. Quinn Mills. Madison, WI: Industrial Relations Research Association, 1981. Pp. 47-98.

_____. *What Do Unions Do?* New York: Basic Books, 1984.

Gay, Robert S. "Union Contract Concerns and Their Implications for Union Wage Determination." Washington: Division of Research and Statistics, Board of Governors of the Federal Reserve System, 1984. Photocopy.

"General Tire Announces Closing of Plant in Akron." *BNA Daily Labor Report*, No. 43, March 4, 1982, pp. A6-A7.

Graham, David R., and Daniel P. Kaplan. "Competition and the Airlines: An Evaluation of Deregulation." Staff Report. Washington: Office of Economic Analysis, Civil Aeronautics Board, 1982.

Greenhouse, Steven. "Steel Moves Off Center Stage." *The New York Times*, May 9, 1984a, p. D1.

_____. "Farm Equipment Hits a Trough." *The New York Times*, November 11, 1984b, Sec. 3, p. 4.

Greenstone, J. David. *Labor in American Politics*. New York: Random House, 1969.

Hendricks, Wallace, Peter Feuille, and Carol Szerson. "Regulation, Deregulation, and Collective Bargaining in Airlines." *Industrial and Labor Relations Review* 34 (October 1980): pp. 67-82.

Holusha, John. "A Race for Greater Auto Profits." *The New York Times*, September 30, 1984, Sec. 3, p. 1.

"How Frontier Airlines Is Getting Outgunned." *Business Week*, August 9, 1984, p. 66.

"How Tiremakers Are Slashing Away at Inefficiency." *Business Week*, February 13, 1984, p. 94.

"Investment Outlook Scoreboard." *Business Week*, March 21, 1984, pp. 107, 109, 110.

Job, Ann M., and Helen Fogel. "Both Sides Win in Chrysler Deal." *TheDetroit Free Press*, October 29, 1985, p. 1A.

Kahn, Mark L. "Airlines." In *Collective Bargaining: Contemporary American Experience*, ed. Gerald G. Somers. Madison, WI: Industrial Relations Research Association, 1980. Pp. 315-72.

Kamm, Thomas. "Michelin Is Revamping its Strategy in Bid to Inflate its Position in the Tire Industry." *The Wall Street Journal*, December 12, 1984, p. 32.

Katz, Harry C. "Shifting Gears: Changing Labor Relations in the U.S. Automobile Industry." Cambridge, MA: Massachusetts Institute of Technology, 1984. Photocopy.

Kochan, Thomas A., Robert B. McKersie, and Peter Cappelli. "Strategic Choice and Industrial Relations Theory." *Industrial Relations* 23 (Winter 1984): pp. 16-39.

"A Labor Package Gives Republic Room to Maneuver." *Business Week*, July 16, 1984, p. 28.

Lawrence, Robert Z. *Can America Compete?* Washington: Brookings Institution, 1984.

Levinson, Harold M. "Trucking." In *Collective Bargaining: Contemporary American Experience*, ed. Gerald G. Somers. Madison, WI: Industrial Relations Research Association, 1980. Pp. 99-149.

Levitan, Sar A., and Martha R. Cooper. *Business Lobbies*. Baltimore: Johns Hopkins University Presss, 1984.

Lienert, Paul. "Chrysler Posts Record Quarter." *The Detroit Free Press*, July 20, 1984, p. 1A.

McKersie, Robert B., and Janice A. Klein. "Productivity: The Industrial Relations Connection." In *Productivity Growth and U.S. Competitiveness*, eds. William F. Baumol and Kenneth McLennan. New York: Oxford University Press, 1985. Ch. 6.

McLennan, Kenneth. "Industry Perspectives or Adjustment to Economic Change." In *American Jobs and the Changing Industrial Base*, eds. Eileen Collins and Lucretia Dewey Tanner. Cambridge, MA: Ballinger, 1984a.

_____. "Policy Options to Facilitate the Reemployment of Displaced Workers." In *Displaced Workers: Implications for Educational and Training Institutions*, eds. Kevin Hollenbeck, Frank C. Pratzner, and Howard Rosen. Columbus: National Center for Research in Vocational Education, Ohio State University, 1984b.

Moore, Thomas Gale. "Rail and Truck Reform—The Record So Far." *Regulation* (November/December 1983).

"National Rubber Bargaining Completed With URW Ratification of Big Four Pacts." *BNA Daily Labor Report*, No. 98, May 21, 1985, p. A5.

"New Job Security Concepts Included in UAW's Settlement at Harvester." *BNA Daily Labor Report*, No. 18, January 28, 1985, p. A7.

"The New LTV Steel: How Republic Will Fit In." *Business Week*, April 16, 1984, p. 129.

Norsworthy, J. R., and C. A. Zabala. "Responding to the Productivity Crisis: A Plant-Level Approach to Labor Policy." In *Productivity Growth and U.S. Competitiveness*, eds. William F. Baumol and Kenneth McLennan. New York: Oxford University Press, 1985. Ch. 5.

Northrup, Herbert R. "The New Employee Relations Climate in Airlines." *Industrial and Labor Relations Review* 36 (January 1983): pp. 167–81.

O'Boyle, Thomas F. "Bethlehem Sets Sights on Diversifying in Bid to End Heavy Dependence on Steel." *The Wall Street Journal*, May 17, 1984, p. 10.

Orr, Ann C., and James A. Orr. "Employment Adjustments in Import Sensitive Industries—1960-1980." *Proceedings of the 36th Annual Meeting, Industrial Relations Research Association*, 1983. Madison, WI: IRRA, 1984. Pp. 230–38.

Orr, Ralph, Helen Fogel, and Billy Bowles. "UAW Hails 'Excellent' Accord." *The Detroit Free Press*, September 22, 1984, p. 1A.

Petzinger, Thomas Jr., and Betsy Morris. "Tenneco to Buy Farm-Gear Unit from Harvester." *The Wall Street Journal*, November 11, 1984, p. 2.

"Pilot Group Negotiates New Pact at American." *BNA Daily Labor Report*, No. 217, November 8, 1983, pp. D7–D8.

Pine, Art. "U.S. Sets Pacts to Curb Imports of Finished Steel." *The Wall Street Journal*, December 20, 1984, p. 20.

Piore, Michael J. "Can the American Labor Movement Survive Re-Gomperization?" *Proceedings of the 35th Annual Meeting, Industrial Relations Research Association*, 1982. Madison, WI: IRRA, 1983. Pp. 30–39.

"Plan to Purchase Bethlehem Mill." *The New York Times*, August 2, 1984, p. 27.

"President Reagan Signs Bankruptcy Bill Including 'Bildisco' Labor Clause." *BNA Daily Labor Report*, No. 134, July 12, 1984, pp. A9–A11.

"The Radical Surgery Keeping Harvester Alive." *Business Week*, December 10, 1984, p. 41.

"Reagan Seeks Cut in Steel Imports Through Accords." *The New York Times*, September 19, 1984, p. 1.

"Republic Airlines: One Union Down and Five to Go." *Business Week*, April 9, 1984, p. 33.

"Republic Airlines, Unions in Accord." *The New York Times*, July 3, 1984, p. 34.

"Revisions in Firestone URW Agreement Approved in Memphis, Rejected in Indiana." *BNA Daily Labor Report*, No. 248, December 23, 1980, pp. A7–A8.

Roberts, Markley. "A Labor Perspective on Technological Change." In *American Jobs and the Changing Industrial Base*, eds. Eileen L. Collins and Lucretia Dewey Tanner. Cambridge, MA: Ballinger, 1984. Ch. 8.

"Rubber: Short-run Prosperity Ahead." *Business Week*, October 4, 1976, p. 82.

"The Rubber Talks May Show Some Give." *Business Week*, February 8, 1982, p. 38.

"Rubber Workers at Uniroyal Agree to Take Pay Cut for 17 Months." *BNA Daily Labor Report*, No. 151, July 23, 1980, p. A12.

"Rubber Workers, Firestone Sign No-Strike, No-Lockout Agreement." *BNA Daily Labor Report*, No. 213, November 1, 1979, pp. A17–A18.

"Rubber Workers, Goodrich, Reach Tentative Agreement in Pattern-Setting 3-Year Pact." *BNA Daily Labor Report*, No. 117, June 15, 1979, pp. AA1-AA2.

Ruben, George. "Development in Industrial Relations." *Monthly Labor Review* 105 (April 1982a): pp. 62–64.

—————. "Clothing Workers Get New Contract." *Monthly Labor Review* 105 (June 1982b): p. 62.

—————. "Southern Textile Workers Get Wage Increases." *Monthly Labor Review* 105 (December 1982c): pp. 47-48.

Salpukas, Agis. "New Era for Eastern's Unions." *The New York Times*, April 20, 1984a, p. D1.

—————. "Changing American's Rules." *The New York Times*, April 25, 1984b, Sec. 3, p. 6.

Sockell, Donna. "Two Decades of Mandatory-Permissive Distinction in Bargaining: Reflections on the Wisdom of *Borg-Warner*." New York: Graduate School of Business, Columbia University, 1984. Photocopy.

Somers, Gerald G., Edward L. Cushman, and Nat Weinberg, eds. *Adjusting to Technological Change*. IRRA Series, No. 29. New York: Harper & Row, 1963.

"Steel Companies Will End 30-Year Practice of Joint Negotiations With Steelworkers." *BNA Daily Labor Report*, No. 87, May 6, 1985, p. A10.

"Steel Forges a Japanese Connection." *Business Week*, May 7, 1984, p. 30.

"Steel Imports Fell 2%, Totaled 31% of Market in U.S. in December." *The Wall Street Journal*, February 2, 1985, p. 3.

Stepanek, Marcia. "Quarterly Profit Sets Ford Record." *The Detroit Free Press*. July 27, 1984a, p. 1A.

—————. "Baldridge Alters Quota Stand." *The Detroit Free Press*, August 9, 1984b, p. 7B.

Stieber, Jack. "Steel.'" In *Collective Bargaining: Contemporary American Experience*, ed. Gerald G. Somers. Madison, WI: Industrial Relations Research Association, 1980. Pp. 151–209.

"Study Finds Garment Jobs Up by 5000." *The New York Times*, December 26, 1984.

"Summary of United Auto Workers-Ford Agreement as Prepared by UAW." *BNA Daily Labor Report*, No. 205, October 23, 1984, pp. D1–D23.

"Tentative Accord Reached in URW-Goodrich Contract Talks." *BNA Daily Labor Report*, No. 75, April 19, 1982, pp. A1–A2.

"Time Runs Out for Steel." *Business Week*, June 13, 1984, p. 84.

Troy, Leo. *Trade Union Membership, 1897–1962.*. National Bureau of Economic Research Occasional Paper No. 92. New York: NBER, 1965.

"The Trying Times for Continental Aren't Over Yet." *Business Week*, March 19, 1984, p. 44.

"UAW Summary of Proposed New Contract with General Motors." *BNA Daily Labor Report*, No. 188, September 27, 1984, pp. D1–D24.

"United Gets a Break at the Bargaining Table." *Business Week*, July 2, 1984, p. 26.

"URW Accepts Firestone Accord as Pattern-Setting Agreement." *BNA Daily Labor Report*, No. 158, August 12, 1976. pp. A9–A10.

U.S. Civil Aeronautics Board. *Air Carrier Traffic Statistics*. Washington: The Board, December 1983.

U.S. Department of Labor, Bureau of Labor Statistics. *Directory of International Unions and Employee Associations*. Washington: U.S. Government Printing Office, 1973.

—————. "Industry Wage Survey: Textiles." Bull. 1945. Washington: U.S. Government Printing Office, 1975.

—————. "Employment and Earnings, 1909–1979." Bull. 1312-11. Washington: U.S. Government Printing Office, 1980.

—————. "Industry Wage Survey: Men's and Boys' Shirts and Nightwear." Bull. 2131, Washington: U.S. Government Printing Office, 1981.

—————. "Productivity Measures for Selected Industries, 1954–1981." Bull. 2155. Washington: U.S. Government Printing Office, 1982.

_____. "Hourly Compensation Costs for Production Workers in Iron and Steel Manufacturing—20 Countries, 1975–1983." Washington: U.S. Department of Labor, Office of Productivity and Technology, 1984a. Photocopy.

_____. "Leading Suppliers of U.S. Imports by Major 2-Digit SIC-Based Group 1984." Washington: U.S. Department of Labor, 1984b. Photocopy.

_____. Occupational Earnings and Benefits, Men's and Boys' Suit and Coat Manufacturing. Washington: U.S. Government Orinting office, 1984c.

_____. "Trade Monitoring System: U.S. Imports Compared to Domestic Production by 4-Digit SIC Code." Washington: U.S. Department of Labor, 1984d. Photocopy.

_____. "Trade Weighted Output per Hour, Hourly Compensation, and Unit Labor Costs in Manufacturing, Seven Countries, 1960–1983." Washington: U.S. Department of Labor, Office of Productivity and Technology, December 1984e.

United Steelworkers of America. The Future of Steel: Challenges and Opportunities, 1983 Basic Steel Settlement. A special report. Pittsburgh: undated.

Wayne, Leslie F. "Big Steel's Puzzling Strategy." The New York Times, July 10, 1983, Sec. 2, p. 1.

"Western Airlines Seeks Further Cuts in Wages and Other Concessions." The Wall Street Journal, May 14, 1984, p. 56.

"What Could Deflate RubberTalks?" Business Week, January 28, 1985, p. 46.

"Why Johnstown's Steel Workers Voted Away Their Jobs." Business Week, March 19, 1984, p. 33.

Wilson, Graham K. Unions in American National Politics. London: The MacMillan Press, Ltd., 1979.

Winter, Ralph E. "Tire Concerns, Rubber Workers, Conciliatory About Achieving New Pact." The Wall Street Journal, January 2, 1985, p. 8.

Witkin, Richard. "Continental Air's Gains and Fears." The New York Times, May 14, 1984, p. D1.

Zieman, Mark, and Alex Kotlowitz. "Harvester-Tenneco Bid to Merge Units Anguishes Dealers, Towns." The Wall Street Journal, January 21, 1985, p. 4.

Chapter 11

The Response of Industrial Relations to Economic Change

Mark Thompson
University of British Columbia

Hervey A. Juris
Northwestern University

As Tabatoni chronicles in the opening chapter, 1973-1983 was indeed a decade of significant economic change. The introduction of flexible exchange rates in 1972-1973, the two oil shocks and the subsequent recessions, the rise of the third world as competitors in markets once the sole province of the major powers, the high interest rate policy of the United States, and the recession of 1981-1982 affected each of the nations studied in this volume. The chapters that precede this one document the effect of these changes on the industrial relations system of each country. In this chapter we will review the individual country responses, looking for patterns which might have emerged and for explanations of those patterns.

In setting the context for this review, Tabatoni reminds us that it was not just economic change, but technological change and the absence of an orthodox and agreed-upon response which helped make the decade so difficult. The lack of a dominant theoretical framework for response led to a muddling through the 1970s which produced a stagflation, protecting many countries, industries, and unions from the ultimate day of reckoning. With the 1980s, says Tabatoni, came an emerging consensus that a monetarist fiscal policy to dampen inflation, some reductions in the welfare state, and an increased emphasis on local management of resources by companies can restore some degree of competitiveness to a country's export position. Still, while the search for a response was going on, there was a technological revolution which led to a reordering of world trade, a shift in power from the Atlantic to the Pacific. The unanswered question for Tabatoni is how the current developed countries will remain major players in future world markets, especially in the production of goods.

Responses to Change

If the criterion by which we ordered the summary to follow were "which industrial relations systems coped with change with the least disruption," Japan, as of this writing, would set the standard by which all industrial relations systems would be judged. Germany would be second. Japanese industrial relations adapted to a new economic climate, while the existing German system was capable of dealing with altered circumstances with little structural change. We include Sweden in the first group as well, not for what the Swedish industrial relations system accomplished, but rather for the fact that the Swedish model in place in 1973 should have dealt with change as effectively as the Japanese and German models but in the end did not.

Japan

Taira and Levine attribute the Japanese response to the adoption of flexible exchange rates, the two oil shocks, and the subsequent recession to a mechanism for tripartite and bipartite discussion and consultation that was emerging in 1973. The key event in this scenario was the lesson the government learned from the year-long strike it endured at the Mitsui Miike coal mines in 1960. When it decided to substitute petroleum for coal as the chief source of industrial energy, several hundred thousand miners were suddenly displaced from their jobs. The resulting strike dramatized to political and industrial leaders the need to prepare carefully for major labor force readjustments, as Japan subsequently experienced rapid industrial growth and shifts in industrial structure in the 1960s. From this event came not only an expanding network of joint consultations, but also the development of the Japanese form of worker participation which increases employer-employee interaction without challenging the legitimacy of the collective bargaining process. Thus, when the first oil crisis hit, there was a response mechanism in place. The mechanism and the government's willingness to stay within the collective bargaining framework while moving towards more market determination not only moderated wage demands but also smoothed the transition from an economy dominated by heavy industry to one emphasizing lighter microelectronic industry. The authors also credit management's restraint in the 1970s (not using the shift in market-generated bargaining power to rescind union gains in the 1960s) with contributing to transitions. They document how the flexibility of the internal labor markets of large Japanese enterprises were used instead to absorb the shocks. All of these activities—information-sharing, consultation, nonconfrontation over givebacks, and job security—facilitated a trusting relationship that the parties have used to achieve their current dominant position in certain world markets. The authors, however, are not sanguine about the future. In the changing industrial structure and demographics, they see strains that may make the current system untenable.

Germany

A close contender for best-coping mechanism would be the Federal Republic of Germany. Jacobi says that while the end of the postwar boom, the rise in competition from other nations, and the new technologies have caused higher unemployment in the Federal Republic, neither these economic events, nor a political shift towards conservatism, nor the change in social power favoring employers has caused or should cause a fundamental change in German industrial relations. He cites two reasons for this stability: the existing social consensus among government, employers, and the banks that Germany will promote national competitiveness through technological superiority and overcome barriers to innovation by integrating the unions into the change process; and second, the fact that the efficiency and legitimacy of collective bargaining has been maintained because the participants utilized the existing system flexibly.

The tests of this commitment have been severe. Recessions in 1966–1967, 1974–1975, and 1981–1982 have led to high unemployment and a two-tier employment system, with a core of highly skilled workers and a peripheral labor force of women and part-timers. The departure of guest workers did take up some of the slack. Unlike some other countries, however, government policy post-1974–1975 sought to check the acceleration of inflation through monetary control while promoting innovation and investment. Thus we have the German model of promoting international competitiveness by producing technologically advanced goods and overcoming social barriers to innovation through trade union involvement. After the 1981–1982 recession, the new conservative government maintained the German model but deemphasized the social welfare state in favor of more market discipline, encouraging flexibility and innovation. While structural changes in German industry have caused losses in trade union membership, labor's strength has not declined proportionately because the core workforce still has great bargaining power. Thus, wage and income sacrifices have been small for core workers and pattern bargaining continues. Unlike some other countries, the shift to a conservative government in 1982 did not produce a change in the general principles of economic policy since the earlier recession had already prompted a significant switch by the previous social democratic government. Even the formula approach to wage-setting (productivity plus cost-of-living adjustment) had been abandoned during the period of the social democrats. While there is not the animus towards unions by the conservatives as there is in the U.K. and the U.S., the government has tended to limit the role of trade unions in political and economic decision-making. Employers have not shared this hostility towards labor. The legitimacy of unions comes from their role as mediators of social interests vital to the continued functioning of the system.

Jacobi attributes a great deal of the stability of the German industrial relations system to the centralized structure of bargaining. Since union decision-making and bargaining is centralized at the industry level, is not formally involved with the state, and cannot be questioned by the rank and file, macroeconomic considerations carry great weight. Microadjustments occur at the enterprise level, where works councils can work out local details but cannot strike or consider issues not referred or ceded to them by the parties to the bargain. Finally, Jacobi observes that while unions would like to be doing something about the impact of economic change on changes in their jobs and wages, they defer to the overall need to remain competitive. Regardless of rhetoric, the union wage policy in practice does not inhibit structural change, but does provide a temporary "soft landing" for those currently affected. Unions do not create obstacles or disincentives to technology and productivity; rather, they promote adjustment systems. Because of this, employers are not willing to provoke the unions too much for fear of radicalizing them and losing them as social partners. Thus, unlike the Swedish model, the German model persists.

Sweden

Swedish industrial relations were to the 1950s and 1960s what the Japanese model is to the 1970s and 1980s. Yet at the time when it might have adjusted most effectively to a deteriorating economic situation, the Swedish model was partially abandoned. Peterson describes some attributes of the model: consultation, participation, pragmatism and cooperation, and a commitment to free collective bargaining. Bargaining was centralized and, says Peterson, there was general agreement that the sector of the economy most exposed to international competition should be the wage leader. After years of successful economic performance, the Swedish experience during the decade under study was dismal. Sweden suffered from the effects of the first oil shock because it must import 100 percent of its oil. Moreover, public-sector expenditures, which had accounted for 45 percent of the gross domestic product in 1970, rose to 70 percent in 1982; industrial wages and unit labor costs were higher than those in Japan and the U.S.; inflation was double-digit, and exports decreased considerably.

Why did the Swedish model perform so poorly during this period, given its earlier success? Peterson points to a number of factors. One was the pressure from high-wage workers (particularly the miners) that had been building within the LO, reflecting their dissatisfaction with LO's wage policy to narrow differentials. A second factor was LO's shift from a movement content to let private capital manage while it concentrated on collective bargaining, to a more politically active role promoted by an increasingly militant left within the labor movement and the Social Democratic party. Thus LO turned from bargained solutions to legislated solutions and, in the process, introduced rigidities into the system that made adjustments to changed conditions more difficult. A conservative government in the mid-1970s was replaced with another socialist government, and the idea of worker-earner funds was added to the factors that had already changed the Swedish system. LO's insistence on wage-earner funds seems to have clouded the future and cemented the ideological break with the old system. There no longer appears to be the consensus that provided the foundation for the Swedish system. Taira and Levine express a similar concern about a loss of consensus in Japan.

If Japan, Germany, and Sweden should be considered together

because of the high regard in which foreign observers have held their industrial relations systems, then France and Great Britain should also be grouped together because of the similarity of the effect of change on the structure of collective bargaining in each country.

France

Economic change had two significant effects on the French industrial relations system, according to Sellier. The first, which is still in a nascent stage, is a decentralization of the bargaining process with respect to hours of work, quality of work, organization of work, and other nonwage issues. The second is a shift in relative strength from the radical to the less radical unions. This second change is linked with the economic developments of the decade through employers' and employees' mutual understanding of the need to adjust at the level of the firm or workplace, plus the reluctance of the left-wing unions to go along with these employee and employer interests.

Sellier paints a picture of an economy increasingly dependent on exports, with a decline in industrial employment during the decade and a rise in unemployment (partly associated with a lack of new jobs, partly with a large increase in the labor force). French governments vacillated in their macroeconomic approach to these changes. The conservative government in office in 1974 tried to stimulate economic growth and reduce unemployment, but inflation and export deficits forced a reversal. By 1976 the government sought to limit wages, which improved the balance of trade but did not slow inflation or unemployment. The socialist government elected in 1981 reversed policy again, emphasizing public-sector job creation, shorter hours, and income maintenance. Although employment stabilized, a rise in prices together with a decline in exports led the government to reverse policy yet again in June of 1982. Wages and prices were frozen for six months, and the government declared that the purchasing power of wages should be reduced. To compensate labor for this loss, a number of laws were passed to enhance the power of unions and plant-level consultative committees.

Sellier explains that French governments are reluctant to antagonize the unions; instead they seek to reduce the potential for conflict. This approach introduced rigidities into the system which managers have found they can reduce by working with employees and committees at the enterprise level. The French employers previously opposed enterprise-level unionism. Then, centralized wage bargaining and national legislation of benefits put pressure on managers to effect economies at the plant level. As groups of employers and employees have seen the benefits of working together locally, the legitimacy of unions has risen at the plant level among managers, while the importance of the radical unions has declined because they resisted change.

Great Britain

Brown portrays the industrial relations system of Great Britain as having been fundamentally affected by declining economic competitiveness, by an abrupt rise in and continued high unemployment, and by the first government in this century to be explicitly hostile to collective bargaining. He details the nature of the economic decline, attributing Britain's problems to a poor domestic economy (inflation, low investment, and high wages) and an overvalued currency which led to a lack of competitiveness in world markets. Since 1979 the Conservative government, says Brown, has pursued a policy designed to make the U.K. more competitive in world markets, including a monetarist policy to reduce inflation, privatization of some nationalized industries, a reduction in some transfer payments, and legislation to restrict union power. Employers, however, have shown less hostility towards unions than has the government, preferring to work with them at the enterprise level in an attempt to make local adjustments necessary to compete in world markets. Characteristics of the new industrial relations system include decentralization of bargaining, lower levels of conflict, a reduced political role for unions, a trend towards de facto enterprise unionism, and the creation of core and peripheral labor forces within the enterprise. The core workers exchange job security for negotiated agreements on job redesign, reduction of craft distinctions, and new pay arrangements. Brown notes that even in the face of government animus towards unions, employers see them as an effective way of maintaining contact with the workforce. Ultimately, he questions whether the observed changes (which in fact have led to improved economic perfor- mance) are so fundamental as to be durable or whether it is the shocked response of a fearful workforce that will fade as attitudes adjust to a harsher labor market.

Two other countries that might be considered together are the United States and Canada. The common thread is that both are market economies and both have long been considered as having many similarities, including their industrial relations systems. However, economic pressures have driven them to different responses, perhaps emphasizing differences that have always existed but which have not necessarily been recognized explicitly.

United States

Consistent with the idea that the industrial relations system in the United States is essentially market driven, Block and McLennan present a market framework for understanding the changes in that system over the decade. They identify four major sources of change: import penetration in basic manufacturing industries, innovation in traditional industries, deregulation of several domestic industries, and declining demand worldwide in some mature markets. Taken together, in the context of the overall changes over the decade, these factors undermined previously sheltered markets in which labor and management had negotiated agreements with high wages and restricted flexibility which helped reduce productivity differences between U.S. firms and their foreign competitors.

In a series of industry studies they show how much variance occurred in the response of different labor-management relationships to these challenges. The lesson they draw from these studies is that management has chosen to reallocate corporate assets in response to a structural adjustment in the economy. In the U.S. such decisions have been a management prerogative. While pattern bargaining and wage comparability had previously constrained management, the growth of the nonunion sector, the emergence of global competition, the convergence of productivity levels among industrialized nations, and existing labor laws have recently limited unions' ability to influence these resource reallocation decisions. The authors believe that in the future the parties will have to find ways to be more flexible within the enterprise and within the labor market. They cite experience elsewhere in the world, such as that discussed above, to show that flexibility is associated with adjustments that reduce unemployment, while inflexibility is associated with extended duration of unemployment for laid-off workers and few new jobs for new entrants to the labor force. They indicate that in some industries this type of flexibility is already seen in the United States (in their sample, in automobiles, airlines, trucking, and farm equipment), while in others there has not been this kind of adjustment.

In taking this approach to understanding the American experience, the authors may have disappointed some who would attribute a larger role to antiunion attitudes of employers and government. The approach they have taken suggests not that such animus does not exist. Rather, in the context of a market economy and an industrial relations system emphasizing collective bargaining over politics, where unions used available bargaining power to secure the maximum member benefits, it is not surprising that a shift in market power means that employers and promanagement government are now using this period to "get even" or adjust, or regain what was lost in the 1950s and 1960s. This system contrasts with Japan, where unions and management show restraint, nor is it like Germany, where export industries set the standard. If we read the authors correctly, they are saying that those who live by the sword must be prepared to die by the sword. Their call is for new solutions within the bargaining context.

Canada

The response of the Canadian system differed greatly from that of the U.S., according to Adams. He sees the 1973–1983 decade as encouraging labor, management, and the federal government in Canada to develop a North American industrial relations system drawing on European experience. While Canada suffered economically during the decade, the major problems during the first half of the period were seen to be high rates of inflation and unemployment in the face of economic growth. Almost as serious, in the opinion of government, was a record number of labor disputes. Government responses included wage and price controls, consultation with the parties, experiments to ease labor conflict, and legislation to improve substantive conditions of work. Unlike in the U.S., union membership in Canada increased during this period. Canadian employers adopted a tougher stance at the bargaining table although, according to Adams, they seldom had available the weapon of a nonunion alternative to pressure their unionized workers. Thus, Canadian unions more successfully resisted give-backs than did their U.S. counterparts.

The Canadian system was not inflexible, however. Wage and price increases slowed significantly in 1983, and by 1984 wages and prices were advancing at the slowest rate in two decades. Canadian authorities had little choice but to emulate U.S. monetary policies. Governments imposed public-sector wage controls. Employers reduced their labor forces sharply, creating unemployment rates far above the "excessive" levels of the 1970s. The uniquely Canadian changes Adams sees are the increased role of the CLC in response to government-imposed controls in 1974, the formation of the BCNI in response to the CLC role, and the six years of minuets these two have danced with government in efforts to mold a consultative framework. So far each dance has ended when one of the three finds an excuse to drop out. Other responses include moves towards worker participation without undermining the union's representa-tion role and the trend towards labor courts. Some of these changes fly in the face of the Canadian industrial relations system, with its decentralized bargaining, autonomous unions, provincial jurisdic-tion over labor law, and close contractual regulation of workplace behavior. In addition, conservative provincial governments in the West have rejected consultation, and the federal government itself moved against the public employees.

The last two countries discussed here are paired not because they have something in common with one another, but rather because both are outliers from the population mean. Brazil, a country moving from legislated corporatism to plant-level collective bargaining, is shifting toward the mean. Australia, an industrialized Western democracy, is moving away.

Australia

As Dabscheck and Niland indicate, what makes Australia different are the institutional constraints of the industrial relations system and the logic of the parties which, from a market perspective, seemed counterintuitive. The well-known distinguish-ing feature of the Australian system is the reliance on tribunals at the federal, industry, and state levels which can determine wages when the parties disagree and validate agreements when they do occur. The authors describe a system of wage determination which in the 1950s and 1960s was decentralized and seemed to be responsive to market forces. The tribunals were cooperative and, within the context of the Australian system, they seemed to work. The departure came in 1974, when the ACTU responded to the recession and rising unemployment with a request for national wage determination. The demand was granted a year later. With the exception of a short period during the recovery of 1980–1981, the national tribunal has set the floor for Australian wages in every year since.

The authors also describe two periods of indexation which occurred during the decade and the current accord between the ACTU and the new labor government which formalizes the previously informal commitment to maintain real wages irrespective of the level of inflation or the number unemployed. They point out that employers feel frozen out of this decision-making process, although in passing they acknowledge that employers do have means of coping with the effects of maintaining real wages such as raising prices or transferring capital. To this list they might have added reducing output and increasing redundancies. Given the system they describe, no macroeconomist would be surprised that while the labor force increased 23 percent during the period 1971–1983, employment increased only 13 percent and unemployment 635 percent. The authors state that the opposition might attempt deregulation when it regains power, but they indicate that such a dramatic change is unlikely.

In conclusion the authors point out that probably alone among Western industrial nations during this decade, Australian unions maintained real wages, did not lose members, and increased their political power. A 1984 High Court decision giving increased powers to the federal tribunal and legislature and new laws on redundancy reaffirmed the centralized structure. The interesting question is what form the inevitable adjustments to specific labor and product market conditions will take after the system has been in place through several economic cycles.

Brazil

Brazil represents an interesting contrast to Australia. In Australia a labor government chose maintenance of real wages rather than the reduction of inflation as their goal. In Brazil, pressure from the International Monetary Fund (a result of recession-induced loan repayment problems) forced reductions in inflation at the expense of unemployment and put pressure on the government-run industrial relations system to keep real wages from rising. The industrial relations system in Brazil, as outlined by Pastore and Skidmore, is a pure corporatist system dominated almost completely by the government through various mechanisms. The authors highlight the pressures for a free labor movement which coincided with the easing of political restraints (*abertura*) by the military government. Consistent with *abertura*, the government sporadically facilitated the development of bilateral industrial relations by the parties in heavy industrial sectors. This process has been uneven and upset by a variety of adversities—occasional government and employer hostility, the economic recession, and the unions' own political agendas.

Brazil is quickly becoming a world industrial power and a direct competitor of domestic manufacturers in developed nations. In the tradition of most developing countries, industrial relations there are still highly politicized, and the continuation of the trend towards negotiation is likely to depend greatly on political decisions. But the Brazilian case study does demonstrate that, even in a negative political climate, while pressures for participation from labor may not actually force government and employers to deal with workers, unions can make their continued exclusion from decision-making very unattractive.

An especially interesting question for North Americans arising from the Brazilian experience is the extent to which similar pressures from labor will be felt in other nations pursuing comparable economic development strategies. Several other developing nations have based development on an export-oriented economy which severely restricts labor costs. Various mechanisms, including Brazilian-style corporatism, are used to control industrial workers. Can these systems endure in the face of sustained economic growth and modernization? Conventional pluralist theory suggests not, and the recent experience of Brazil provides limited support for that position.

Models of Industrial Relations Responses

While each nation studied had unique responses to the economic "shocks" of 1973–1983, a comparative volume such as this offers special opportunities for generalization.

The responses of the parties, including government, during the decade can be put into two general categories for analytical purposes. At one extreme is the "corporatist" model of industrial relations, while the "market" model is at the other.

A corporatist system of industrial relations relies on major interest groups—that is, labor and management—and the government agreeing on basic economic and social policy. The involvement of interest groups in the formulation of public policies is a characteristic of democratic societies, so consultation per se does not indicate a corporatist system. Corporatism implies more than occasional contacts, however significant they may be. It entails an institutionalized system for reaching major public policy decisions by the state and "peak associations," each of which represents a major producer group and each of which has authority over its constituents. The peak associations are national bodies accorded a monopoly on representation for their interests by government and are integrated into the policy-making apparatus. Moreover, they engage in a joint consultative process together with the government, rather than approaching political leaders separately as interest groups normally do. If they are sufficiently strong, private interest groups may extract concessions from the government in return for supporting its policies. (When governments are dominant, the corporatist model extends its influence over economic policy by using private bodies to implement its decisions, as happened in Brazil.) The results of these consultations are binding on all parties, with the peak associations expected to regulate their members to ensure that the decisions are implemented (Crouch 1977).

The most common forms of corporatist industrial relations have been tripartite bodies to establish or administer incomes policies, or agreements such as the "Social Contract" between the British Trades Union Congress and the Labour Party in 1975. These arrangements require that unions restrain their economic power in exchange for a major role in public policy, guarantees of a measure of economic protection for their members, and the adoption of some public policies that benefit working people generally. Employers gain a respite from union wage pressure, plus the hope (or expectation) of improved prospects or expanding markets. But in return business usually has to restrain prices. Governments hope to maintain both full employment and price stability, while avoiding the need for wage and price control legislation which, in any case, may be difficult to enforce without the cooperation of labor and management.

The market model of industrial relations[1] implies that government will avoid extensive intervention in economic affairs, including relations between labor and management. Essentially, economic and political decisions are separated. Workers' rights to organize for collective bargaining are protected, but they advance their interests through economic action in a pluralistic framework or through lobbying government on specific issues. A degree of conflict is accepted and may be regulated, but economic outcomes of negotiations are not controlled. There are few nonlegislative bodies for making public policy, and when they exist, labor is seldom accorded a formal role. Legislative protections for labor, as an interest group or as a social class, are limited. Unorganized workers are represented only through the political system. Since economic policies are made without direct participation of interest groups, a low level of organization by either labor or management is not seen as an impediment to policy-making (Crouch 1977).

A market system of industrial relations may exist under governments that favor collective bargaining or oppose it. In the former case, official policies usually emphasize full employment and a conciliatory approach to labor disputes. When governments oppose collective action by workers, they weaken the limited protections that exist by legislation or administrative neglect. A high level of unemployment may in itself be a significant restraint on labor militancy.

This brief description of the two models highlights sets of policies and structures found in the industrial relations systems in the nine countries discussed in this volume.

If one puts these countries on a spectrum between the two ideal types, the corporatist model best describes Germany, France, Australia, and Sweden, with Japan and Canada evolving from the market model towards corporatism. The purest examples of the market model are the United States and the United Kingdom, with Brazil moving away from corporatism towards the market system. The direction of the evolution of these systems has been highly uneven. For instance, Swedish industrial relations, long held out as an ideal example of cooperation at the level of peak associations,

---

[1] Crouch (1977) refers to this as the "liberal" model. For purposes of this chapter, the adjective "market" is more appropriate.

has experienced stresses that may lead to the breakup of corporatist structures. Brazil, the only nation with a statutory system of corporatism, is attempting to release unions from highly restrictive political constraints.

Japanese industrial relations in the early 1970s were focused at the level of the enterprise, one of the least propitious settings for corporatist forms. Yet within ten years multilateral consultation at the national level, which began in the 1960s, was well developed, without removing the locus of decisions from the corporation and its union. Canada, with a weak national government and major internal economic disparities, was an equally unlikely location for such activities. However, successive federal governments, representing both major political parties, have attempted to use corporatist structures to address major economic problems. Australia, also a fragmented industrial relations system, capitalized on the centralizing tendencies of the Arbitration Commission and close government-labor ties to establish the rudiments of a corporatist system. French governments, employers, and moderate unions overcame the traditional intransigence of left-wing unions and many managers to forge new relations at all levels of the system.

The two market-oriented systems represent the greatest and least change in forms of interest group representation. In the United Kingdom, plant-level industrial relations traditionally have been free of legal regulation, but during the postwar era corporatist structures emerged to deal with a wide array of national economic issues. The persistent combination of inflation, low economic growth rates, and dependence on exports caused successive governments to establish incomes policies and economic development plans, virtually all with the direct participation of labor and the business community (see Thomson 1979). The Thatcher government is determined to dismantle these systems as completely as possible in favor of reliance on the market and government action without consultation, despite opposition from both labor and many employers.

The United States, where recognition of unions as a significant interest group has always been less important than in other industrialized nations, always had the market model. By international standards, government economic intervention has been limited, and neither politicians nor interest groups themselves favored a continuing role for labor and business in the formulation of economic policy. But the Reagan administration has moved even further in that direction by its macroeconomic policies and attitude towards organized labor. The combination of high interest rates, the promotion of a strong currency, and deregulation has seriously weakened the position of organized labor in its traditional centers of strength, which also are disproportionately concentrated in declining industries and regions. The inability of unions to organize in the service sector and Sunbelt states further undermined its position. Politically, the government has excluded labor from its policy deliberations and weakened enforcement of labor legislation. The combination of economic and political policies has left labor in a vulnerable or even marginal position.

Forces for Change

One would like to be able to explain how these alignments came about. However, the papers in this volume suggest that movement in either direction is a subtle interplay among politics, economics, and industrial relations in each situation rather than a formula applicable to all. For example, except for Australia, no electorate discussed here made fundamental political choices based on industrial relations issues. The election of Thatcher, Reagan, Kohl, and Mitterand, for instance, resulted from a mixture of their campaign styles, prevailing political climates, their stands on foreign affairs and economic policy, or the skills of their opponents, not on the labor issue. Yet once in office, all of these governments put their stamp on industrial relations policies.

Similarly, the partisan composition of government was associated with consultation in the social democratic countries, but was not a predictor of direction in the more conservative countries. The conservative governments in the U.S. and the U.K. were committed to fundamental change in key economic policies, but they froze their respective labor movements out of the decision-making process. By contrast, conservative governments in Japan and Germany did not seek fundamental transformation of these relationships. Instead, they favored the cooperation of major interest groups in change.

The political complexion of the Swedish, Australian, French, and Canadian governments strongly favored the corporatist approach. The first two were more social democratic, as was

France under Mitterand. The Trudeau regime in Canada was definitely more centrist, but was still progressive during most of its life. When social democratic parties govern, their close ties to labor almost invariably foster the corporatist model. However, once established, the corporatist system can survive the demise of a social democratic government, as occurred in Sweden and Germany. The parties and government come to rely on consultation and do not want to destroy the process because of transitory shifts in the balance of power. (See Lange et al. 1982).

Nor was choice of economic policy a good predictor. The basic choices of economic policy for most governments were clear—either the monetarist goals of stimulating private investment and reducing inflation, or the neo-Keynesian emphasis on maintaining employment levels and protecting the welfare state. Yet these fundamental policy choices did not in turn lead automatically to a predictable set of industrial relations policies. The characteristics of the national industrial relations systems were highly salient to the approach of government and the private parties towards their mutual relations.

Where the labor movement was strongly entrenched, even the most conservative governments moved cautiously against unions or not at all. In Britain, for instance, the Thatcher government, aware of the heavy price previous governments had paid for choosing a direct confrontation with the labor movement, relied on a series of relatively minor pieces of legislation aimed at reducing the strength of unions, changes in the position of public employers on industrial relations, plus broader economic and social policies designed to assist private investors. It also exercised the discretionary authority to exclude labor from the policy-making process. Similarly, in Germany while the rising rate of unemployment left the labor movement open to attack from employers and the government, Chancellor Kohl was unable to weaken the corporatist structures of the German industrial relations system because opposition from both labor (which was predictable) and employers (which was not predictable) forced him to abandon his plans. By contrast, the Hawke government in Australia relied upon the combination of the organizational power of labor and the Prime Minister's own close ties with labor to change the direction of Australian economic policy. In Sweden the labor movement played a similar role. In Western Europe and North America, however, labor appeared unable to develop any strategy to cope with its new circumstances. Clearly, the role of employers was crucial in the transition. The Thatcher and Kohl governments were hampered in their efforts to shift the balance of power by the reluctance of employers to cooperate with them. In both cases employers viewed unions as channels of communication with their workforces—British employers at the plant level, German employers at the industry and national levels. French employers, on the other hand, surprisingly cooperated with government efforts to strengthen tripartite consultation and collective bargaining.

By contrast, many American employers took advantage of the shift in market power to eliminate or reduce union power. The cases described by Block and McLennan, where employers worked successfully within the framework of collective bargaining to deal with economic problems, were not the modal cases. Leading firms invested heavily in management systems designed to reduce the propensity to unionize. In companies or industries where unions were not strongly entrenched, employers undermined them or avoided them where possible by aggressive management techniques. When they expanded, these firms opened new plants in regions hostile to unionism. The policies of the Reagan administration—exclusion of organized labor from any consultative role and lax enforcement of existing labor legislation—created a climate which at least was consistent with, if not a stimulus to, such employer policies. The Reagan administration did not have to take special action to attack organized labor. A combination of less strict enforcement, conservative macroeconomic policies, high unemployment, and the hostility of employers accomplished the same result.

In Australia, employers saw themselves as junior partners in the centralization of industrial relations and apparently participated reluctantly, although they are committed to a tripartite industrial relations system. Should they choose to resist the government and labor movement, the consensus necessary for effective corporatist systems will probably disappear. The fissures in the Swedish system caused by labor efforts to socialize the private sector via the wage-earner fund and extend worker participation also illustrate the importance of employers to the maintenance of a national consensus.

The perceived impact of the industrial relations system on

national economic performance also appeared to be associated with pressure for change. In Britain and Canada high strike rates were perceived as impairing national economic performance. In the U.S. union wages and workrules were seen as the reason for noncompetitiveness. In France government legislation with respect to labor was the villain. In each of these cases market forces were given free (or freer) rein. By contrast, in Japan and Germany the industrial relations systems were viewed as positive factors in an era of generally satisfactory economic performance. Sweden is the interesting intermediate case. At the beginning of the 1970s industrial relations were perceived as contributing to the economic well-being of the country. Neither government nor management pressed for change. Rather, it was the labor movement which was unhappy with the status quo and pushed for changes which, as Peterson points out, threaten to undo the earlier cooperation.

While it is difficult to anticipate where corporatism might arise, there are certain obstacles to corporatism on the North American continent which would suggest that a corporate solution is not likely to occur under current circumstances.

In the United States, checks and balances among branches of government limit the executive's ability to agree with private parties. American political culture also resists such arrangements. The parliamentary system in Canada largely eliminates conflict within the national government, but provincial powers to regulate most economic activity and industrial relations restrict the role of the federal government to coordination of private groups and provincial governments. Moreover, as Adams points out, provincial governments themselves may prefer the market model to the corporatist system within their own jurisdictions.

In neither nation in North America are there strong peak associations—bodies with power to represent their members and bind them to the results of any deliberations (Salisbury 1979). The difficulties in forging corporatist relations are especially apparent on the employers' side. Not only are businesses reluctant to commit themselves to corporatist policies, but most are hostile to economic planning. The focus on consultations in Canada has been to influence government policy to benefit private parties. Groups like the Business Council on National Issues have never been asked to secure support for government policies their members may oppose. The American government is philosophically disposed to diminish the regulatory role of government, and in times of declining rates of inflation and high unemployment, the traditional motives of government to consult with private parties—the reduction of inflation or limitation of wage increases—are absent. Even if North American governments and management wanted to enter such consultations, as they have from time to time in the past, the ability and willingness of labor centrals to respond is always questionable. Trade union structures in the two countries, developed primarily to meet the demands of collective bargaining, are ill-suited for what is essentially political bargaining. Not only are national centers relatively weak, but workplace organization is strong and relatively autonomous, and many important unions, especially in the public sector, are unaffiliated.

Changes in the Structure of Collective Bargaining

If any strong pattern emerged from the study of changes in industrial relations in these countries, it was this: In every case, except Australia, Germany, and Japan, where changes in bargaining structures occurred, there was a movement towards decentralization. The trend was strongest in Britain, where the former pattern of industry-wide bargaining seems to be disappearing in the private sector. There are also signs of fissures in the Swedish system of national bargaining, and in Brazil and France, where the role of government in determining the outcome of collective bargaining has always been strong. In the U.S. and Canada bargaining traditionally has been decentralized relative to Europe, but even here the number of industry- or area-wide bargaining arrangements has decreased. In the province of British Columbia in Canada, for instance, where industry-wide bargaining was more common than in any other region on the continent, employers withdrew from several such structures when economic pressures weakened labor resistance and when the law permitted. In both Canada and the U.S. the locus of decision-making has shifted from industry to company and from company to plant. Germany and Japan, with centralized structures and good performance, maintained what they had. In Australia centralization of industrial relations decisions took place under the auspices of the Arbitration Commission to the detriment of industry-wide and company-wide over-award bargaining.

The causes of these changes in structure fall into two categories.

In France and Brazil the governments traditionally had favored wider bargaining units. When their participation in bargaining declined, unions and employers were left to work out structure in the context of market considerations, as was the case in all other countries where structure was free to fluctuate. Where the market has been competitive, unions have lost the whipsawing threat which encouraged wider bargaining units in the first place. Moreover, employers found that differences among them accentuated by competitive markets and a prolonged recession hastened the disintegration of bargaining groups in which strong employers were more willing to buy labor peace than their brothers who were more exposed to market forces.

The United States in a Comparative Context

From this overview of the country chapters in this book, the unusual nature of U.S. industrial relations becomes apparent. For decades scholars have examined "U.S. exceptionalism," generally in terms of the characteristics of the American labor movement. This literature focuses on the lack of a labor or socialist political party and the relatively conservative ideology of American unions. These characteristics of the American labor movement remain exceptional, but other features of the U.S. industrial relations system are equally unusual when viewed from a comparative perspective in the 1980s.

Among the nations examined in this volume, the United States (and to a lesser extent the United Kingdom) experienced the sharpest decline in union membership. Unions everywhere were weakened by a severe economic recession, high unemployment rates, and, in several nations, conservative governments. In general, however, membership held up if one takes into account job losses in industries that were heavily organized. Perhaps as a result of these developments, strikes and labor unrest declined in most nations in the sample. In the U.S., however, union penetration fell to the lowest levels of any of the developed nations covered. Especially noteworthy was the increased size of the nonunion sector in traditionally organized industries, such as airlines, trucking, construction, and basic steel production. The chapter on the U.S. points out that the labor movement has not been able to make any substantial progress in organizing these companies or operations, despite the threat they pose to existing negotiated labor standards.

While it is difficult to measure the extent of concession bargaining, these events certainly were prominent in the industries discussed in the U.S. chapter. Other national industrial relations systems experienced declining living standards as wage increases failed to match rates of inflation, but only in the U.S. were there nominal reductions in wages and conditions of employment previously negotiated between the parties. The unusual nature of these developments was illustrated by the experience of the auto industry in the U.S. and Canada. Chrysler workers in both countries agreed to concessions when the survival of the company seemed threatened. General Motors then demanded and received concessions in the U.S. but failed to win similar gains in Canada. When the United Automobile Workers international president attempted to pressure Canadian locals into accepting the American pattern, they refused and subsequently seceded from the union.

Viewed comparatively, American employers seem more hostile to unions and collective bargaining than their peers elsewhere. As noted above, British employers resisted the efforts of the Thatcher government to undermine the dominant role of collective bargaining in wage determination. While British employers were anxious to increase their bargaining power relative to labor, especially at the level of the plant or shopfloor, they did not seek to eliminate unions from their organizations. German employers opposed attempts by the Kohl government to make structural changes in the industrial relations system that had grown up after World War II. Even in France, where employer resistance to collective bargaining encouraged political action by unions, management joined both the conservative and socialist governments and labor in economic consultation. In Australia, Brazil, Japan, Canada, and Sweden, employers joined or continued to participate in corporatist-style consultative mechanisms aimed at combatting the effects of the recession. There were no such macro-level activities in the U.S. Clearly, there are cultural factors at work there not found elsewhere in developed countries.

Finally, the lack of general innovation in the American system of industrial relations in the past decade was noteworthy. Other nations, including Japan, Canada, and Australia, experimented with tripartism. In Sweden, the labor movement proposed several plans to use wage-earner funds to extend the ownership of private industry to workers. The political decision in Brazil to adopt *abertura* encouraged the parties to begin the dismantling of a corporatist industrial relations system that was over 40 years old. French governments and employers established new industrial relations training programs, strengthened collective bargaining and improved some social legislation linked closely to industrial relations.

During the decade of economic change, the major changes in U.S. industrial relations were an acceleration of the trend towards union-free workplaces, a variety of workplace committees designed to improve quality or raise productivity, reductions in negotiated conditions in exchange for greater employee security or influence on policies, and an increasing reliance on the courts by employees seeking redress or protection. Unions became involved in managerial decisions in a few industries, but the impact of these experiments is uncertain (Kochan, McKersie, and Katz 1985). In many cases they were based on successful institutions of a similar nature that have long existed in Japan or Western Europe, so, on a comparative basis, they were not especially innovative. One unusual factor in the American experience, however, is the lack of any legislative support for consultation at the workplace. Similar arrangements in France, Germany, and Canada, for instance, all are stimulated by law. American experiments may be more meaningful when they occur than are other initiatives because they result from voluntary actions of the parties, but this lack of institutional support in public policy also makes them vulnerable to temporary changes in the parties' priorities. Finally, unlike the 1960s, there did not seem to be a great deal of protective labor legislation during this decade of economic crisis. There was, however, an increase in litigation probably due to economic conditions, as was an increased interest in unjust-dismissal legislation.

Future Developments

If there is one lesson reinforced by this volume's authors, it is that one cannot punctuate history. Many of the changes in industrial relations systems documented here began prior to 1973 and none seemed complete by 1983. However, the isolation of this decade of economic turmoil has helped identify the interplay between industrial relations and economic forces.

It appears that the relatively rapid economic changes of this period put a high premium on flexibility in an industrial relations system. Systems with highly centralized bargaining structures, strongly entrenched work practices, lacking consultative mechanisms at all levels, or where the parties maintained rigid political positions were at risk, while systems with the opposite characteristics fared well. If world economic developments are equally discontinuous in the next decade, Japan and Germany should still be seen as successful industrial relations systems. Japan combines adaptable practices at the level of the workplace and corporation with arrangements for achieving consensus at the macro level. In Germany moderately centralized bargaining isolates wage determination from the rank-and-file workers, who still have access to works councils to resolve day-to-day issues. Above this structure is a network of consultative schemes that have preserved unity of economic purpose extraordinarily well.

The future seems less promising for Sweden and Australia. Both have very centralized bargaining structures and consultation is either breaking down or still to be firmly established. Strongly held political positions may well inhibit the spirit of compromise so necessary to bring about change in an industrial relations system.

Canadian industrial relations also seem destined for turmoil when faced with economic instability. While structures are decentralized, the attention to protection of local work practices, the sporadic record of consultation, and strong political positions by elements in labor, management, and some provincial governments contain few of the elements of smooth transition.

In Brazil and France, one is left with the impression that the future will respond more to political than to economic developments. The decision to liberalize Brazilian industrial relations is still not a permanent one and was based on broad political objectives. To be sure, the growing militancy of the labor movement was a factor in the government's decision, but Pastore and Skidmore point out that the legal tools for reinstituting a coercive form of corporatism in Brazil remain. In France, government again has been an initiator of change in industrial relations, through the many mechanisms by which it intervenes in the economy as well as its role in the industrial relations system. Out of this has come some acceptance of unions by employers, but given the volatility of French politics, even under President Mitterand, the course of any reforms in industrial relations is likely to be uncertain.

Both political and economic developments seem likely to determine the future of British industrial relations. As Brown points out, the changes in private-sector industrial relations seem to be promoting economic recovery, especially in the manufacturing sector. But the breakdown in consultation at the level of the economy has removed a significant adjustment mechanism. The obvious hostility of the Thatcher government for organized labor threatens to politicize private-sector industrial relations, much as it has already been politicized in steel and coal and other industries in the public sector. Under the leadership of a more sympathetic government, the emerging British industrial relations system may well surmount difficulties posed by economic change.

As Block and McLennan describe the U.S. industrial relations system, most of the industries where collective bargaining is well established have demonstrated the adaptability of the institution. It is difficult to imagine a combination of peacetime economic events that would be more challenging than those of the decade considered here. Yet bargaining systems evolved in ways that seem suitable for the future. Consultation in some industries has increased, while bargaining structures were decentralized and work practices were altered. However, outside of the industries discussed in the chapter in this volume, the employer antiunion offensive, supported by the national and some state governments, continues. It remains to be seen to what extent collective bargaining will prove a more viable option than employer-provided mechanisms or employees' turning to the courts for redress of their grievances.

References

Crouch, Colin. *Class Conflict and the Industrial Relations Crisis.* London: Heinemann, 1977.

Kochan, Thomas A., Robert B. McKersie, and Harry C. Katz. "U.S. Industrial Relations in Transition: A Summary Report." *Proceedings of the 37th Annual Meeting, Industrial Relations Research Association.* Madison, WI: IRRA, 1985. Pp. 261–76.

Lange, Peter, George Ross, and Maurizio Vannacelli. *Unions, Change and Crisis: French and Italian Union Strategy and the Political Economy, 1945-1980.* London: George Allen & Unwin, 1982.

Piore, Michael J. "Can the American Labor Movement Survive Re-Gomperization?" *Proceedings of the 35th Annual Meeting, Industrial Relations Research Association. Madison, WI: IRRA, 1983. Pp. 30–39.*

Salisbury, Robert. "Why No Corporatism in America?" In *Trends Toward Corporatist Intermediation*, eds. P.C. Schmitter and G. Lembruch. Beverly Hills, CA: Sage, 1979, Pp. 213–29.

Thomson, A.W.J. "Trade Unions and the Corporate State in Britain." *Industrial and Labor Relations Review* 33 (October 1979): pp. 36–54.